DRESS DESIGN

WITH DEBBY BLACK

SECOND EDITION

A STEP-BY-STEP GUIDE TO MODERN PATTERN DRAFTING

© Deborah Elizabeth Ann Black 2019, 2022

Reprinted 2021

Second Edition 2022

Reprinted 2023

ISBN 978-0-6397-4644-9

Dress Design with Debby Black

A step-by-step guide to modern pattern drafting

First published by Deborah Black 2019

Velddrif, Western Cape, South Africa

debbyblack30@gmail.com

ISBN 978-0-620-85902-8

eISBN 978-0-620-85903-5

2 4 6 8 10 9 7 5 3 1

All rights reserved. No part of this publication may be reproduced, stored in a retrieval system, or transmitted in any form by any means electronic, mechanical, photocopying, recording, or otherwise without the written permission of the copyright owner.

CONTENTS

CHAPTER 1: PATTERN MAKING
- Blocks and patterns — 13
- Marking patterns — 14
- Pattern notches — 16
- Taking measurements — 33

CHAPTER 2: DARTLESS BODICE BLOCKS
- The basic bodice block — 36
- A-Line dress — 38
- Handkerchief hem dress — 42
- Boxy jacket — 48

CHAPTER 3: DESIGNING WITH DARTS
- The shoulder dart — 50
- Dart manipulation — 53
- Dart positions — 54
- Basic shift dress — 56

CHAPTER 4: SLEEVES
- The basic set-in sleeve — 58
- Bishop sleeve — 66
- Kimono sleeve — 67
- Basic raglan sleeve — 71

CHAPTER 5: NECKLINES
- Halter-neck dress — 76
- Scalloped neckline — 79
- Slanted neckline dress — 84
- Cowl neck top — 90

CHAPTER 6: PANELS
- Panels — 92
- Princess style dress — 94
- Boat neck dress — 96
- Off-the-shoulder dress — 100

CHAPTER 7: DRAPES
- Gathered drapes — 104
- Pleated drapes — 108

CHAPTER 8: STRAPLESS GARMENTS
- Bra-top bodice — 112
- Boning tutorials — 115

CHAPTER 9: COLLARS
- Collar terminology — 119
- Shirt collars — 120
- The shawl collar — 128
- Sewing the shawl collar — 140

CHAPTER 10: SHIRTS AND TOPS
- Casual shirt — 142
- The shirt sleeve — 144
- Sewing shirt cuff plackets — 150
- Peasant blouse — 160

CHAPTER 11: SKIRTS
- The basic skirt — 165
- Skirt with godets — 174
- Tiered skirt — 178
- Circular skirts — 192

CHAPTER 12: TROUSERS
- Basic trouser draft — 196
- Basic jeans — 208
- Jumpsuit — 210
- Basic culottes — 212

CHAPTER 13: SPORTSWEAR
- Sports bra — 219
- Tracksuit top with hood — 232
- Leggings — 236
- One-piece swimsuit — 242

CHAPTER 14: MATERNITY WEAR
- Maternity skirt — 244
- Maternity pants — 245
- Maternity top — 246
- Empire waist dress — 248

PATTERN MAKING EQUIPMENT

The following is a list of essential tools and equipment required to draft patterns:

Working Surface: A table is required with a height between **76 cm** and **90 cm (30 - 35½ in)**.

Paper: A roll of strong paper is required for pattern drafting. Durable cards such as poster board should be used for pattern blocks that are frequently used.

Pencil and Rubber: Use hard pencils such as **3H** and **4H**. Use colour pencils to outline certain style lines.

French Curves: These are used to shape necklines and armholes and are available in a variety of shapes and sizes.

Flexible Curve: Measures necklines and armholes accurately, but a tape measure held on its edge also works well.

Hip Curve or Vary Form Curve: Curve rulers are used for shaping the hipline and waistline curves, as well as shaping lapels.

Tracing Wheels: The blunt prong tracing wheel is used with carbon paper to transfer sewing marks to fabric. The sharp prong tracing wheel is used to trace pattern sections off.

Metre Stick: This **1 metre (39 ½ in)** long ruler is used for ruling long lines on patterns.

Metric Sewer's Ruler: These are usually **60 cm (23 ½ in)** long and **12** to **16 cm (4 ¾ - 6 ¼ in)** wide.

L-Square and Triangle Set Square: These measure, rule, and square lines on pattern drafts.

Paper Scissors, Sellotape, and Calculator.

Pattern Notcher: This tool marks sewing/balance points by snipping out a section of the pattern.

Pattern Punch and Hooks: The punch makes circular holes in patterns so that they can hang on hooks.

Pattern Weights: These are used to keep the pattern flat on the fabric. There are a variety of weights available to buy, but painted garden pebbles work well.

Tape Measure and Pins.

Awl: This tool makes holes in patterns to mark dart points or buttonhole placements.

PATTERN MAKING EQUIPMENT

French Curve Set

Flexible Curve

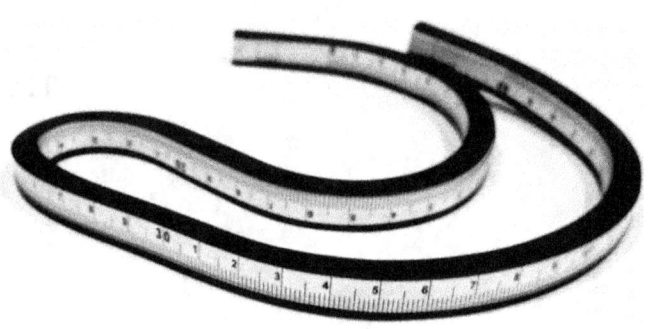

Multipurpose French Curve

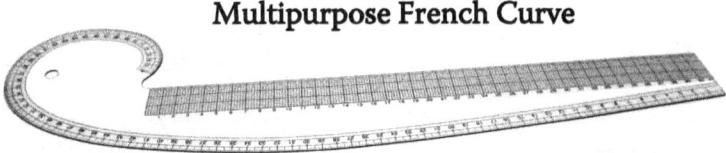

Pattern Notcher

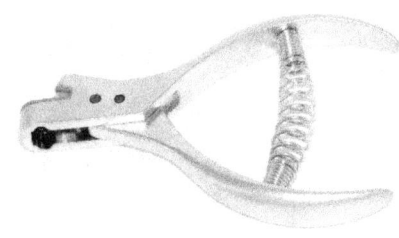

Vary Form Curve

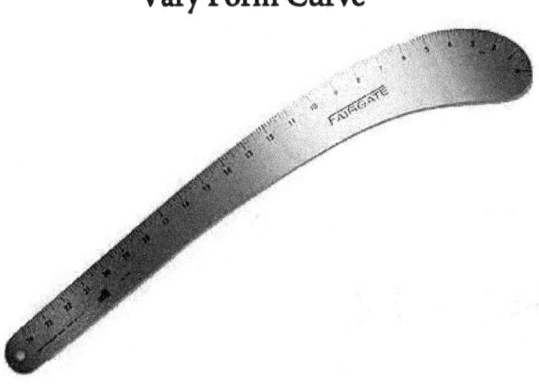

Hip Curve

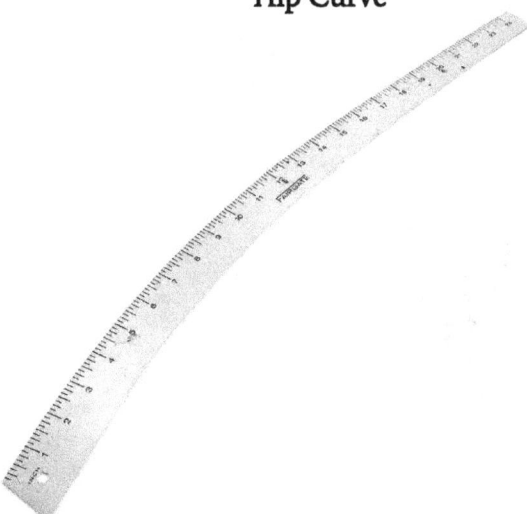

PATTERN MAKING EQUIPMENT

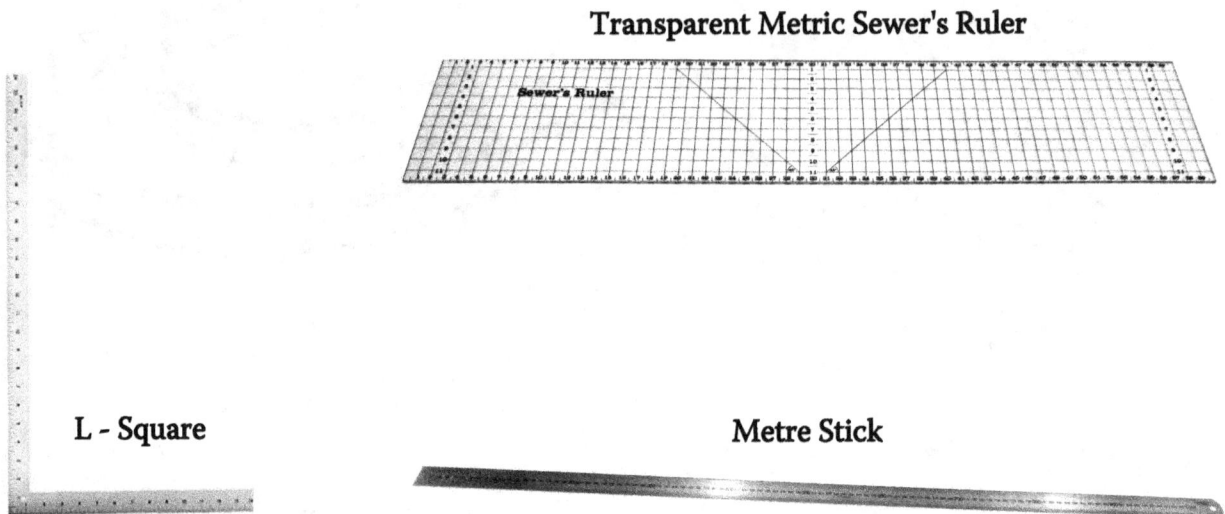

Transparent Metric Sewer's Ruler

L - Square

Metre Stick

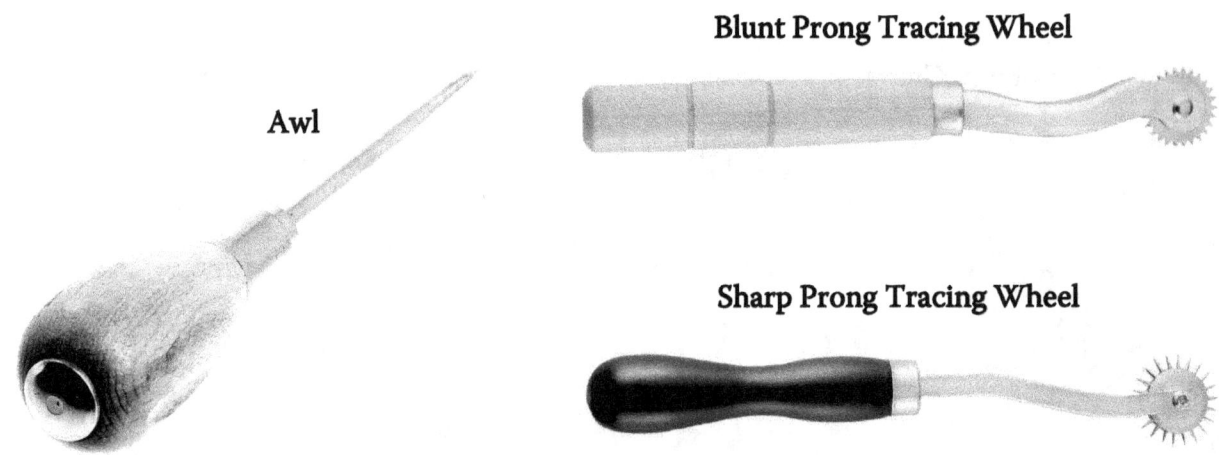

Blunt Prong Tracing Wheel

Awl

Sharp Prong Tracing Wheel

THE FRENCH CURVE

French curves are used in pattern drafting to shape armholes, necklines, sleeve heads, hip lines, and more. There are quite a few types and sizes of French curves available and some come with a grading rule and seam allowance guide. Below are a few examples of using a French curve.

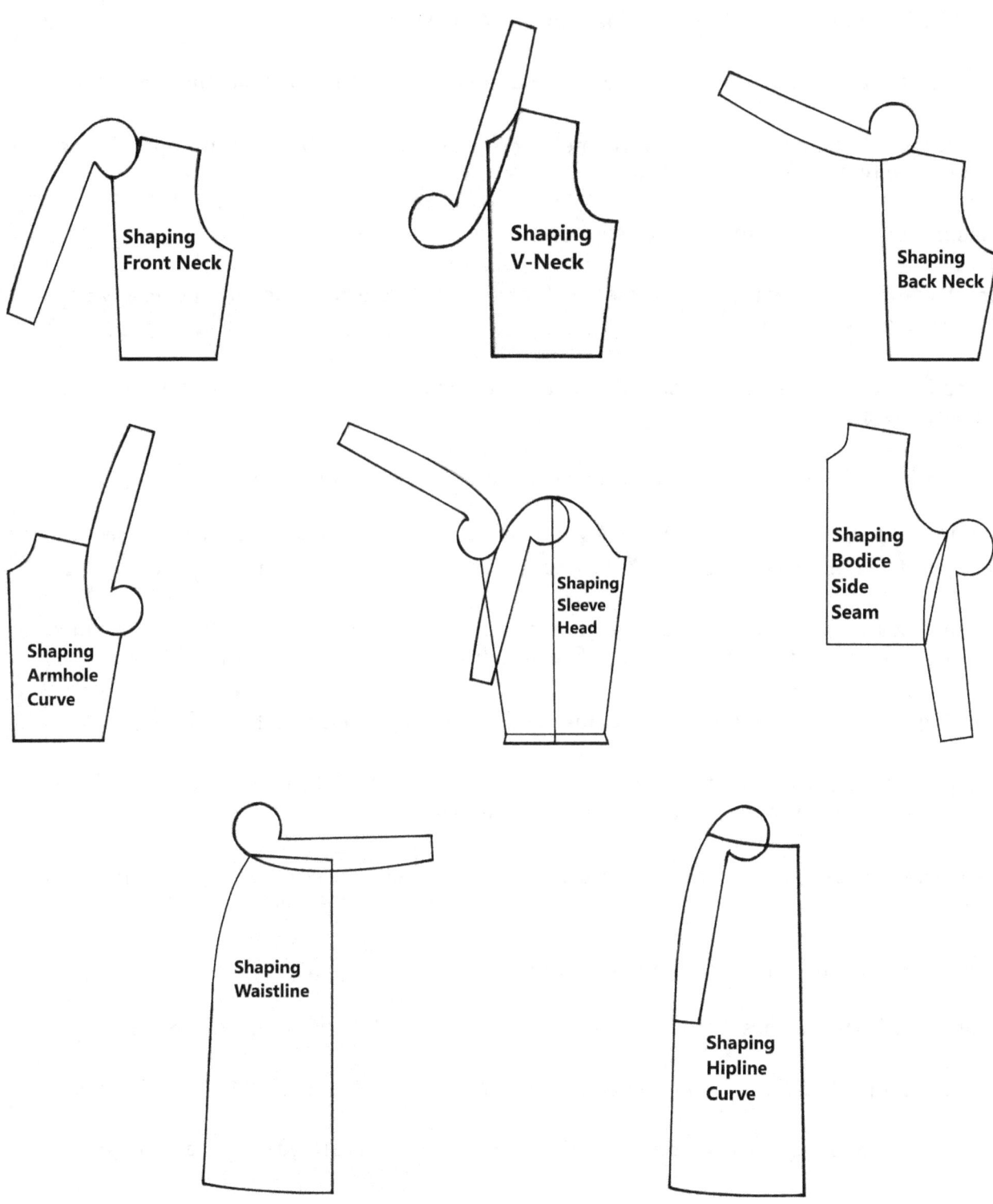

SEWING TOOLS AND SUPPLIES

There are many sewing aids available to choose from. Listed below are a few essential tools and supplies that might come in handy for general sewing.

Straight Pins and Pin Cushion: A pin cushion holds the pins and needles safe and ready for use.

Thimble: A thimble will protect your finger during hand sewing.

Needle Threader: The needle threader makes the threading of hand and machine needles easier.

Seam Ripper: These are used to cut machine-made buttonholes and to cut seams open. The sharp point is used to unpick stitches that have been sewn wrong.

Bodkin: A bodkin is used to thread elastic or cord through a casing.

Tape Measure: The tape measure is essential for taking accurate body measurements as well as measuring fabric and seams.

Sewing Gauge: This is a small ruler with a sliding marker and is ideal for measuring hems, pleats, and button-spacing.

Tailor's Chalk: These come in several colours and are used to mark the fabric.

Pens and Pencils: There are different types of marking pens and pencils. They are all used to make construction markings on fabric, for example, buttonhole placement and pleats.

Dressmaker's Carbon Paper: A pack of carbon paper contains a few sheets of different colours. The carbon paper is used with a tracing wheel to transfer construction marks to fabric.

Point Turner: This handy tool is used to push out the points of collars, cuffs, and more.

Rotary Cutter: The rotary cutter is used with a cutting mat and can be used to cut through thick layers of fabric, as well as fabric that is difficult to cut with sewing shears.

Dressmaker's Shears: These have long blades which make them ideal for cutting out fabric pattern pieces.

Thread Clipper: The clipper quickly cuts sewing threads while sewing.

Embroidery Scissors: These are useful for clipping threads and cutting delicate fabric pieces.

Sewing Machine Needles: Choose a selection of good-quality machine needles in different sizes.

Hand Sewing Needles: Choose a selection of needles that are best suited to the task at hand.

SEWING TOOLS AND SUPPLIES

Straight Pins and Pin Cushion

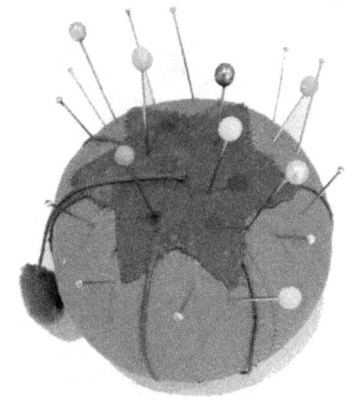

Needle Threader

Seam Rippers

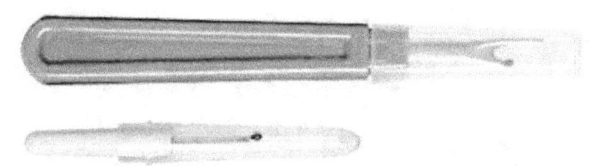

Bodkins

Tape Measure

Pens and Pencils

Sewing Gauge

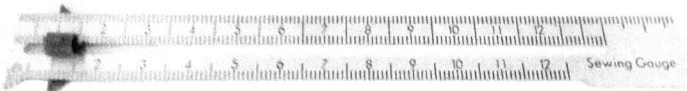

SEWING TOOLS AND SUPPLIES

Tailor's Chalk

Point Turner

Rotary Cutter
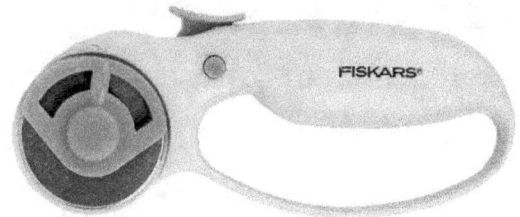

Dressmaker's Shears
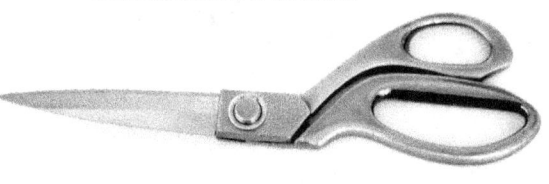

Thread Clipper
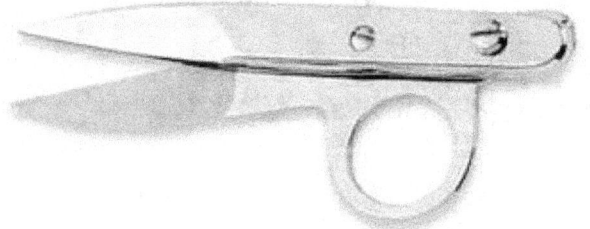

Embroidery Scissors
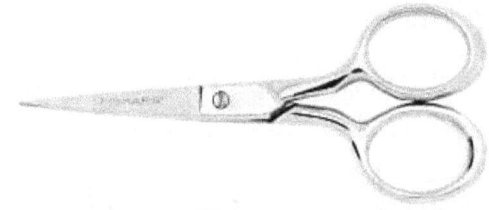

PATTERN MAKING TERMINOLOGY

Apex: The highest point of a curve, such as a dart point.

Armscye: The (armhole) section of a pattern into which a sleeve is fitted.

Base Pattern: This is an industry term that refers to the original pattern created (usually the middle of the size run). In the home setting, the base pattern is the pattern you are working with.

Bias: This is a diagonal line across the grain of fabric when a pattern is placed at a **45-degree angle**.

Blend: Blending is the process of smoothing and shaping angular and curved lines on a pattern.

Blocks: The block is an outline of the body on paper. These outlines form a bodice, skirt, or sleeve from which different styles can be created. Blocks do not have seam or hem allowances.

Dart: Darts are the triangular elements of a pattern. When sewn into the fabric, it takes the shape of a curved figure.

Dart Intake: The intake is the excess fabric between the dart legs. When sewn, the excess is removed and shape is created in a garment.

Dart Leg: These are the two lines that come to a specific point on the pattern to form a dart.

Draping: Draping is a method of pattern making that involves creating a mock-up pattern, which is also known as a TOILE. Calico or other cheap fabric is used to drape directly to the body, or a dress form. The outline and markings of the mock-up are then transferred to the paper pattern.

Ease: This is the extra amount added to a pattern, for example, to the sides, to ensure a comfortable fit.

Grain: The direction of the fabric that runs parallel to the selvage.

Notch: Notches are marks or symbols (like large dots, triangles, squares, or diamond shapes) used on patterns to indicate cutting lines, joining points, hems, dart legs, CF (centre front), and CB (centre back).

Truing: This is a process of checking that all measurements, seam lengths, and darts are correct on the pattern.

ABBREVIATIONS

The basic abbreviations that can be used on pattern pieces are as follows:

AC.F - Across Front
AC.B - Across Back
AH - Armhole
BL - Back Length
BP - Bust Point
CB - Centre Back
CF - Centre Front
CH - Chest
GL - Grainline or Grain Line
HL - Hem Line or Hemline
NL - Neckline
RB - Round Bust
RA - Round Arm
RN - Round Neck
RW - Round Waist
SA - Seam Allowance
SB - Side Back
SF - Side Front
SH - Shoulder
SL - Sleeve Length
SS - Side Seam
WL - Waist Length

Below are some abbreviations that are often used in sewing.

FL - Fold Line
FOE - Fold Over Elastic
RST - Right Sides Together
RTW - Ready To Wear
RSU - Right Side Up
SA - Seam Allowance
WST - Wrong Sides Together
WS - Wrong Side
WOF - Width Of Fabric
ZZ - Zigzag Stitch

BLOCKS AND PATTERNS

BLOCKS

There are two methods to create a pattern. One is by draping fabric around a dress form, and the other is by drafting a pattern. The block pattern is the first stage of creating a pattern. It is only an outline of the body, drafted from body measurements. Block patterns usually consist of waist- and hip-length bodices, skirts, sleeves, and trousers. Blocks have no seam allowances. Patterns are usually made of paper, but the basic block can also be made of durable card, such as poster board, for repeated use. Blocks made of card must be outlined on paper with a pencil. It is best to make nicks on the edge of the card that corresponds with construction lines to make it easier to transfer the lines to paper.

The second stage is where the basic block outline is converted into a chosen design by adding style lines, for example, necklines, tucks, dart placement, etc. This final draft must never be cut.

During the third stage, all the pattern pieces must be traced off from the final draft, which is also known as the **master draft. Grain lines, notches, hem, and seam allowances** must be added to all pattern pieces. A ruler must be used for straight lines and a tape measure or French curves must be used around all the curved outlines of the pattern piece. Facing must be traced off where necessary. Pattern pieces must be cut out neatly. Shoulder darts must be folded closed and secured with sticky tape.

MARKING PATTERNS

All pattern pieces need to have all the information on them that is required for cutting out the garment pieces. Complete each pattern piece to indicate the following:

- The name of each pattern piece, for example, front, side front (SF), back, side back (SB), centre front (CF), and centre back (CB).

- The amount of pieces that must be cut.

- The fold of fabric placement

- Grain line

- Seam allowances

- Hem Allowances

PATTERN NOTCHES

Notches are small marks or symbols made on a pattern to make the assembling of a garment faster and more accurate. These marks can be large dots, circular holes made with an awl or punch, and indents made with a pattern notcher. On commercial patterns, notches are indicated with dots, small circles, squares, triangles, and diamond shapes. The notches are marked on patterns to indicate zipper placement, the dart apex, pocket placement, buttonhole placement, pleats, tucks, and the gathering section on sleeve heads. Notches are also placed where armholes, shoulders, and panel seams should align.

Single notches are used to indicate the front pattern pieces. Side front and side back seams that are sewn together are also marked with a single notch. A double notch usually indicates the back of a pattern, for example, the back armhole, the back section of a sleeve, or the waistline. The shoulder marking is usually a notch, a perforation, or a circle. The underarm of a two-piece sleeve is marked with a nick, circles, or small squares. In some instances, patterns will have groups of three or four notches. These groups of notches are used when a garment has multiple seams or style lines.

PATTERN NOTCHES

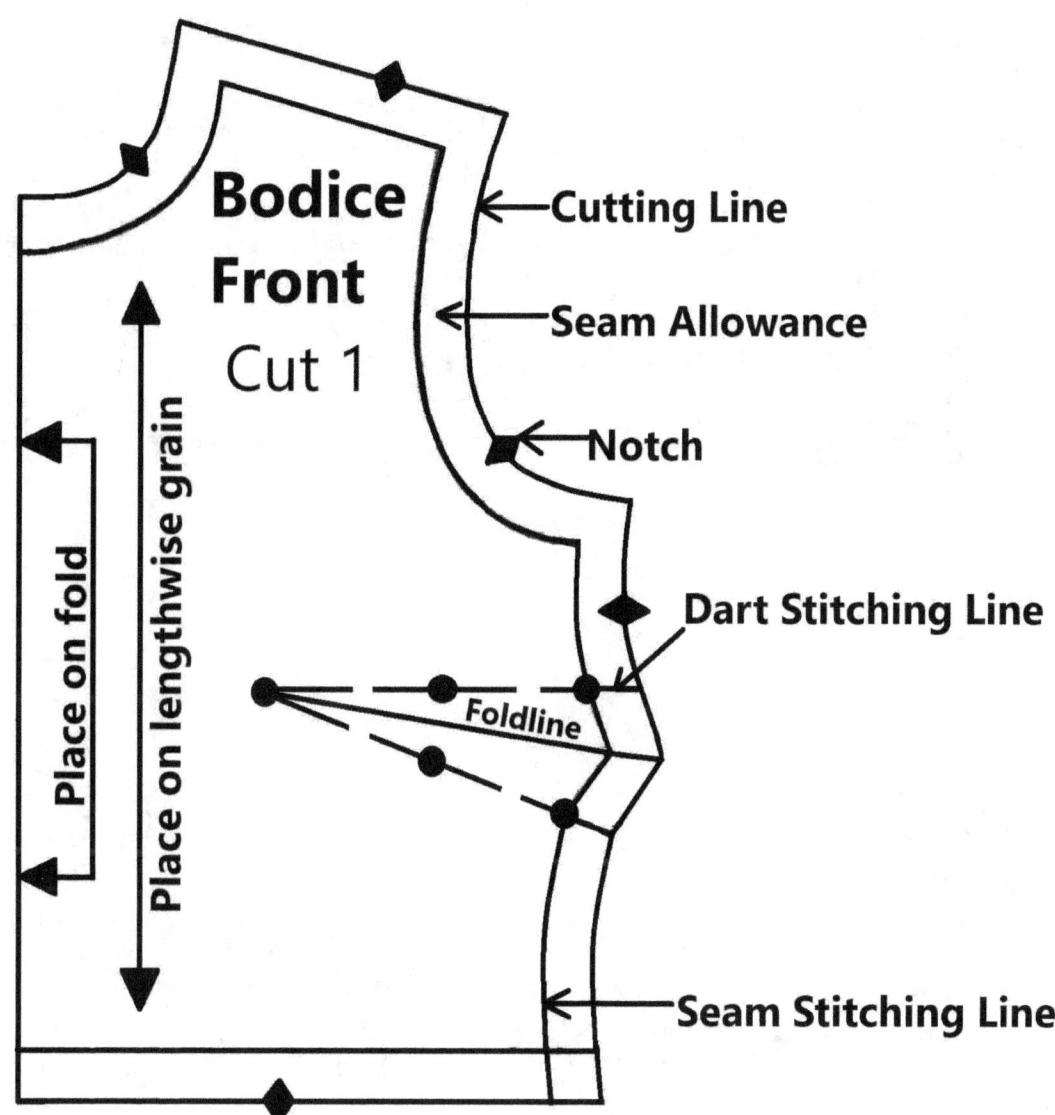

PATTERN NOTCHES

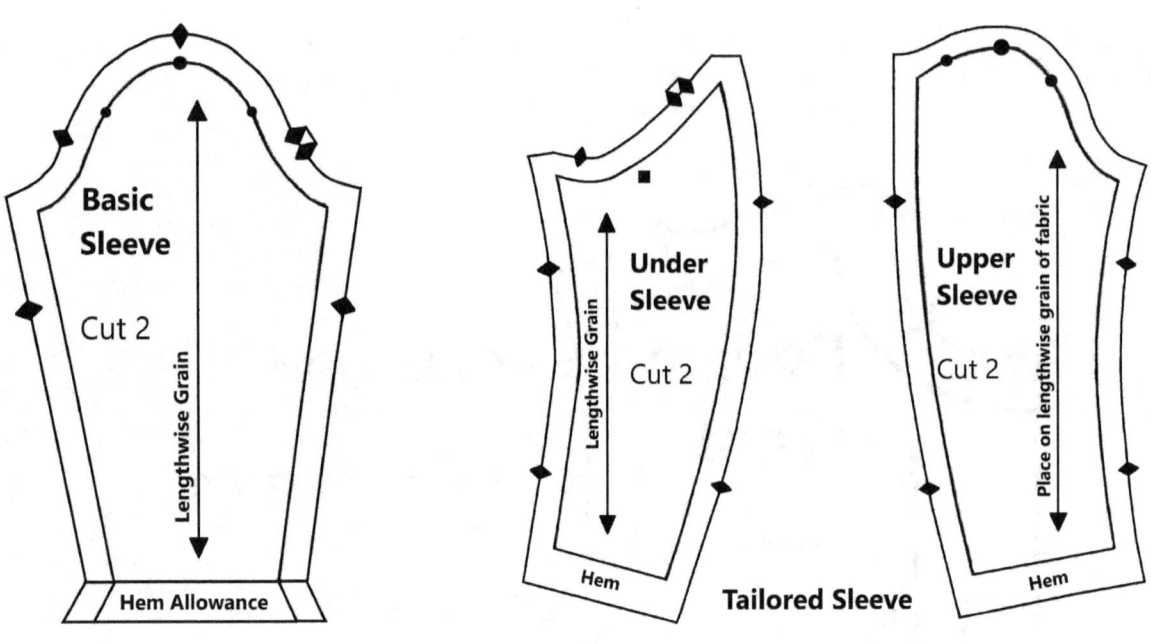

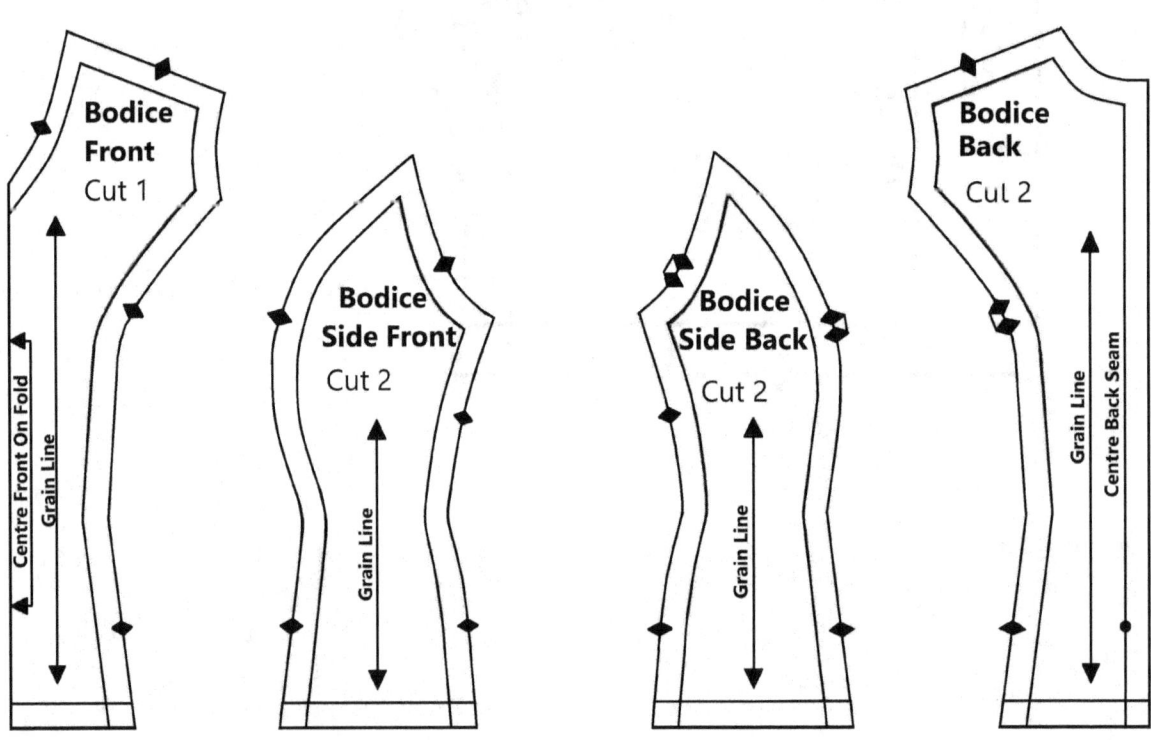

PATTERN NOTCHES

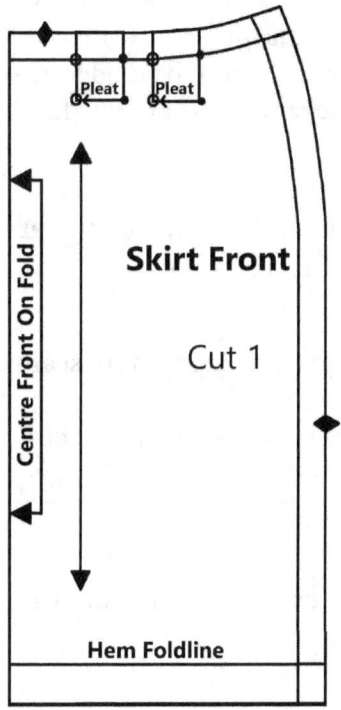
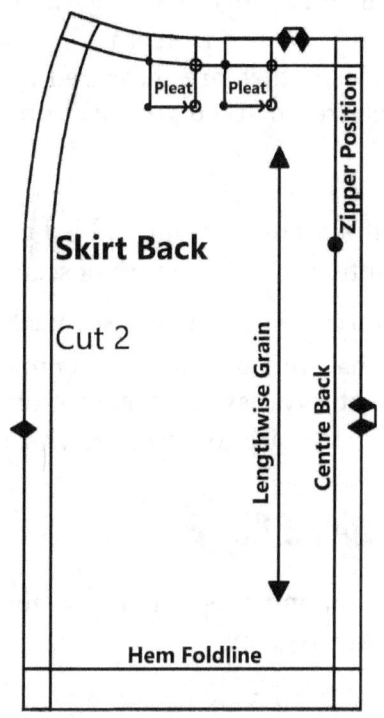
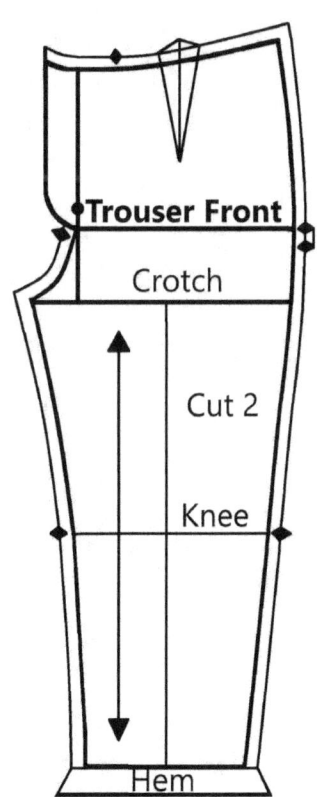
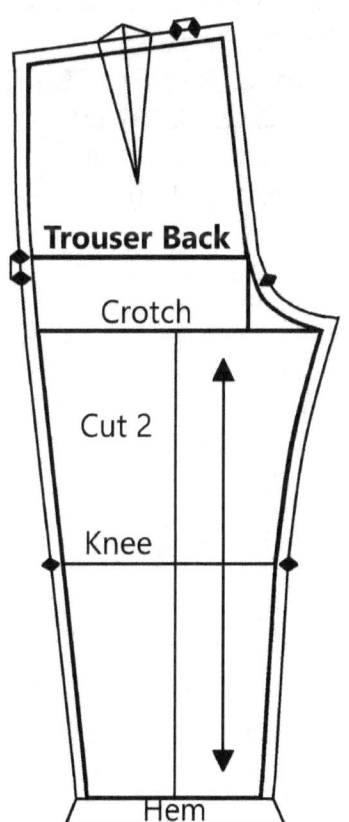

SEAM ALLOWANCES

Seam allowance is added where garment shoulders, necklines, armholes, side seams, and centre back seams will be sewn together. Most sewing machine needle plates are marked with seam allowance lines, which are measured from the machine needle. The fabric edge should line up with the preferred marked guideline on the needle plate while sewing to obtain the desired seam allowance.

The amount of seam allowance added to a pattern depends largely on personal preference. Many factors can influence the amount of seam allowance you need to add to a pattern.

- Bulky fabric will require less seam allowance.
- Fabrics that shift around, for example, Chiffons, and Georgette, require more seam allowance.
- Fabric that frays easily will need more seam allowance.
- Garments that are constructed with an overlocker use very small seam allowances.

SEAM ALLOWANCE GUIDE

The most commonly used seam allowance on a garment is **1.5 cm (⅝ in)**. The following is a good guide to go by:

- Necklines: **1 - 1.5 cm (⅜ - ⅝ in)**
- Shoulder Seams: **1 - 1.5 cm (⅜ - ⅝ in)**
- Centre Back Seams: **1 - 2 cm (⅜ - ¾ in)**
- Waist Seams: **1.5 cm (⅝ in)**
- Style Line Seams: **1 - 1.5 cm (⅜ - ⅝ in)**
- Facings: **1 - 1.5 cm (⅜ - ⅝ in)**
- Collars and Cuffs: **1 cm (⅜ in)**
- Hems: **1 - 5 cm (⅜ - 2 in)**

SEAM ALLOWANCES

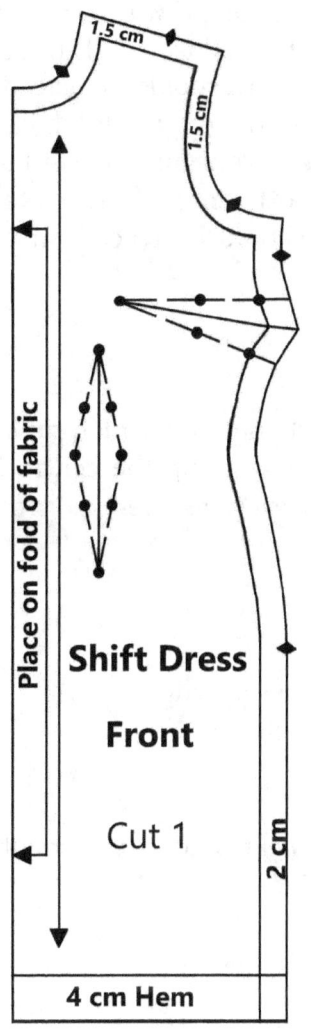
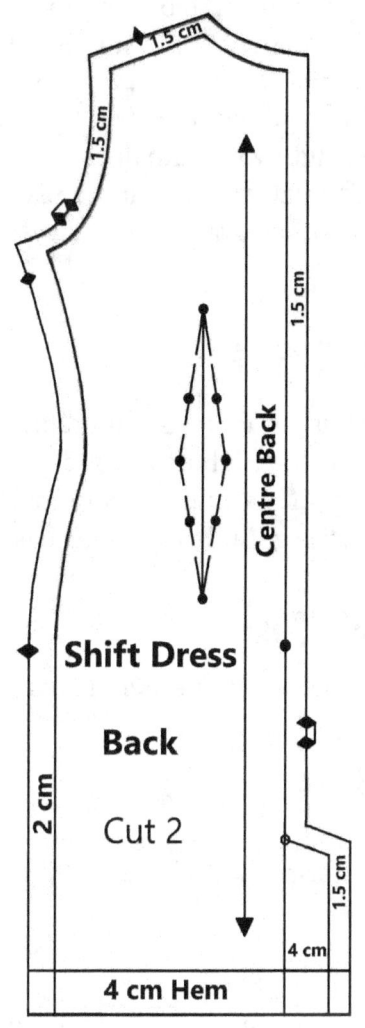
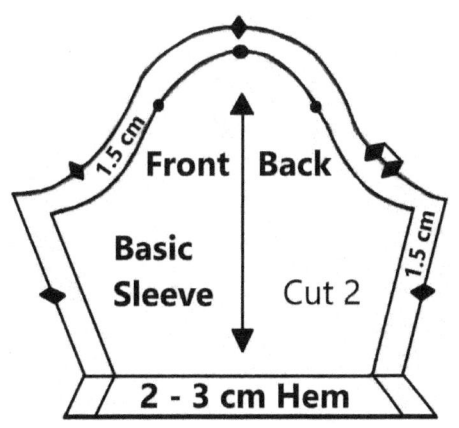
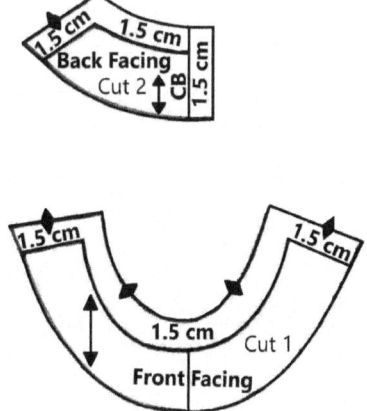

GRAIN LINES

The grain in woven fabric is indicated by the yarn that runs **lengthwise (warp yarns)** and **crosswise (weft yarns)**. It is for this reason that grain lines must be added to all traced pattern pieces, as the grain lines on patterns indicate the direction the pattern should be placed on fabric before cutting. Long lines with arrowheads should be drawn on the entire length of a pattern piece. **The lengthwise grain lines** are drawn parallel to the centre front and centre back of the pattern. **The pattern should be placed an equal distance on both ends of the selvage of the fabric**. The other grain line indicates that the pattern piece should be placed on the fold of the fabric.

LENGTHWISE GRAIN

The lengthwise grain (straight grain) is the most commonly used grain line which runs vertically from the top to the bottom of a pattern piece. This grain line runs up the centre front and centre back of garments and up through the centre of sleeves, as well as trouser legs. The lengthwise grain in garments has very little give or stretch.

CROSSWISE GRAIN

The crosswise grain is perpendicular to the lengthwise grain, or selvage edge.

BIAS GRAIN

This refers to the pattern being placed on fabric at a **45-degree angle**. Bias-cut garments are very flexible, flattering, stretchy, and drape to the contour of the body.

SELVAGE

The tightly woven strip along each lengthwise edge of fabric is called the selvage. These tightly woven edges prevent the sides of the fabric from fraying.

GRAIN LINES

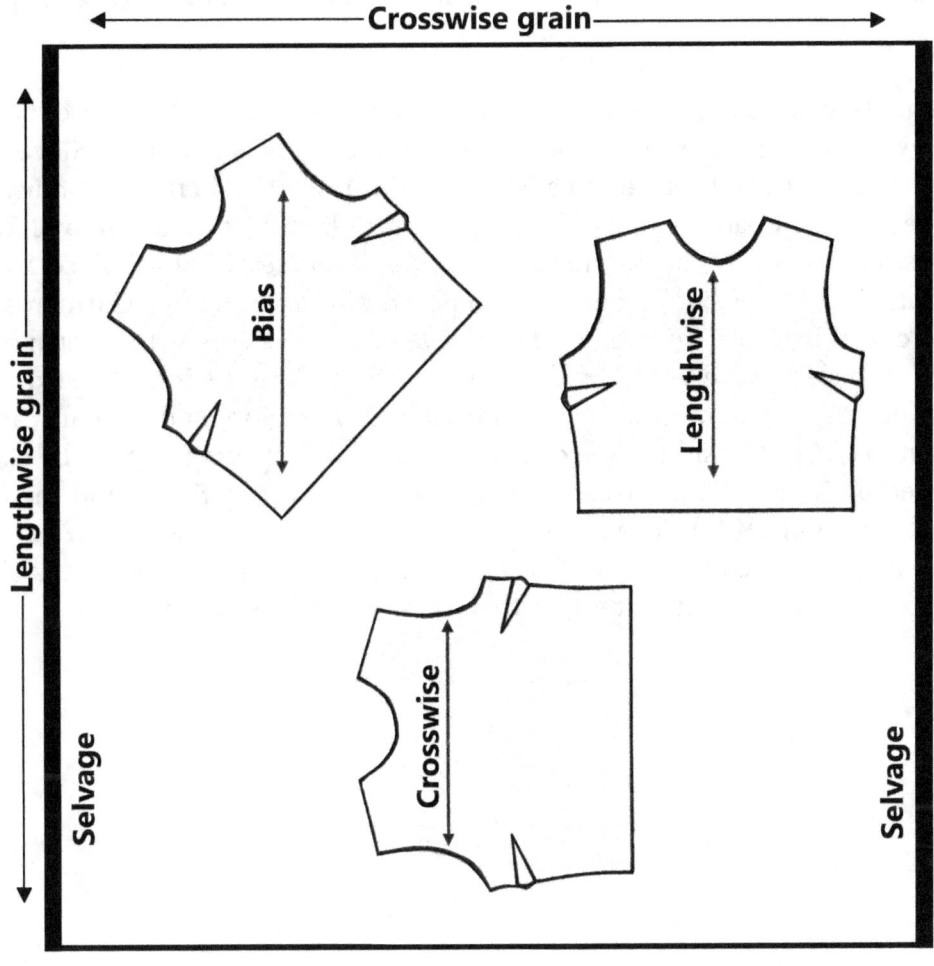

PATTERN GRADING

Pattern grading essentially means creating larger or smaller sizes of a base pattern, while maintaining the same style, shape, and fit. The different grades between sizes usually have an increment of **5 cm (2 in)** per size. It is important to keep the increment the same from size to size. The increment amount is evenly distributed by the bust, waist, and hip. Most garment and pattern companies set their own base pattern measurements and grading rules. It is for this reason that the same size garment will differ from one company to the next. The illustrations demonstrate grading a base pattern one size up. **The method illustrated here is for personal use only.**

To grade a base pattern size **92 cm (36 in)** bust up to a size **97 cm (38 in)** bust, use the **5 cm (2 in)** difference and evenly distribute it along the side front and side back seams. Since the pattern consists of a left and right front, as well as a left and right back, the **5 cm (2 in)** must be divided into 4 parts. The half-front pattern and half-back pattern, will each be increased by **1.25 cm (½ in)** along the side seams. The neck, shoulder, and armhole curves of the bodice block can be increased by **5 mm (¼ in)**. The bodice hemline can be lengthened by **5 mm**. Garments are usually lengthened by **1 cm (⅜ in)** in between sizes. The sleeve head and sleeve hemline can be increased by **5 mm (¼ in)**. The sleeve side seams can be increased by **1.25 cm (½ in)**. The skirt is adjusted in the same manner. The skirt waistline can be raised by **5 mm (¼ in)** and the dart can be shifted to the side by **5 mm**. The skirt side seams can be increased by **1.25 cm (½ in)**. The skirt hemline can be lengthened by **5 mm**. The trouser waistline can be raised by **5 mm** and the dart can be shifted to the side by **5 mm (¼ in)**. The trouser side seams can be increased by **1.25 cm (½ in)** and the hemline can be lengthened by **5 mm**. Collar sizes must be adapted to the neck size. Follow the lines on the pattern to continue grading further sizes, using the same amounts.

PATTERN GRADING

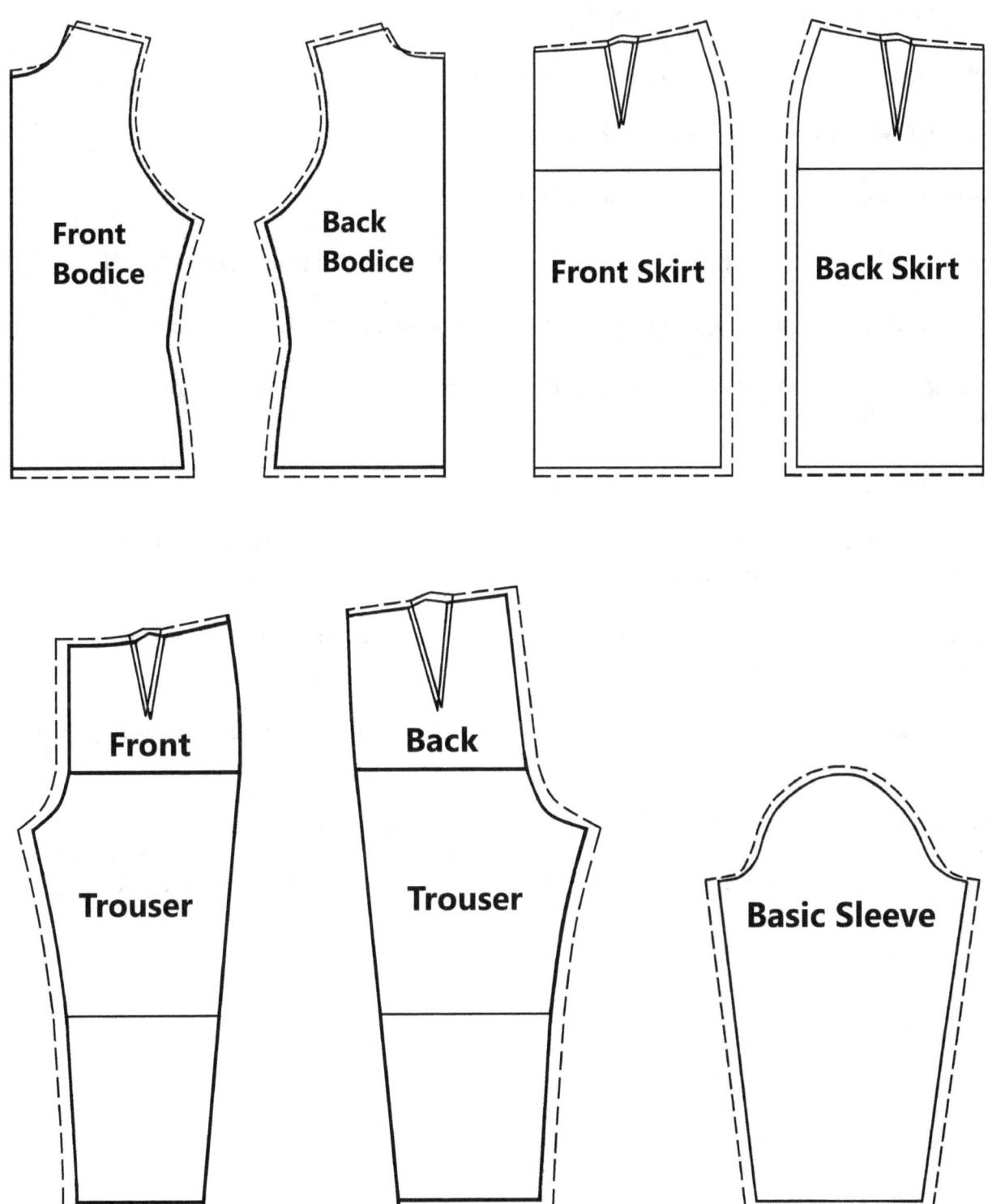

PREPARING FABRICS FOR CUTTING

Wash or dampen woven fabric before cutting. Dampen drycleanable fabric and lay it on a flat surface to dry. This is to preshrink the fabric when shrinkage possibilities are unknown.

Press the fabric to get rid of any wrinkles.

Determine the right side of the fabric before cutting.

Smooth fabrics are usually shinier or softer on the right side.

Textured fabrics stand out more on the right side.

Straighten the fabric ends to fold it evenly and ensure that the grain is properly aligned.

Fold the fabric right sides together, from selvage to selvage, for a lengthwise cutting layout.

Shifting of slippery fabric can be prevented by pinning the selvages together or by dampening the fabric before cutting.

Align plaids, prints, and stripes before cutting.

Pin the pattern to the fabric, or use pattern weights to keep the pattern flat on the fabric. Place the pattern with the grain line, parallel to the centre fold or selvage of the fabric.

Always keep the fabric flat on the work surface and keep one hand firmly on the pattern while cutting with the other hand.

Cut the fabric with sharp scissors or a rotary cutter. Never cut paper with your sewing scissors, as it will make them dull.

Directional fabrics can only be laid in one specific direction for cutting. Examples of directional fabrics are those that are described as "with nap" and include fabrics with pile, such as velvet and corduroy, one-way designs, and fabrics that reflect light in different ways, such as satins.

PATTERN LAYOUT FOR CUTTING

STANDARD LENGTHWISE FOLD

This is done on the lengthwise grain, with selvages matching along one edge, as illustrated below.

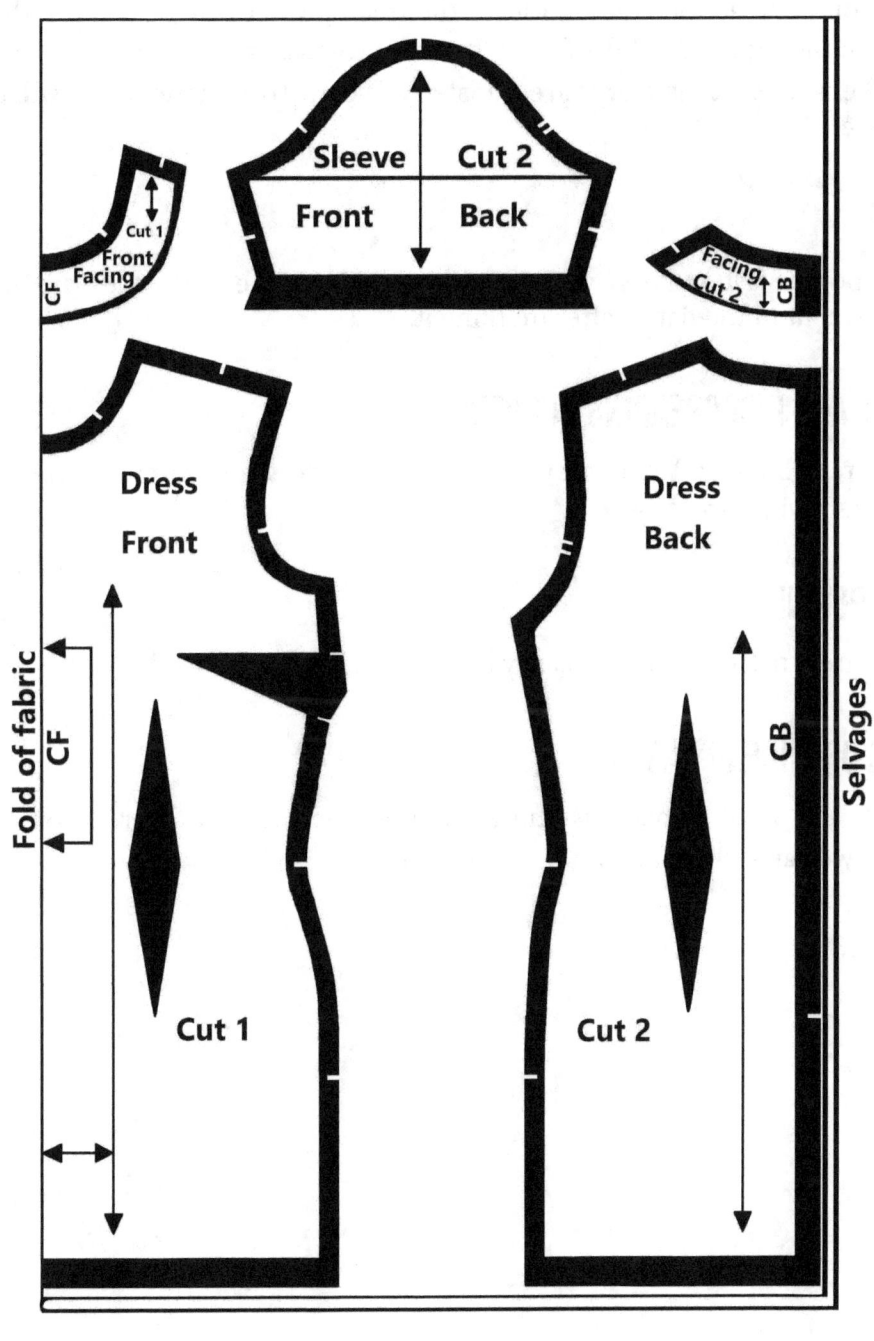

MARKING FABRIC

The most commonly used markings to transfer to fabric are darts, pleats, button placement, tucks, fold lines, and pocket placements. Marking takes place after cutting and before the pattern is removed. Below are a few common methods and tools used to mark fabric.

DRESSMAKER'S CARBON PAPER AND TRACING WHEEL

The carbon paper is used along with a tracing wheel. The waxed side of the carbon paper must be placed on the wrong side of the fabric. It works fast and well on plain and opaque fabrics. This method is not recommended for sheer fabric, as the tracing wheel might damage the fabric and the marks will show on the right side of the fabric. **It is best to place a hard board under the fabric while tracing. This will ensure that the marks are transferred correctly and the board will prevent damage to the work surface.**

TAILOR'S CHALK

Tailor's chalk is another fast and easy way of marking fabric. The chalk does rub off easily and it is best to sew the garment immediately after marking it.

WATER-SOLUBLE AND DISAPPEARING INK PENS

These make accurate lines and it is easy to make small dots and circles. The marks generally disappear completely with time or water.

DRESSMAKER'S PENCILS

These pencils are great markers and can easily be removed with a damp cloth.

TAILOR'S TACKS OR THREAD BASTING

This is probably the most time-consuming method, but it works great on sheer and very delicate fabric, as well as quilted and multicoloured fabric.

INTERFACING

Interfacing is a type of fabric that is applied to the wrong side of sections of a garment to give it support, body, and shape. In some instances, an entire garment can be interfaced, but it is mostly applied to certain areas such as collars, cuffs, front or back openings, facings, pocket flaps, and lapels.

There are three different types of interfacings: **woven**, **nonwoven**, and **knit**. Each type is manufactured in different widths, weights, and weaves. Interfacing comes in light, medium, and heavy grades. Lightweight interfacings can be used on most lightweight fabrics such as rayon, cotton, and chiffon. Mediumweight interfacings can be used on fabrics such as gabardine, shantung, and linen. Heavy grades are most often used in heavy fabrics for coats and jackets.

Woven interfacing has a lengthwise and crosswise grain and can be made from natural, synthetic, or a blend of both fibres. Woven interfacing has no stretch in the width or length and is usually cut with the pattern grain lines.

Nonwoven interfacing is made from synthetic fibres and is readily available and cheap to buy. Nonwoven interfacing does not have an actual grain line and pattern pieces can be cut in any direction. It is best to cut pattern pieces that require more stability, in the lengthwise direction.

Knit interfacings are mostly fusible and the amount of stretch in knit interfacings differs. Some have less stretch while others have more stretch. Knit interfacings can also be used on woven fabric as interfacing or underlining. Some of the knit interfacings that are readily available are Tricot and Fusi Knit which have a crosswise stretch and are made from polyester, and Soft Knit which is an all-bias knit interfacing made from nylon.

Fusible interfacing is either woven, nonwoven, or knit. Interfacing is made fusible with the added adhesive it has on one side. The side with adhesive should be placed on the wrong side of fabric. A pressing cloth should be placed over the interfacing and then pressed with a steam iron.

Non fusible interfacing is also known as **sew-in interfacing** because it does not have adhesive on the back, which adheres to the fabric when pressed. This type of interfacing must be hand or machine stitched to the fabric pieces.

Fabrics such as fur, synthetic leather, velvet, beaded fabrics, sheers, metallics, and some brocades require sew-in interfacing because these fabrics do not react well to heat. Examples of sew-in interfacings that are commonly used are organza, netting, and hair canvas.

Always choose interfacing that is compatible with the weight or stretch of the fabric you are working with.

FACINGS

A facing is the fabric used to finish the raw edges of a garment's neckline, armholes, and front and back openings. A bias facing is a strip of fabric cut on the bias so that it can be shaped to the curved edge where it will be sewn to. A shaped facing is cut from a pattern to the same shape as the edge it will be sewn to. Both bias and shaped facings can be cut from a lighter fabric than that of the garment to reduce bulk.

Use an average width of **4** to **5 cm (1 ½ - 2 in)** for a separate neck and armhole facing. Facing and button stand widths of jackets and shirts can vary from those given in illustrations in this book. The size of the button to be used must be taken into consideration when adding a button stand and facing to a pattern.

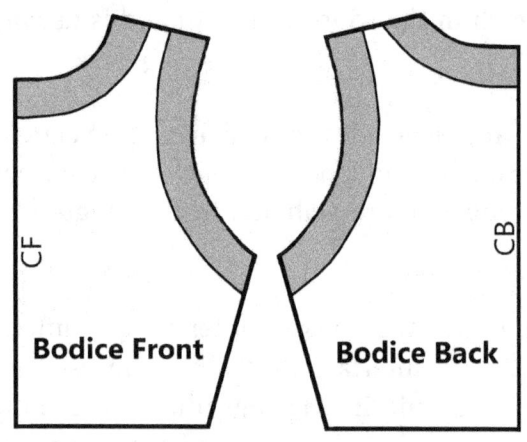

Separate Neck and Armhole Facing

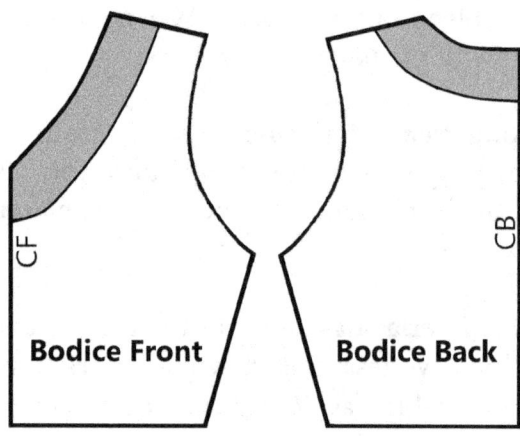

V-Neck and Back Facing

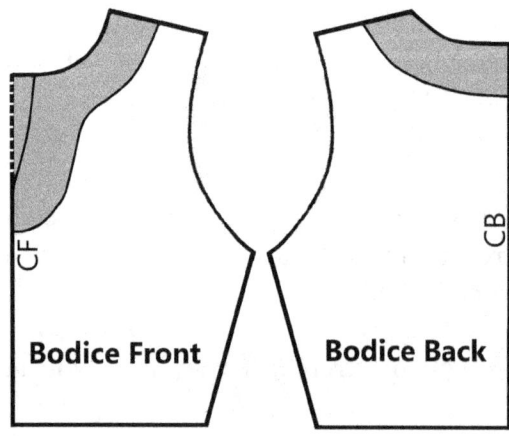

Keyhole Neckline and Back Facing

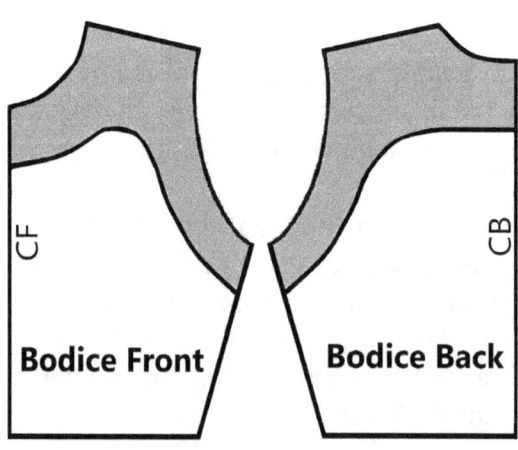

All-In-One Neck and Armhole Facing

FACINGS

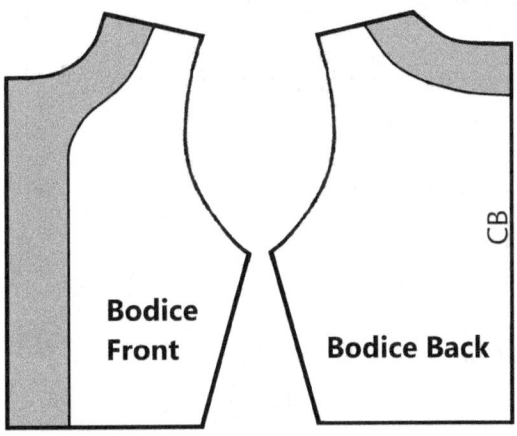
Neck and Separate Front Facing

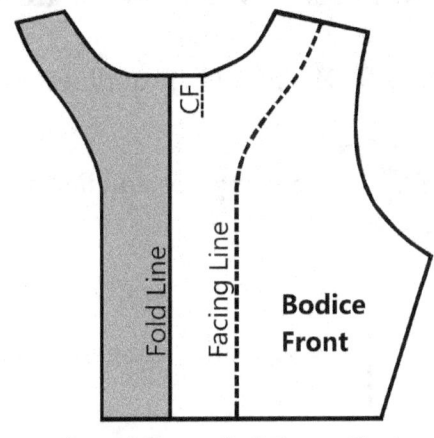
Neck and Extended Front Facing

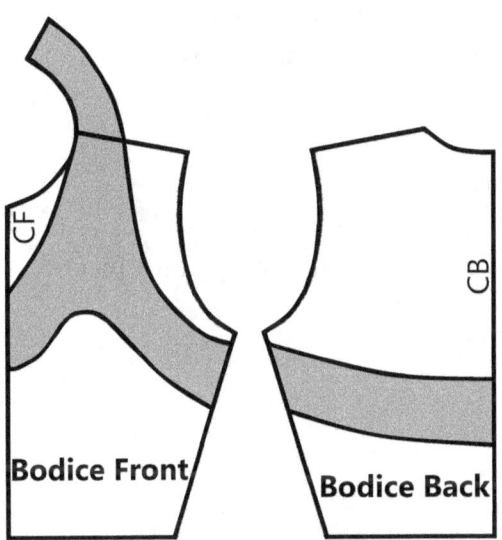
Halter Neckline and Back Facing

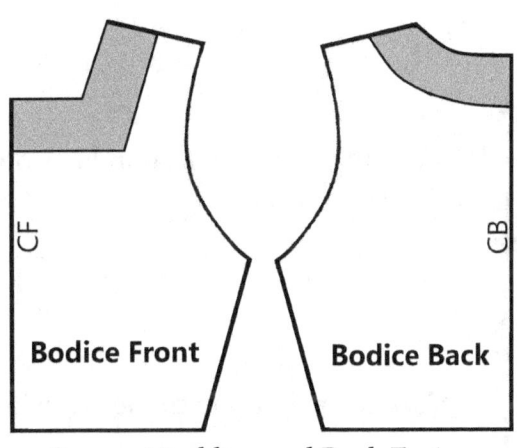
Square Neckline and Back Facing

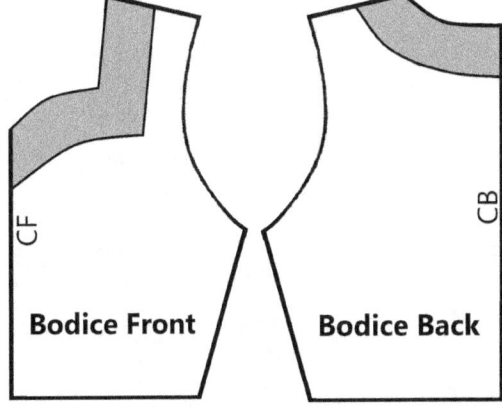
Sweetheart Neckline and Back Facing

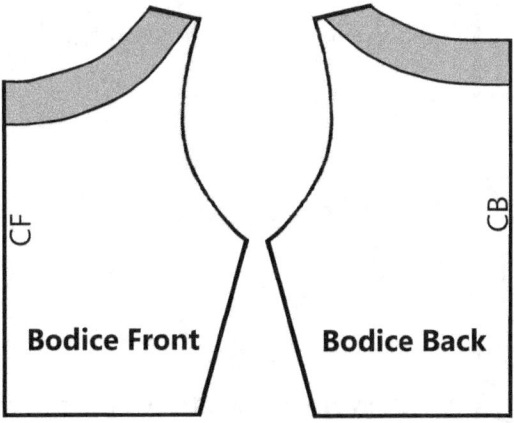
Boat Neckline and Back Facing

SYMBOLS

The symbols illustrated below are used throughout the book.

 Thick black outlines on patterns in this book indicate seam and hem allowances.

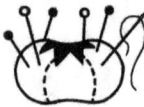 Sewing tips and instructions are indicated by this symbol.

 Special drafting instructions are indicated by this symbol.

 Shaded areas on necklines, front, and back openings indicate facings. Dotted lines indicate pattern variations, adjustments, and adaptations.

 This symbol indicates grain lines on patterns and must be added to all pattern pieces before cutting fabric.

 Slash the pattern up to the arrowhead.

 Place the pattern piece on the fold of the fabric.

 Cut the fabric on the bias.

 This symbol indicates where interfacing should be applied.

SHOULDER DROP CHART

The chart below indicates the amount the front shoulder **F** and the back shoulder edge **R** should be dropped from the top line when drafting the basic front and back bodice blocks. Select the required bust size and the corresponding amount by which the shoulder line should be dropped. Amounts are shown in **centimetres** with an approximate equivalent in **inches.**

Chest/Bust Measurement		Shoulder Drop Guide	
Centimetres	Inches	Centimetres	Inches
56	22	3	1¼
60	23⅝	3	1¼
64	25⅛	3	1¼
68	26¾	3.5	1⅜
72	28¼	3.5	1⅜
76	29⅞	3.5	1⅜
80	31½	3.5	1⅜
84	33⅛	4	1½
88	34⅝	4	1½
92	36⅛	4	1½
97	38⅛	4	1½
102	40⅛	4	1½
107	42⅛	4.5	1¾
112	44⅛	4.5	1¾
117	46	5	2
122	48	5	2
127	50	5.5	2⅛
132	52	5.5	2⅛

MODIFIED BODY MEASUREMENT CHART FOR LADIES

SHOWN IN CENTIMETRES WITH AN APPROXIMATE EQUIVALENT IN INCHES WITH 4 cm (1 ½ in) and 5 cm (2 in) INCREMENTS (Ease is not included)

THIS CHART MUST BE USED AS A GUIDE WITH THIS BOOK ONLY

SIZE CODE	6	8	10	12	14	16	18	20	22	24
S-M-L	S	S	M	M	L	L	XL	XL	XXL	XXL
BUST CM IN	80 31½	84 33⅛	88 34⅝	92 36⅛	97 38⅛	102 40⅛	107 42⅛	112 44⅛	117 46	122 48
WAIST	62 24⅜	66 26	70 27½	74 29⅛	79 31⅛	84 33⅛	89 35	94 37	99 39	104 41
HIPS	88 34⅝	92 36⅛	96 37¾	100 39⅜	105 41¼	110 43¼	115 45¼	120 47¼	125 49¼	130 51⅛
WIDTH ACROSS CHEST	31 12⅛	32 12½	33 13	34 13⅜	35 13¾	36 14⅛	37 14⅝	38 15	39 15⅜	40 15¾
SHOULDER LENGTH	11.5 4½	12 4¾	12.5 4⅞	12.5 4⅞	13 5⅛	13 5⅛	13.5 5¼	14 5½	14.5 5¾	15 5⅞
NECK SIZE	33 13	34 13⅜	35 13¾	36 14⅛	37 14⅝	38 15	39 15⅜	42 16½	44 17¼	44.5 17½
FRONT SHOULDER TO WAIST	40 15¾	41 16⅛	42 16½	42.5 16¾	43 16⅞	43.5 17⅛	44 17¼	44.5 17½	45 17¾	45.5 17⅞
SHOULDER TO BUST POINT	25 9⅞	26 10¼	27 10⅝	27.5 10¾	28.5 11¼	29.5 11⅝	30.5 12	31.5 12⅜	32 12⅝	33 13
WIDTH ACROSS BACK	32 12⅝	33 13	34 13⅜	35 13¾	36 14⅛	37 14⅝	38 15	39 15⅜	40 15¾	41 16⅛
NAPE TO WAIST	38 15	39 15⅜	40 15¾	40.5 16	41 16⅛	41.5 16¼	42 16½	42.5 16¾	43 17	43.5 17⅛
CROTCH DEPTH	22 8¾	23 9	24 9⅜	25 9¾	26.5 10⅜	27.5 10¾	29 11⅜	30 11¾	31.5 12⅜	32.5 12¾
SLEEVE HEAD DEPTH	10 4	10.5 4⅛	11 4¼	11.5 4½	12.5 4⅞	13.5 5¼	14.5 5¾	15.5 6⅛	16.5 6½	17.5 6⅞
SLEEVE LENGTH	56.5 22¼	57 22⅜	57.5 22⅝	58 22¾	58.5 23	59 23¼	59.5 23⅜	60 23⅝	60.5 23⅞	61 24
TOP ARM (BICEP)	25 9⅞	26 10¼	28 11	30 11¾	31 12¼	32 12⅝	33 13	34 13⅜	36 14⅛	38 15
WRIST	14.5 5¾	15 5⅞	15.5 6⅛	16 6¼	16.5 6½	17 6¾	17.5 6⅞	18 7⅛	18.5 7¼	19 7½
WAIST TO HIP	18 7⅛	18 7⅛	18 7⅛	18 7⅛	18 7⅛	18 7⅛	18 7⅛	18 7⅛	18 7⅛	18 7⅛
WAIST TO KNEE	57.5 22⅝	58 22¾	58.5 23	59 23¼	59.5 23⅜	60 23⅝	60.5 23⅞	61 24	61.5 24¼	62 24⅜
WAIST TO ANKLE	98 38⅝	99 39	100 39⅜	101 39¾	102 40⅛	103 40½	104 41	105 41⅜	106 41¾	107 42⅛
SIDE WAIST TO FLOOR	103 40½	104 41	105 41⅜	106 41¾	107 42⅛	108 42½	109 42⅞	110 43¼	111 43¾	112 44⅛

TAKING MEASUREMENTS

It is essential to take accurate measurements, as inaccurate measurements will result in unnecessary fittings and re-cutting of the garment. Skill in taking measurements will be achieved with practice on a dress form (dressmaker's dummy). Make a note of the posture of the figure, whether erect, with sloping shoulders, or a rounded back (hunch back). It is best to wear fitted garments such as a T-shirt and tights while taking measurements.

Take all measurements closely, but not tightly. Use a pencil to write all measurements taken on the body measurement chart. Do not allow ease while taking measurements, as ease will be added while drafting the pattern. Keep the shoulder to waist length the same for the front and the back, as this will eliminate problems while drafting the bodice block. Tie tape or string around the waist to help while taking measurements. The average adult hip position is about 18 cm (7 in) to 24 cm (9 ½ in) below the waist level, but in this book we use 18 cm (7 in) hip depth from bust size 80 cm (31 ½ in) and up.

1. **Shoulder length:** Measured from the side of the neck to the end of the shoulder bone.
2. **Centre front to waist:** Measured from the throat (clavicle) to the waist.
3. **Width across the chest:** Measured at a level approximately **7.5 cm (3 in)** down from the throat (clavicle), from armhole to armhole, where the crease of the armhole begins.
4. **Bust point:** Measured approximately **3 cm (1¼ in)** from the base of the neck, down to the centre of the bust.
5. **Bust circumference:** Measured from the back, under the arms, to the centre front bust.
6. **Front shoulder to waist:** Measured from the base of the neck, where the garment shoulder seam is located, over the bust point, and down to the tape at the waist.
7. **Front shoulder to empire:** Measured from the top of the shoulder, next to the neck, to just under the bust.
8. **Empire (under bust) circumference:** Measured from the back and under the arms to just under the bust and centre front area.
9. **Waist circumference:** Measure the waist from the back to the front at tape level.
10. **Waist to hip:** Measured at a level **18 cm (7 in)** below the waist for all adults.
11. **Hip circumference:** Measure the widest part of the hip.
12. **Crotch depth:** Measured from the waist to the base of the flat surface.
13. **Neck size:** Measure around the base of the neck, from the front to the back.
14. **Width across the back:** Measured at a level approximately **14 cm (5 ½ in)** down from the top neck bone, from armhole to armhole (to the garment armhole seam).
15. **Nape to waist:** Measured from the top neck bone at the back of the neck, down to the tape at the waist.
16. **Depth of sleeve head:** Place a ruler high up under the armpit and measure from the tip of the shoulder bone, down to the upper edge of the ruler as illustrated.
17. **Top arm circumference:** Measured around the widest part of the upper arm (bicep).
18. **Sleeve length:** Place the arm on the hip and measure from the tip of the shoulder bone, down over the elbow, to just below the wrist bone.
19. **Wrist measurement:** Measure the wrist circumference with slight ease.

BODY MEASUREMENT CHART

BODY	MEASURE	QUARTER	HALF	EASE
THE FRONT				
1. SHOULDER LENGTH				
2. CENTRE FRONT TO WAIST				
3. WIDTH ACROSS THE CHEST				
4. SHOULDER TO BUST POINT				
5. BUST CIRCUMFERENCE				
6. FRONT SHOULDER TO WAIST				
7. SHOULDER TO EMPIRE LINE				
8. EMPIRE CIRCUMFERENCE				
9. WAIST CIRCUMFERENCE				
10. WAIST TO HIP				
11. HIP CIRCUMFERENCE				
THE BACK				
12. CROTCH DEPTH				
13. NECK SIZE				
14. WIDTH ACROSS THE BACK				
15. NAPE TO WAIST				
ARM MEASUREMENTS				
16. DEPTH OF SLEEVE HEAD				
17. TOP ARM CIRCUMFERENCE				
18. SLEEVE LENGTH				
19. WRIST CIRCUMFERENCE				

BODY MEASUREMENTS

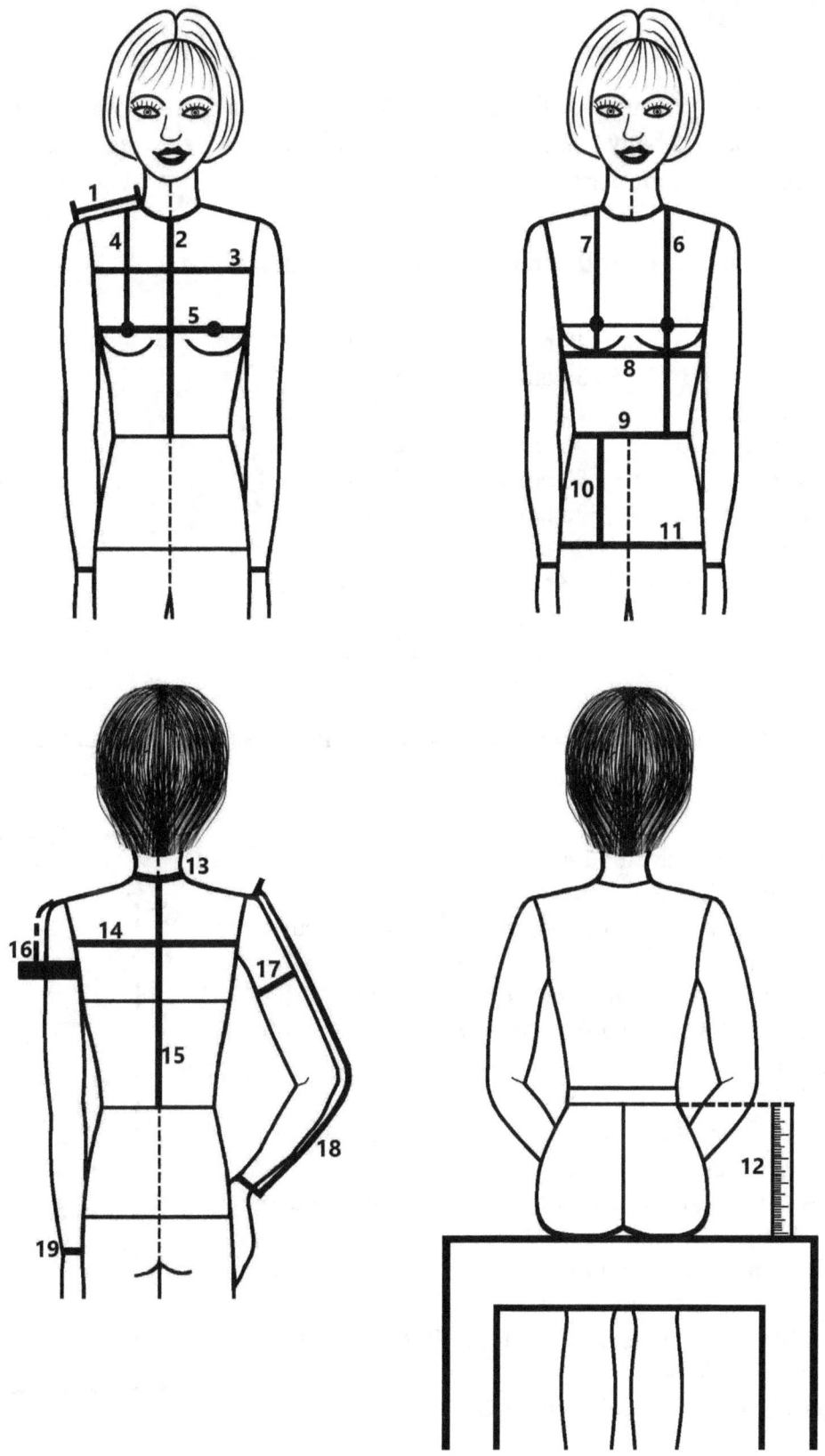

THE BASIC BODICE BLOCK

THE FRONT BODICE

The instructions given throughout the book are for an average figure with a bust size of **88 cm (34 in)** from the **modified body measurement chart for ladies**. Other sizes are constructed in the same way, using the exact measurements that are given for the basic front and back bodice drafts.

Measurements required to draft the basic front and back bodice blocks:

Front shoulder to waist	42 cm	16 ½ in
Neck size	35 cm	13 ¾ in
Shoulder length	12.5 cm	4 ⅞ in
Shoulder drop from chart	4 cm	1 ½ in
Bust circumference	88 cm	34 ⅝ in
Waist circumference	70 cm	27 ½ in
Hip circumference	96 cm	37 ¾ in
Waist to hip length	18 cm	7 ⅛ in
Width across chest	33 cm	13 in
Width across back	34 cm	13 ⅜ in

Draft half the front bodice block by ruling lines down and across from A, as illustrated below.

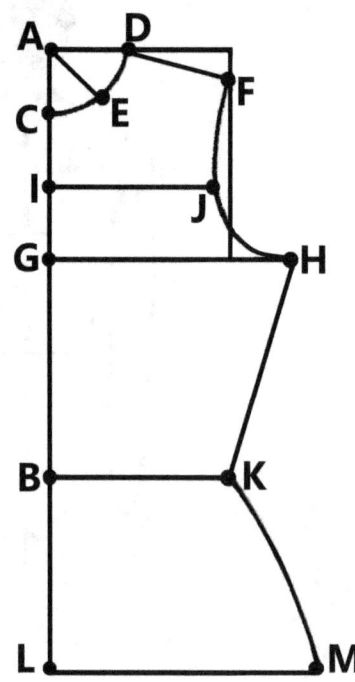

A-B: Front shoulder to waist length.
A-C: One fifth of neck size plus **1 cm (⅜ in)**.
A-D: One fifth of neck size.
A-E: The same length as **A-D** plus **6 mm (¼ in)**. Draw a curve with the French curve from **C** to **D** for the front neck.
D-F: The shoulder length. **F** must be **4 cm (1 ½ in)** below the top line for bust size **88 cm (34 in)**. Refer to the shoulder drop chart on page 31.
B-G: Half of **A-B**.
G-H: Quarter of the bust circumference plus **2.5 cm (1 in)**.
G-I: Half of **C-G**. Rule a line across from I.
I-J: Half across the chest. Draw a curve with the French curve from **F** to **J** and **H** for the armhole.
B-K: Quarter of the waist circumference. Rule a line from **H** to **K** for the side seam length (underarm to waist).
B-L: Waist to hip length, measured at **18 cm (7 in)** below the waistline from size **6 (31 ½ in)** and up.
L-M: Quarter of the hip circumference. Connect **K** and **M** with the hip curve.

~ 36 ~

THE BASIC BODICE BLOCK

THE BACK BODICE

Draft half the back bodice block by ruling lines down and across from N, as illustrated below.

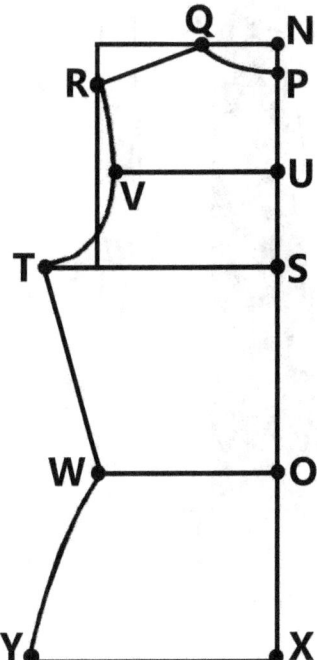

N-O: The same measurement as **A-B** for the front.
N-P: Drop **2 cm (¾ in)** for the **basic** back neck.
N-Q: One fifth of neck size.
P-Q: Draw a curve with the French curve for the back neck.
Q-R: Shoulder length. Draw this line **4 cm (1 ½ in)** below the top line.
O-S: Half of **N-O**.
S-T: Quarter of the bust measurement. Do not add **2.5 cm (1 in)** here. Rule a line across.
P-U: Half of **P-S**.
U-V: Half across back. Draw a curve from **R** to **V** and **T** for the back armhole.
O-W: Quarter of the waist circumference. Rule a line from **T** to **W** for the side seam length.
O-X: Waist to hip length, measured **18 cm (7 in)** below the waistline.
X-Y: Quarter of the hip circumference. Connect **W-Y** with the hip curve.

DARTLESS BODICE BLOCKS

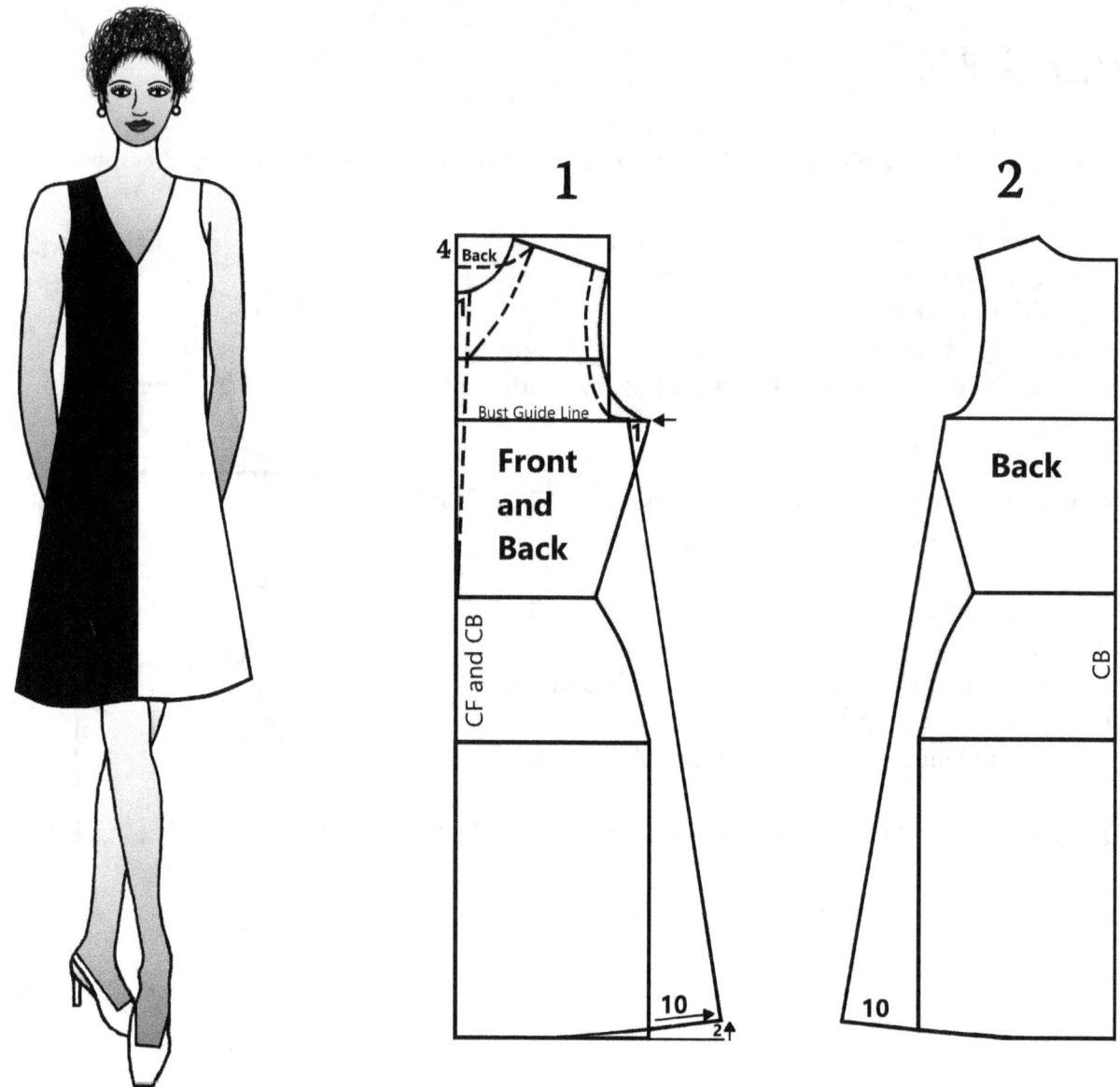

A-LINE SLEEVELESS DRESS

1. Draft the basic front bodice block on the left side of a large sheet of paper. Lengthen the bodice for the required dress length. Draw a line **1 cm (⅜ in)** from the centre front neck, disappearing at the waist level. This will eliminate a gaping neckline. Draw the V-neck **3 cm (1¼ in)** from the neck edge, ending at a desired depth. Measure **4 cm (1 ½ in)** down at the centre front and draw the back neck from the new neckline, using a French curve. Measure **1 cm (⅜ in)** in at the side of the bust guide line and mark. Use a tape measure to scoop the armhole by **1.5 cm (⅝ in)** or as desired. Use the French curve to blend the armhole curve. Measure **10 cm (4 in)** out at the side seam and lift the hemline by **2 cm (¾ in)**. Rule a line from the armhole down to the hemline as illustrated. Use the hip curve to draw the hemline.
2. Place the right-hand side of the paper underneath the front draft and trace the back pattern from the front draft on the original centre front line. This completes the master draft.

A-LINE SLEEVELESS DRESS

3. Place a sheet of paper under the master draft and secure the top section with pins. Trace the front and back pattern pieces off. Draw neckline and armhole facings (shaded areas) and trace it off. Add grain lines, notches, hem, and seam allowances to the pattern pieces. Cut the pattern pieces out with the seam allowances. This pattern works well with stretch or bias-cut fabric.

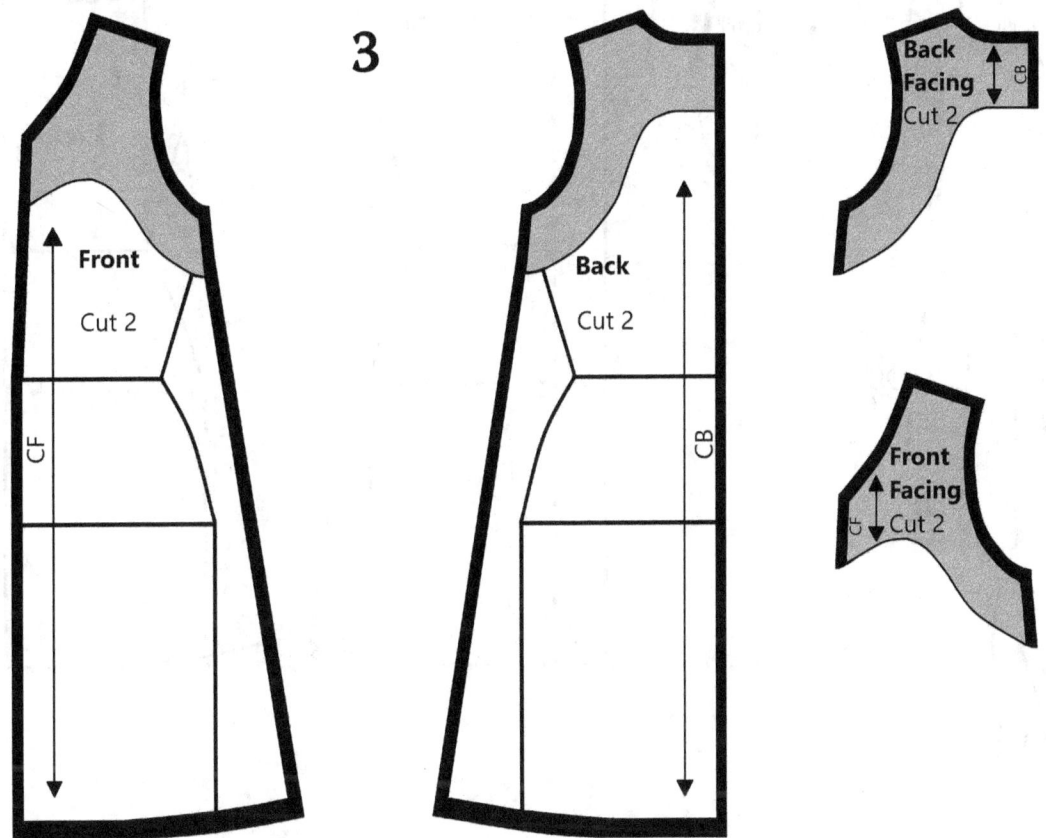

The front and front facing sections can be cut on the fold if using the same colour fabric. Cut the garment sections out. Neaten the shoulders, centre back, centre front, and side seams of the dress sections with overlocking or a zigzag stitch. Pin and stitch the centre front seam, right sides together. Press the seam open. Pin and stitch the front and back shoulders together. Press the seams open. Interface the facing pieces. Pin and stitch the facing centre front seam, right sides together. Press the seam open. Pin and stitch the facing front and back shoulders, right sides together. Press the seams open. Pin and stitch the facing to the dress neckline. Trim, grade, and clip the seam allowances. Press the facing. Understitch through the facing and seam allowances. Press. Pin and stitch the facing to the armholes. Trim, grade, and clip the seam allowances. Pull the back panels through the shoulders and right side out. Understitch the armhole facings. Press. Pin and stitch the dress centre back seam, right sides together. Pin and stitch the side seams and facings. Press. Overlock the hem edge. Turn the hem up and hand stitch in place. Press the garment.

DARTLESS BODICE BLOCKS

HALTER-NECK DRESS

Trace the basic front bodice block. Lengthen the block to the required amount. Draw the basic back neck at the front. Measure **2 cm (¾ in)** in at the side of the bust line and mark. Draw the new armhole as illustrated by the dotted line. Trace the back from the front including the new armhole. Draw the neck band (shaded area) by measuring **5 cm (2 in)** or a desired amount from the basic front neck. Measure **8 cm (3 ⅛ in)** out at the centre front and side seam. Lift the hemline by **2 cm (¾ in)** at the side seam. Rule a line at the front and side seam as illustrated. Redraw the hemline. Repeat the same for the back. Trace all the pattern pieces off. Add grain lines, notches, hem, and seam allowances.

HALTER-NECK DRESS

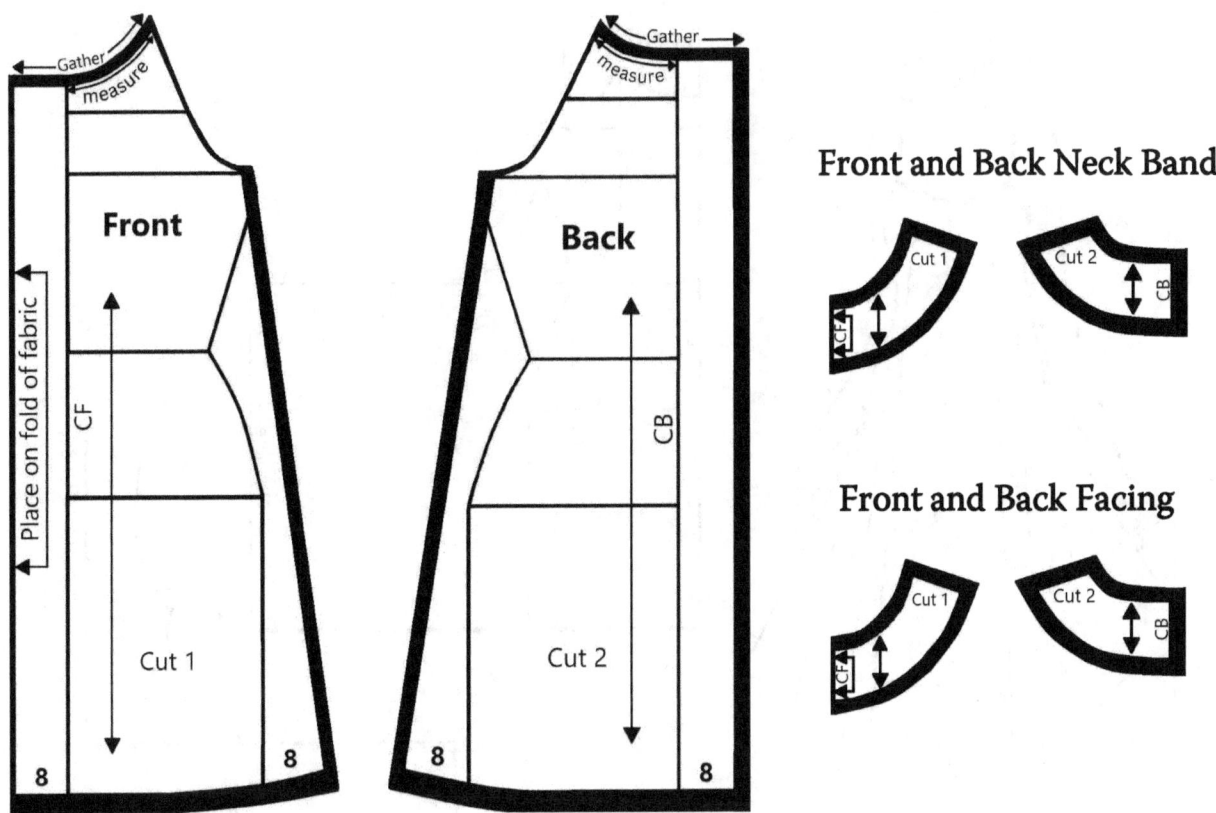

Staystitch the front and back armholes to prevent stretching. Sew two parallel rows of stitches in the seam allowance of the front and back necklines for gathers. Overlock the front and back side seams, as well as the centre back. Pin and stitch the centre back seam right sides together, up to the marked opening. Topstitch around the back opening. Pin and stitch the front and back side seams, right sides together. Press the seams open. Pin and stitch bias binding around the armholes. Measure the distance from the centre front neck to the upper edge of the armhole and record. Pull up the bobbin threads to measure the same as the recorded amount. Secure the thread ends. Repeat the same for the back sections. Apply suitable interfacing to the neck band sections. Mark notches. Pin and stitch the neck band sections along the shoulder seams. Press the seams open. Repeat for the facing sections of the neck band. With right sides together, pin and stitch the neck band and facing together along the outer neck edge. Trim, grade, and clip the seam allowances. Press the bottom seam allowances of the band and facing to the wrong side. Matching notches up, pin and stitch the neck band to the front and back necklines. Make button loops from a bias strip and secure it on the right side of the neck band at the back opening. Fold the facing and neck band right sides together along each centre back edge and stitch in place. Turn the facing to inside and tack or pin in place. Edgestitch in place from the right side of the garment. Turn the hem up and stitch in place. Press the garment.

DARTLESS BODICE BLOCKS

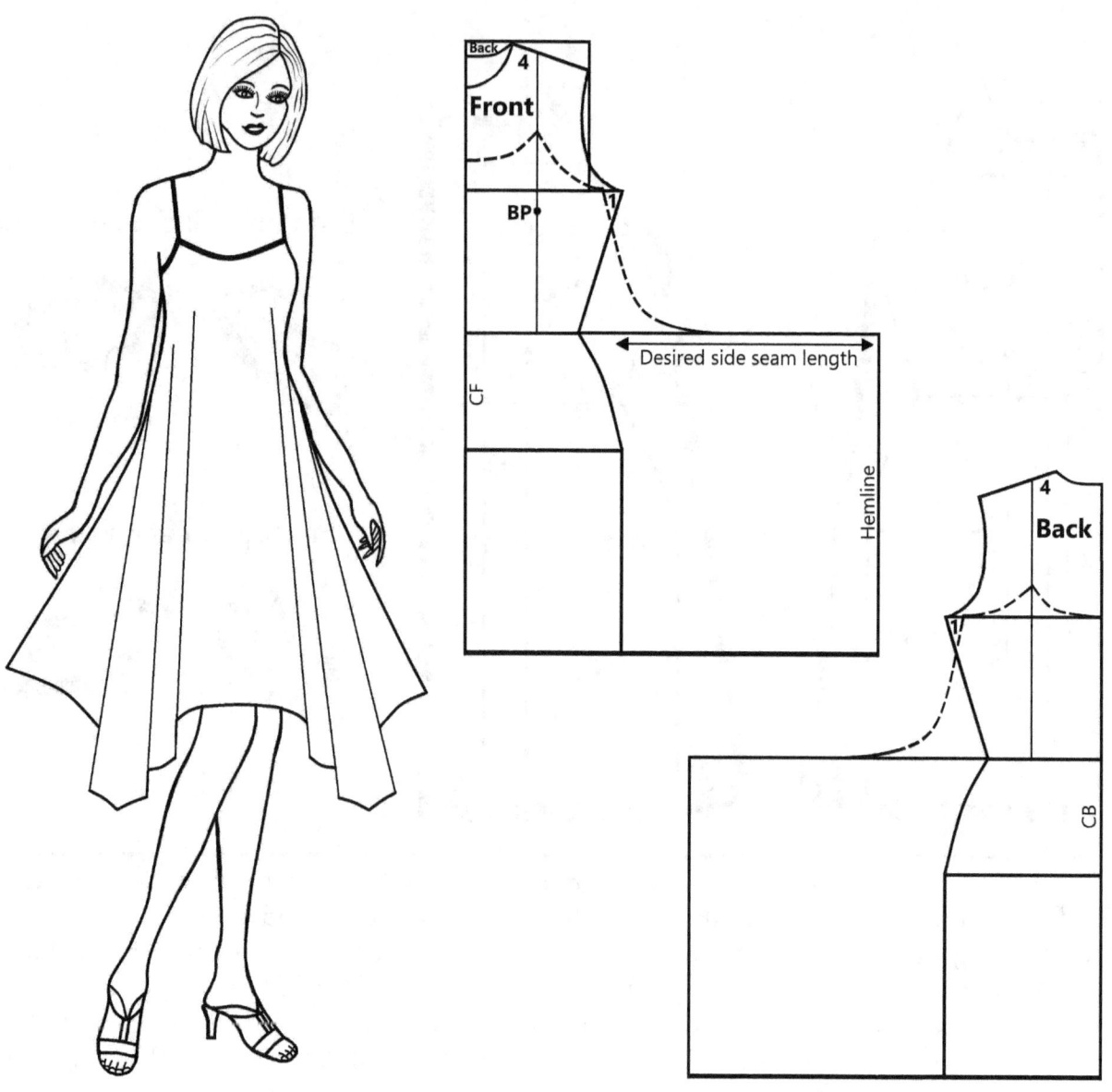

HANDKERCHIEF HEM DRESS

Draft the basic front bodice block. Lengthen the bodice as desired. Draw the back neck at the front. Trace the back from the front bodice. Rule a vertical line **4 cm (1 ½ in)** from the neck edge, down to the waist. Mark the bust point level on the line. Measure the required front neckline depth and mark. Measure **1 cm (⅜ in)** in at the side of the bust line and mark. Draw the neckline and armhole with the French curve as illustrated. Rule a horizontal line from the waist out for a desired side seam length. Rule a line down to the hemline. Draw a curved line from the bust guide line down to the waistline as illustrated by the dotted line. Repeat the above instructions for the back pattern. Trace the pattern pieces off. Add grain lines, notches, hem, and seam allowances.

~ 42 ~

HANDKERCHIEF HEM DRESS

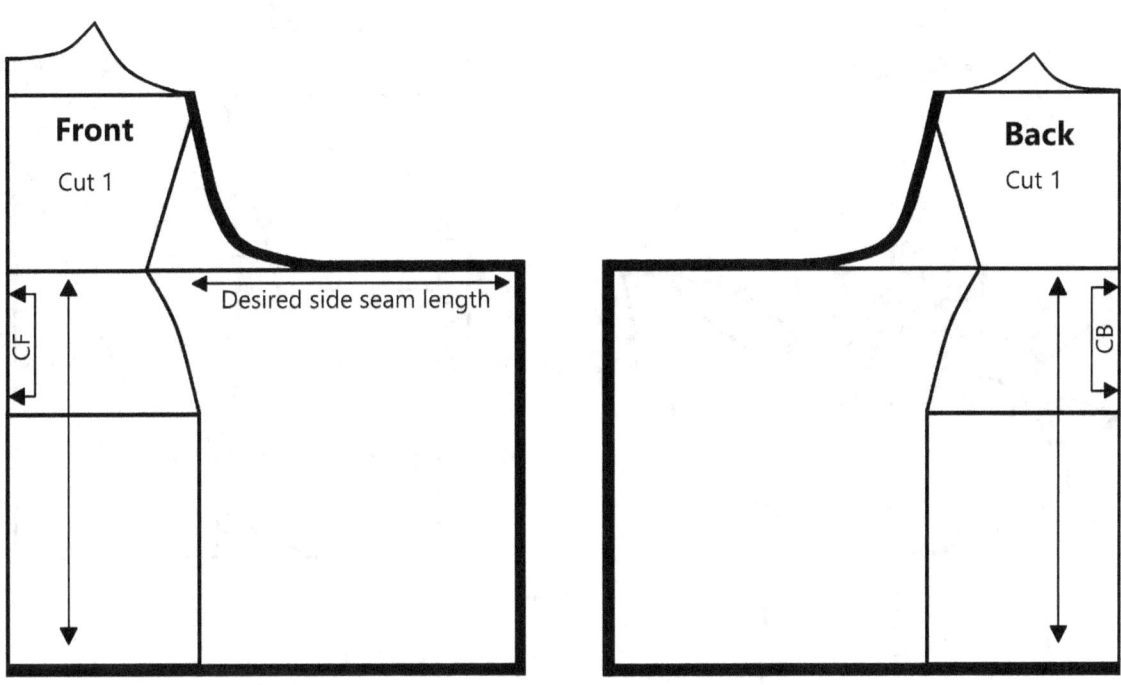

Cut the front and back panels out. Make bias binding for the front and back neckline as described on page **195**. Measure the front neckline and cut binding to that length. Pin and stitch the right side of the binding to the wrong side of the front neckline. Fold the binding to the right side of the garment and pin and stitch it in place. Press. Repeat for the back neckline. Measure the strap length and armhole curve and add **4 cm** (**1 ½ in**) to the length. Cut two straps from bias binding. Starting at the side seam, pin the right side of the strap to the wrong side of one front armhole edge and stitch in place. Repeat for one back armhole. Fold the binding to the right side of the garment and pin or tack it in place from the front armhole, continuing across the shoulder, and down to the back armhole. Sew it in place in one continuous motion. Repeat for the opposite side of the garment. With right sides together, pin and stitch the front and back side seams, matching notches up. Overlock the side seams. Sew the hem, using a rolled or narrow hem, depending on the type of fabric used. Press the garment.

DARTLESS BODICE BLOCKS

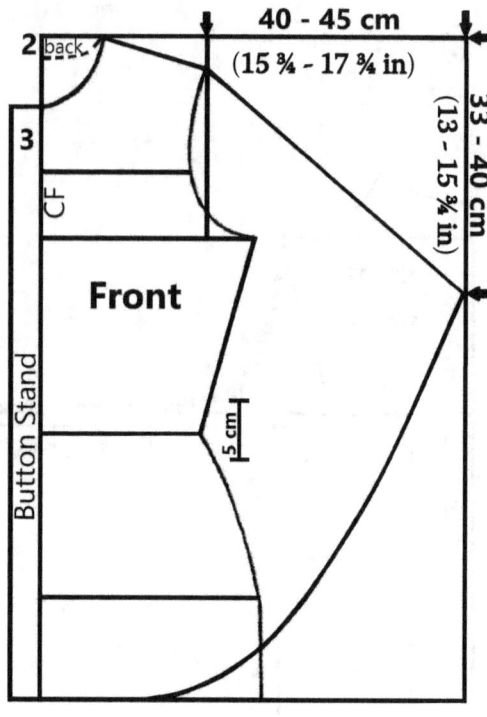

1

40 - 45 cm
(15 ¾ - 17 ¾ in)

33 - 40 cm
(13 - 15 ¾ in)

2 back
3
CF
Button Stand
Front
5 cm

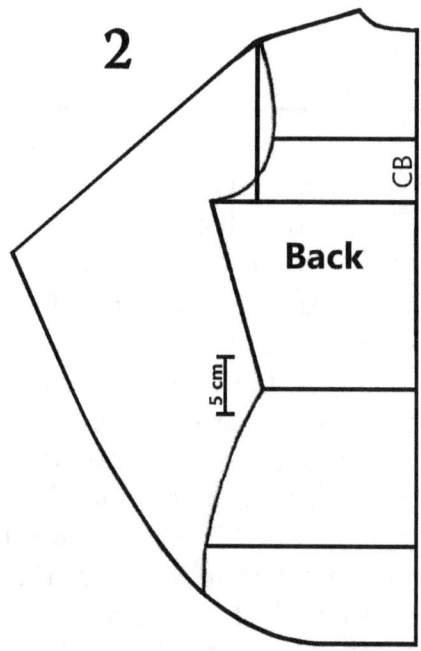

2

CB
Back
5 cm

BELTED CAPE

1. Draft the basic front block. Lengthen the block as desired. Add **3 cm (1 ¼ in)** to the centre front for a button stand. **The width of the button stand should be equal to the diameter of the button that will be used.**
Draw the back neck. Rule lines across and down the bodice block as illustrated. Draw the style lines. Mark a belt opening **5 cm (2 in)** long to the side of the waist.
2. Trace the back pattern from the front.

BELTED CAPE

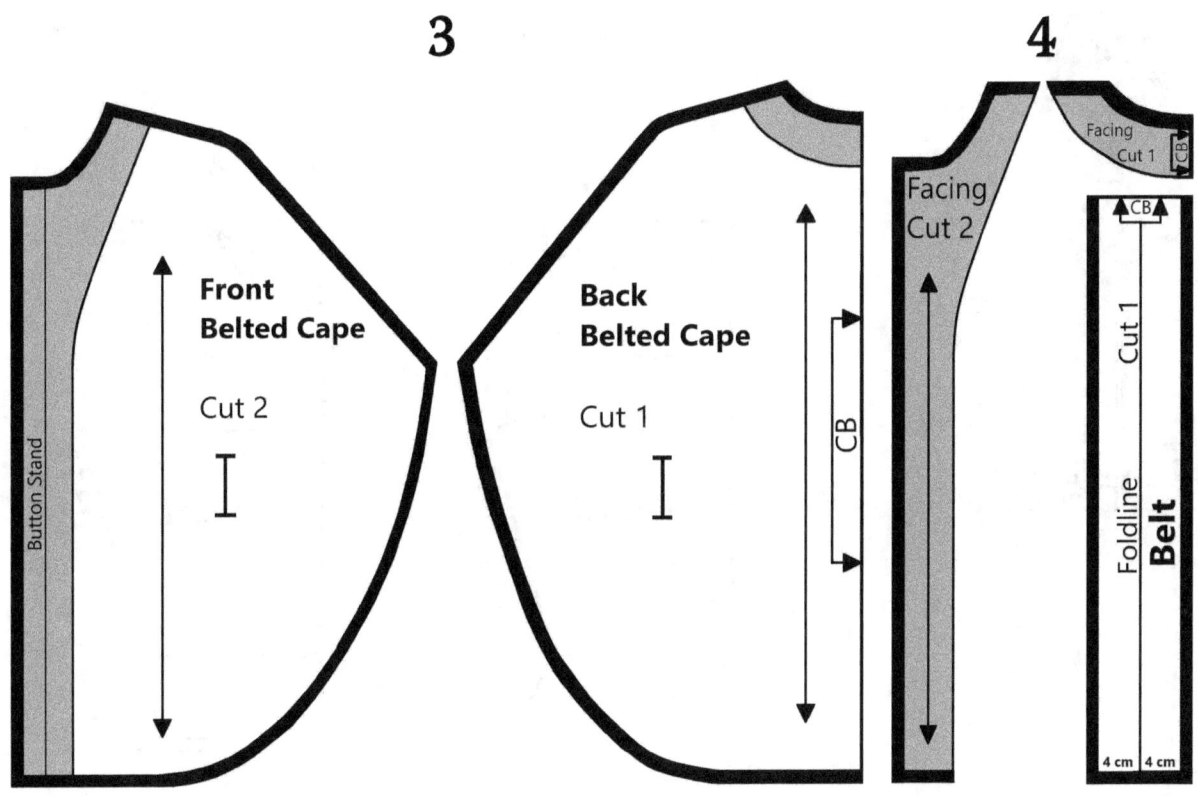

 3. Trace the front and back off on a new sheet of paper. Draw front and back facing (shaded areas) as illustrated. Add grain lines, notches, hem, and seam allowances.
4. Trace the facings off and cut the pattern pieces out. Draw a rectangle for a belt measuring **8 cm (3 ⅛ in)** wide and to the desired length. Add seam allowance to the belt pattern.

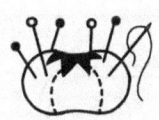 Iron fusible interfacing on the wrong side of the facing panels. Cut the cape panels out and mark the belt opening on the front panels, using dressmaker's carbon paper or tailor's chalk. With right sides together, pin and stitch the shoulder seams. Sew the front and back shoulder seams of the facing together. Press the seams open. Pin and stitch the facing to the neckline and front panels, right sides together. Cut the corners on the front edges diagonally. Trim, grade, and clip the neckline seam allowances. Press the seam allowance toward the facing. Understitch by stitching through the facing and the seam allowance, close to the seam. Finish the hem off with bias binding, or machine stitching. Pin each front panel to the back panel, wrong sides together, and stitch on the marked lines to secure them in place. Make a buttonhole on each marked line for the belt opening. Make a belt from the same fabric as the cape, or as desired. Mark and sew buttonholes on the right front panel. Mark and sew buttons on. Press the cape.

DARTLESS BODICE BLOCKS

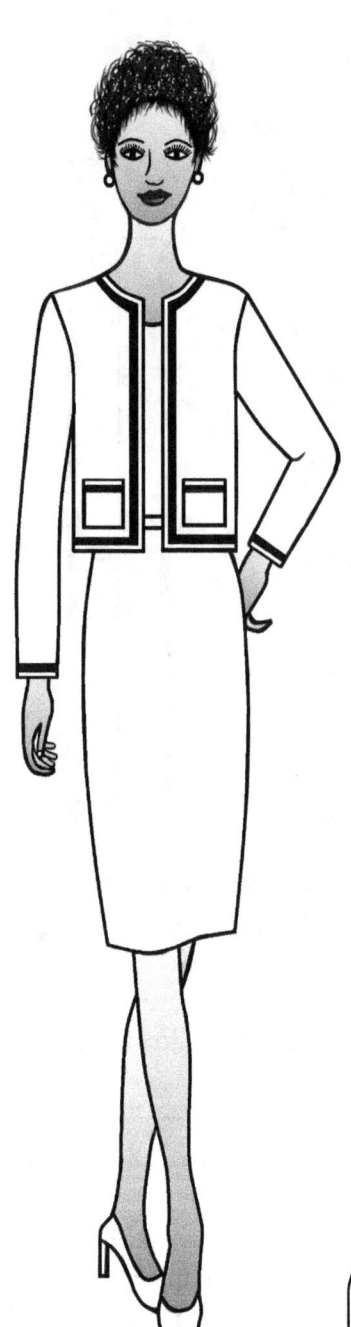

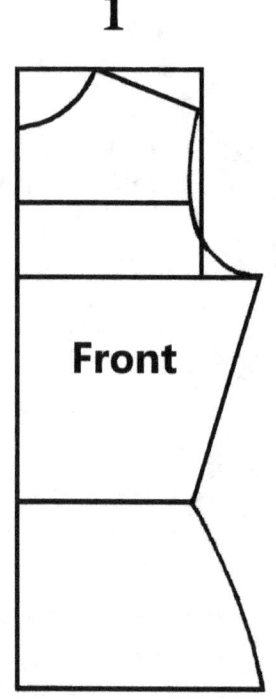

1

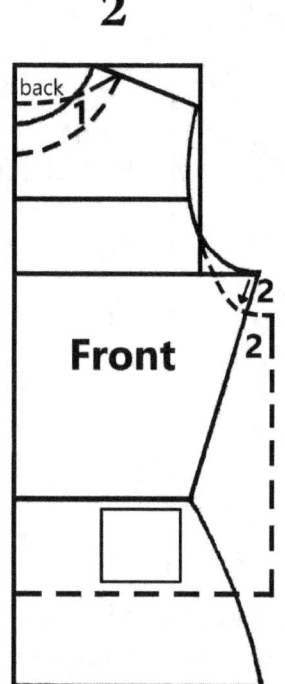

2

CHANEL STYLE JACKET

1. Draft the front bodice block as illustrated.
2. Scoop the neckline by **1 cm (⅜ in)**. Drop **2 cm (¾ in)** at the centre front and draw the back neck. Shorten the bodice as desired. Drop **2 cm (¾ in)** along the side seam line and measure **2 cm (¾ in)** out or as desired. Redraw the armhole with the French curve. Rule a line down and across as illustrated by the dotted line. Draw the pocket.

CHANEL STYLE JACKET

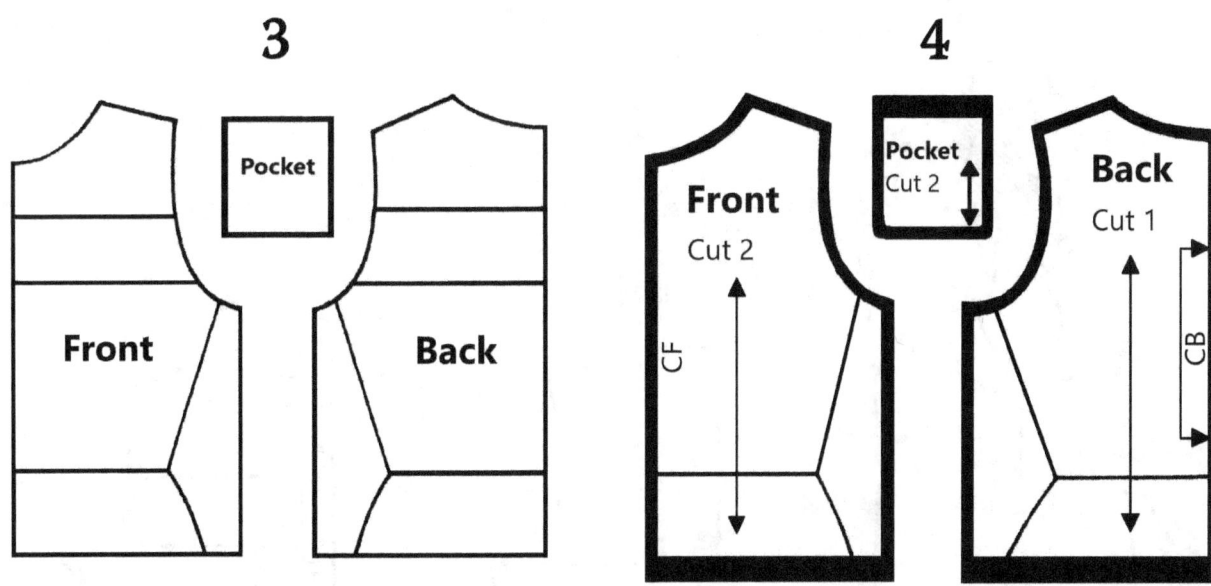

 3. Trace the front, back, and pocket patterns from the master draft.
4. Add grain lines, notches, hem, and seam allowance. Draw front and back facing as illustrated on the facings page and the belted cape. Trace the facing off and cut the pattern pieces out. Draft the basic set-in sleeve on page **58** to complete the pattern.

Cut the jacket panels out in Tweed or other suitable fabric. Attach medium-weight fusible interfacing to the front and back facings. Pin and stitch the facing shoulder seams, right sides together. Pin and stitch bias binding to the long edges of the facing, right sides together. Fold the binding to the wrong side and stitch in place from the right side. Pin and stitch the jacket shoulder seams, right sides together. Neaten the seams with binding. Press the seams open. Pin and stitch the jacket sides seams, right sides together. Neaten the side seams with binding and press. Pin and stitch the sleeve seams and neaten them with binding. Press the seams open. Use a stitch length of **5** and sew two rows of stitches along the sleeve head for gathers. Pin and stitch the sleeves into the armholes, right sides together. Neaten the armhole with binding. Pin and stitch the facing to the jacket, right sides together. Trim the facing side of the seam allowance to half its width. Notch the seam and turn the facing to the wrong side. Press. Understitch the facing. Bind the bottom edge of the sleeve. Fold the sleeve hem **2 cm (¾ in)** up and hand stitch in place. Press. Bind the bottom edge of the jacket excluding the facing. Turn the hem **4 cm (1 ½ in)** up and hand stitch in place. Turn under the lower edge of the facing and hand stitch in place. Pin decorative ribbon trim to the neck, centre front, hemline, and sleeves. Topstitch in place close to the trim edges. Turn under **2 cm** of the top edge of the pocket and stitch it in place. Pin decorative ribbon trim along the pocket edge and topstitch in place. Press the pocket seam allowance to the wrong side. Pin the pockets to the jacket and stitch in place. Press.

DARTLESS BODICE BLOCKS

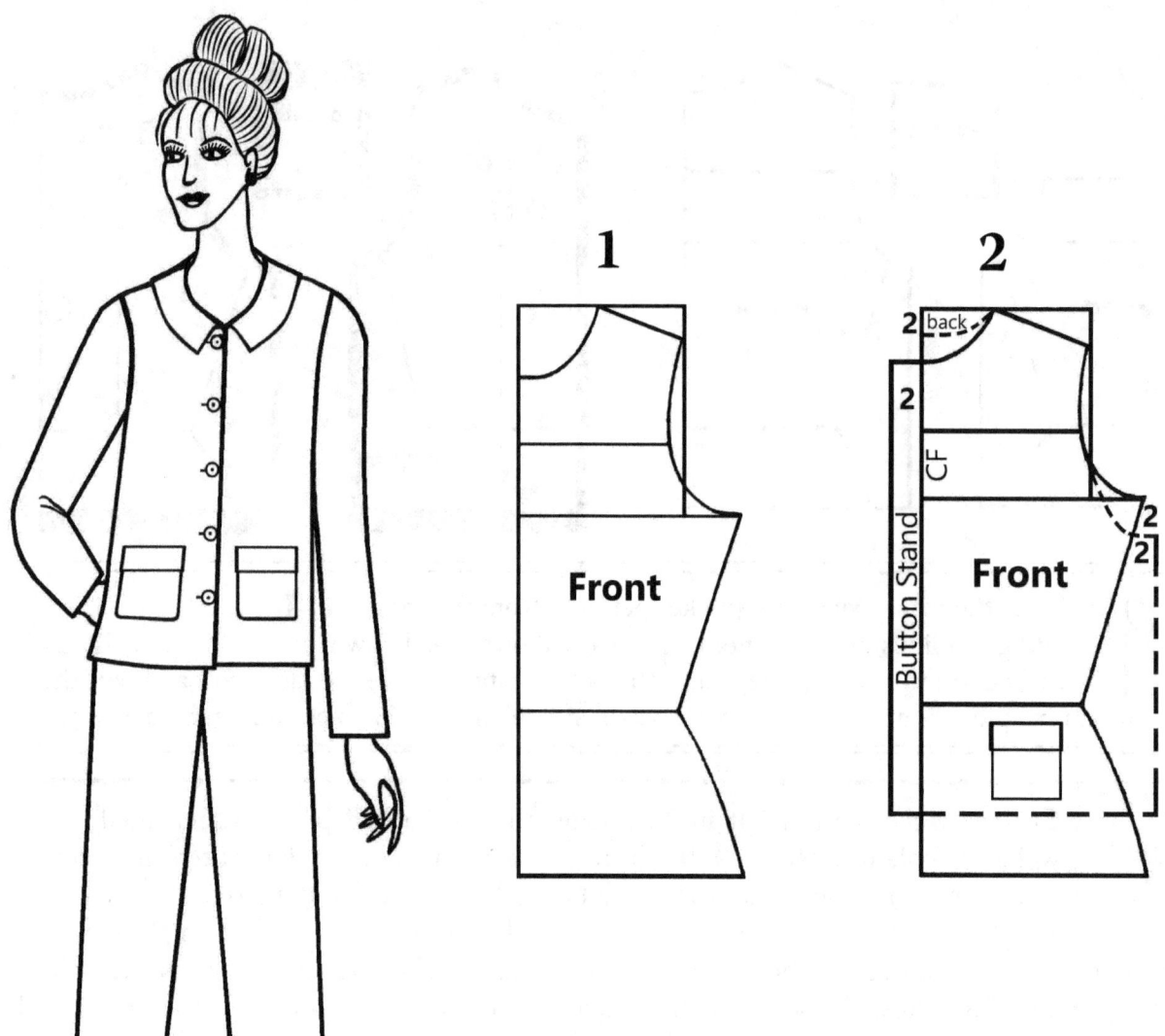

BOXY JACKET

1. Draft the basic front bodice block as illustrated.
2. Drop **2 cm (¾ in)** at the centre front and draw the back neck as illustrated. Add **2 cm (¾ in)** to the centre front for a button stand. Drop the armhole **2 cm (¾ in)** and measure **2 cm (¾ in)** out or as desired. Redraw the armhole with the French curve. Draw a line down from the armhole and across the hip line, to a desired length. Draw the pocket and flap.

BOXY JACKET

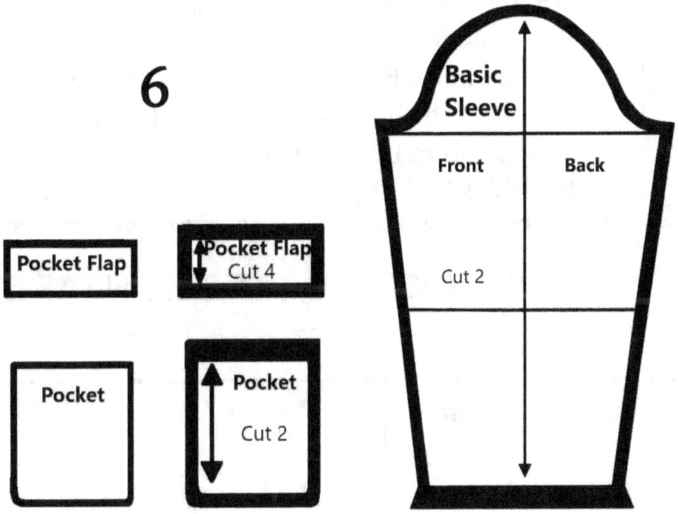

3. Trace the front and back pattern off. Measure the front and back necklines of the bodice blocks and record. Draw facing as illustrated before.

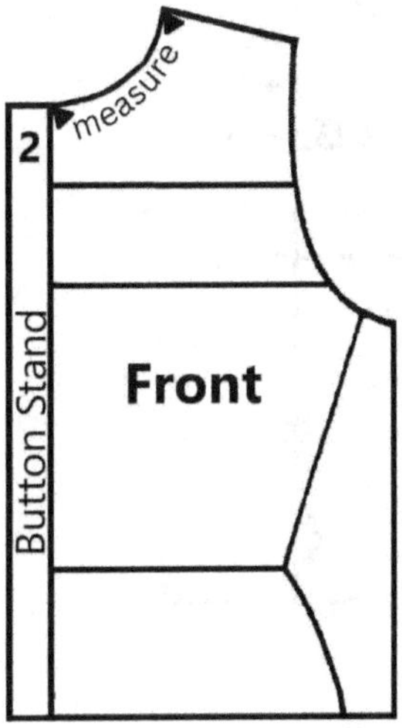

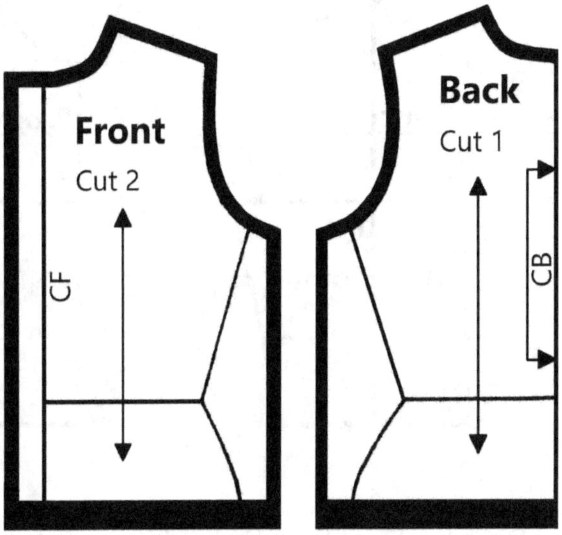

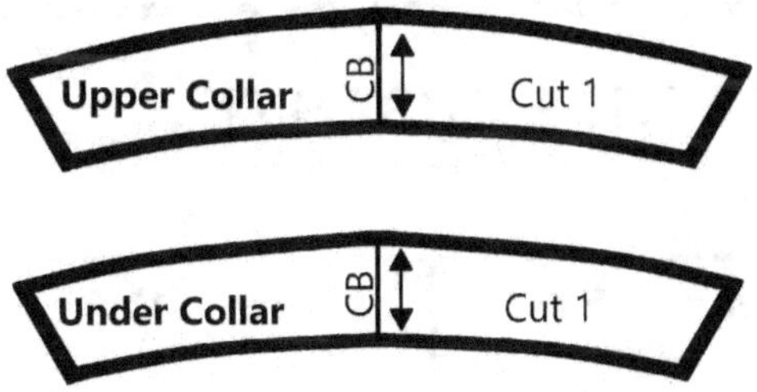

4. Add hem and seam allowances, notches, and grain lines to all pattern pieces.

5. Draw the straight collar variation as explained on pages **120** and **121**.

6. Trace the pocket and flap off and add seam allowance. Trace the basic set-in sleeve to complete the pattern.

DESIGNING WITH DARTS

The width of the shoulder dart differs from size to size. The chart below indicates a guide to different dart sizes. Choose a dart size that is suitable for the bust size.

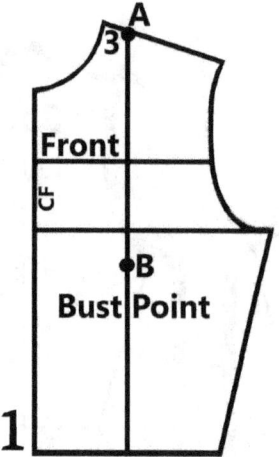 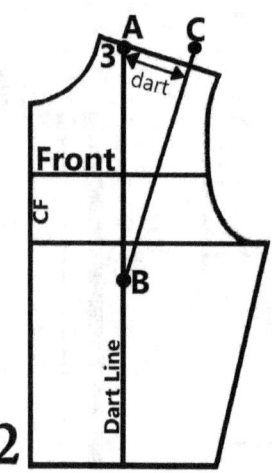 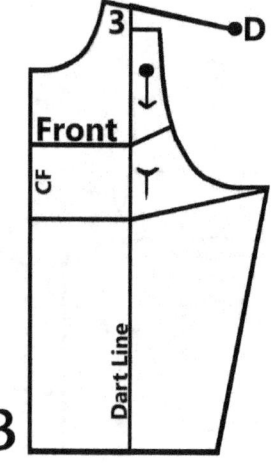

1. Draft the basic front bodice block. Rule a vertical line **3 cm (1 ¼ in)** from the base of the neck, down to the waist. **A** to **B** is the length from the shoulder to the bust point.
2. Measure the required dart size from **A** and mark. Rule a line from **B** to **C**, measuring the same length as **A** to **B**.
3. Fold the dart line **CB** lengthwise and place it on dart line **AB**. Secure it in place with a pin. Place a ruler at the base of the neck in line with the **3 cm** section of the shoulder line and rule a line down to **D**. The shoulder line from the base of the neck to **D** must measure the same length as the original shoulder of the bodice block.

CHOOSE A DART SIZE NEAREST TO THE BUST SIZE			
80 cm = 5.5 cm	92 cm = 7.5 cm	107 cm = 10.5 cm	122 cm = 11.5 cm
31½ in = 2⅛ in	36⅛ in = 3 in	42⅛ in = 4⅛ in	48 in = 4½ in
84 cm = 6.5 cm	97 cm = 8.5 cm	112 cm = 10.5 cm	127 cm = 12 cm
33⅛ in = 2½ in	38⅛ in = 3⅜ in	44⅛ in = 4⅛ in	50 in = 4¾ in
88 cm = 7 cm	102 cm = 9.5 cm	117 cm = 11 cm	132 cm = 12 cm
34⅝ in = 2¾ in	40⅛ in = 3¾ in	46 in = 4¼ in	52 in = 4¾ in

THE SHOULDER DART

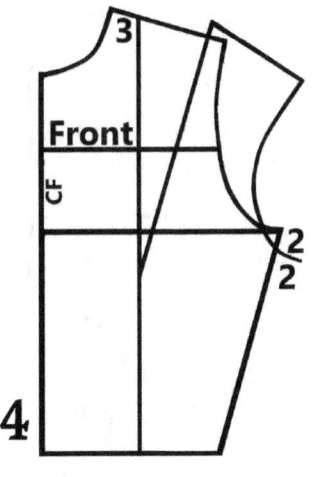 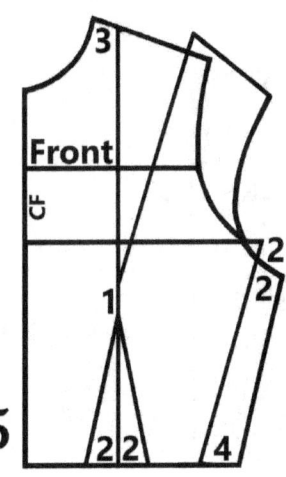

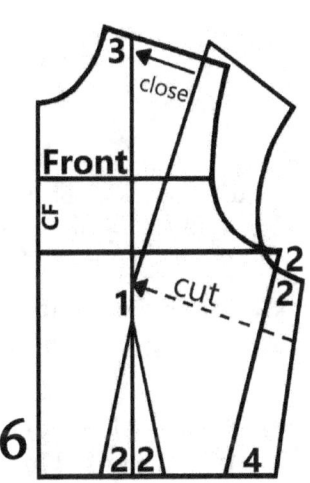 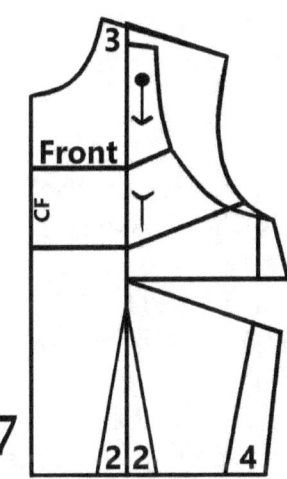

4. Measure **2 cm (¾ in)** down along the bodice side seam and **2 cm (¾ in)** outwards. Redraw the armhole with the French curve.
5. Place a waist dart **1 to 3 cm (⅜ - 1 ¼ in)** below the bust point as illustrated. The waist dart can vary from **2 cm (¾ in)** to **4 cm (1 ½ in)** deep, **1 or 2 cm (⅜ or ¾ in)** on both sides of the centre dart line. This depends on the style of the garment and the size of the person.
6. Add the dart allowance to the side of the waist. This allowance should be equal to the width of the waist dart when a fitted garment is required. Add more to the side seam when a looser fitting garment is required. Draw the new side seam as illustrated. Rule a line from the side seam to the bust point, approximately **10 cm (4 in)** from the top edge of the new side seam.
7. Cut the line up to the bust point so that the shoulder dart can be closed, to obtain the side bust dart, or to draw other style lines. Secure the shoulder dart with a pin, or sticky tape.

THE BACK BODICE BLOCK

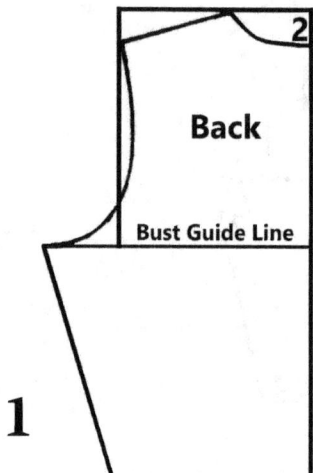

1

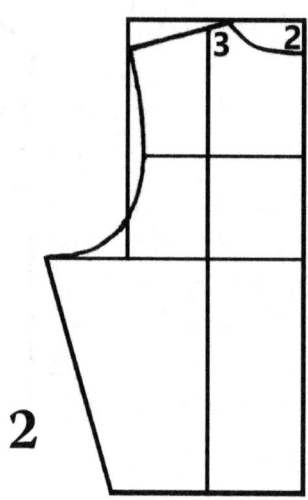

2

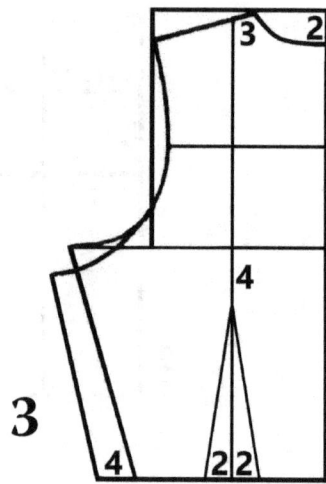

3

1. Drop **2 cm (¾ in)** for the **basic back neck curve** on all back bodice blocks. This amount of drop only differs when the style requires the front and back necklines to be scooped for wider or lower necklines.
2. Draw a vertical line **3 cm (1 ¼ in)** from the base of the neck. This is a standard position for the dart line in this book. The dart line may be moved more to the side when different designs are required.
3. Draw the end (apex) of the dart a minimum of **4 cm (1 ½ in)** below the bust guide line if a fitted garment is required. Draw the end (apex) of the dart between **5 cm (2 in)** and **10 cm (4 in)** below the bust guide line for a looser fit, depending on the body size. Draw the dart as illustrated and add the same amount to the side of the waist when a fitted garment is required. Add more to the side of the waist when a looser-fitting garment is required. **Ensure that the back side seams measure the same as the front side seams.**

Keep the back shoulder to waist length the same as the front shoulder to waist length when drafting the basic bodice blocks. Opt for a shorter shoulder to waist length when drafting blocks for larger and rounded figures.

DART MANIPULATION

The bust dart which initially starts in the shoulder can be moved to any position, provided it runs from an outer edge to the bust point. This is called the **Pivot Principle.** Relocating a dart does not alter the fit of a garment as long as the **focal point** of the dart and the **intake (the amount of fabric taken in, or removed)** remain the same.

Darts are folds sewn into the fabric to provide shape to a garment, especially over the bust area. A variety of design features such as gathers, pleats, and tucks can be created with the dart excess/intake. Darts can also be concealed in seams which form part of the design of a garment, provided that the seam passes over or close to the bust point. Darts are usually cut away on basic blocks to enable them to be outlined. Darts on patterns can also be transferred to fabric with dressmaker's carbon paper.

Trace copies of the front bodice block up to the waist. Draw lines to indicate the different dart positions, as illustrated on page **55**. Cut along the lines up to the bust point. Close the shoulder dart edges together and secure it with sticky tape. The darts will open in different positions, once the shoulder dart is folded close.

Although the dart on the block extends to the bust point, the darts on a pattern must be **shortened** to allow ease over the bust point and to make it less conspicuous. The size of the dart and the amount by which it is shortened depends on personal preference.

Shorten the side bust dart (French dart) by measuring 3 cm (1 ¼ in) down from the bust point, or as required. The waist dart can be shortened by measuring 1 - 3 cm (⅜ - 1 ¼ in) down from the bust point, or as required.

DART POSITIONS

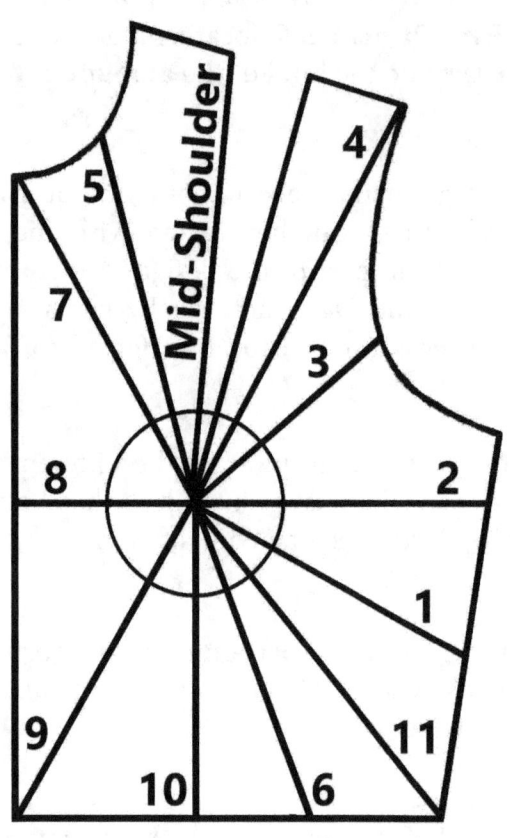
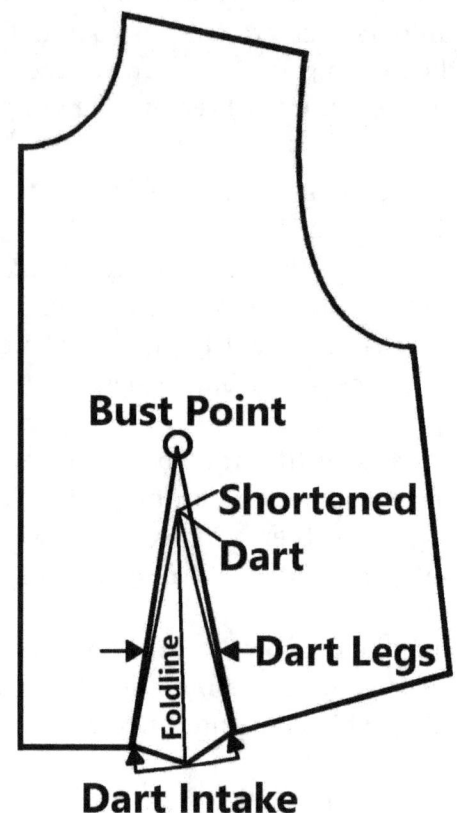

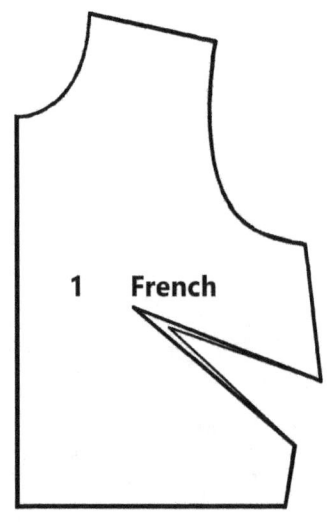
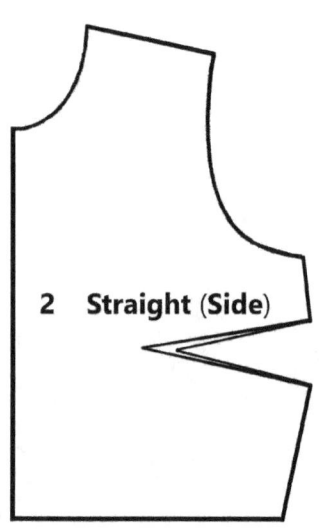

DART POSITIONS

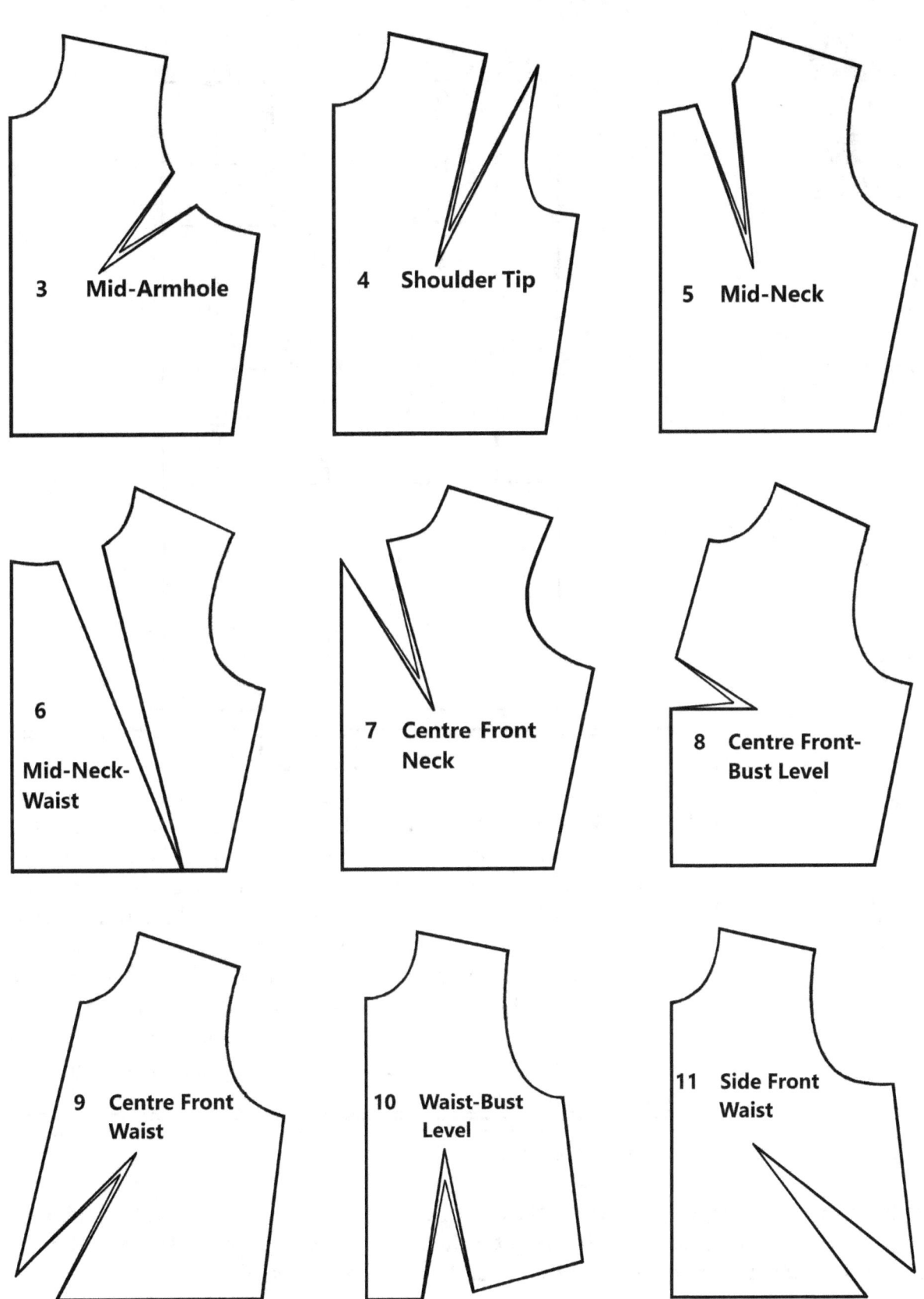

DESIGNING WITH DARTS

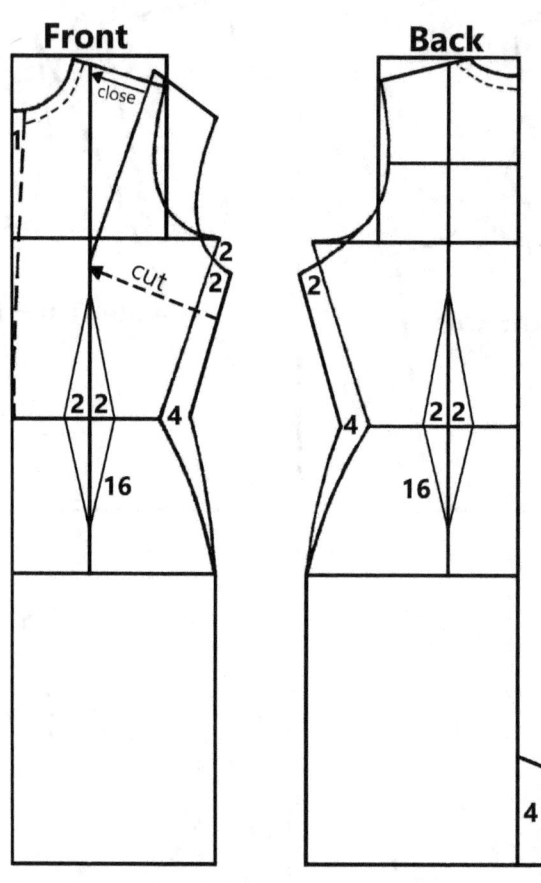

BASIC SHIFT DRESS

Draw the front bodice block with the shoulder dart on page **50** and the back bodice block on page **52**. Lengthen the bodice block for a required dress length. Scoop the front and back neck as desired. Drop the armhole by **2 cm (¾ in)** and measure **2 cm (¾ in)** out. Repeat for the back. Add the waist dart as illustrated and add the dart amount to the side seam for a fitted dress. Add a desired amount of ease to the side front and side back when a looser fit is required. Add **4 cm (1 ½ in)** at the centre back for a slit or vent. Trace the front, back, and facing patterns off. Draft the basic set-in sleeve on page **58**. Add grain lines, notches, hem, and seam allowances.

A basic guide to waist dart widths and lengths:

2 cm (¾ in) = 1 cm (⅜ in) on each side of the centre dart line. The dart length is 12 cm (4 ¾ in).
3 cm (1 ¼ in) = 1.5 cm (⅝ in) on each side of the dart line. The dart length is 14 cm (5 ½ in).
4 cm (1 ½ in) = 2 cm (¾ in) on each side of the dart line. The dart length is 16 cm (6 ¼ in).

BASIC SHIFT DRESS

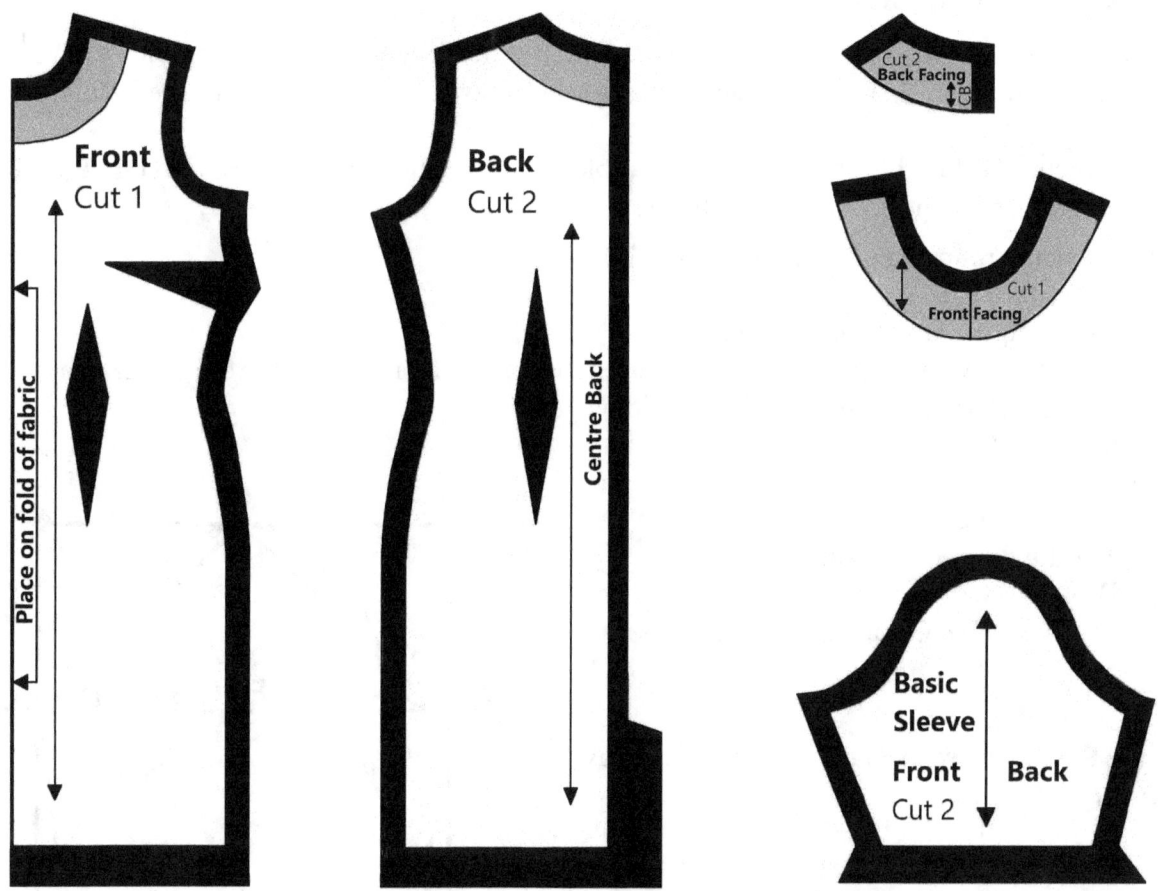

Cut the lining and dress fabric from the same pattern. Mark and sew the darts in the dress front and back sections. Overlock the shoulders and sides seams of the front and back, and the centre back. Stitch the centre back seam up to the marked zipper and vent opening. Stitch a zipper of your choice in the centre back seam. Pin and stitch the dress back to the front at the sides and shoulders, right sides together. Press the seams open. Sew the sleeves as described on page **73** and insert them into the armholes. Complete the lining sections as described for the dress, leaving the marked zipper and vent opening. Baste the lining neckline to the dress, wrong sides together. Apply lightweight interfacing to the neck facing. Pin and stitch the facing shoulder seams together. Press the seams open. Pin and stitch the facing to the garment neckline. Trim, grade, and clip the seam allowances. Understitch the facing. Press. Fold the centre back lining and facing edges under and pin it to the zipper tape. Hand stitch in place. Turn up a **2 cm (¾ in)** hem on both sleeves, tack, and hand stitch in place. Turn up the hem of the sleeve lining and hand stitch in place. Turn up the dress hem **4 cm (1 ½ in)** and hand stitch in place. Trim the lining hemline. Turn the lining hemline **1.5 cm (⅝ in)** under twice and machine stitch in place. Fold the lining under around the vent and hand stitch in place. Secure the lining to the dress on the shoulder seam and underarm seam with hand stitching. Press the garment.

SLEEVES

BASIC SET-IN SLEEVE DRAFT

The basic set-in sleeve block is the basis from which other classic set-in sleeve styles derive. The sleeve head of a set-in sleeve is rounded and slightly larger than the armhole of the garment.

Draw a rectangle for the **basic set-in sleeve** block, using the top arm circumference and the sleeve length. Mark the rectangle as follows:

A-B: Top arm circumference plus **4 cm** (1 ½ in).
A-C: One half of **A** to **B**.
C-D: Sleeve length. Close the rectangle.
C-E: Depth of sleeve head plus **2 cm** (¾ in) ease. Rule a line from **G** to **H** for the underarm.
E-F: One half of **E** to **D**. Rule a line for the elbow position.
Rule a line from **C** to **G** and from **C** to **H**.
G-I: One third of **C** to **G**.
H-J: One third of **C** to **H**.
D-K: Half the desired hemline width.
D-L = **D-K**
Rule a line from **K** to **G** and from **L** to **H**.

SLEEVE HEAD

Use the **French curve** to shape the sleeve head as illustrated on page 7.

Raise the curve **2 cm** (¾ in) between **C** and **I**.
Hollow the curve **1.5 cm** (⅝ in) between **G** and **I**.
Raise the curve **1.5 cm** (⅝ in) between **C** and **J**.
Hollow the curve **1 cm** (⅜ in) between **H** and **J**.

COMPLETE THE SLEEVE

Always measure the sleeve head with a Flexi curve or tape measure held on its edge. The sleeve head should measure **3 cm** (1¼ in) more than the combined front and back armhole measurement of the pattern.

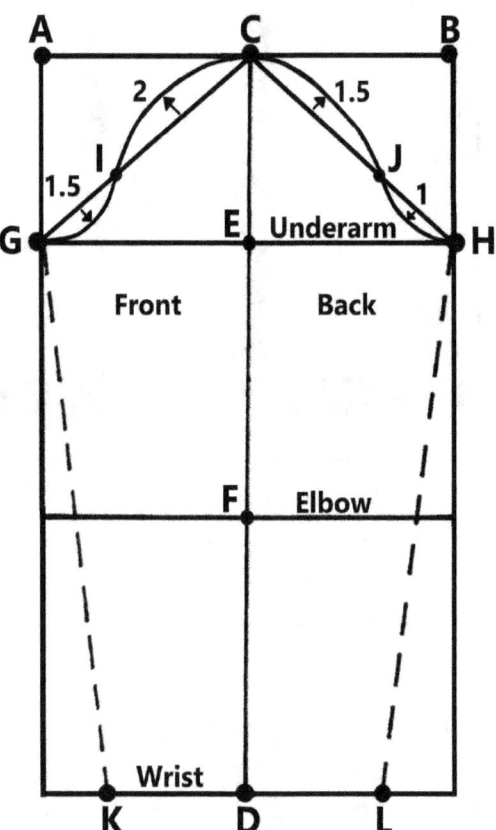

THE BASIC SET-IN SLEEVE

1. Trace the sleeve pattern off and make adjustments as needed by extending and lowering the underarm line as indicated by the dotted line. Blend the sleeve head curves.
2. Add a grain line, notches, hem, and seam allowances to the pattern.

   Sewing the basic set-in sleeve is illustrated on page 73.

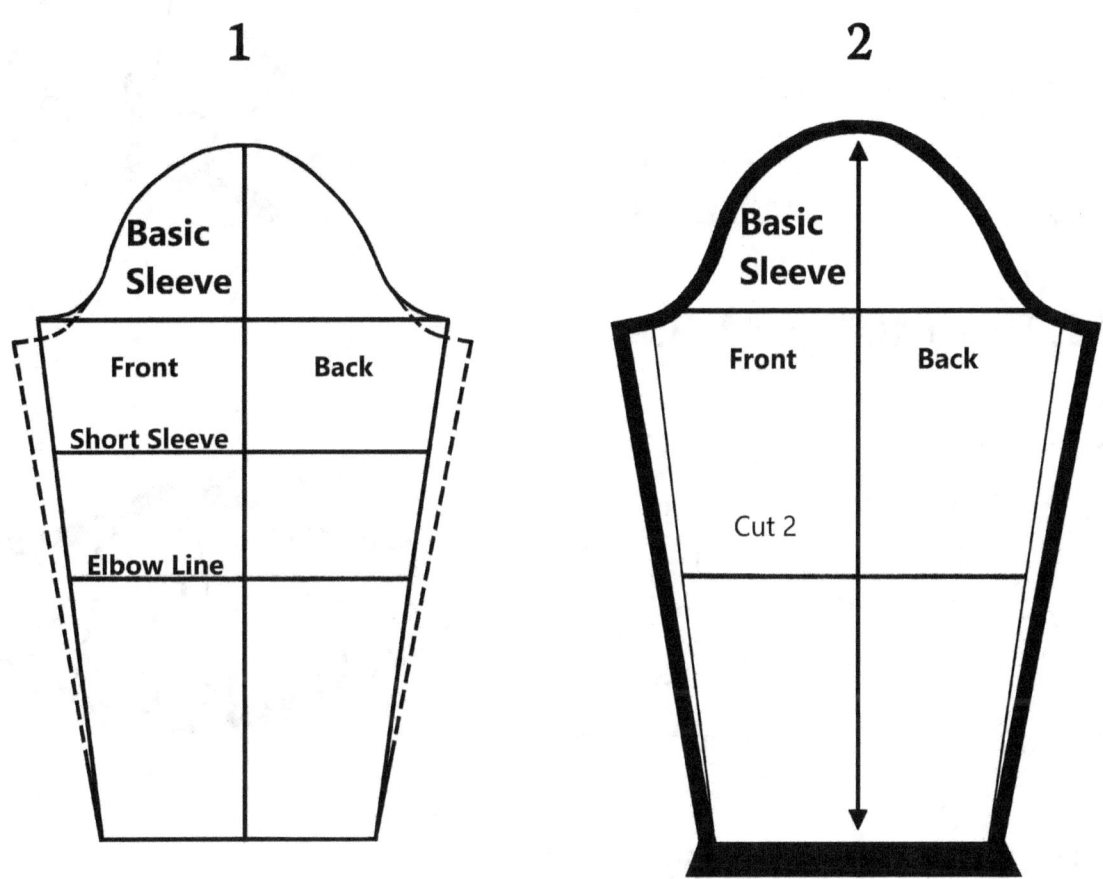

SLEEVES

1. PUFF SLEEVE WITH TOP GATHERS

Draft the basic sleeve and complete the different sleeve variations as illustrated. Slash the pattern up to the arrowheads. Draw a vertical line on a sheet of paper. Place the sleeve on the paper and spread the slashed sections evenly on both sides of the line. Secure with tape. Raise the sleeve head midpoint as illustrated, or to a required amount. Blend the curves and trace the facing off.

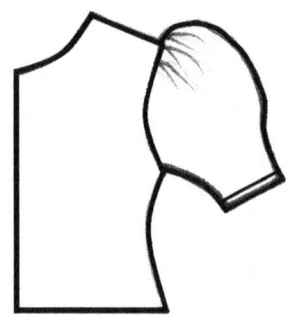 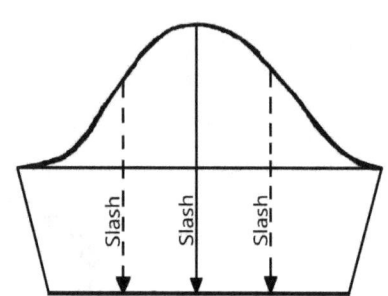 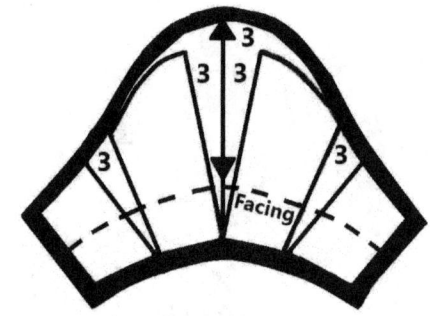

2. PUFF SLEEVE VARIATION WITH BOTTOM GATHERS

 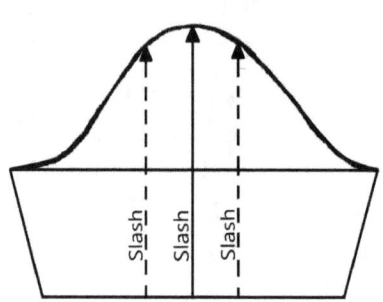 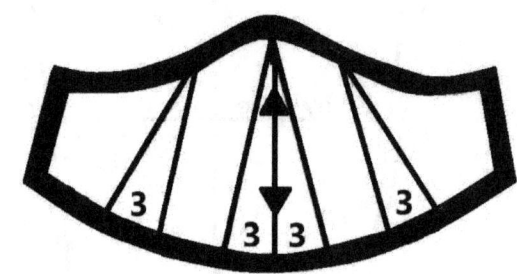

3. PUFF SLEEVE WITH TOP AND BOTTOM GATHERS

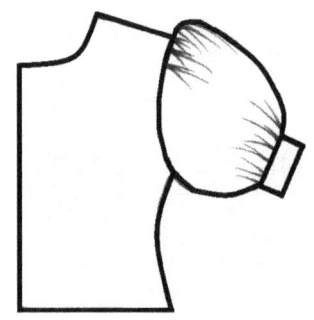 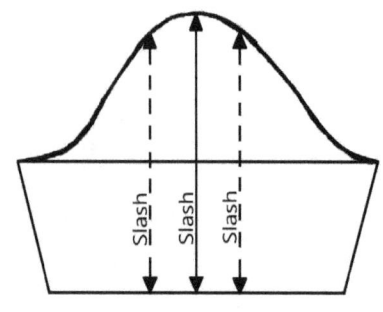 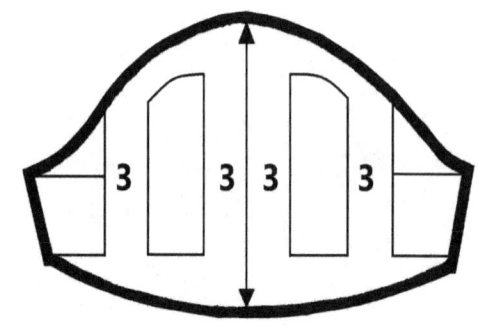

SLEEVES

1. CAP SLEEVE

Trace the basic short sleeve. Draw the cap sleeve and adjust the underarm seam and hemline as illustrated, or as required. Trace the cap sleeve off and add grain lines, notches, hem, and seam allowances.

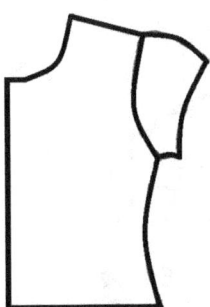 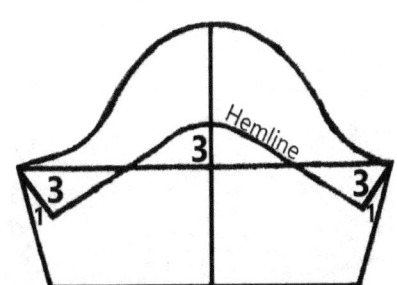 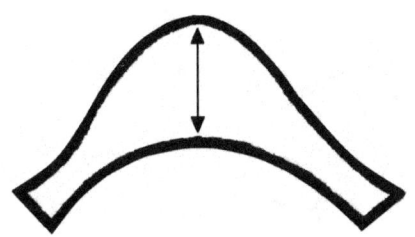

2. CAP SLEEVE WITH TOP GATHERS

Slash up to the arrowheads and spread to the desired amount. Raise the sleeve head as required.

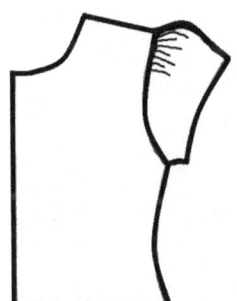 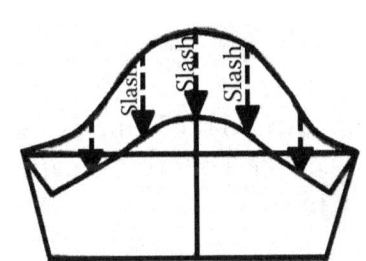 

3. CAP SLEEVE WITH A BOTTOM FLARE

 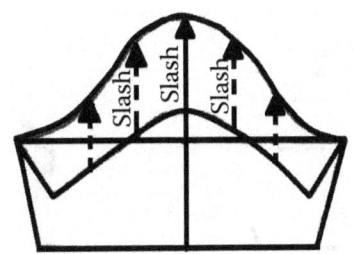 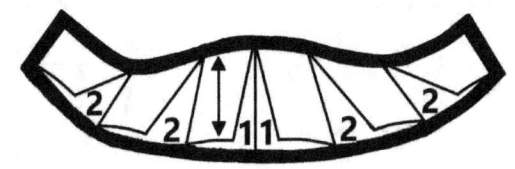

SLEEVES

DRAPED SLEEVES

1. PLEATED SLEEVE

Slash and spread the pattern on paper as illustrated, or to the desired amount to form pleats.

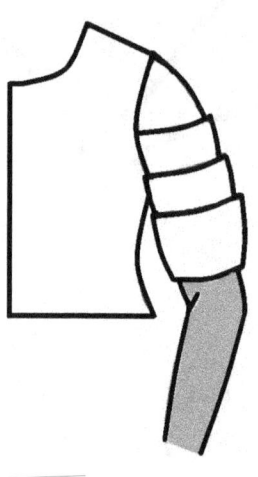 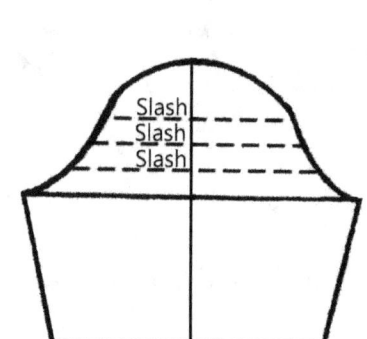 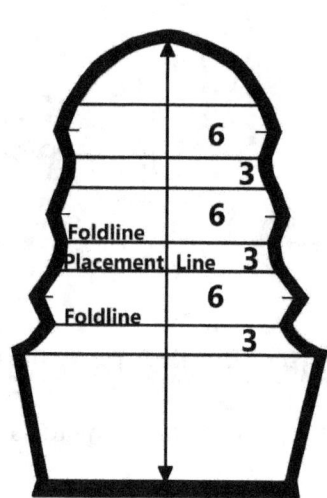

2. COWL SLEEVE

Cut the pattern through the centre and down to the hemline. Slash up to the arrowheads without cutting through the sleeve head. Spread the pattern on paper and secure it with tape. Blend the hemline curve and cut the sleeve on the **bias.**

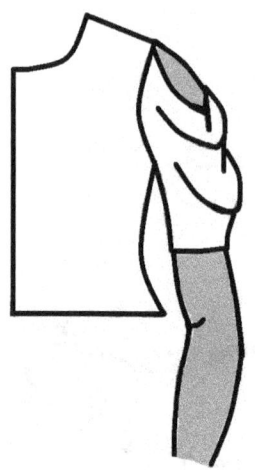 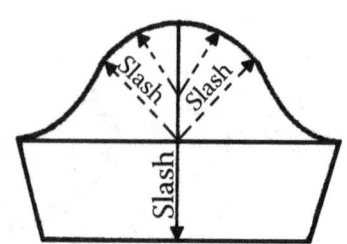 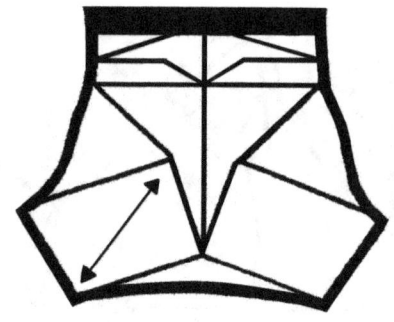

SLEEVES

1. BELL SLEEVE

Trace the basic sleeve. Slash and spread the sleeve patterns on paper to the required width.

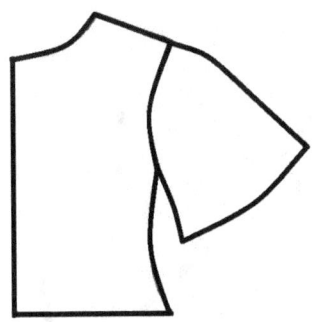 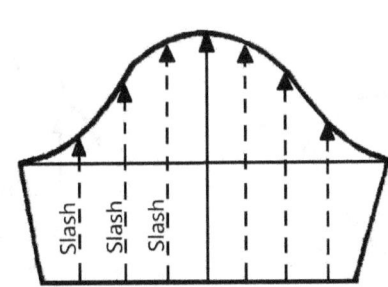 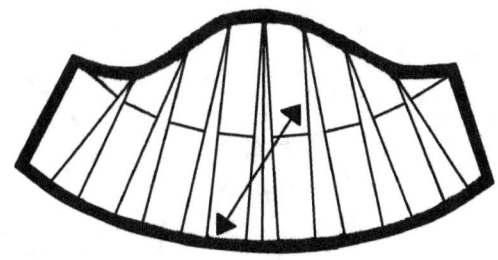

2. BELL SLEEVE VARIATION

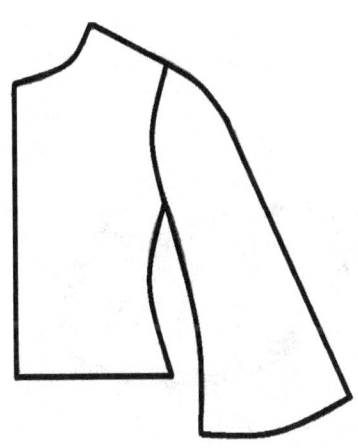 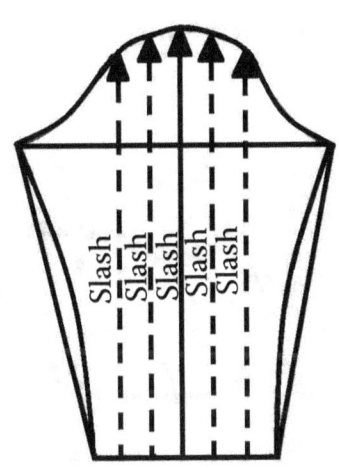 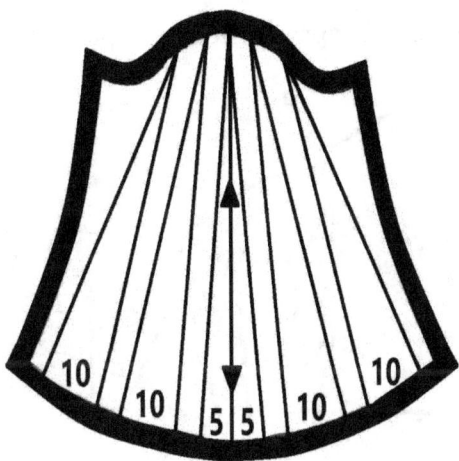

3. CIRCULAR SLEEVE

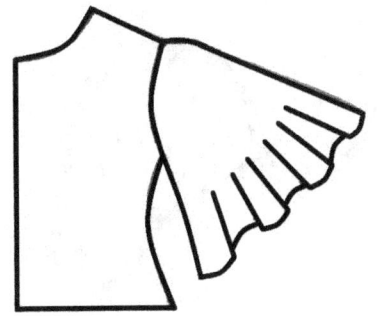 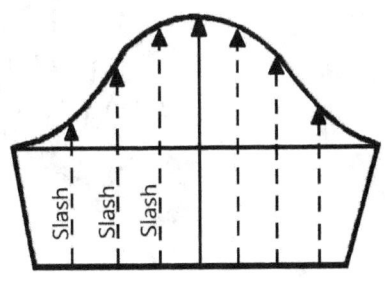 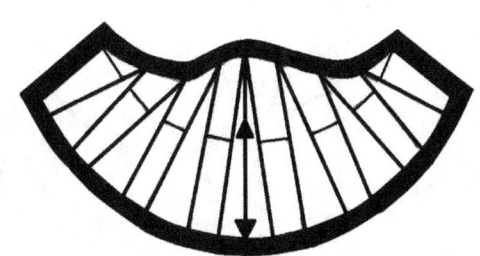

SLEEVES

1. TULIP SLEEVE

Trace the basic sleeve and draw the tulip style lines as illustrated. Trace the front and back sleeve panels off. Notch where the sleeve head overlaps. The sleeve can be lined or unlined.

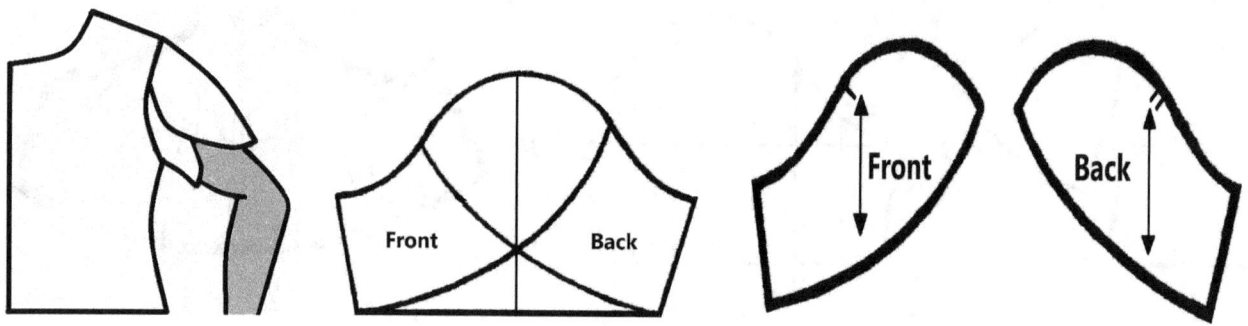

2. TULIP SLEEVE WITH FLARE

Slash and spread the sleeve patterns on paper to a required amount.

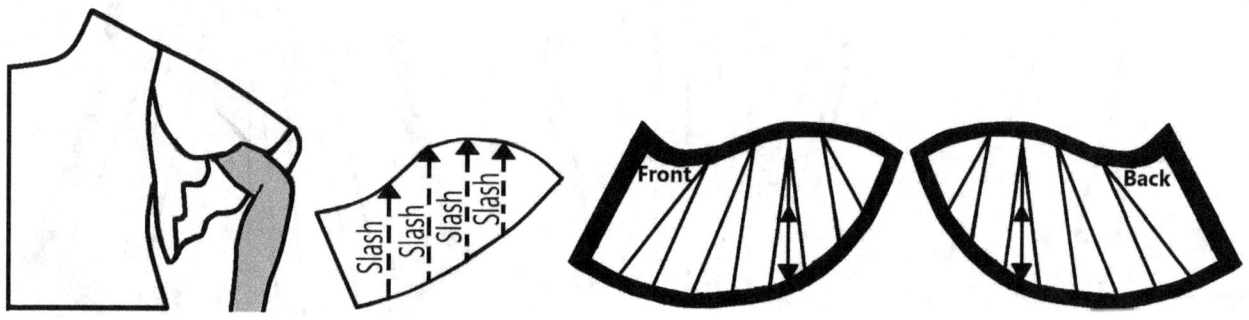

3. TULIP SLEEVE WITH TOP GATHERS

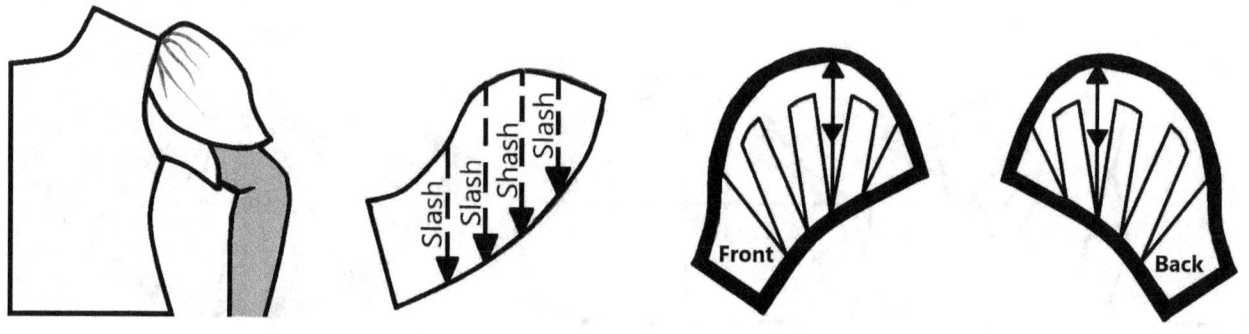

SLEEVES

1. LEG OF MUTTON SLEEVE

Trace the basic sleeve and shape the sides as desired. Slash down the centre of the sleeve head up to the underarm line and into the corners. Slash the pattern with even spaces and without slashing through the pattern. Draw a vertical line on a sheet of paper. Place the centre of the sleeve pattern on the line and secure it in place. Spread the slashed sections evenly on both sides of the line and to a desired amount. Secure with tape. Blend the sleeve head curves.

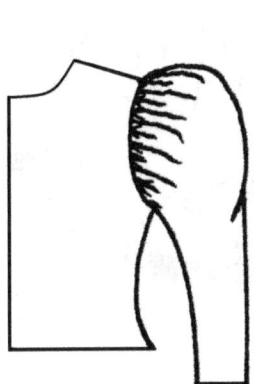
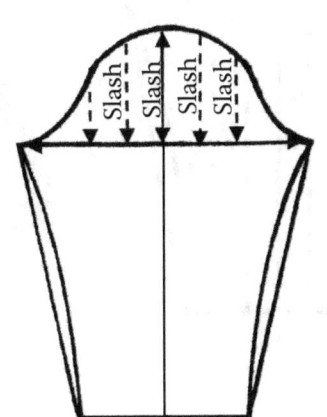
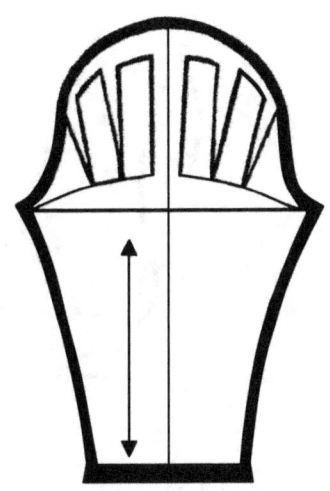

2. LEG OF MUTTON VARIATION

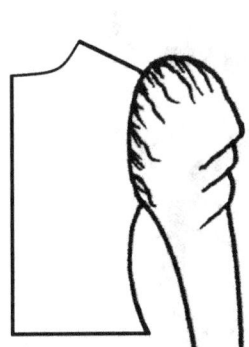
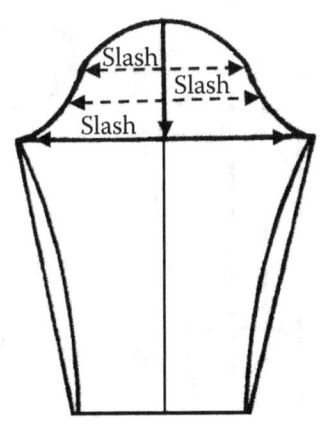
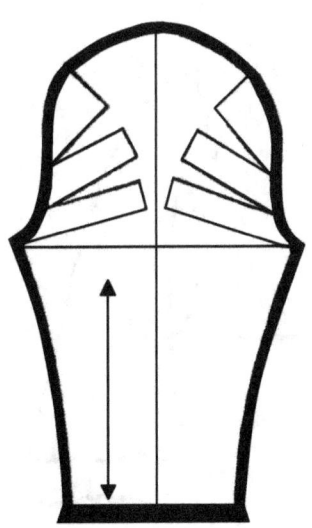

SLEEVES

1. BISHOP SLEEVE

Slash the basic sleeve pattern up to the arrowheads, not through the sleeve head. Draw a vertical line on a sheet of paper and spread the slashes evenly on both sides of the line as illustrated. Secure with tape. Mark a slit **8 cm (3 ⅛ in)** long from the hemline, on the back section of the sleeve.

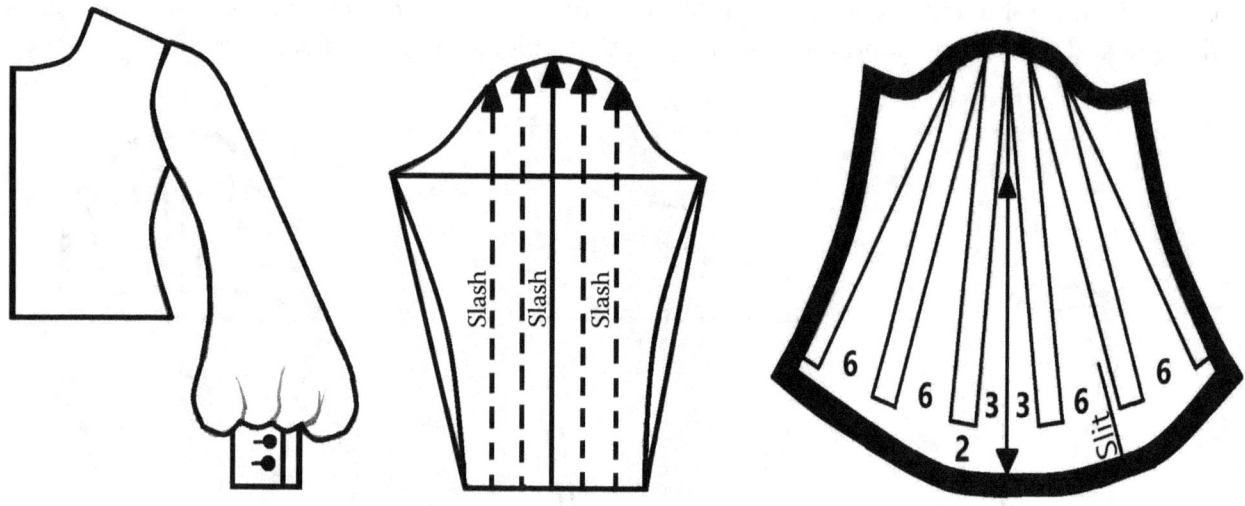

2. LANTERN SLEEVE

Draft the basic sleeve to a desired length. Draw a style line to a desired height from the hemline. Separate the top section from the lower section. Slash the upper sleeve. Place on paper and spread to a desired amount. Secure with tape. Slash the lower sleeve and spread the same amount.

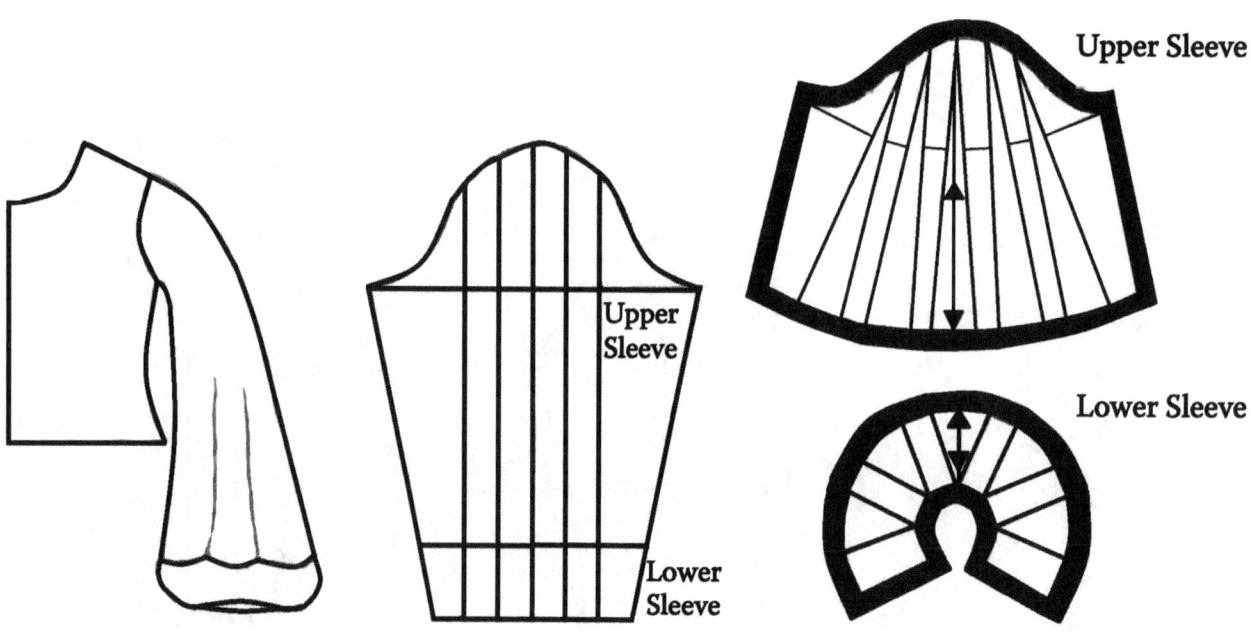

SLEEVES

KIMONO SLEEVE

The kimono block can be adapted for a wide variety of designs ranging from fitted to loose-fitting designs. The shoulders of the kimono pattern can run in a straight line from the base of the neck, or it can have different slant positions. It is important to choose slant positions for the sleeve that will ensure a comfortable fit. Compare your top arm circumference with the draft to ensure that the garment will fit comfortably. Lower the underarm seam when enlargement is required.

BASIC KIMONO BLOCK

Trace the basic front bodice block without the shoulder dart. Draw the back neck at the front. Drop **6 cm (2 ¼ in)** along the side seam and measure **3 cm (1 ¼ in)** out. Draw the new side seam line. Measure **1 cm (⅜ in)** up from the shoulder tip. Rule a line from the neck edge for the full sleeve length, touching the **1 cm** mark. Draw a line that is half of the desired wrist width. Draw the underarm seam line. Shape the underarm seam as desired. Trace the back pattern from the front. Add grain lines, notches, hem, and seam allowances.

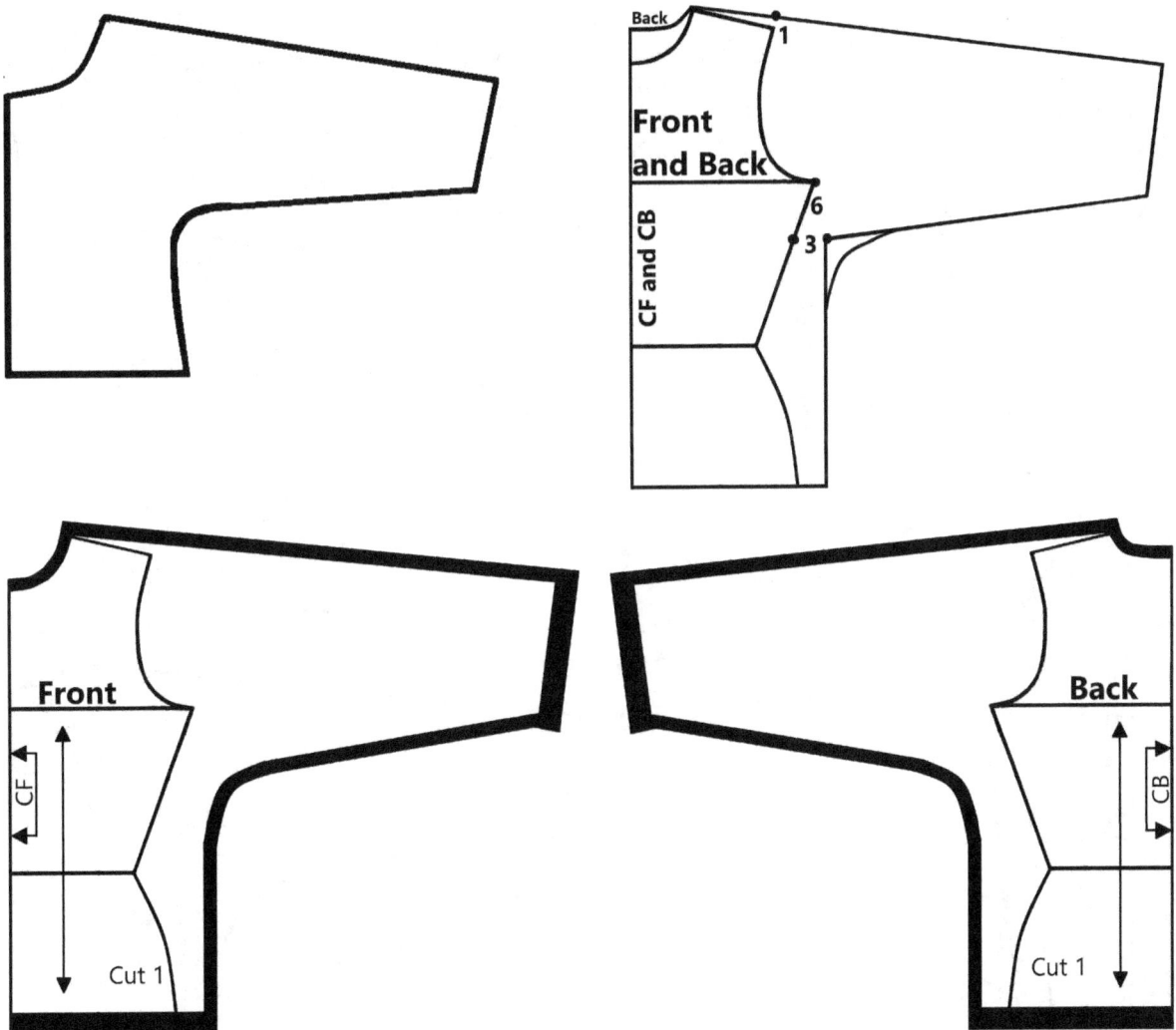

SLEEVES

KIMONO BLOCK WITH A DART

1. Draw the basic front bodice block with the shoulder dart. Measure **1 cm (⅜ in)** up from the shoulder tip and mark. Drop **6 cm (2 ¼ in)** along the side seam and measure **3 cm (1 ¼ in)** out.
2. Draw the side seam line as illustrated. Slash the waist dart up to the bust point. Fold the shoulder dart close and secure it with a pin. Rule a line from the neck edge for the full sleeve length, touching the **1 cm (⅜ in)** mark. Draw the sleeve as described for the basic kimono.
3. Place the pattern on a sheet of paper and secure the centre front and shoulder with pins. Close the waist dart and secure it with pins as illustrated.
4. Trace the back pattern from the front.
5. Transfer the dart to the desired position. Add style lines for your desired design.

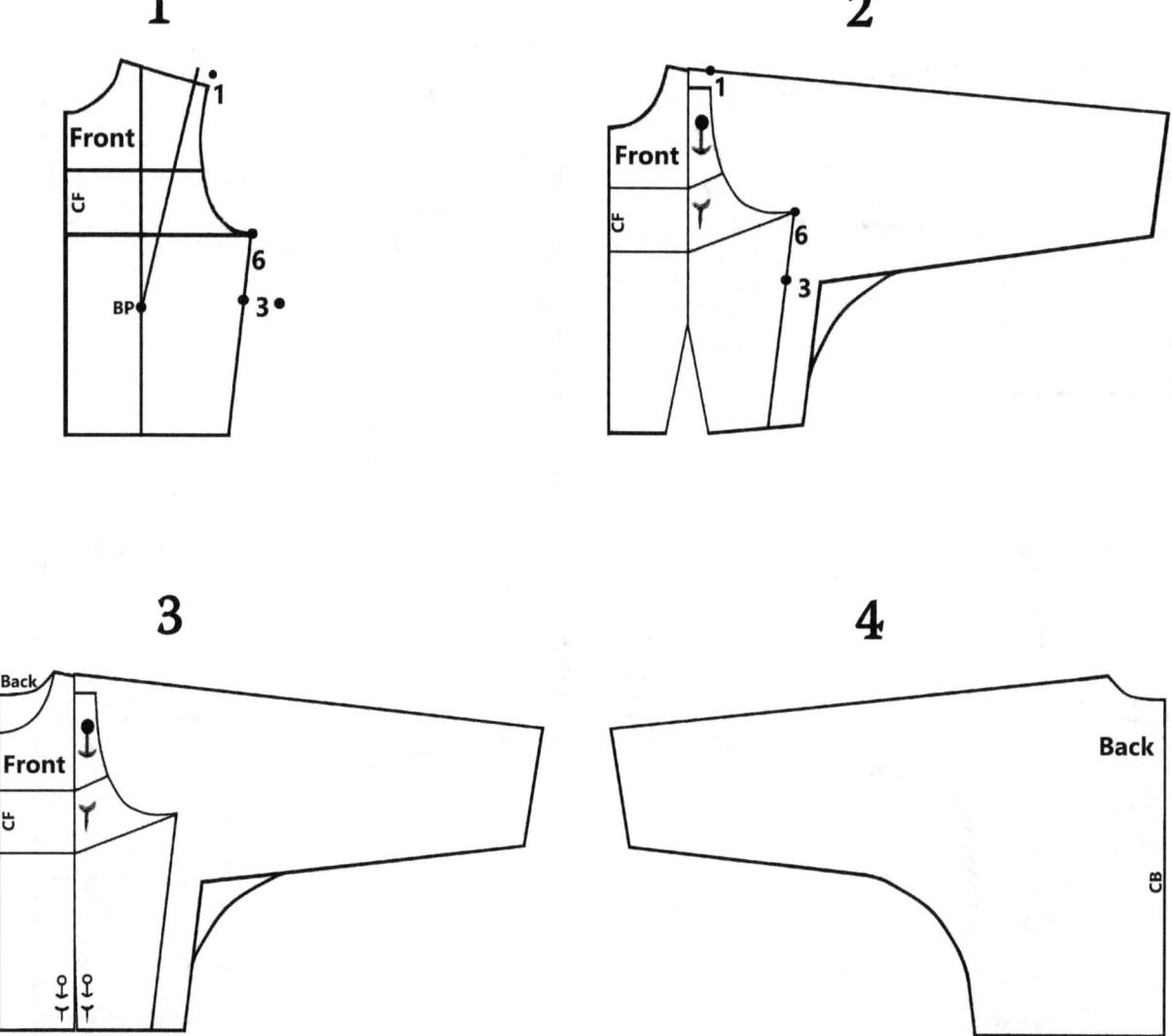

SLEEVES

BATWING SLEEVE

Trace the desired front kimono block. Adjust the underarm and side seam for the desired design. Draw the required underarm curved seam. Add style lines for the desired design. Ensure that the line **A-B** is at least half the top arm circumference plus **4 cm** (1 ½ in). Trace the back from the front pattern as illustrated in the examples below.

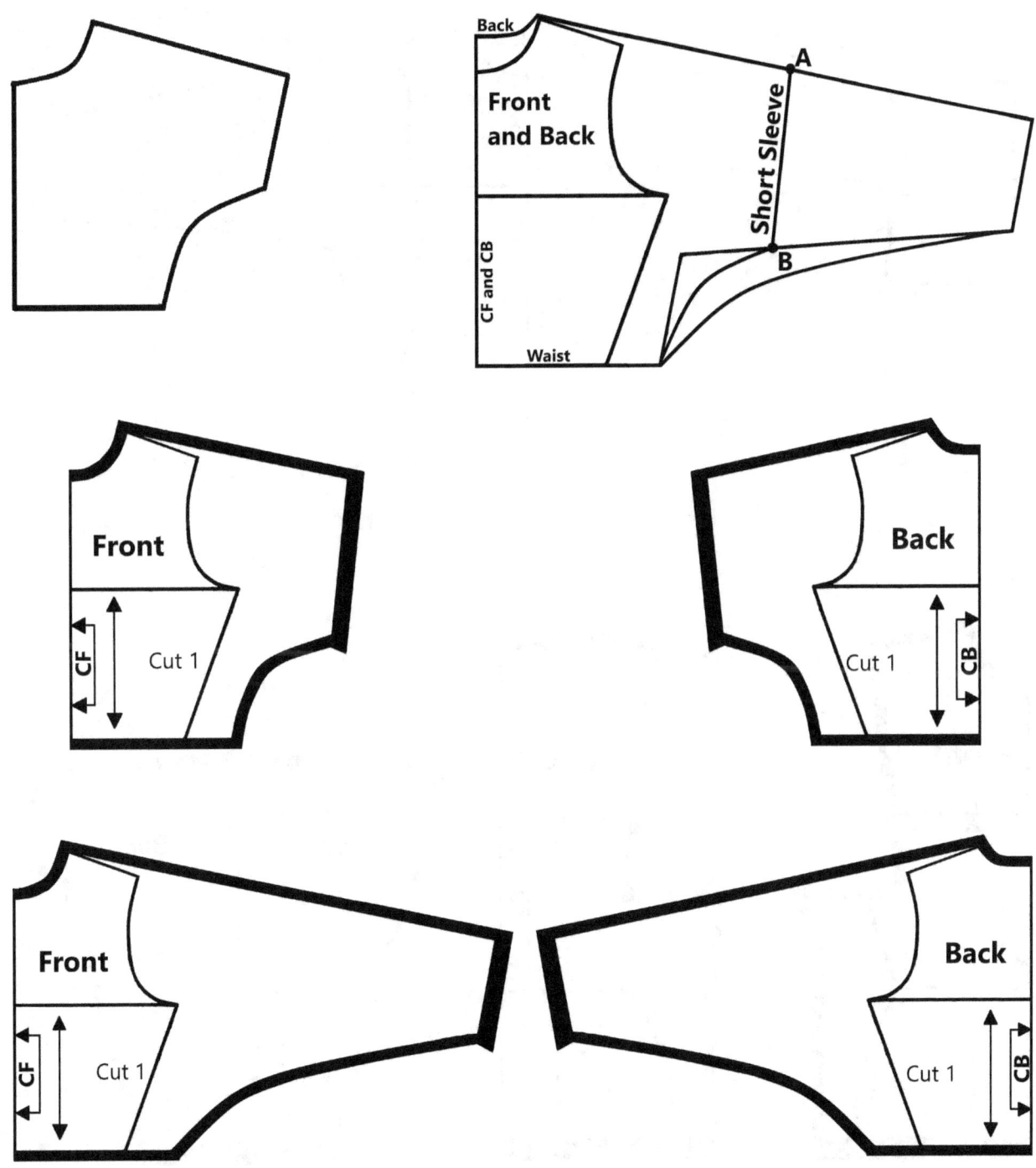

SLEEVES

SQUARE ARMHOLE

Trace the required front kimono block. Draw the square armhole as illustrated. Complete the desired design. Trace the front and back off. Trace the sleeve off on the fold of paper. Add grain lines, notches, hem, and seam allowances to all pattern pieces.

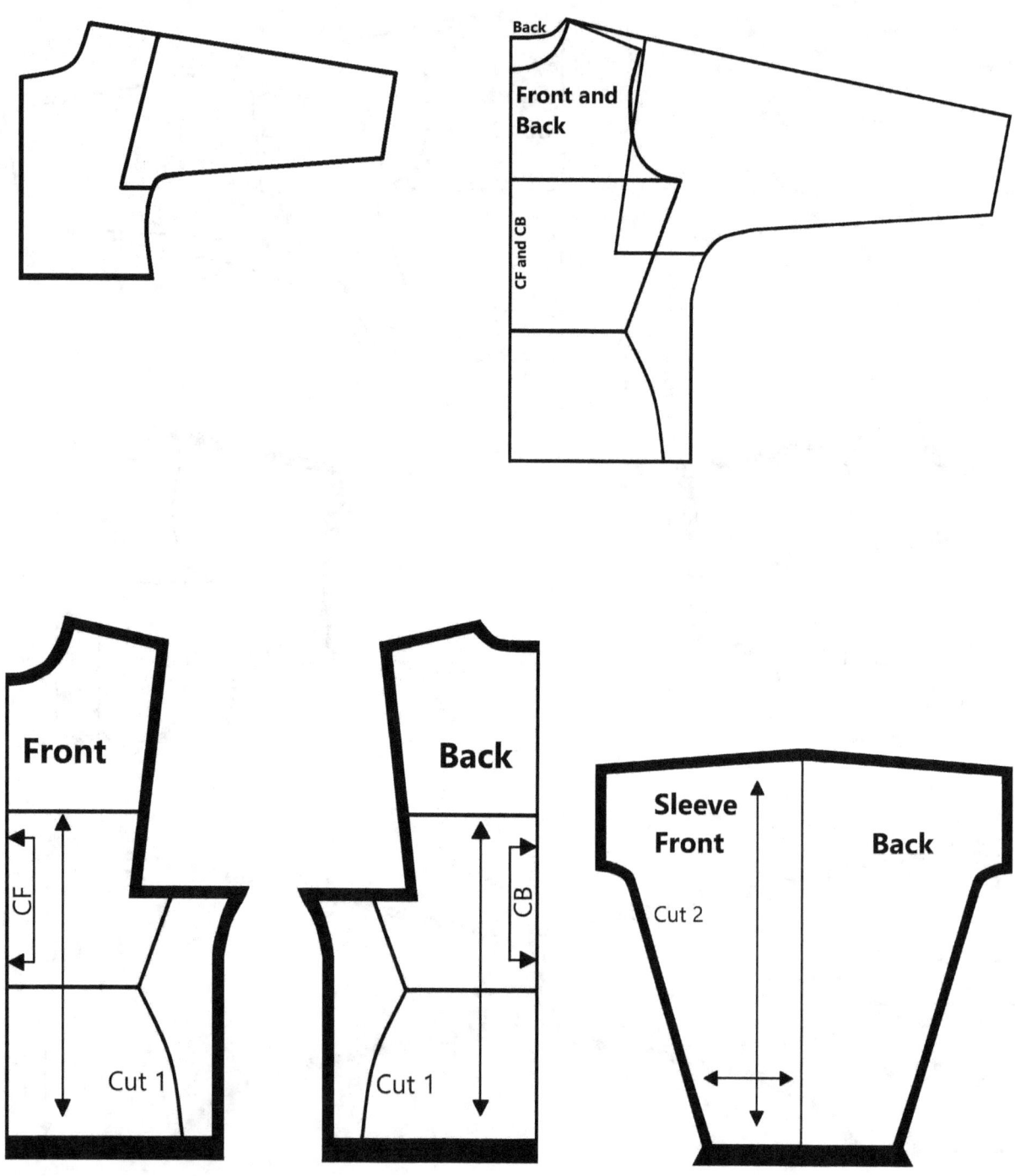

SLEEVES

BASIC RAGLAN SLEEVE

Trace the desired front and back bodice and the basic sleeve block. Lower the armholes for the required design and redraw the armholes with a French curve. Measure **4 cm (1 ½ in)** down from the front and back neck edge. Mark a point **5 cm (2 in)** up from the front and back bust line. Rule a straight line from the neck to the armhole and draw a shallow curved line as illustrated. Repeat for the back. Trace the raglan yokes from the front and back bodice and set them aside. Draw a line through the centre of the basic sleeve. Place the raglan yokes on the sleeve head with the shoulder tips together. Blend the curves with the sleeve head. Extend and or lower the underarm line as needed for the required design.

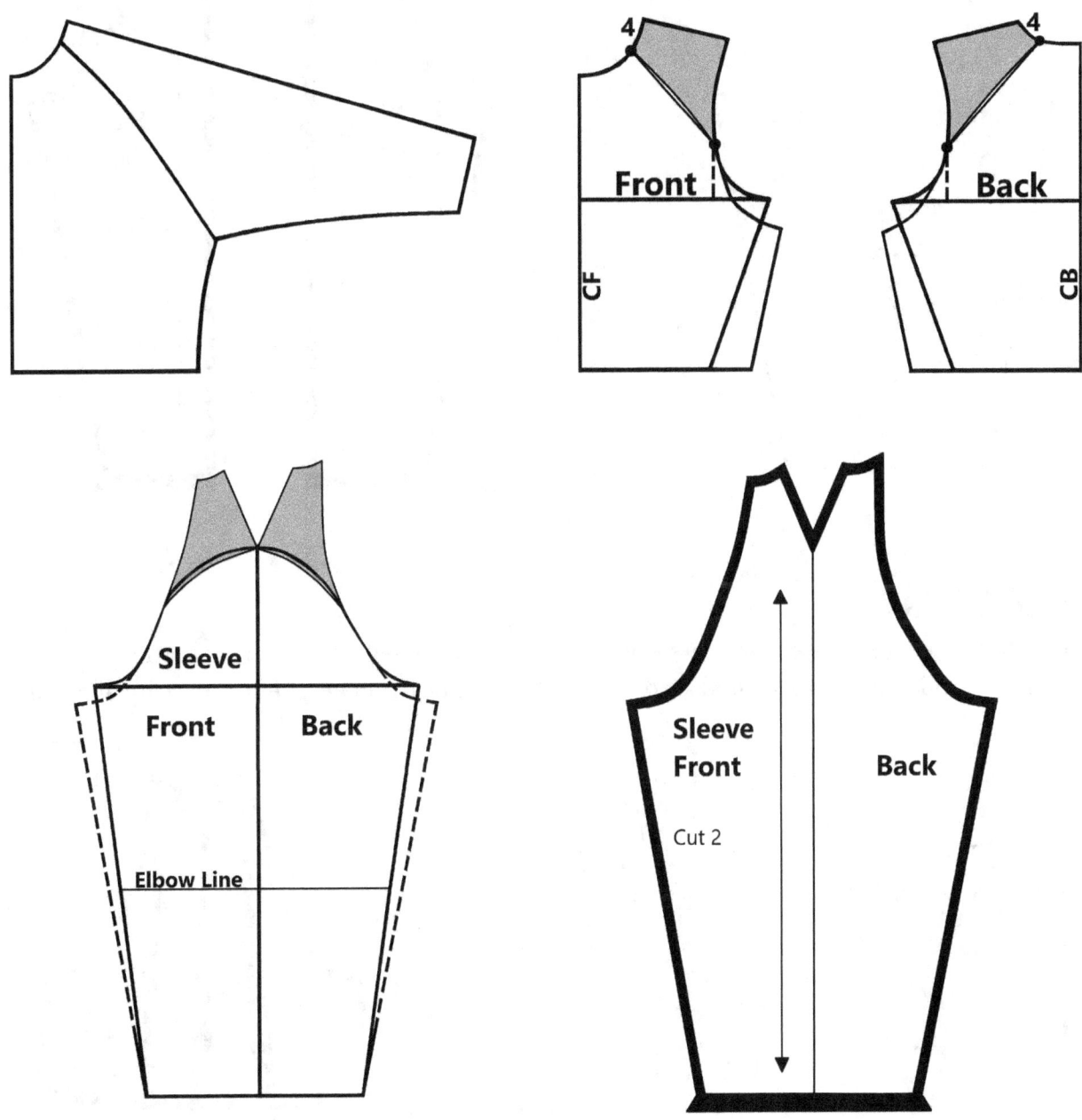

SLEEVES

TWO-PIECE RAGLAN

Trace the basic raglan sleeve. Slash through the centre line to separate the front from the back sleeve. Blend the shoulder tips of each section. Add grain lines, notches, hem, and seam allowances.

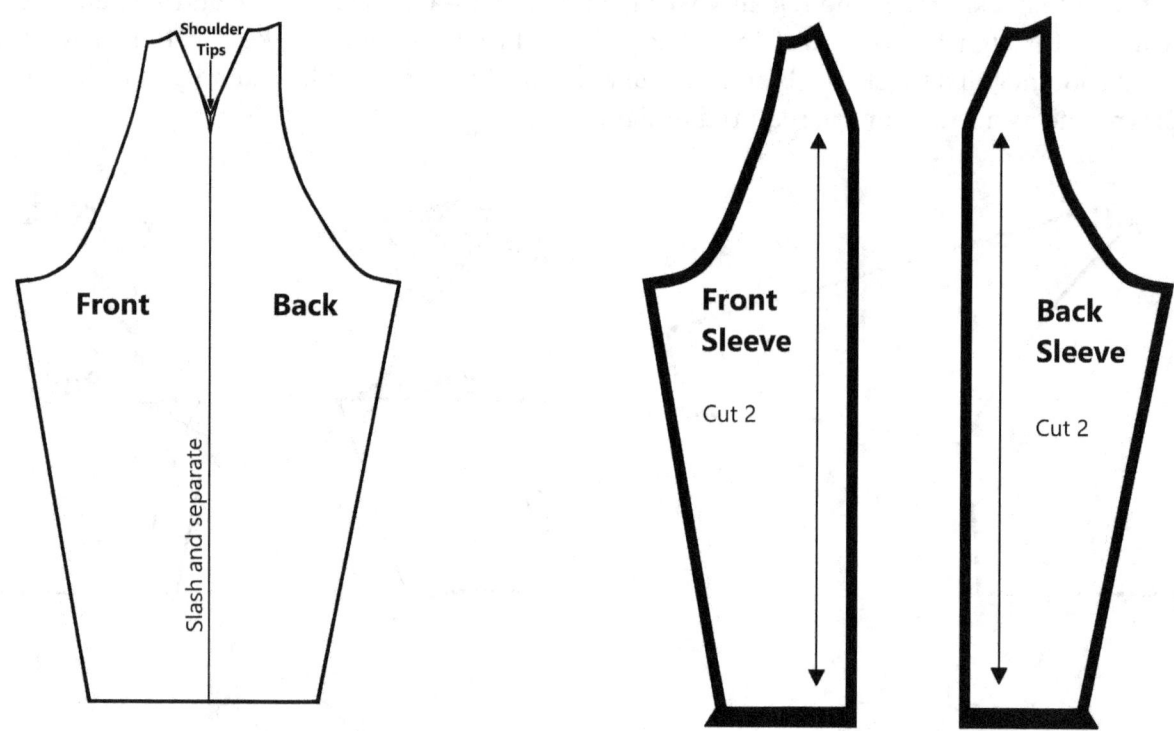

FLARED RAGLAN

Draw slash lines on the one-piece sleeve as illustrated below. Slash each section up to the arrowheads and spread to a desired amount. Add grain lines, notches, hem, and seam allowance.

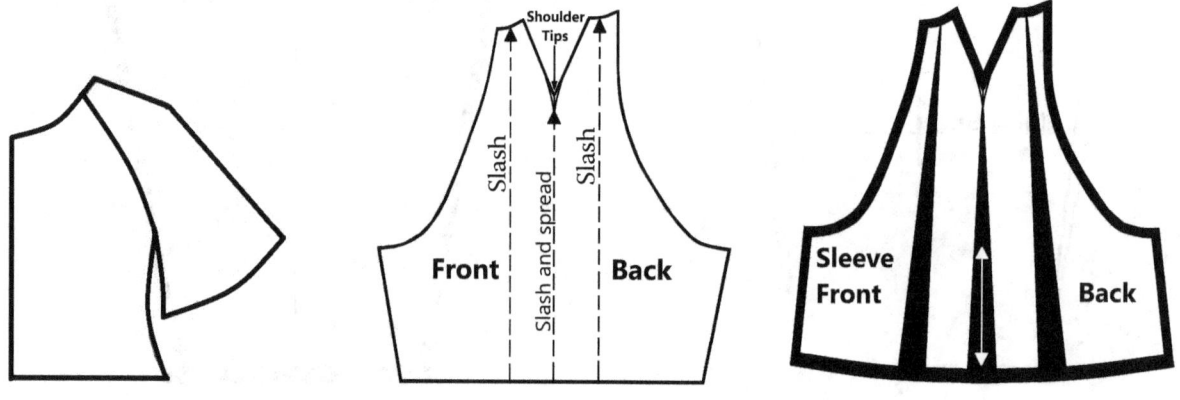

SLEEVES

SEWING THE BASIC SET-IN SLEEVE

1. Neaten the sides and hemline of the sleeve with three-thread overlocking or a zigzag stitch. Sew two rows of easestitching on the right side, around the sleeve head, and between the notches, using long stitches. Sew the first row a thread's width from the seamline and the second row **5 mm** (**¼ in**) above the first row.
2. Pin and stitch the sleeve seam right sides together and press it open.

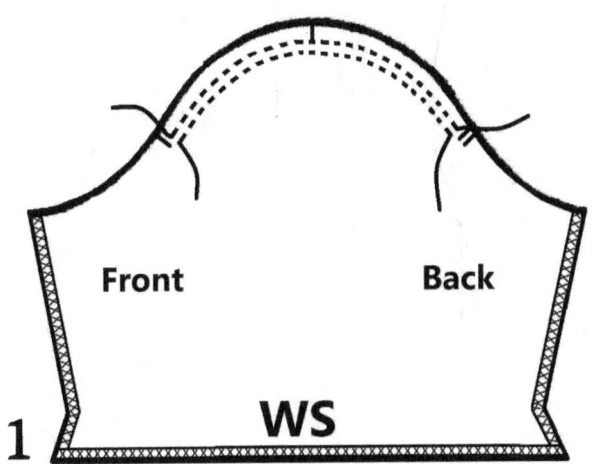
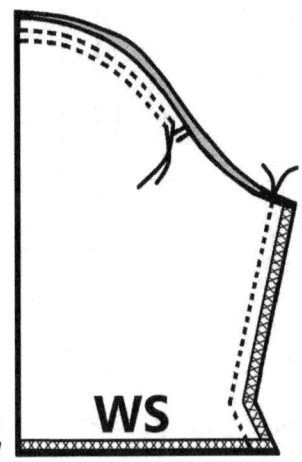

3. With right sides together, pin the sleeve into the armhole matching notches up. Pull up the bobbin threads until the sleeve fits neatly into the armhole. Distribute the fullness evenly around the sleeve head.
4. Stitch the sleeve in place, starting at the underarm seam and within the **1.5 cm** (**⅝ in**) seam allowance. Stitch a second row **1 cm** (**⅜ in**) above the first row. Trim the raw edge close to the stitching. Neaten the raw edge with three-thread overlocking or a zigzag stitch.

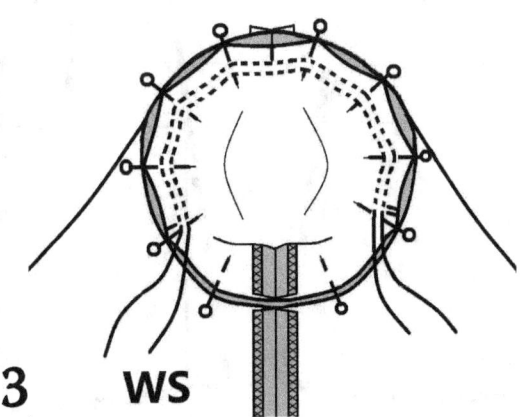
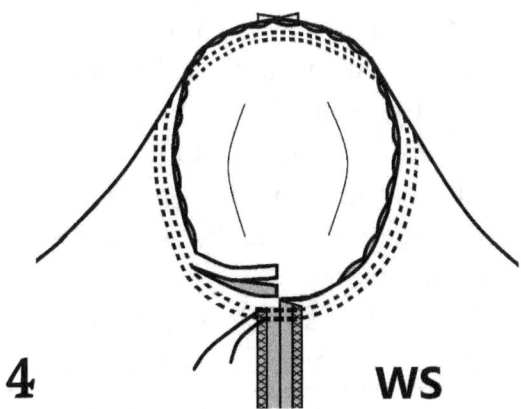

NECKLINES

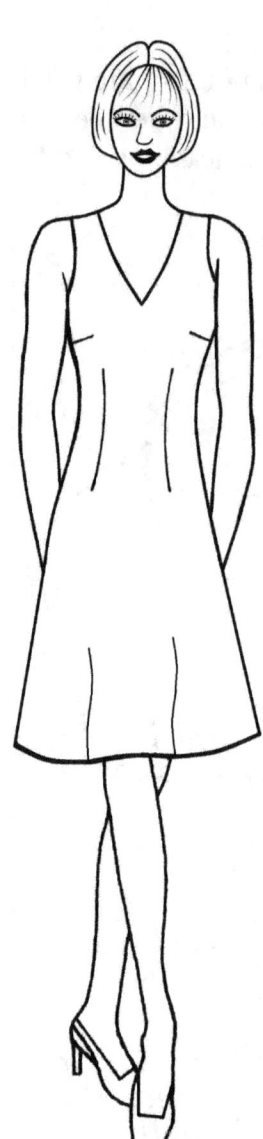
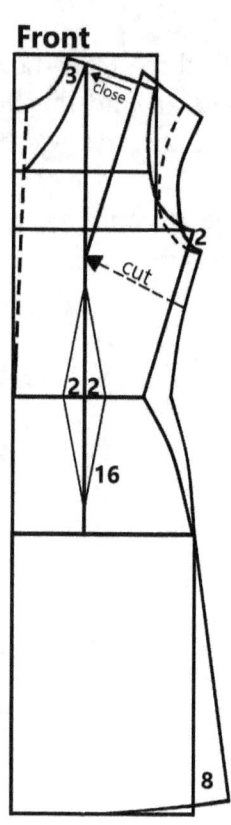
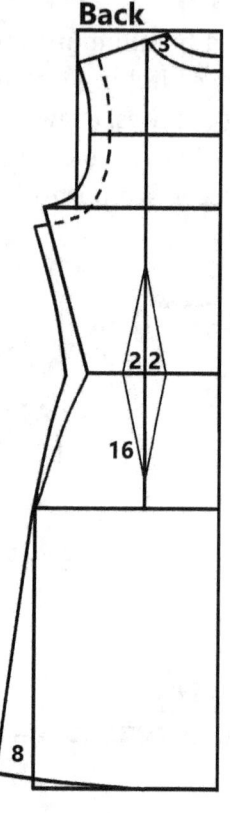
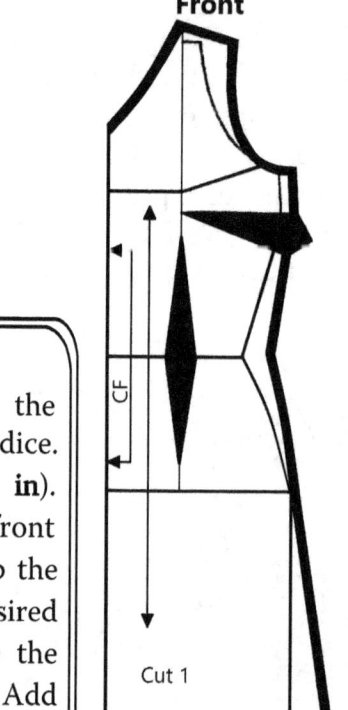
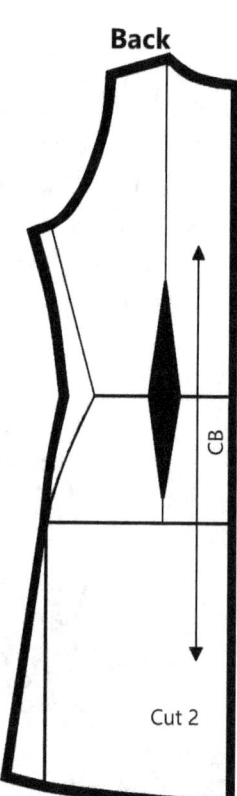

V-NECK DRESS

Draft the front bodice block with the shoulder dart and the basic back bodice. Drop the front side seam line by **2 cm (¾ in)**. Measure **1 cm (⅜ in)** out for ease. Scoop the front and back neck and draw the V-neck. Scoop the front and back armholes as desired. Add a desired amount to the side seams for flare. Trace the pattern off. Draw the facing and trace it off. Add grain lines, notches, hem, and seam allowances.

NECKLINES

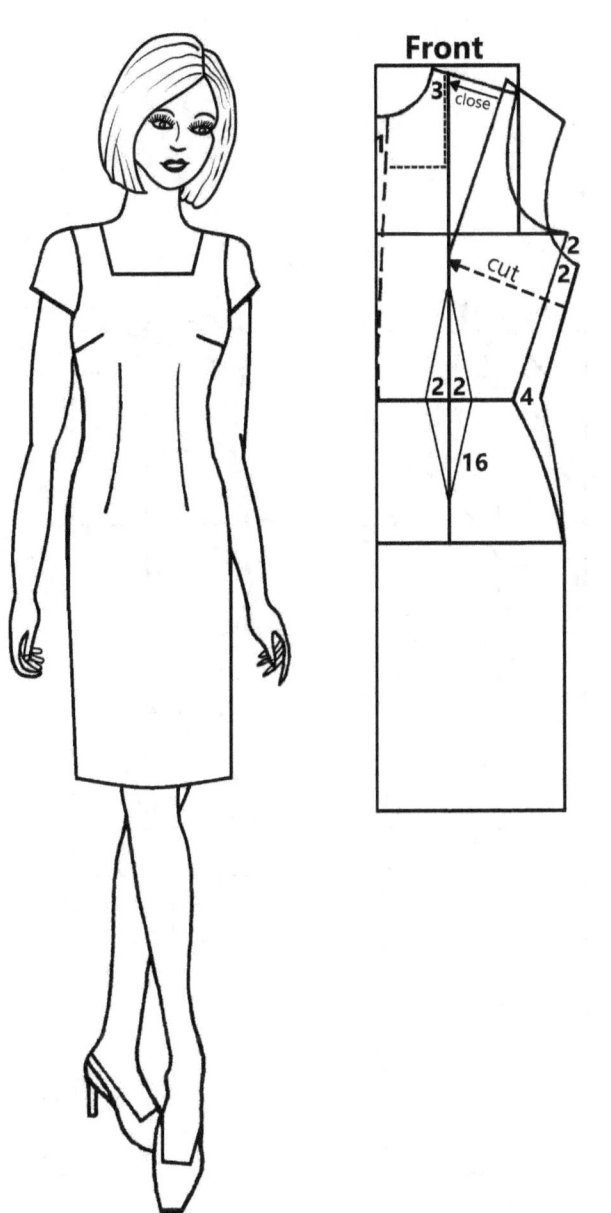
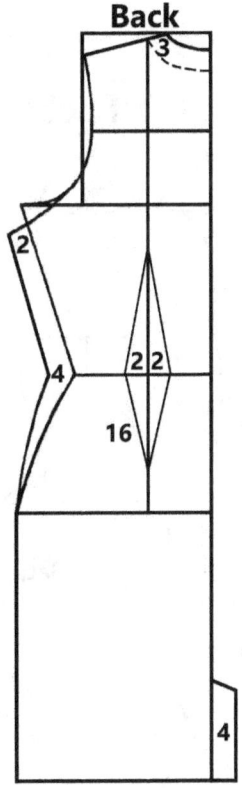
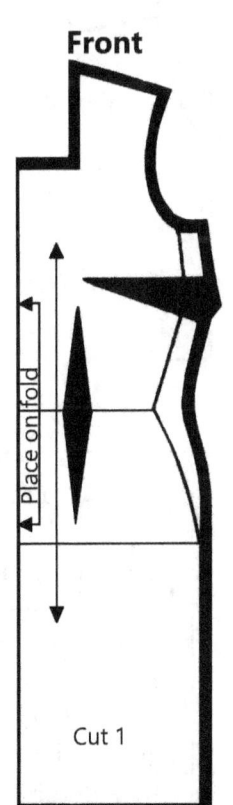
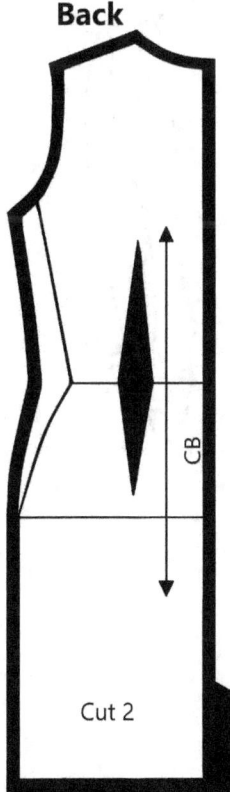

SQUARE NECKLINE

Trace the front bodice block with the shoulder dart and the basic back bodice. Drop the front and back side seams by **2 cm (¾ in)**. Measure **2 cm (¾ in)** out for ease. Draw the square neckline as illustrated. Trace the pattern pieces and facing off. Add grain lines, notches, hem, and seam allowances. Draft a sleeve of choice.

HALTER NECKLINE

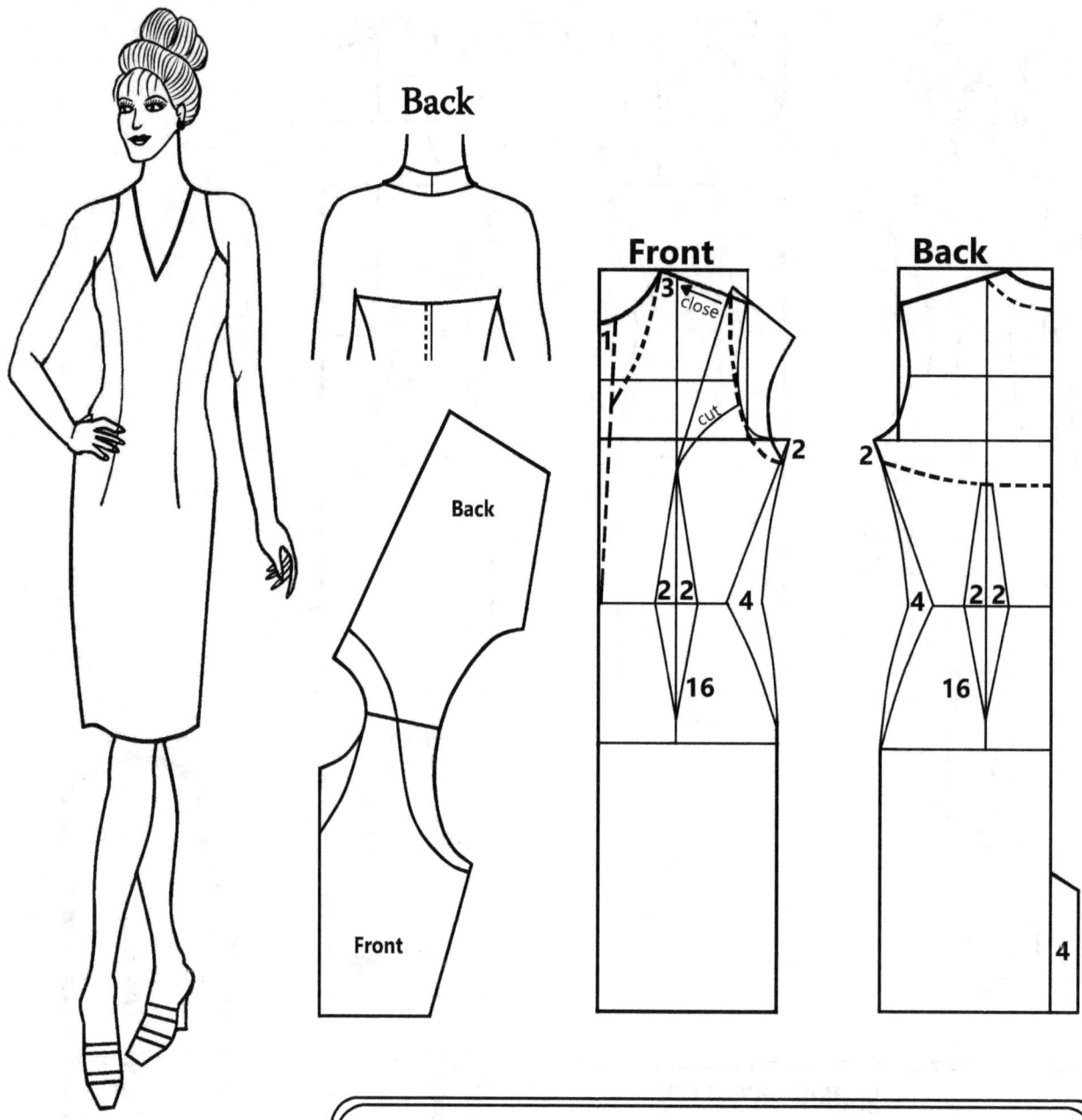

Trace the front bodice with the shoulder dart and the basic back bodice block. Drop **2 cm** (**¾ in**) along the front and back side seam lines. Close the shoulder dart and secure it with a pin. Align the front and back at the shoulder seams and secure it with a pin. Draw the front and back neckline and front armhole as illustrated. Draw the lower back curve. Blend the curves and trace the pattern pieces off. Draw front and back facings as illustrated on page **29** and trace them off. Add grain lines, notches, hem, and seam allowances.

HALTER NECKLINE

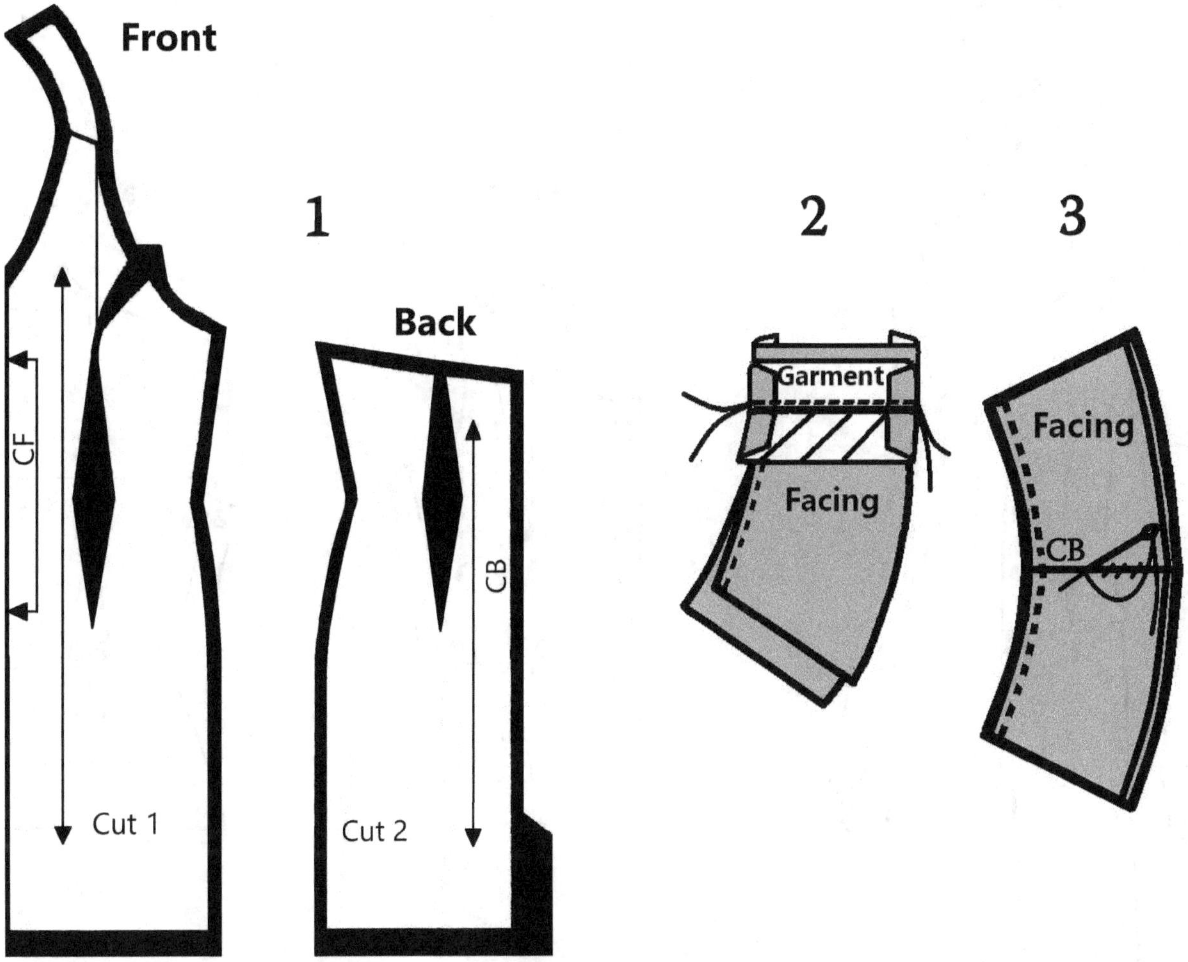

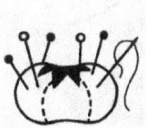

1. Sew the darts in the dress panels. Sew the back panels together up to the marked zipper opening. Insert a zipper in the centre back seam. Interface the back facing. Pin and sew the back facings to the garment's top edges, right sides together. Trim and clip the seam allowance. Turn the facing to the inside and press. Iron interfacing to the front facing. With right sides together, pin and stitch the facing around the neckline, ending **1.5 cm (⅝ in)** from the top edge. Trim and clip the seam allowance. With facing side up, understitch around the neckline. Press. With right sides together, pin and stitch the facing around the armholes and outer neck edges, ending **1.5 cm** from the top edge. Trim and clip the seam allowance. Turn the garment right side out. Press.

2. Pin the garment's centre back neck seams together and stitch, while keeping the facing out of the way. Trim and press the seam open. Tuck the seam allowance inside the opening of the facing.

3. Trim the facing seam allowance to **6 mm (¼ in)**. Turn the facing edges under and slipstitch the centre back neck neatly together.

4. Fold the centre back edges of the facing to the wrong side and hand stitch it to the zipper tapes. Stitch the hem and back slit or vent in place. Press the garment.

RAISED NECKLINE

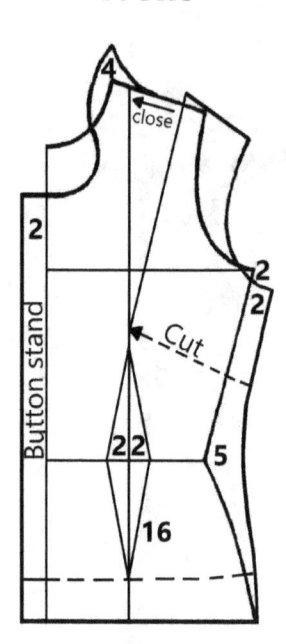

Front

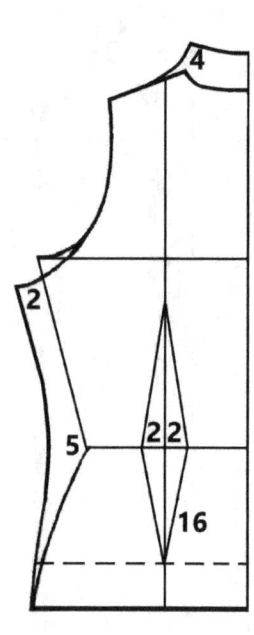

Back

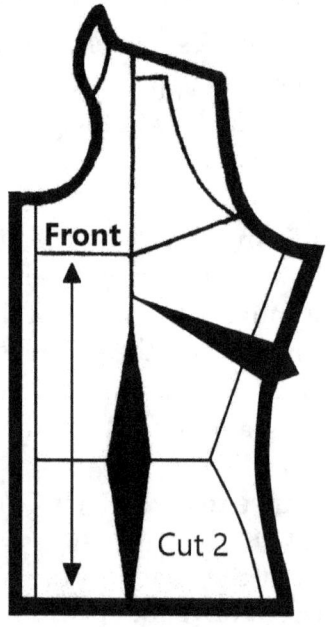

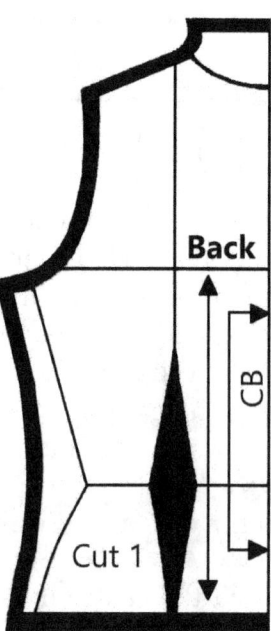

Draft the basic front and back bodice blocks. Raise the front and back necklines between **3** and **4 cm** (1 ¼ - 1 ½ in). Add a button stand to the centre front. Complete the pattern as illustrated. Trace the pattern pieces off. Trace facing off. Add grain lines, notches, hem, and seam allowances. Draft a sleeve of choice.

SCALLOPED NECKLINE

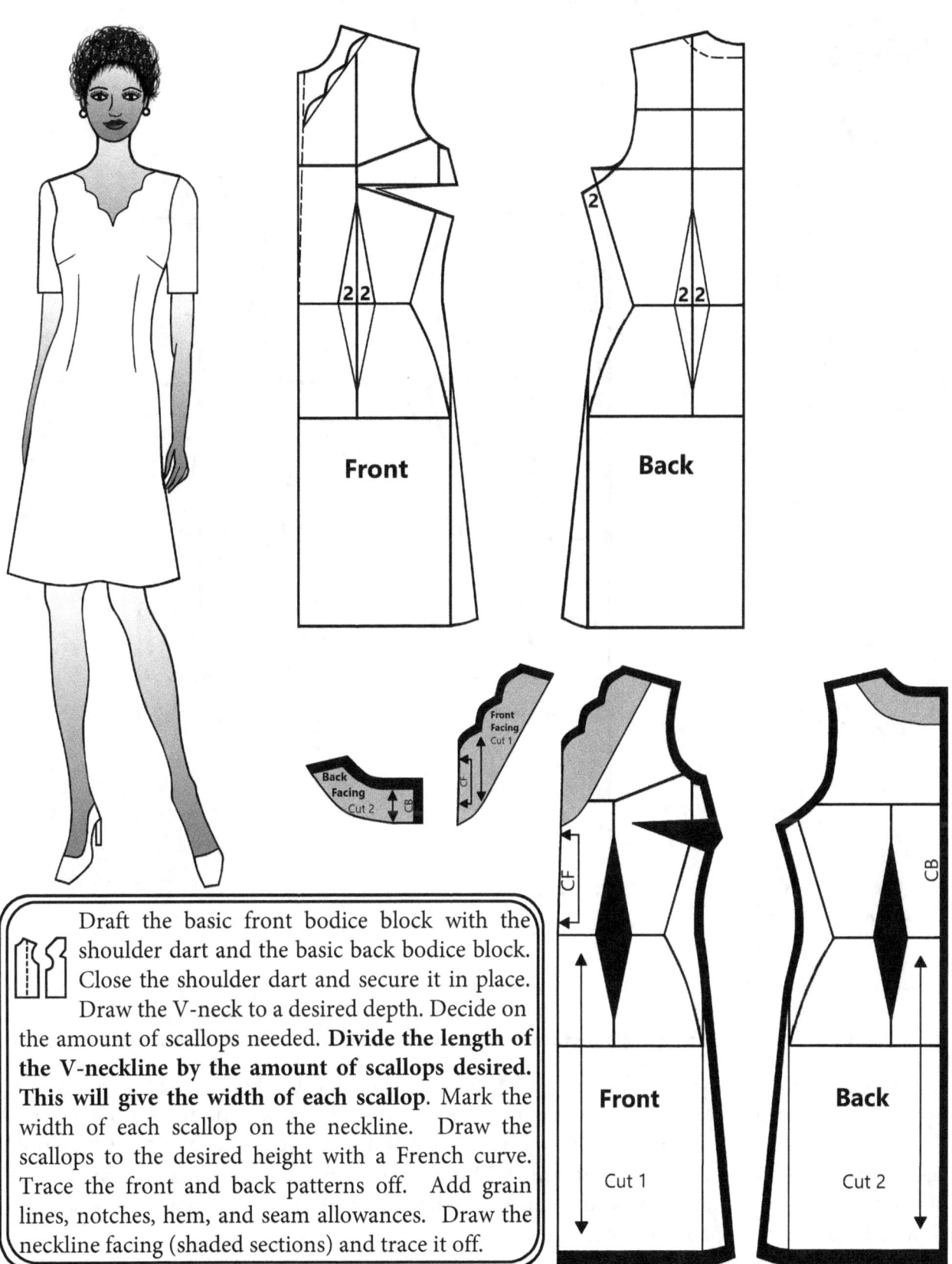

Draft the basic front bodice block with the shoulder dart and the basic back bodice block. Close the shoulder dart and secure it in place. Draw the V-neck to a desired depth. Decide on the amount of scallops needed. **Divide the length of the V-neckline by the amount of scallops desired. This will give the width of each scallop.** Mark the width of each scallop on the neckline. Draw the scallops to the desired height with a French curve. Trace the front and back patterns off. Add grain lines, notches, hem, and seam allowances. Draw the neckline facing (shaded sections) and trace it off.

KEYHOLE NECKLINE

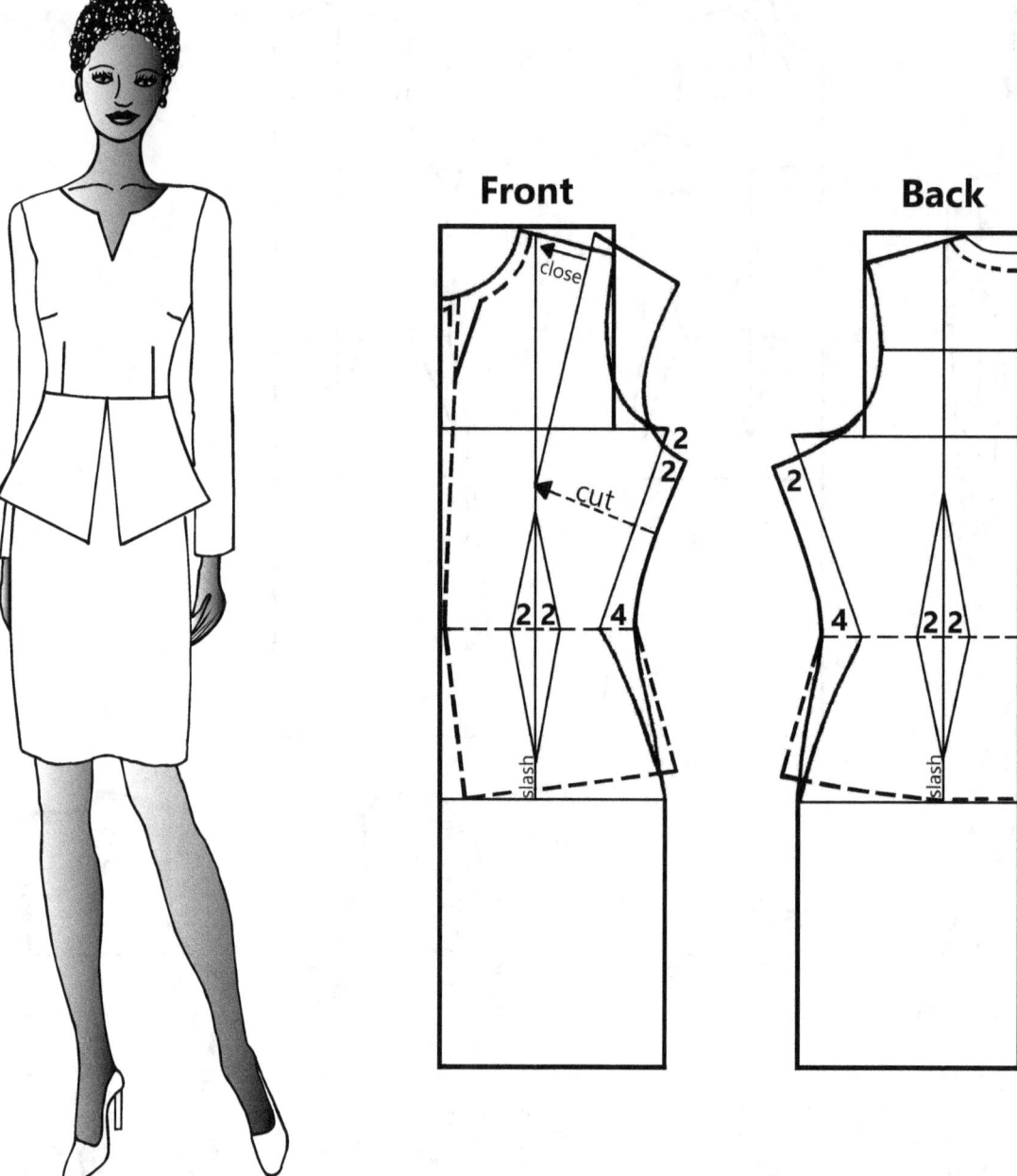

Draft the front bodice block with the shoulder dart and the basic back bodice block. Scoop the front and back necklines by **2 cm (¾ in)**. Reduce the gape at the centre front neck. Draw the style lines as illustrated. Draw front and back facings. Trace the facings, peplum, front, and back panels off. Cut the peplum front and back panels up to the the darts. Close the peplum darts and secure it with tape. Add grain lines, notches, hem, and seam allowances to all pattern pieces.

KEYHOLE NECKLINE

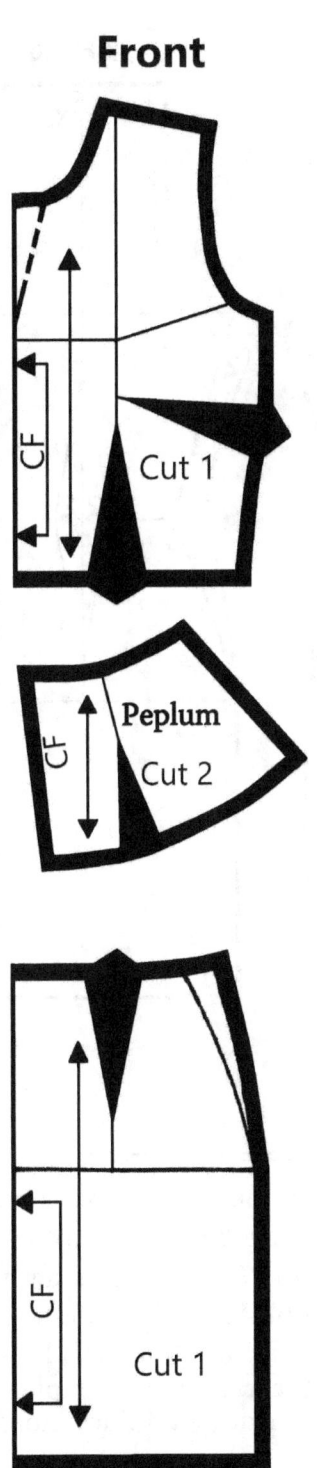

PLEATED NECKLINE

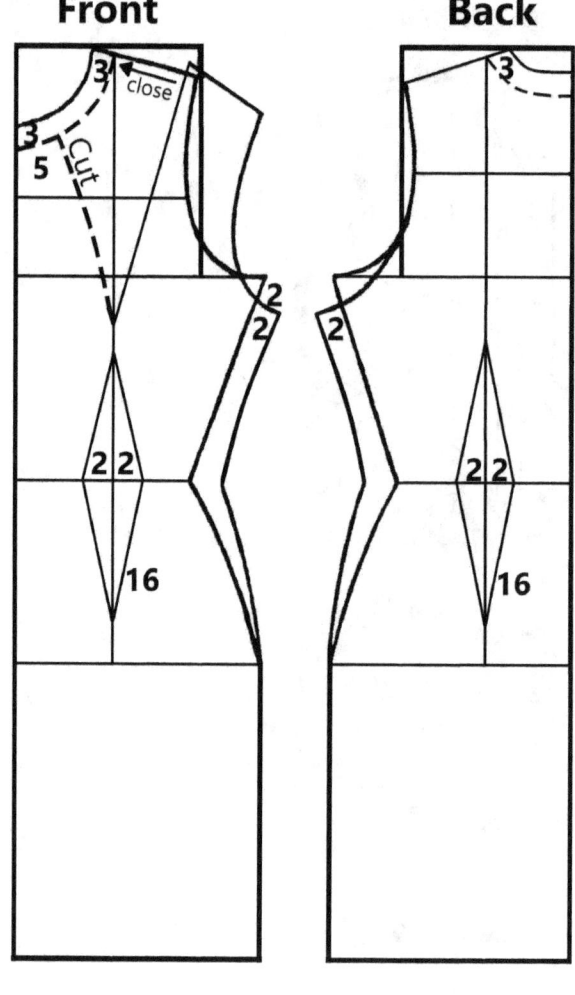

Draft the front bodice block with the shoulder dart and the basic back bodice block. Scoop the front and back necklines by **3 cm (1 ¼ in)**, or as desired. Draw the curve on the front neckline as illustrated. Cut into the curve and close the shoulder dart. A dart will open on the front neckline. Use the dart excess to form pleats on the neckline. Trace the pattern off. Add grain lines, notches, hem, and seam allowances.

PLEATED NECKLINE

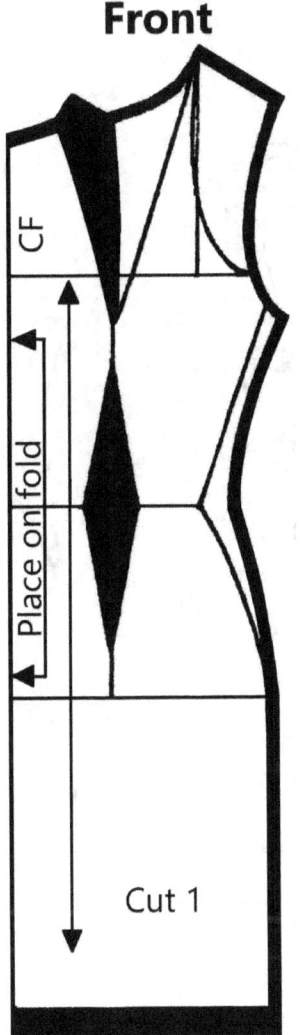

Front

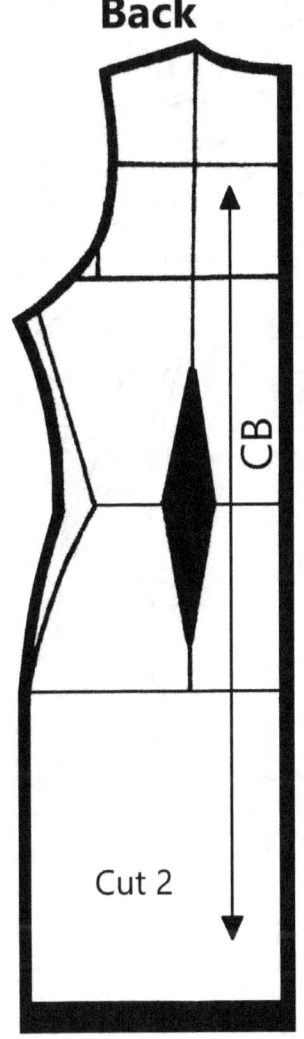

Back

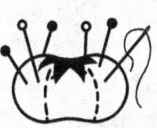

Cut lining from the same pattern if the dress is to be lined. Sew the darts on the front and back panels and press. Make pleats on the front neckline and press to one side. Complete the dress in the manner described on page **85**. Press the garment.

SLANTED NECKLINE

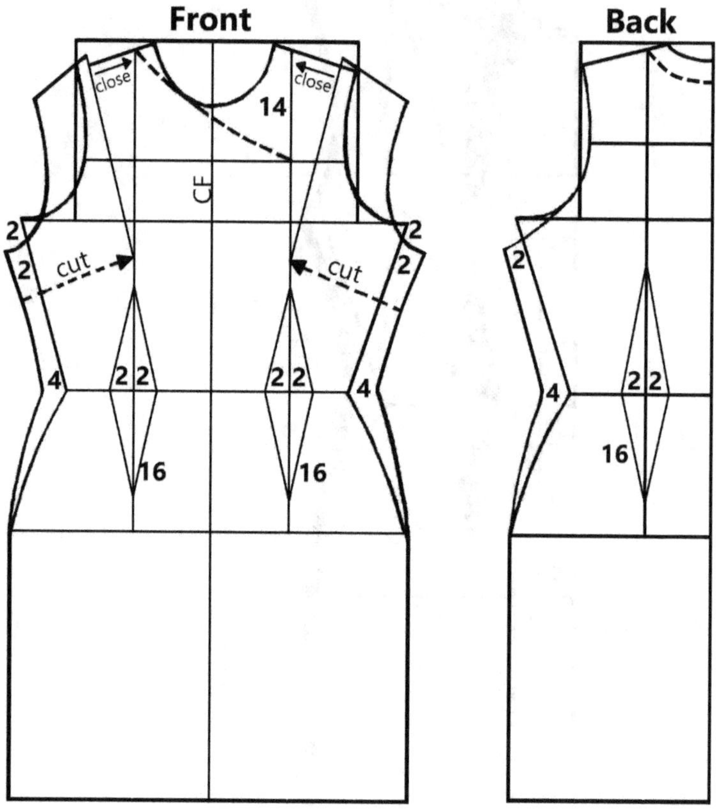

As this is an **asymmetrical neckline**, the front pattern must be drafted on the fold of a sheet of paper. Draft the back bodice block on a separate sheet of paper. Scoop the front and back necklines to the desired amount. Open the front pattern and draw the neckline as illustrated. Draft the basic sleeve on page **58**. Add a flounce as illustrated on page **125**.

SLANTED NECKLINE

Front

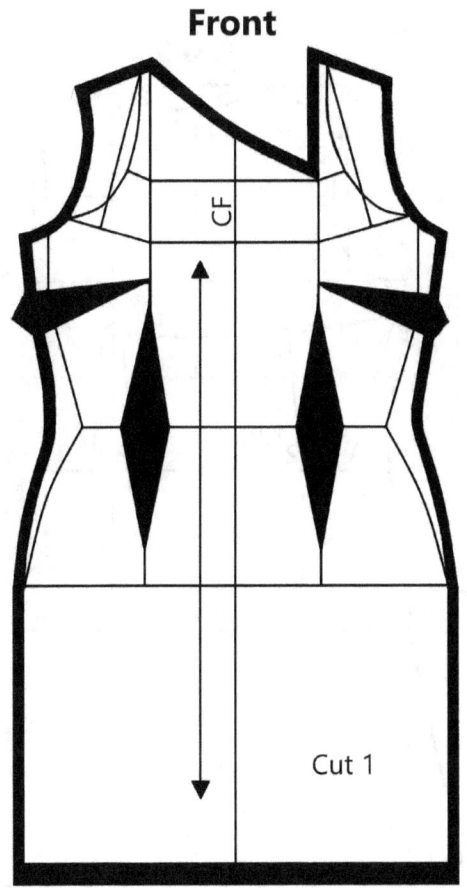

Back

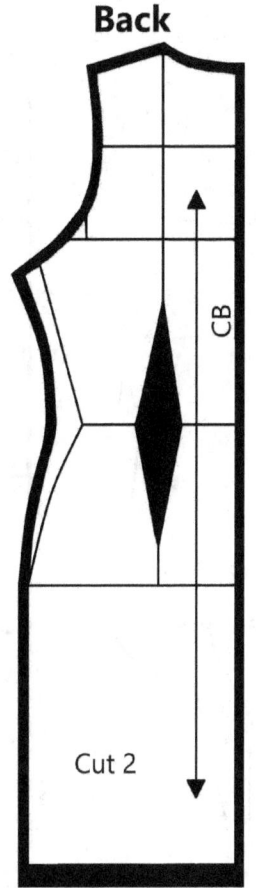

Cut lining from the same pattern if the dress is to be lined. Sew the darts on the front and back panels and press to one side. Stitch the centre back seam up to the marked zipper opening. Stitch a zipper of your choice in the centre back seam. With right sides together, pin and stitch the front and back shoulders and side seams. Sew a flounce to each sleeve. Complete the sleeve as described on page **73**. Interface the neck facing. Pin and stitch the facing shoulder seams together. Attach the facing to the neckline. Trim, grade, and clip the seam allowances. Understitch the facing to the seam allowance, close to the seam. Slipstitch the facing to the zipper tape and shoulder seams. Overlock the hem edge. Turn the hem up and hand sew in place. Press the garment.

ASYMMETRICAL CAMISOLE DRESS

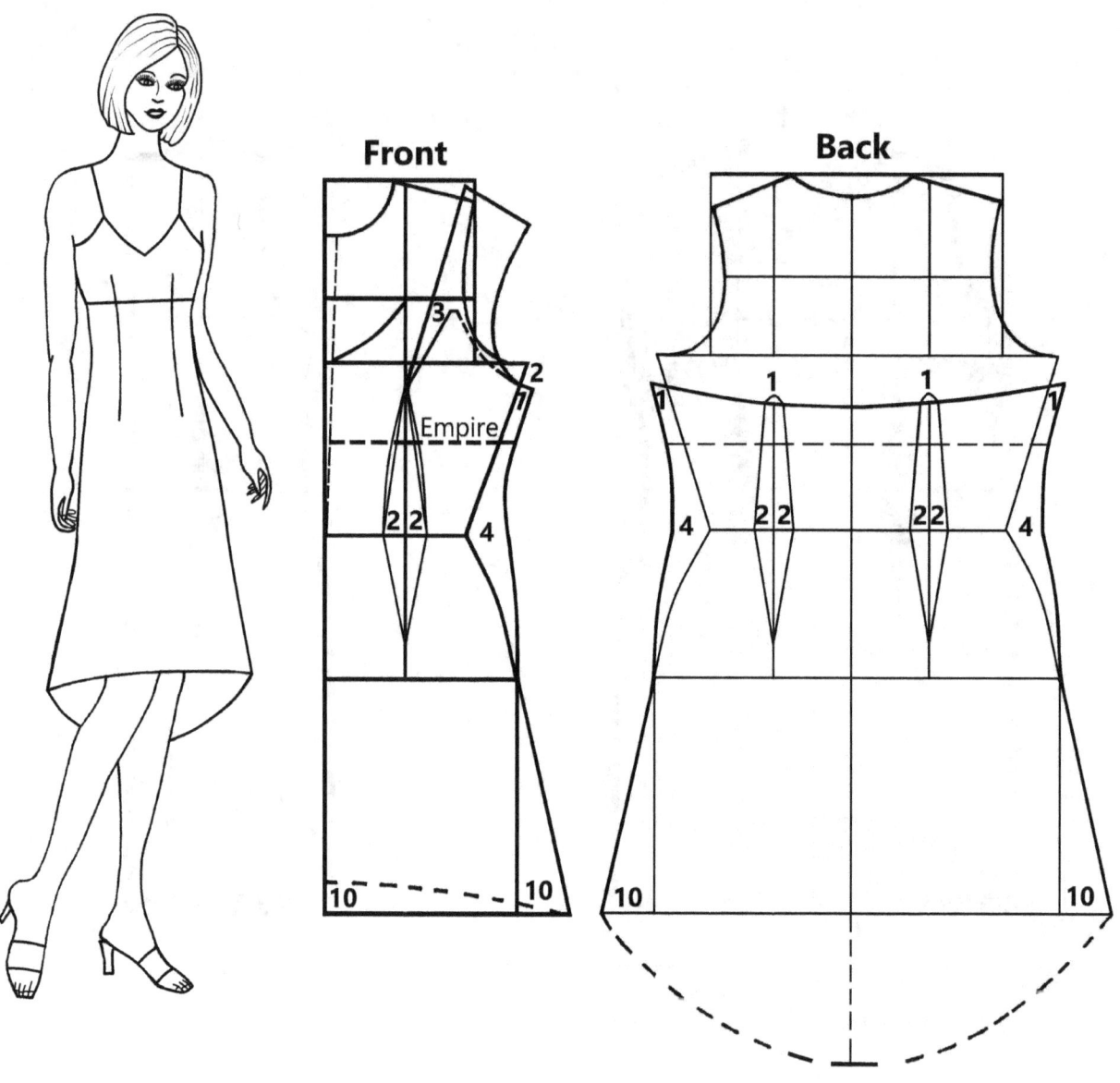

Some asymmetrical styles require the basic blocks to be drafted or traced separately and on the fold of a sheet of paper. Once the basic blocks are completed, the sheet should be opened so that the style lines can be added to the pattern.

Draft the front and back as illustrated. Drop **2 cm (¾ in)** along the front and back side seam line. Draw the V-neck at the desired height. Increase the shoulder dart by **3 cm (1 ¼ in)**. Draw the underarm with a slight curve. Curve the dart below the bust point outward by **6 mm (¼ in)** on each side. Add **10 cm (4 in)** to the side front and side back, or as desired. Lift the hemline at the front as illustrated, or by a desired amount. Measure the distance from the front to the back neckline and draw straps to the desired width. Trace facing and all the pattern pieces off and add grain lines, notches, hem, and seam allowances.

ASYMMETRICAL CAMISOLE DRESS

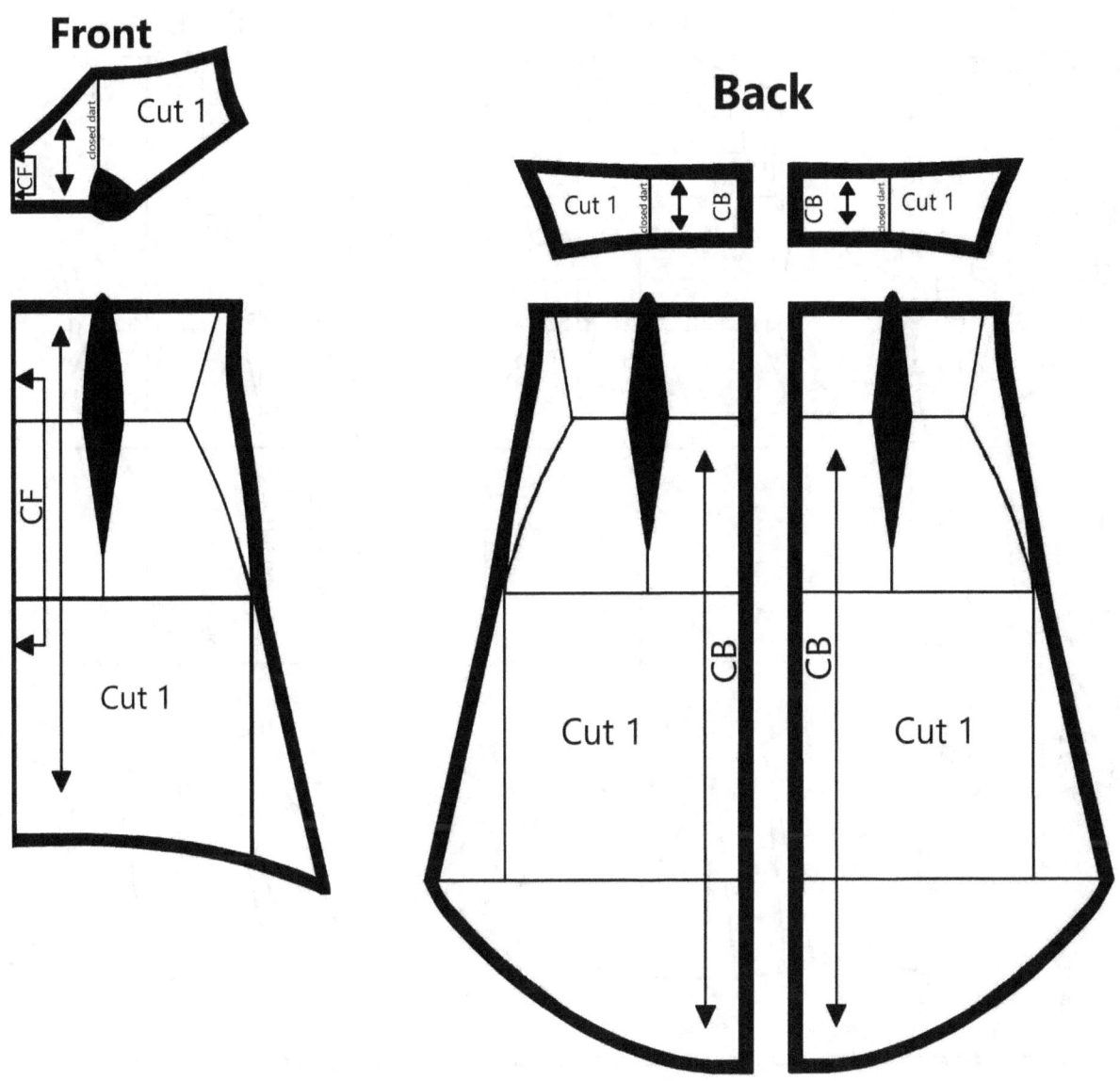

ASYMMETRICAL VARIATION

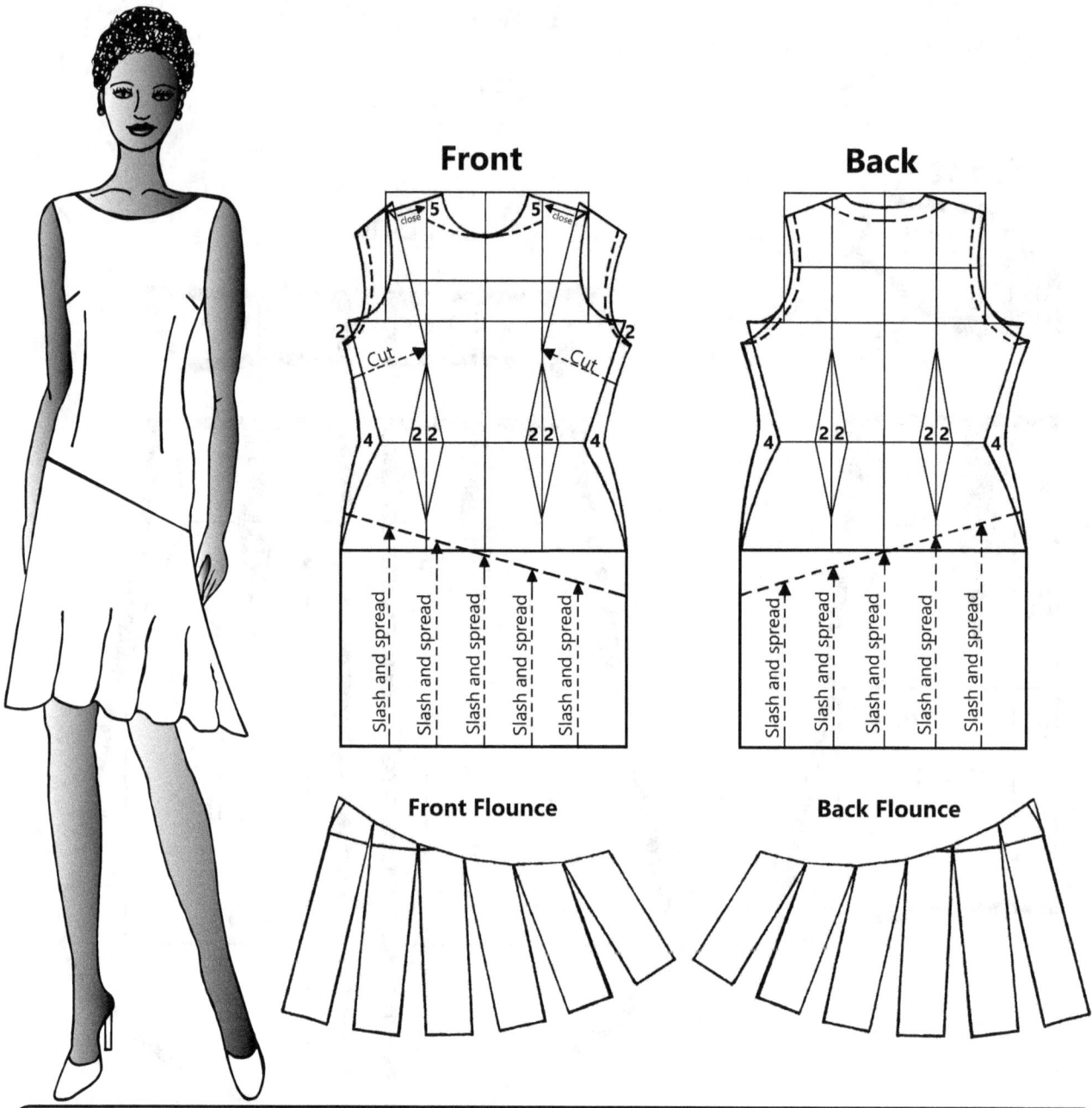

Draft the front and back bodice blocks on the fold of paper. Open the draft and draw the style lines as illustrated. Close the shoulder dart on the front and scoop the neckline by **5 cm** (**2 in**) or as desired. Scoop the back neckline by the same amount. Shorten the front and back shoulder line by **1 cm** (**⅜ in**) and redraw the armhole. Measure the desired height where the asymmetric line should begin and end. Mark this section with equal line spacing. Repeat at the same height for the back. Trace the flounce section off. Put a strip of sticky tape across the top section of the flounce. Slash into the marked sections without cutting through. Spread the sections on a sheet of paper and open it to a desired width and equal amounts. Secure with tape and blend the curves. Add grain lines, notches, hem, and seam allowances.

BOAT NECKLINE

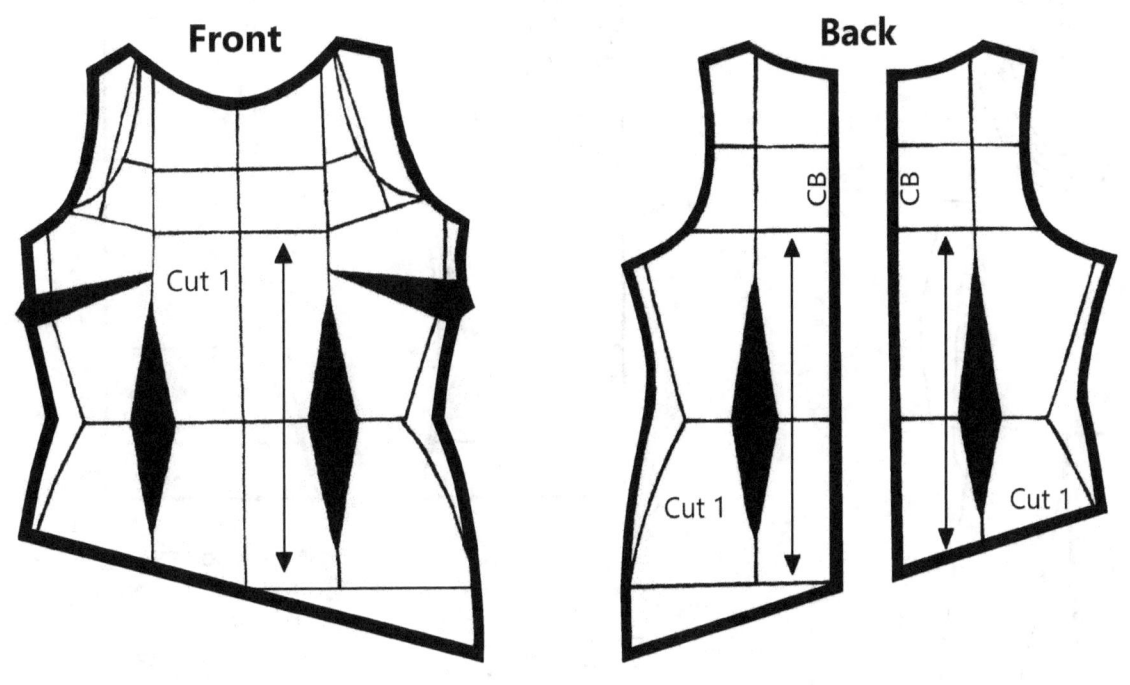

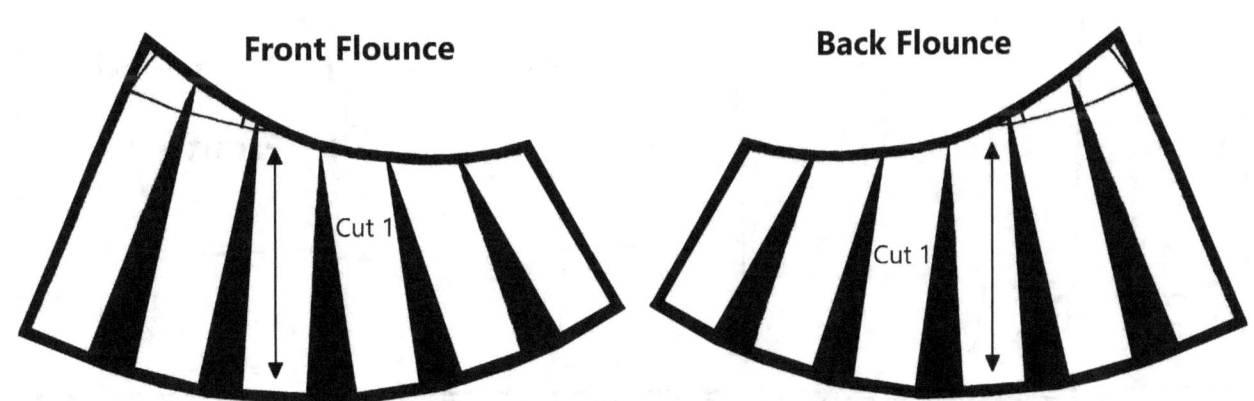

COWL NECKLINE

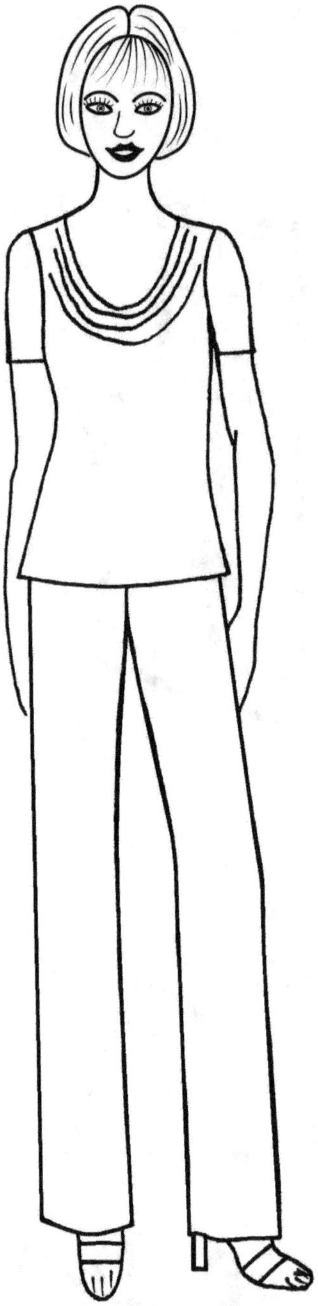

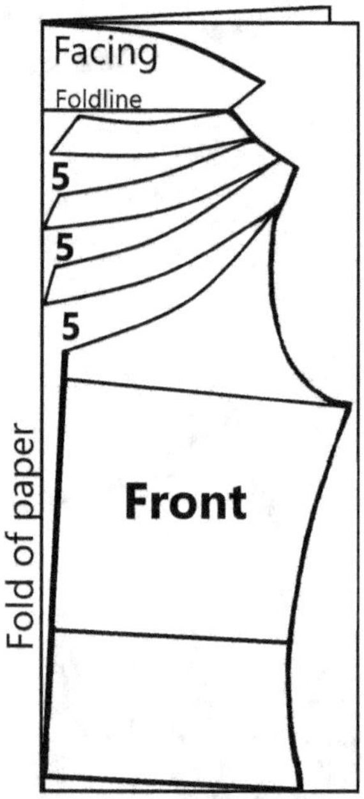

1. Trace the basic front and back bodice blocks and adjust the length. Scoop the front and back necklines as desired. Plan the position of the slash lines and draw them on the front bodice.
2. Slash into the marked cowl sections up to the arrowheads.
3. Place the bodice on the fold of paper and spread the cowl sections as illustrated, or to the desired width. Secure them with sticky tape. Draw the facing as illustrated. Add grain lines, notches, hem, and seam allowances to the front and back pattern.

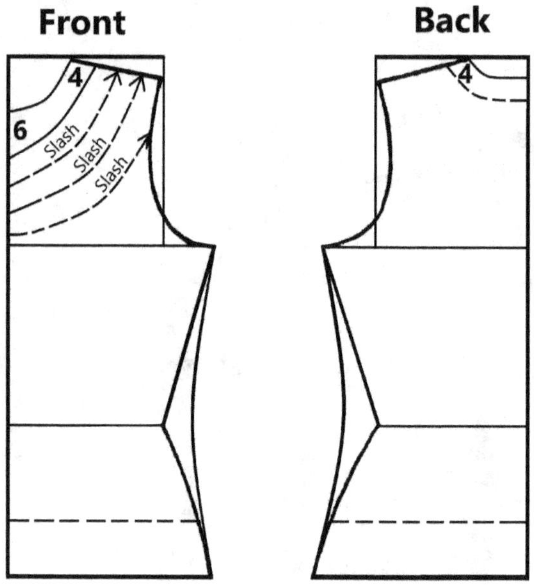

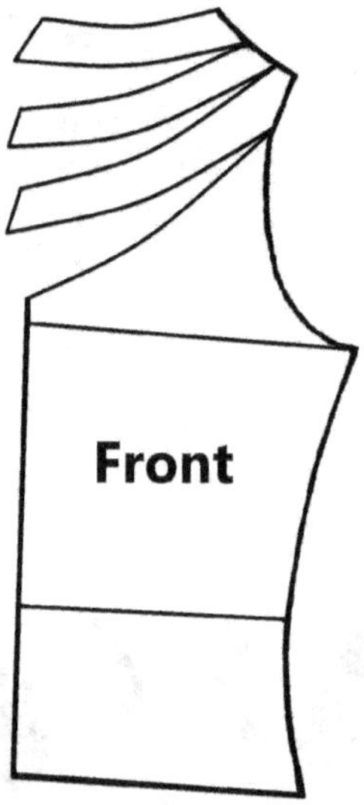

COWL NECKLINE

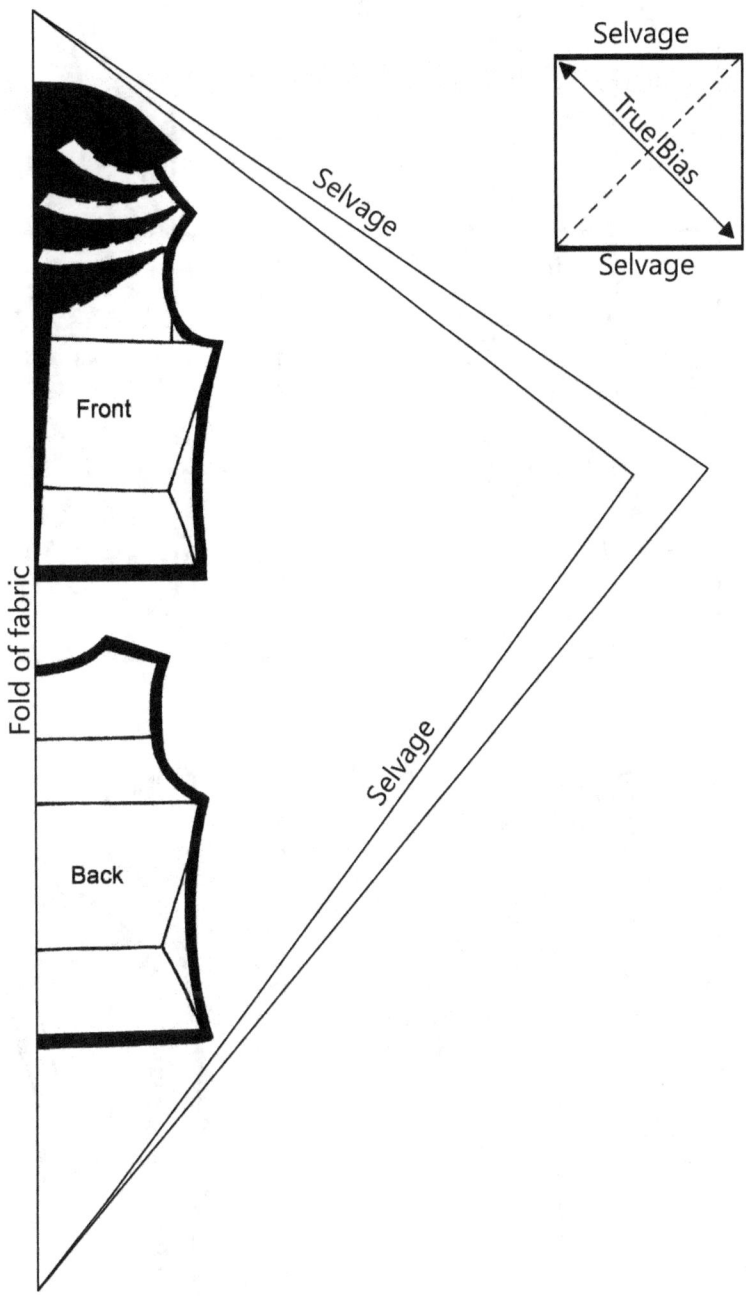

The cowl neckline must be cut on the **True Bias** as illustrated. The fabric must be folded from one corner of the selvage to the opposite corner, at a **45-degree angle**. Place the pattern pieces on the folded edge of the fabric. Both front and back can be cut on the bias, depending on the type of fabric used and the style of the garment. The back neck can be finished off with a facing or binding.

PANELS

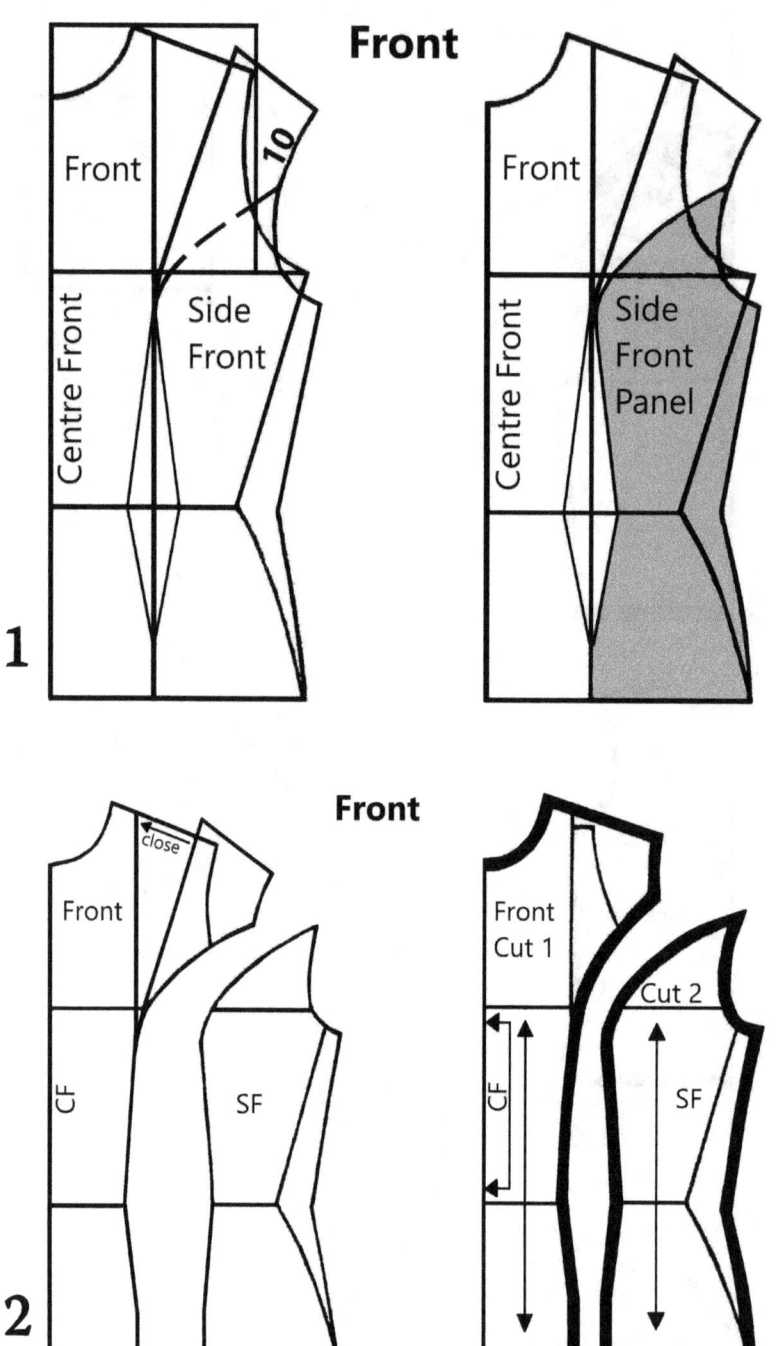

1. Draft the front bodice block with the shoulder dart as illustrated. Draw a curve with the French curve, about **10 cm (4 in)** down from the shoulder line, ending at the bust point. Blend the curve and mark it as the side front panel.
2. Trace the front and side front panels (shaded area) off separately. Close the shoulder dart and secure it with tape. Add grain lines, notches, hem, and seam allowances.

PANELS

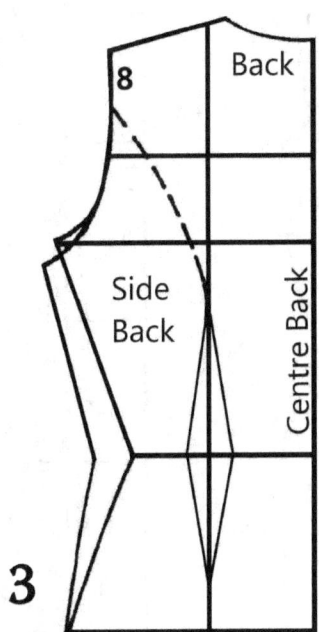
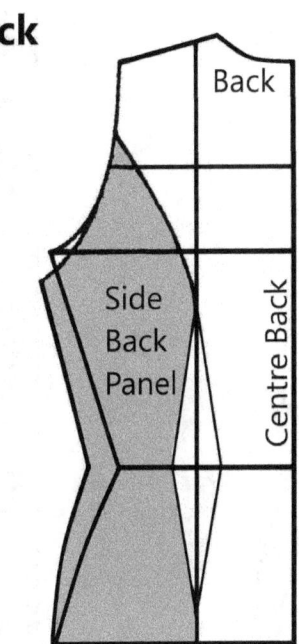

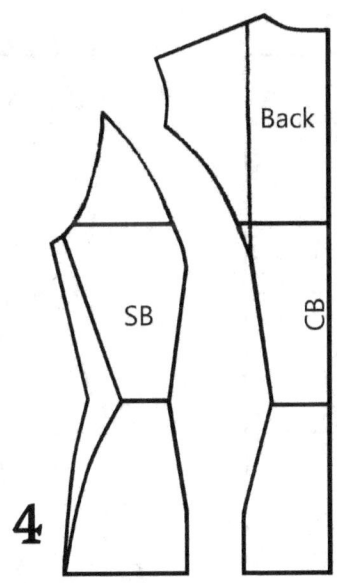
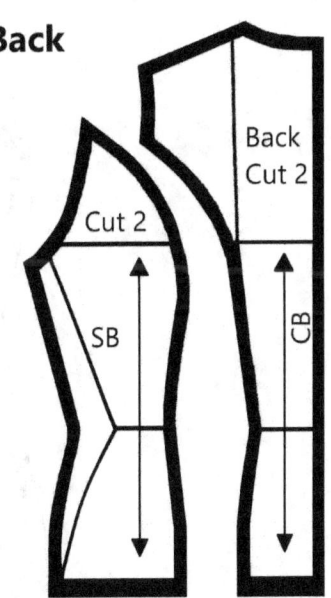

3. Draft the basic back bodice block. Draw a curve about **8 cm** (**3 ⅛ in**) down from the shoulder line, ending at the dart apex. Blend the curve and mark it as the side back panel.

4. Trace the back and side back panels (shaded area) off separately. Add grain lines, notches, hem, and seam allowances.

PRINCESS STYLE DRESS

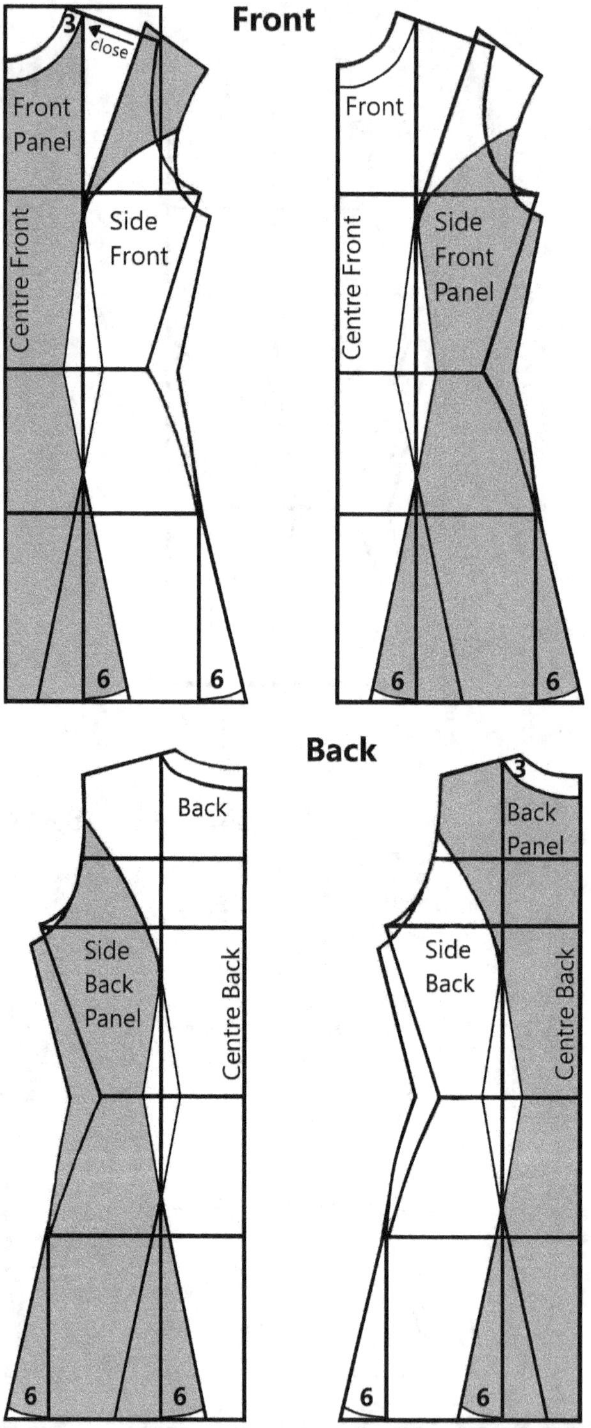

Front

Back

 Draft the front bodice block with the shoulder dart and a basic back bodice block. Draw the front and back panels as illustrated before. Add approximately **6 cm (2 ¼ in)** to the side of each panel for flare as illustrated. The new side seam lines on each panel must measure the same length before flare was added. Trace the panels off. Trace facing off. Add grain lines, notches, hem, and seam allowances.

PRINCESS STYLE DRESS

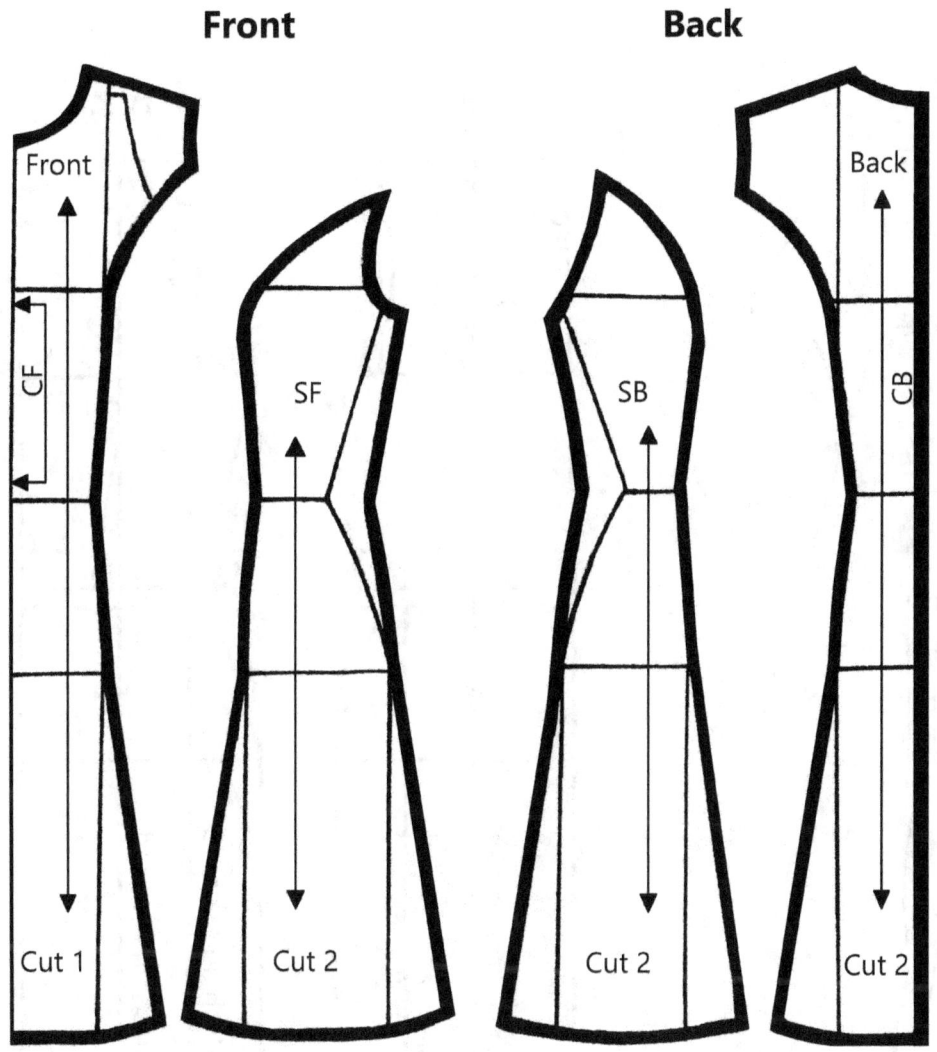

All pattern pieces must be placed on the straight grain of the fabric for cutting. Add **1.5 cm (⅝ in)** seam allowance for the side seams and **2 cm (¾ in)** hem allowance, depending on the amount of flare on the garment. It is best to use a small hem on flare garments. Staystitch the sides of the front panel from the underarm seam to just above the waist level. Clip the seam allowances up to the stitching, without cutting through the stitching. Repeat the same for the back panels. Pin and stitch each side front to the front panel, right sides together, matching notches up. Cut notches (small V's) in the seam allowances of the side front panels. Press the seams open. Repeat for the back panels. Stitch the centre back seams together up to the marked zipper opening. Insert a zipper of your choice in the centre back seam. Sew the front and back shoulders and side seams, right sides together. Lining can be cut from the same pattern and sewn in the same manner. Complete the garment with neck facing and sleeves. Press the garment.

PANELS

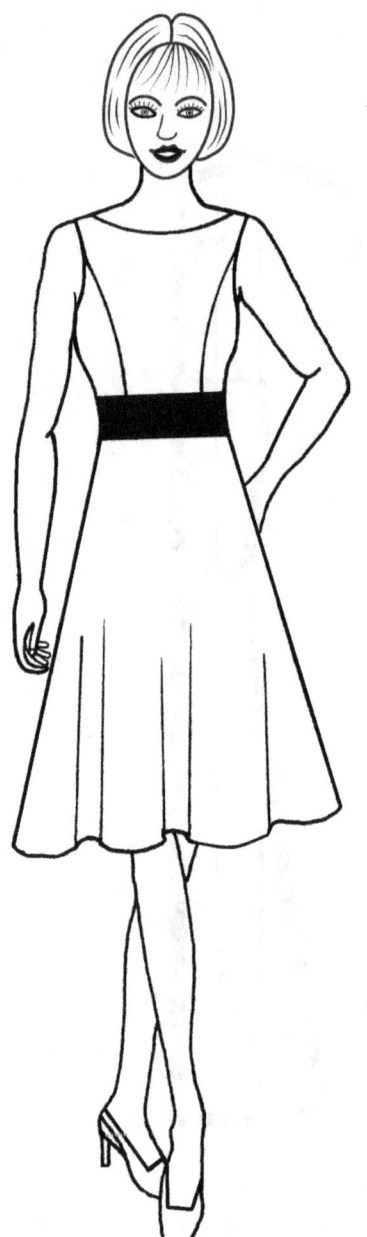

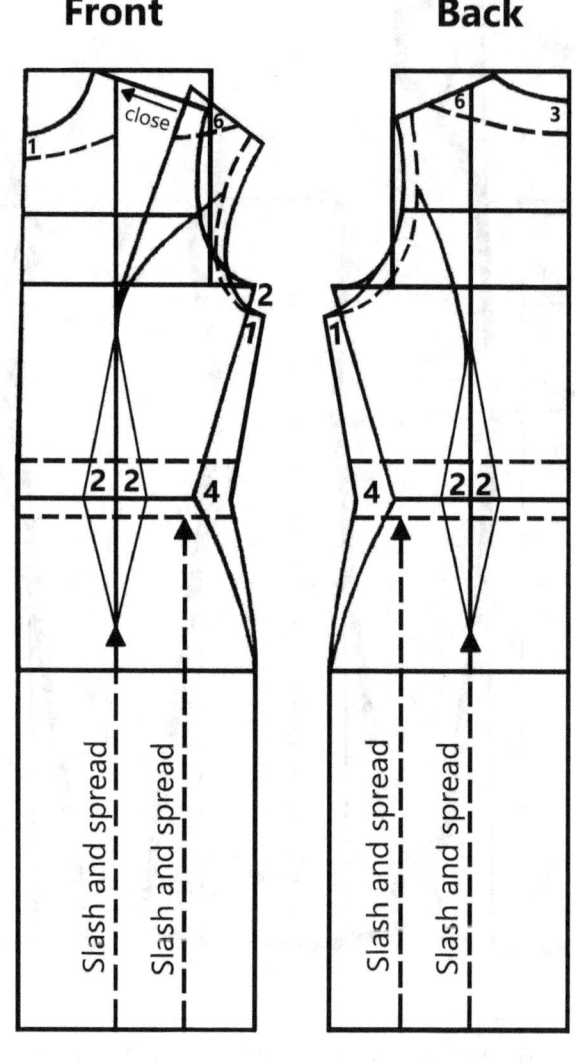

Front   Back

BOAT NECKLINE DRESS

Trace the front and back bodice blocks. Add the desired dress length. Scoop the front and back necklines by about **6 cm (2 ¼ in)**, or as desired. Scoop the armholes as illustrated. Draw and trace the front and back panels, waist panels, and skirt panels off. Draw and trace front and back facings. Slash the front and back skirt panels up to the arrowheads and close the darts. Spread the slashed sections to a desired width. Close the darts on the waist panels and secure it with tape. Add grain lines, notches, hem, and seam allowances.

PANELS

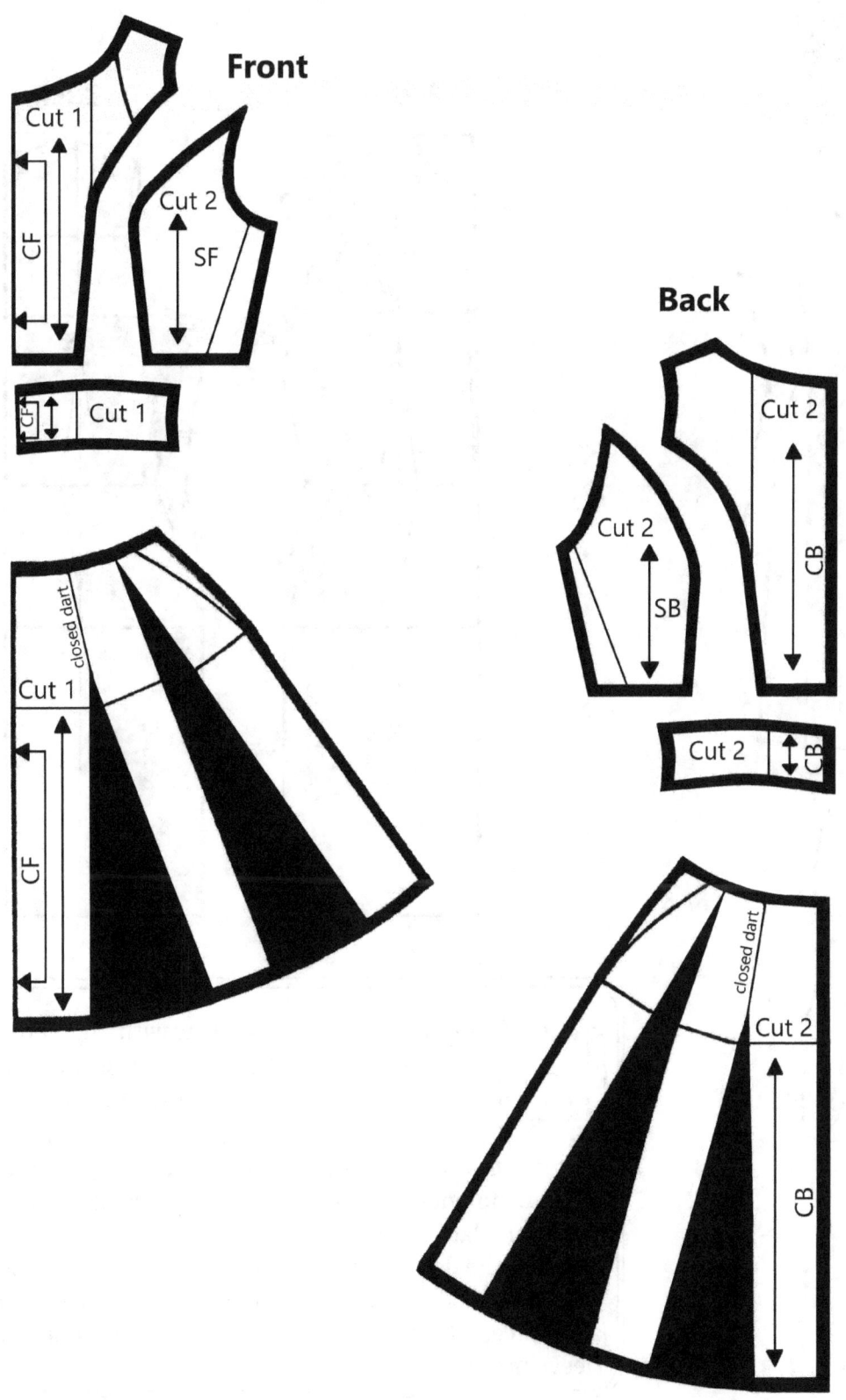

PANELS

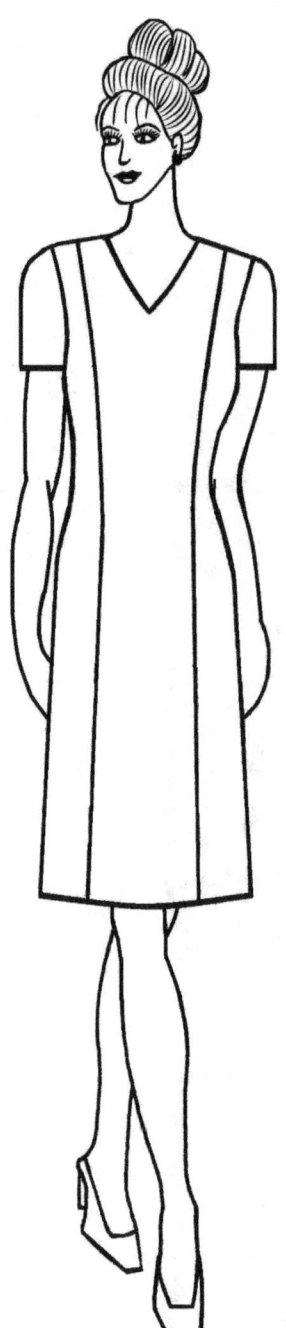

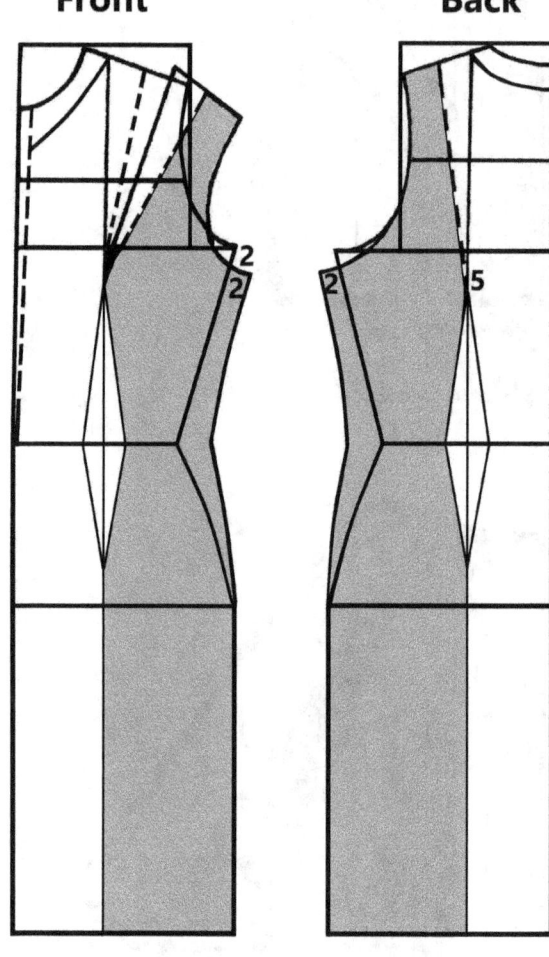

Front   Back

Draft the basic front bodice with the shoulder dart and the basic back bodice as illustrated. Scoop the necklines by a desired amount. Move the back panel line to the centre of the shoulder. Move the front right dart line to the centre of the shoulder line as illustrated. Move the left shoulder dart line further to the right, so that the new shoulder dart position has the same measured space in between the dart lines, as it had in the original position. Trace the panels off. Add grain lines, notches, hem, and seam allowances. Complete the pattern with the basic sleeve or a sleeve of your choice.

PANELS

Front **Back**

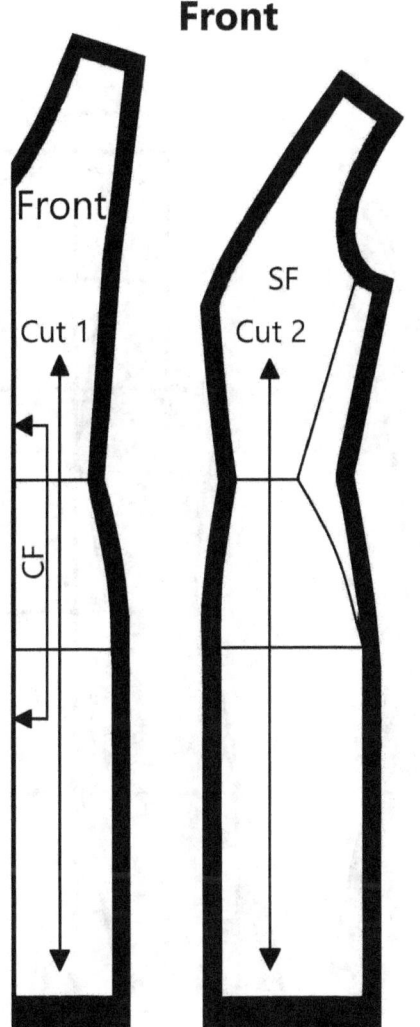
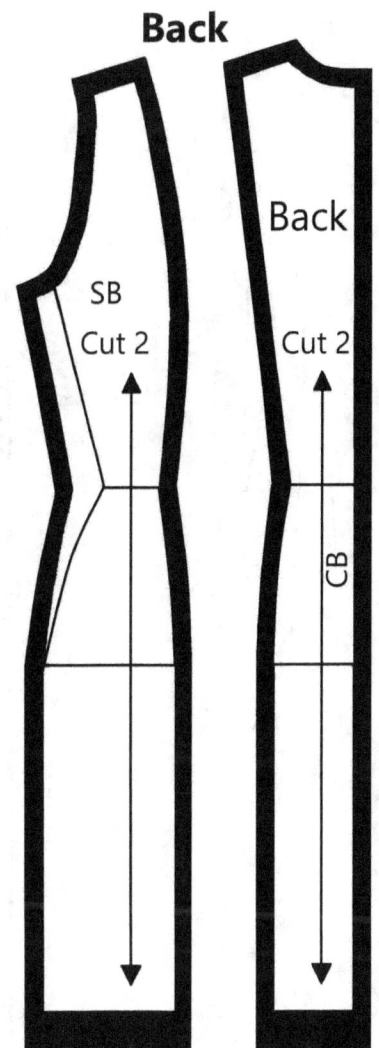

Cut and sew the front panels together as described on page **95**. Sew the centre back panels together up to the marked zipper opening. Stitch a zipper of your choice in the centre back seam. With right sides together, pin and sew the front and back shoulders and side seams. Press. Cut lining from the same pattern if the dress is to be lined. Trace front and back facings off. Complete the dress as described before. Press the garment.

PANELS

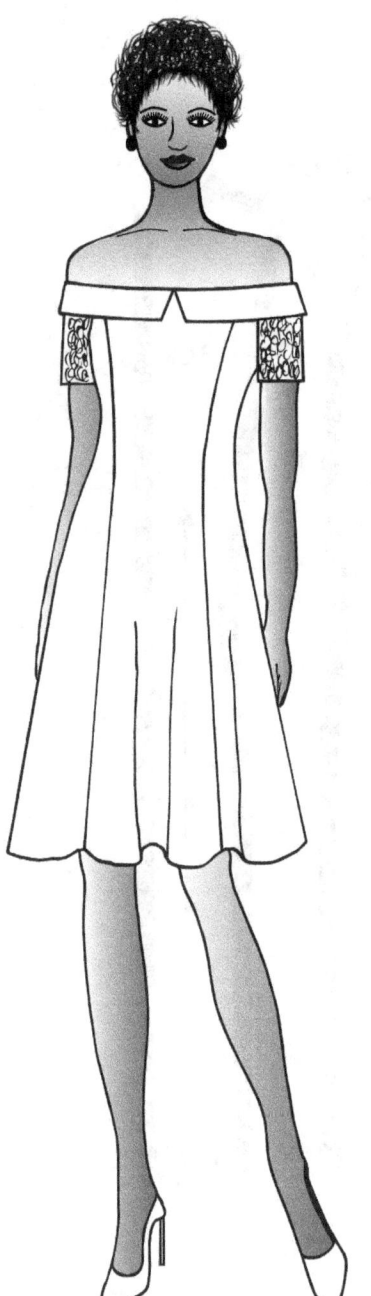 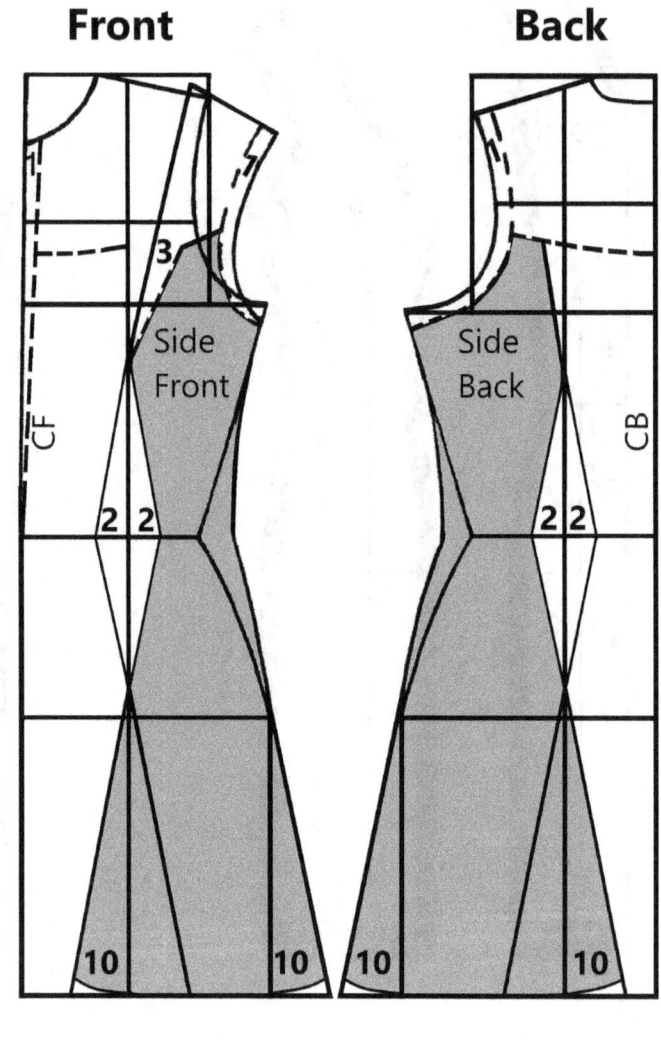

OFF-THE-SHOULDER NECKLINE

Draft the basic front with the shoulder dart and basic back bodice. Draw the front and back neckline at a desired height. Scoop the shoulders and armholes by **1 cm (⅜ in)** to ensure a fitted dress. Draw the new armhole curves. Increase the shoulder dart by **3 cm (1 ¼ in)** as illustrated. Add a desired amount of flare to the sides of the front and back panels. Trace the panels off and add grain lines, notches, hem, and seam allowances.

OFF-THE-SHOULDER DRESS

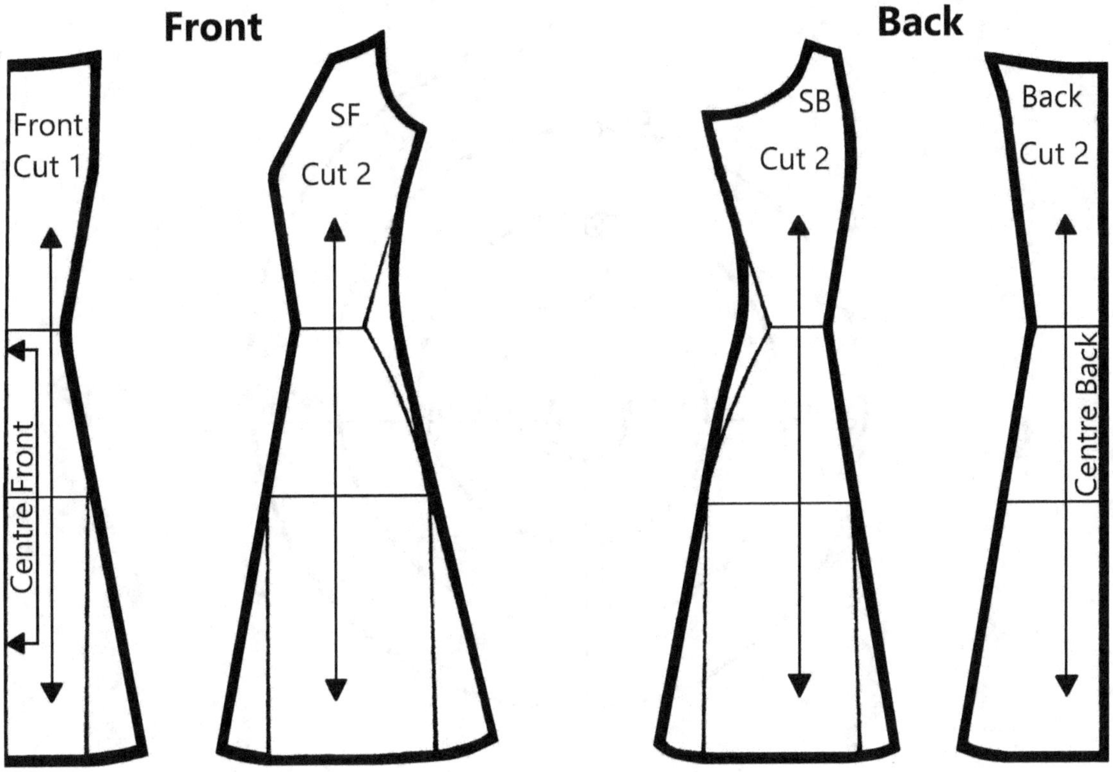

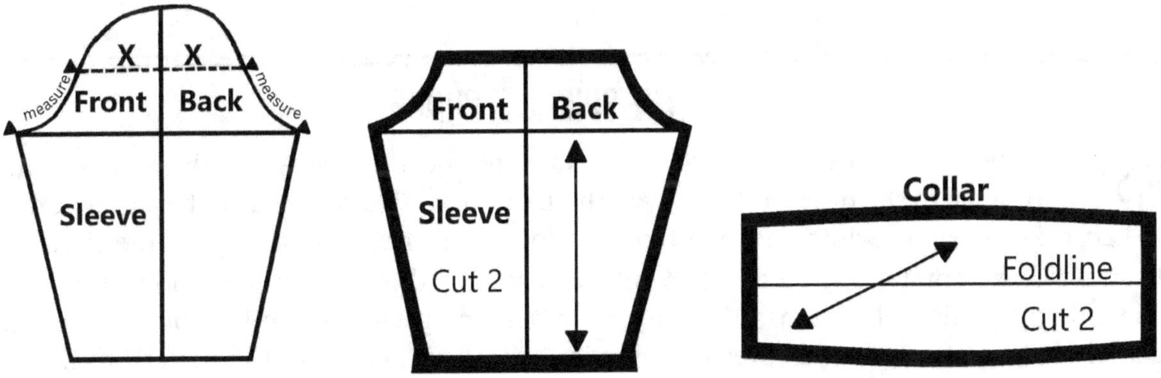

Front   **Back**

Draft the basic sleeve and adjust the width as desired. Measure the two marked sleeve head sections, ensuring that they measure the same length as the front and back armhole curves on the dress pattern. Trace the sleeve off without adding the top section marked **X**. Add grain lines, notches, hem, and seam allowances. Draft a collar to a desired depth by measuring around the upper bodice and arms.

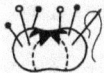

Sew the dress panels in the manner described before. The collar pieces must be cut on the **true bias**.

SPIRAL FLOUNCE

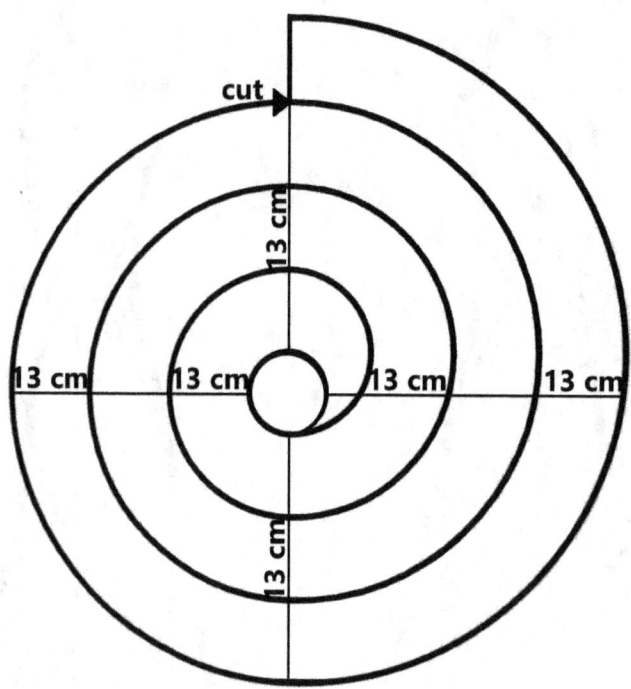

THE SPIRAL FLOUNCE

 Decide on the desired length and width of the flounce. Add hem and seam allowance to the desired flounce width. Draw a small circle as a centre point. Start measuring the width and length of the flounce from the outer edge of the circle as illustrated. An amount of **13 cm (5 ⅛ in)** was used for the width in the above example. The amount of flare diminishes the longer the flounce gets and it might be wise to cut more lengths or to slash and spread the section with less flare. Cut the pattern from the outer edge as illustrated above.

The flounce hemline can be finished off with an overlocker, using the narrow hem or rolled hem setting. The flounce can also be lined with a different colour fabric for a neat and interesting look. The seam of a flounce made with woven fabric should be staystitched and clipped first, before applying it to a garment seam.

DRAPES

Draped styles have various types of folds, pleats, and gathers. Folds, pleats, or cascades can be attached to one side of the garment only. Folds can also be attached at both ends of a garment and will usually be fitted over the body. The fabric should be cut on the bias to ensure a comfortable fit when using the latter method. Graduated folds or pleats can start at one side and disappear on the opposite side of a garment. The outer fold of draped pleats can be made to fold up or down.

It is important to plan when drafting patterns for draped styles. The position and depth of the draped folds, as well as the type of fabric to be used, should all be taken into consideration.

There are two commonly used methods to add drapes to a pattern. The first method is by drawing lines on the pattern in a chosen direction. The lines are slashed up to a certain point and not through the pattern. The slashed sections are placed on paper and then spread apart to the required width. The second method is when the lines are slashed from one end and through the other end. The slashed sections are separated to a required width on a sheet of paper. Both methods are used to obtain folds, pleats, or gathers.

GATHERED DRAPES

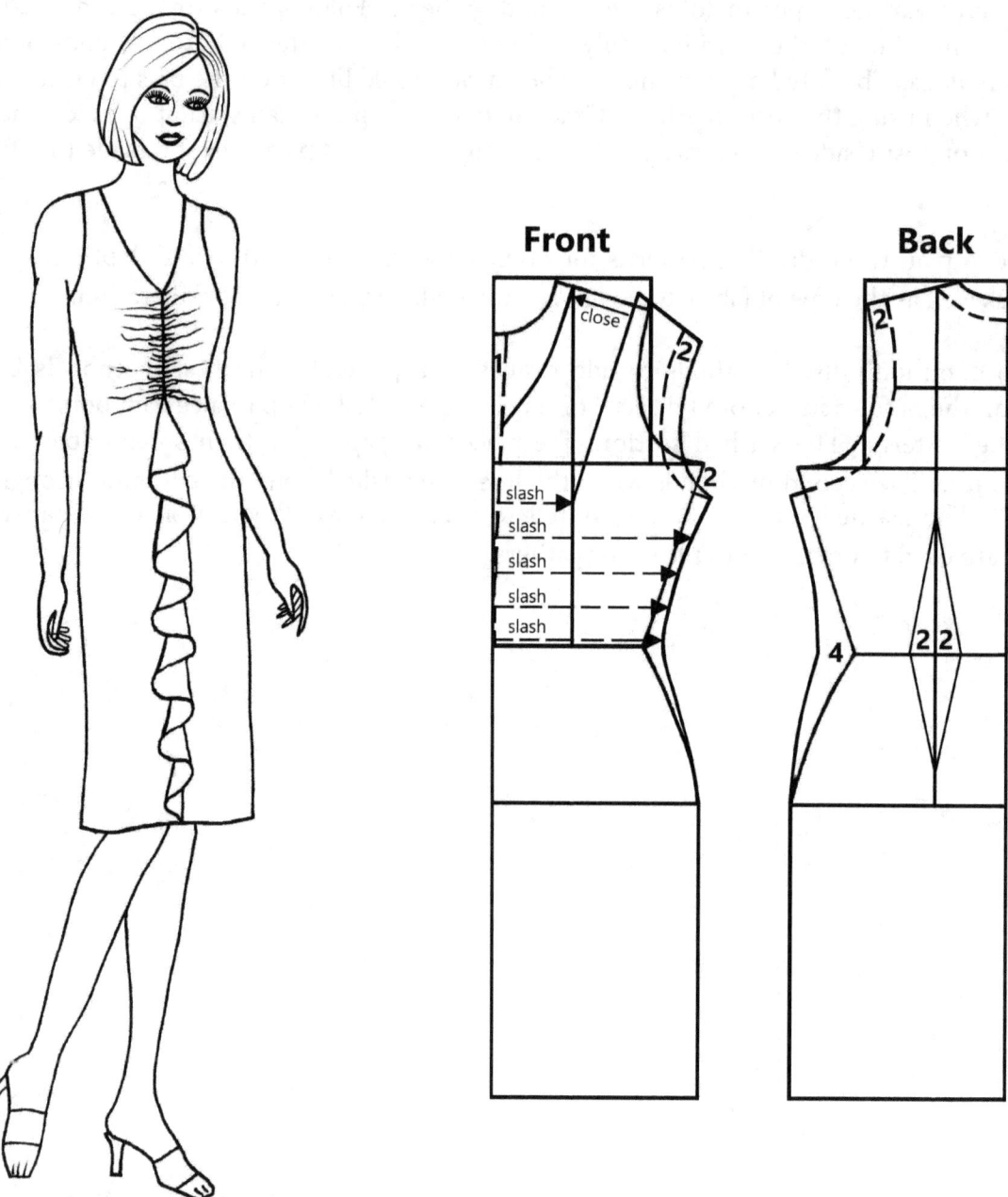

Draft the basic front with the shoulder dart and the basic back block. Scoop the necklines and armholes as illustrated or by a desired amount. Complete the pattern. Trace the front and back off. Draw horizontal lines with even spacing across the front bodice as illustrated. Slash the front bodice up to the arrowheads and close the shoulder dart. Place paper under the slashed sections. Open the slashed sections about **3 cm** (**1 ¼ in**) wide, for gathers over the bust area. Secure the slashed sections in place with tape. Add grain lines, notches, hem, and seam allowances. Draft the spiral flounce for the centre front as illustrated on page **102**.

GATHERED DRAPES

Front

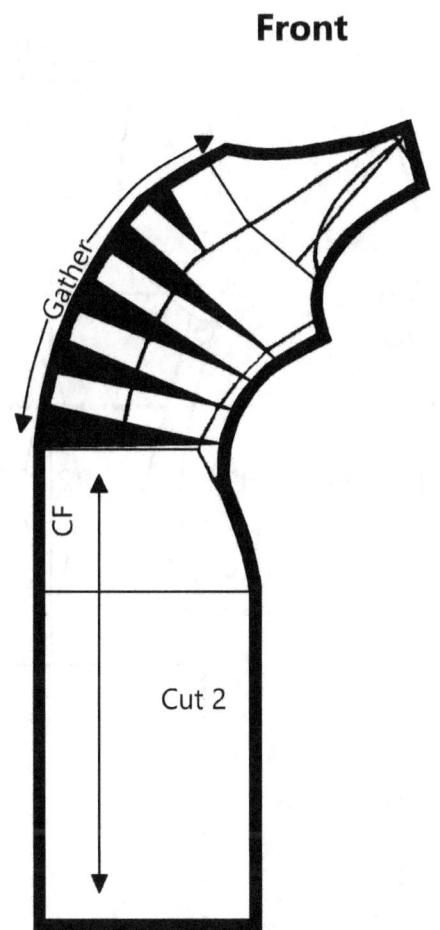

Back

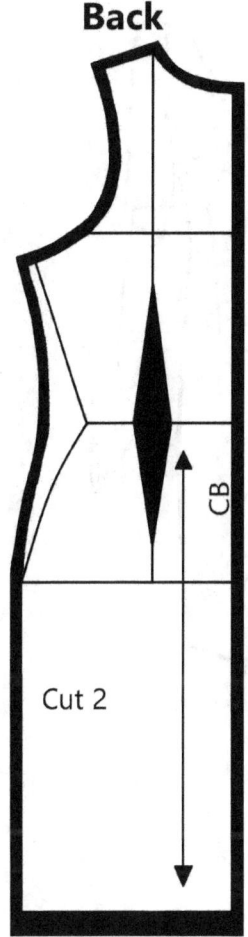

GATHERED DRAPES

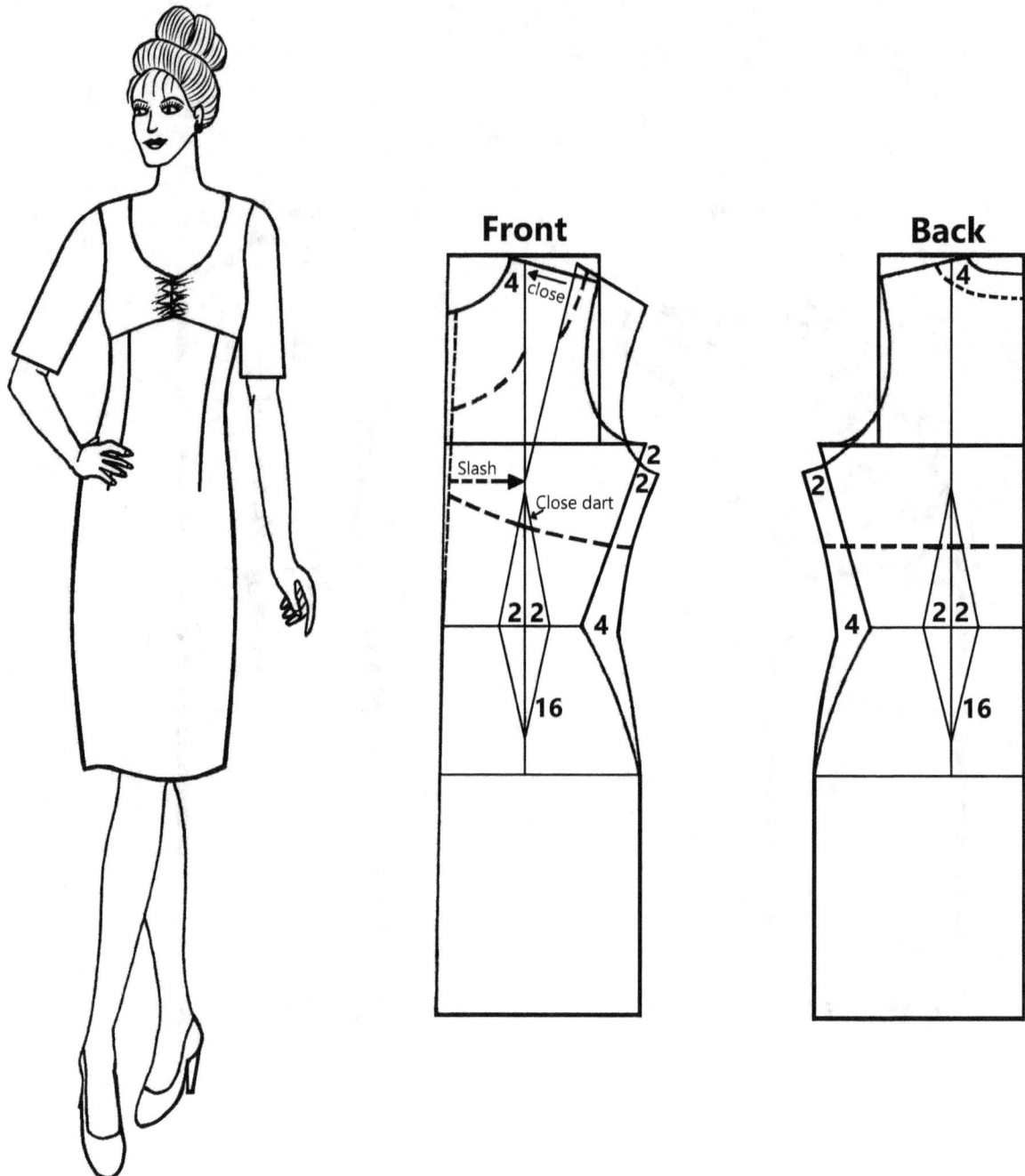

Draft the front and back bodice blocks. Close the shoulder dart with a pin and scoop the neckline as illustrated. Scoop the back neckline by the same amount. Draw the style lines with the French and hip curves. Trace the pattern sections off. Cut the front up to the bust point and close the shoulder dart. Close the small dart on the empire line and secure it with tape. The slashed section on the centre front will open and the dart excess must be used for gathers. Add grain lines, notches, hem, and seam allowances.

GATHERED DRAPES

Front

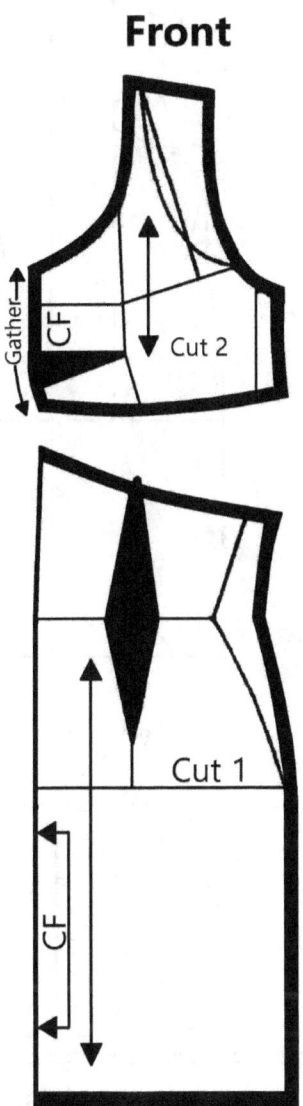

Back

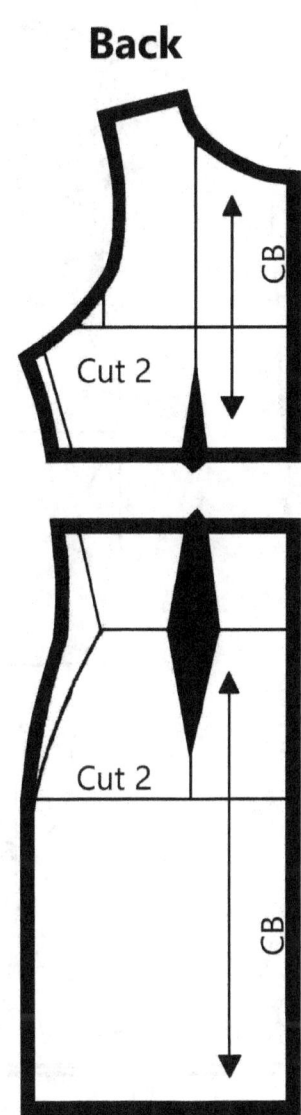

With right sides together, pin and stitch the two front bodice sections. Pull the bobbin threads to gather the seam. Sew the darts on the front and back panels. Neaten raw edges with overlocking. With right sides together, sew the front bodice to the front skirt panel. Sew the back bodice to the skirt back panels. Sew the centre back seam together up to the marked zipper opening. Insert a zipper of your choice in the centre back seam. With right sides together, pin and stitch the front and back shoulders and sides seams. Press. Complete the garment in the manner described before. Press the garment.

PLEATED DRAPES

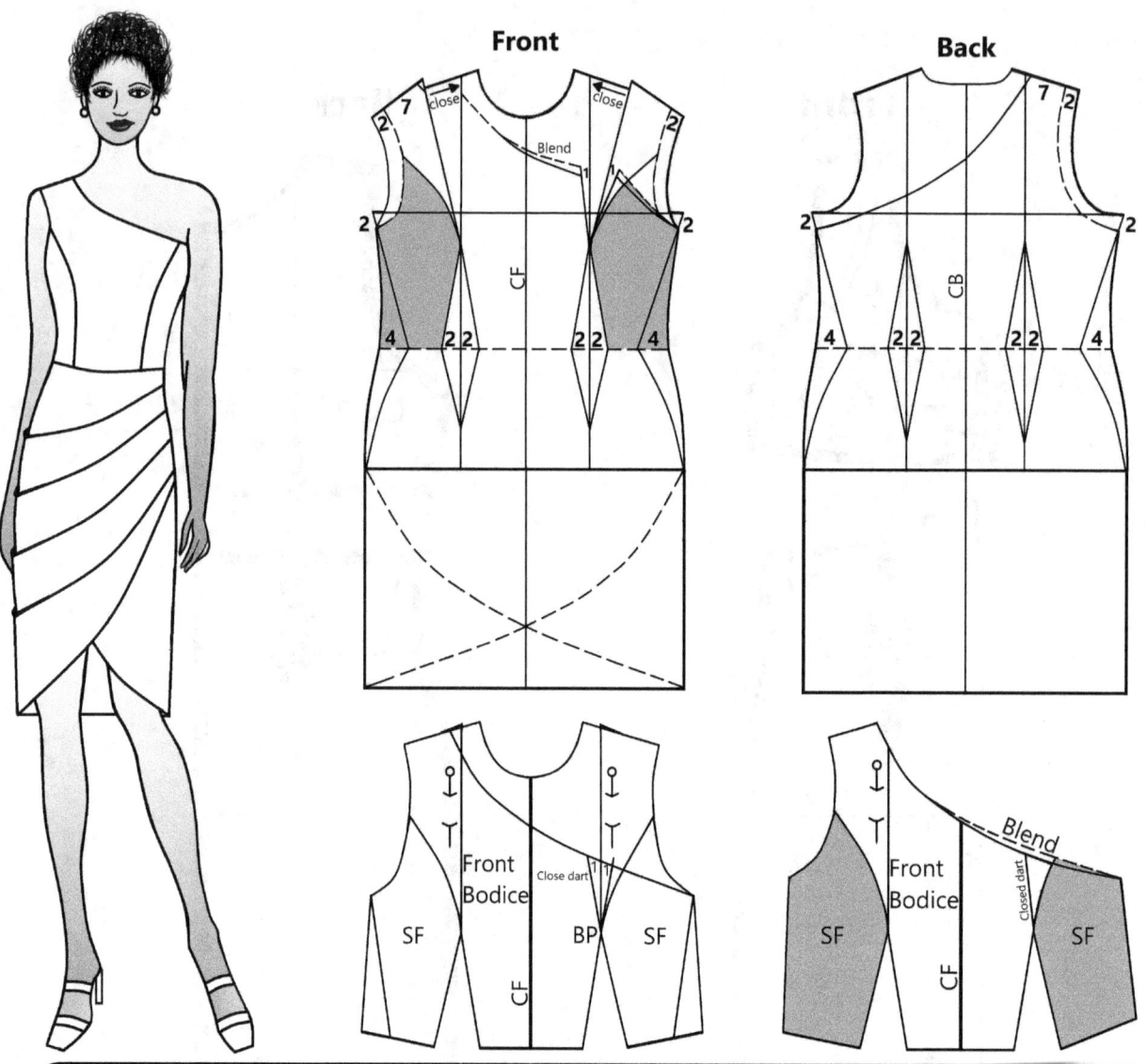

Draft the basic front bodice block with the shoulder dart and on the fold of paper. Trace the lines through. Open the paper and draw the style lines as illustrated. Drop **2 cm (¾ in)** along the side seam. Scoop the armholes by **2 cm** or as desired. Draw the side front panels in. Close the shoulder darts and secure it with pins. Measure **7 cm (2 ¾ in)** in from the scooped armhole for the new shoulder length. Draw the neckline from the shoulder to the armhole as illustrated. Draw a **2 cm (¾ in)** dart on the neckline. Close the dart and redraw the neckline as illustrated by the dotted line. Draft the basic back bodice block on the fold of paper. Trace the lines through. Open the sheet of paper and draw the style lines. Drop **2 cm (¾ in)** along the side seam. Scoop the armhole **2 cm** and redraw the armhole. Measure **7 cm (2 ¾ in)** in from the scooped armhole for the shoulder line. Draw the back neckline as illustrated. Trace the bodice and skirt sections off separately. Draw slash lines on the right front skirt panel. Slash and spread to a desired amount. Add grain lines, notches, hem, and seam allowances.

PLEATED DRAPES

Front

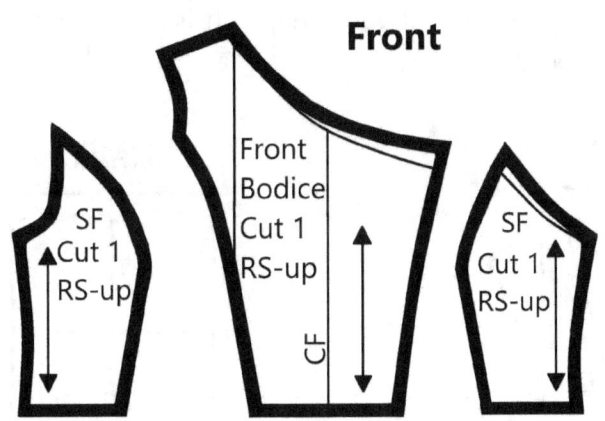

Back

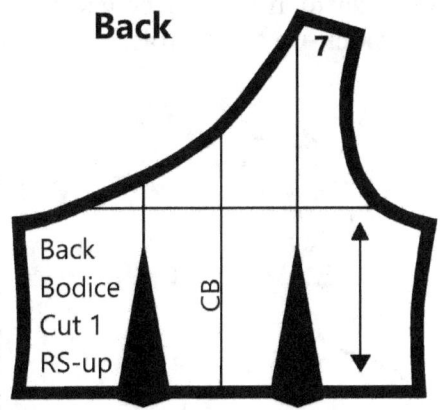

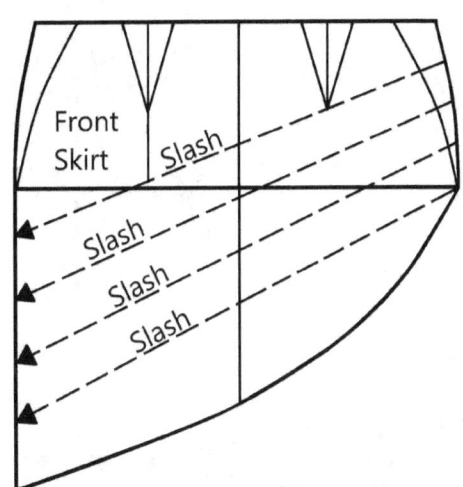

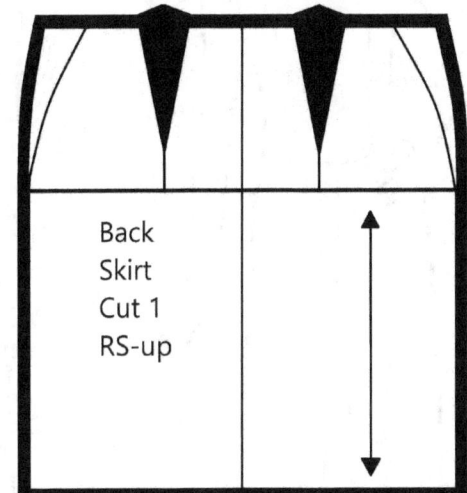

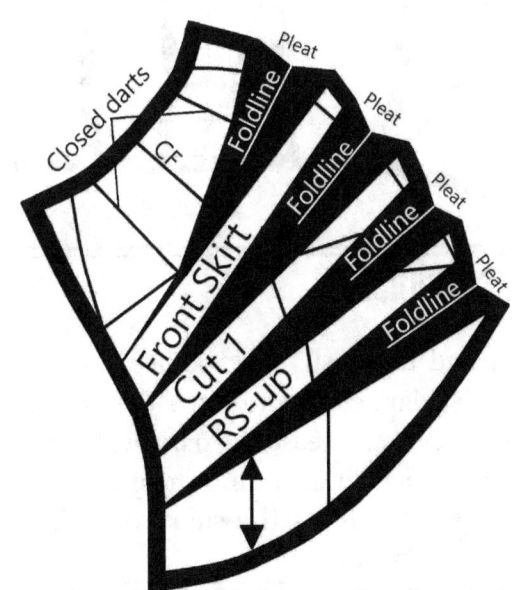

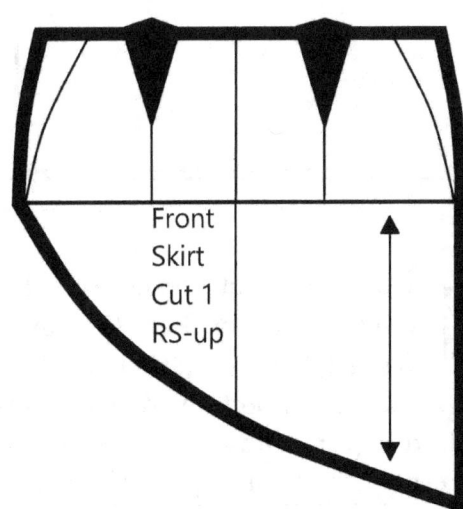

STRAPLESS GARMENTS

Strapless garments are fitted garments that contour the natural body shape. It is always best to make a **mock-up** of a strapless garment to ensure a good fit.

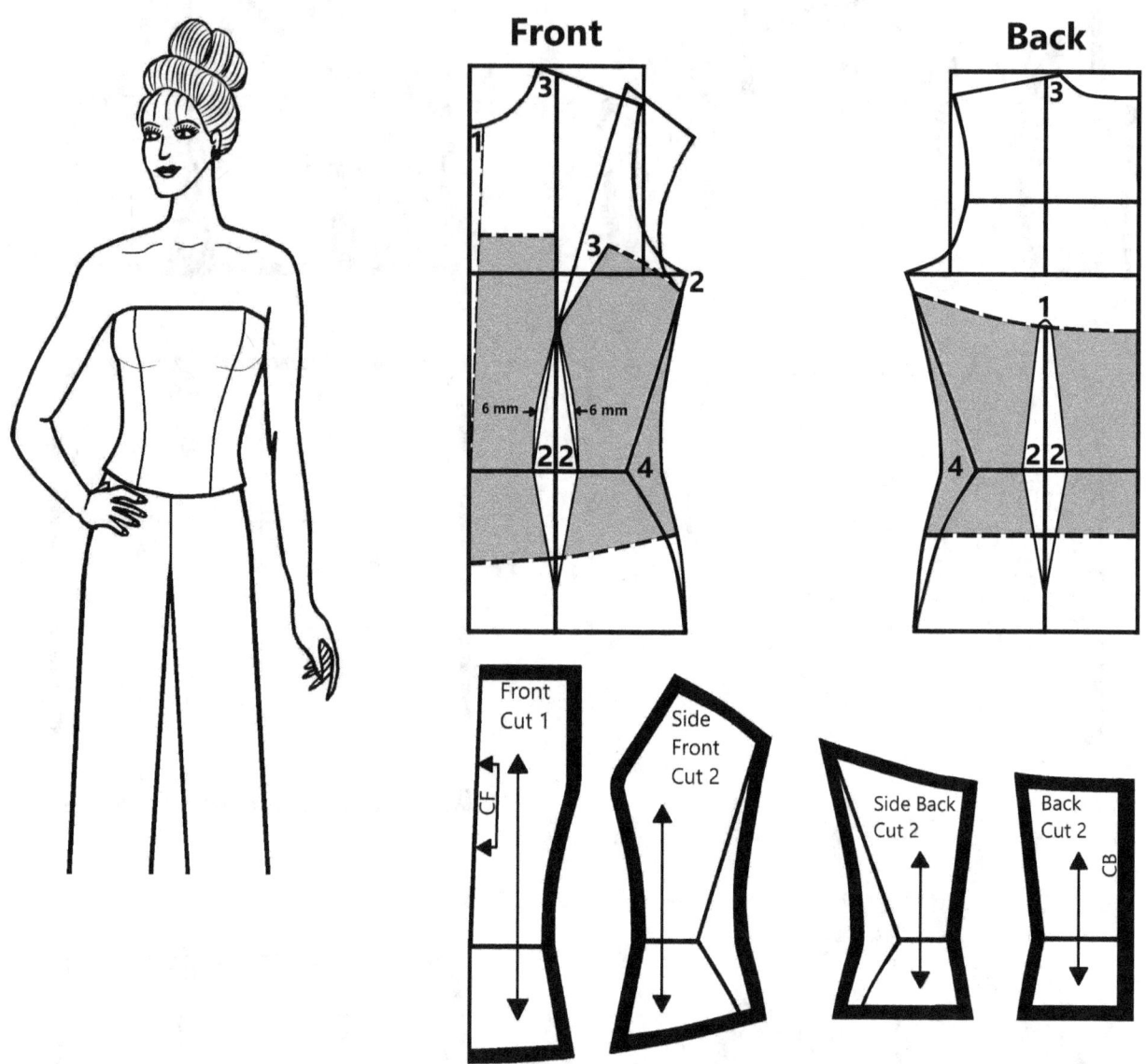

BASIC PRINCESS BODICE

Trace the front bodice with the shoulder dart and the basic back bodice. Increase the shoulder dart by **3 cm (1 ¼ in)**. Fold the shoulder dart close and draw the neckline at a desired depth. Draw curved lines along each dart leg to increase the dart by **6 mm (¼ in)**. Draw the bodice bottom edge as desired. Draw the back neckline, ending the centre back at a desired depth. Draw the back bottom edge at the same height as the side front. Trace the pattern pieces off and add grain lines, notches, and seam allowances.

~ 110 ~

STRAPLESS GARMENTS

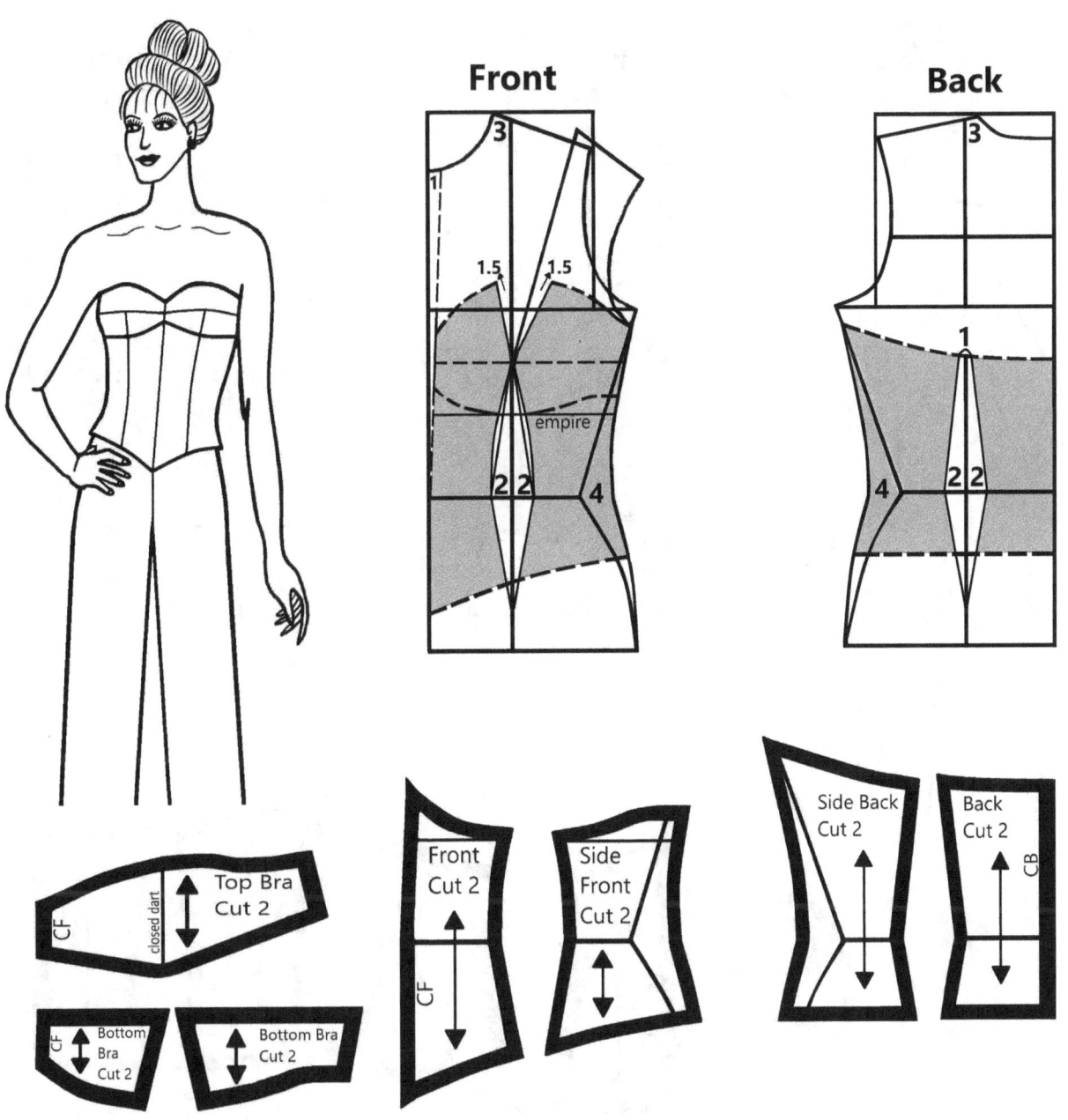

BRA-TOP BODICE

Trace the front bodice with the shoulder dart and the basic back bodice. Draw the bra shape for the top and bottom bra sections. Increase the shoulder dart by **1.5 cm (⅝ in)** on both sides. Draw a horizontal line through the bust point. Draw the front and back bottom edges as desired. Trace the top bra sections off and close the dart. Trace the bottom bra sections and the remainder pattern pieces off. Add grain lines, notches, and seam allowances.

STRAPLESS GARMENTS

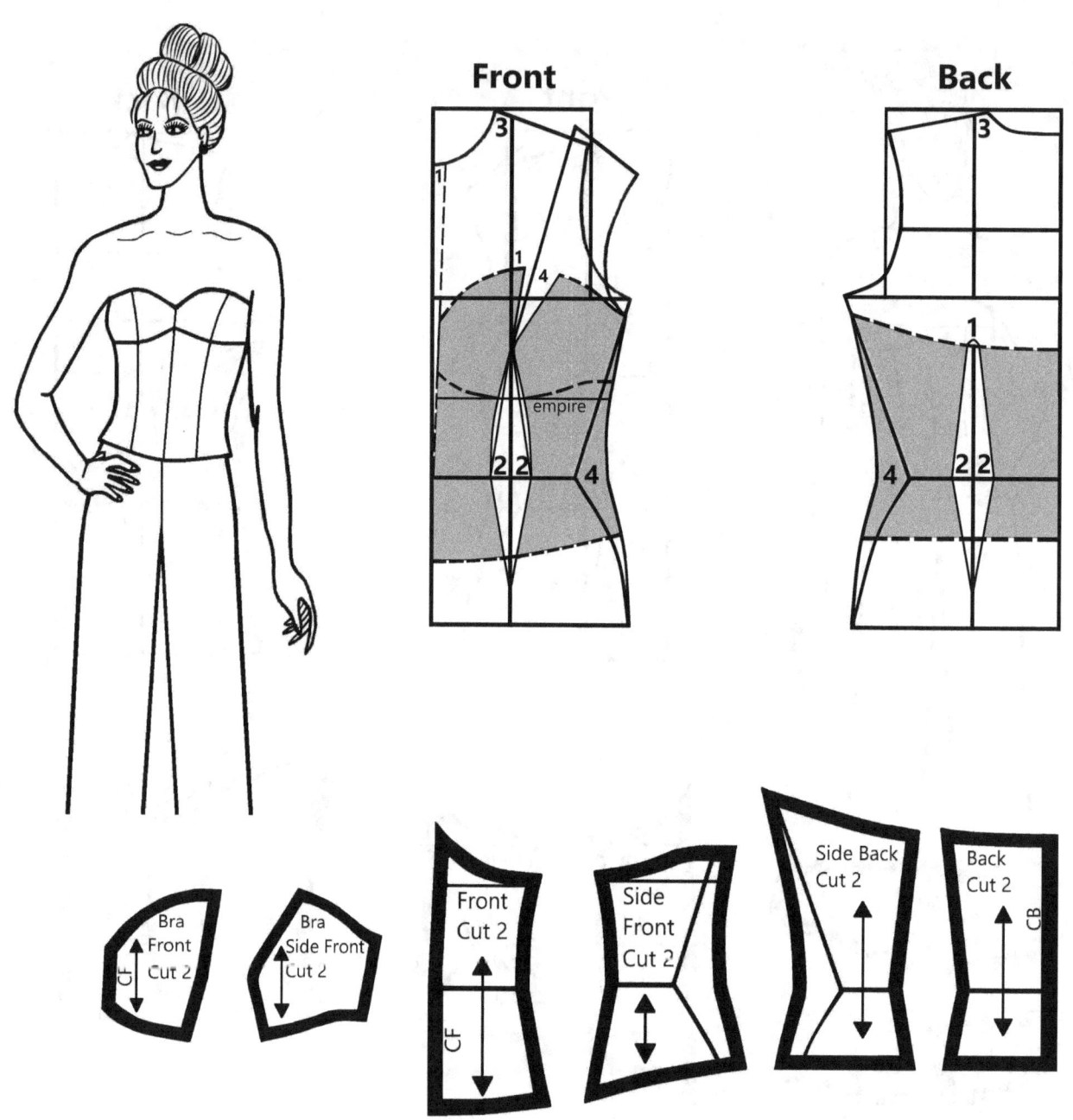

Front

Back

BRA-TOP BODICE VARIATION

Trace the front bodice with the shoulder dart and the basic back bodice. Move the left dart leg **1 cm (⅜ in)** to the right and increase the right dart leg by **4 cm (1 ½ in)**. Draw the bra shape as illustrated. Draw the back neckline. Draw the front and back bottom edges as desired. Trace the bra sections, front, and back bodice sections off. Add grain lines, notches, and seam allowances.

STRAPLESS GARMENTS

BONING

Boning is used to stabilize seams and to give lightweight support and structure to strapless garments. There are different types of boning available, ranging from plastic to metal. Rigilene boning and plastic pre-covered boning are readily available at fabric stores and they are much easier to work with. Both can be purchased per metre and they are available in different widths.

Rigilene boning is flexible, durable, lightweight, and made from polyester. It can be stitched directly onto fabric using a larger size needle. Rigilene boning is used to give shape and support to strapless garments, evening wear, and swimwear.

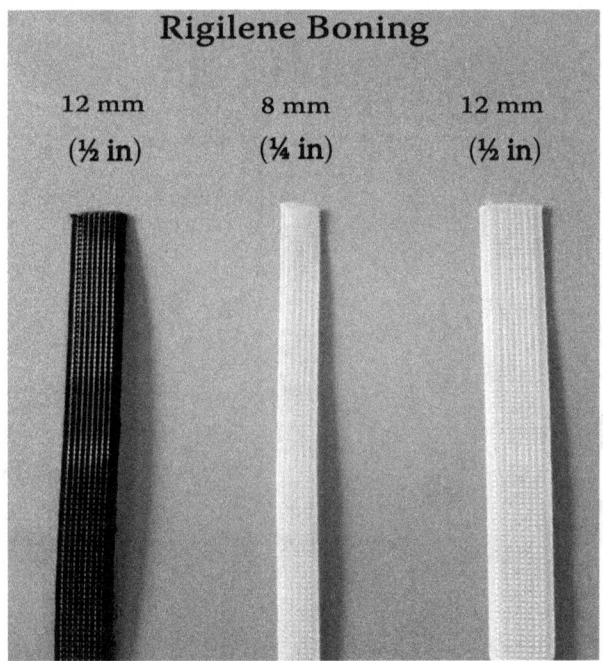

PREPARING THE GARMENT SECTIONS FOR BONING

Strapless garments must be stabilized with fusible or sew-in underlining before stitching the seams and boning. **Underlining** is another layer of fabric or fusible interfacing that is applied to the wrong side of the garment fabric or lining. It helps to stabilize and support fabric and it also helps to reinforce seams. **Lining** provides a neat finish to garments by covering all the construction details.

Boning can be placed in seams as well as in between seams. Plan your design and mark lines for the bone casings onto the underlining with tailor's chalk or thread marks. Do not overlock seams that must be boned to reduce bulk. Use ready-made casings or cotton twill tape, make casings from bias-cut fabric, or use the seam allowance to encase the boning. Make a mock-up of your chosen design. After fitting and alterations have been done, the length of each bone casing should be measured from the marked top stitching line to the bottom stitching line. Subtract a minimum of **12 mm** (½ in) from this measurement to get the length of bone that is needed for that casing. Make a note of each bone length that is needed.

STRAPLESS GARMENTS

There are various ways to attach boning to a garment. Four different methods are illustrated below, using **Rigilene boning**.

BONING STITCHED DIRECTLY TO THE SEAM ALLOWANCE

The end of a bone can be finished off by either melting it with a flame (**1a**) or by binding the ends with fabric (**1b**). This will prevent the sharp ends from poking through the garment. Press the seam allowance open. Centre the boning directly over the seamline, ensuring that the boning is at least **6 mm (¼ in)** from the marked top and bottom stitching line. Pin and topstitch the boning to both sides of the seam allowance as illustrated in (**1c**) and (**1d**).

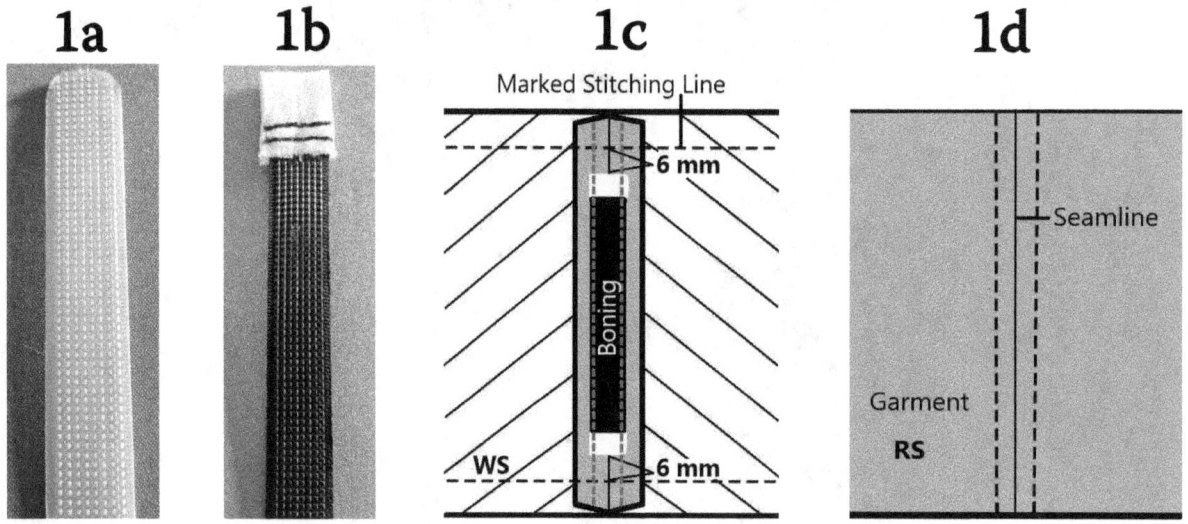

BONING IN CASING

Stitch across the bottom of the casing **6 mm (¼ in)** from the bottom stitching line. Centre the casing over the seam and pin it in place. Edgestitch it on both sides of the seam allowance. Trim **12 mm (½ in)** from the top end of the boning and insert it into the casing (**2a**) and (**2b**).

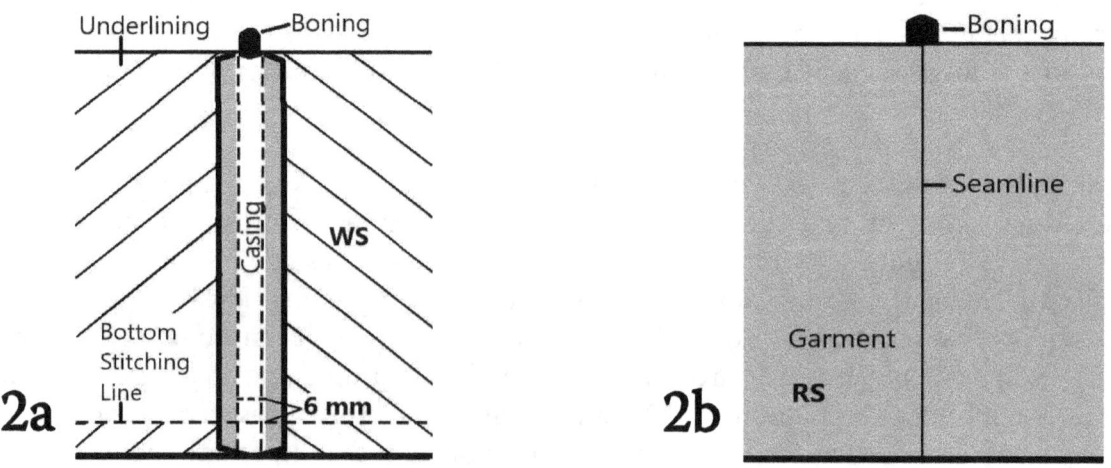

~ 114 ~

STRAPLESS GARMENTS

BONING IN THE SEAM ALLOWANCE

Press the seam allowance open. Topstitch the seam allowance edges to the garment to form casings for the boning (**3a**). Cut the boning shorter than the casing and insert it in both casings. This method can be used for the outer fabric as a design feature (**3b**).

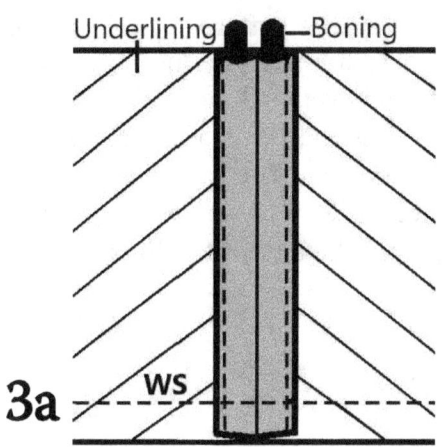
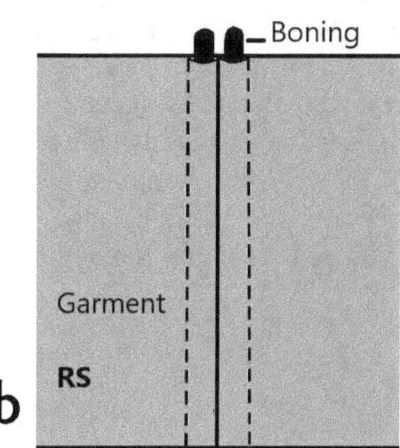

BONING IN FLAT-FELLED SEAMS

This method can be applied to the outer fabric. This type of seam is very durable and the boned seams will be highlighted on the outer fabric as a design feature. Use a seam allowance of at least **2 cm** (**¾ in**) and boning with a width of **12 mm** (**½ in**) for this sample. Sew the seams of the outer fabric wrong sides together, and press the seam allowance open. Trim one side of the seam allowance to **3 mm** (**⅛ in**) to reduce bulk. Press under the edge of the left-hand seam allowance **3 mm** (**⅛ in**) (**4a**). Fold the pressed edge over the trimmed seam allowance and edgestitch it in place (**4b**). Insert the boning (**4c**).

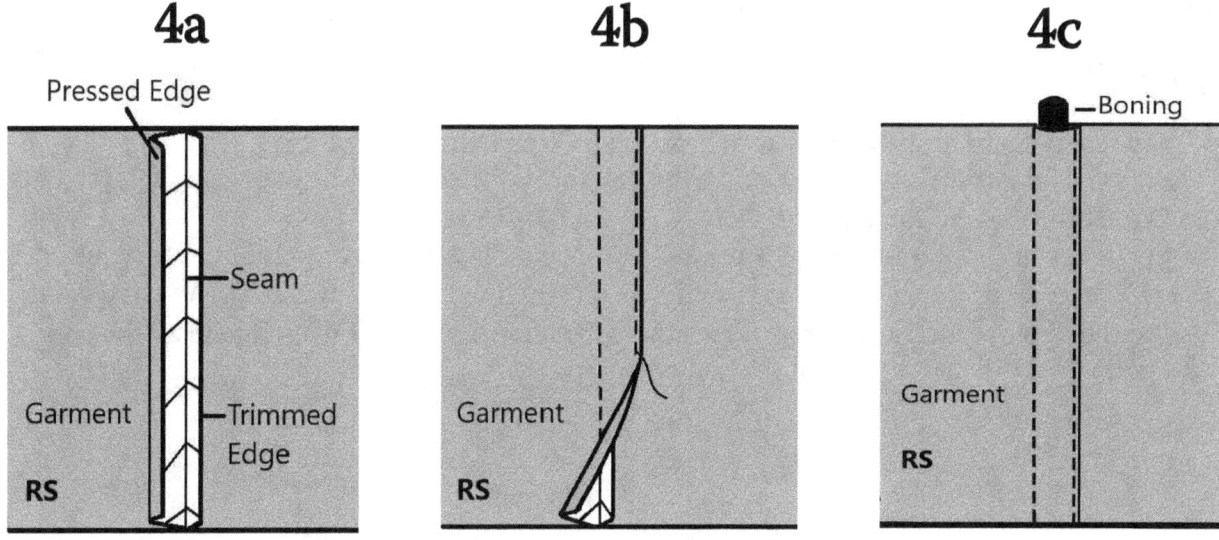

THE TAILORED SLEEVE

UPPER SLEEVE

The tailored sleeve is mostly used in jackets, coats, and blazer dresses. Draw identical grids for the upper and under sleeve. **Ensure that the upper and under sleeve curve measurement combined, is 3 cm (1 ¼ in) more than the armhole measurement of the pattern.** The extra 3 cm is used for ease around the sleeve head. It provides a rounded appearance once the bobbin threads from the easestitching have been pulled up and distributed evenly along the sleeve head. It would be best to make a **mock-up** of this sleeve to obtain the desired fit. Add an extra **1 to 2 cm (⅜ - ¾ in)** to the sleeve hemline for winter jackets and coats. Lift the sleeve head on the sleeve block and the shoulder edge on the bodice block, between **1 and 2 cm**, when shoulder pads are required. Measure the depth of the shoulder pad to obtain the amount of lift needed.

STEP ONE

Rule lines down and across from **A** to **C**.
A-B: The sleeve length.
A-C: Half the upper arm (top arm) circumference plus **2 cm (¾ in)**. Close the grid.
B-D: Half the desired hemline circumference. Mark.
A-E: Sleeve head depth plus **2 cm (¾ in)**. Rule a line from **E** to **F**.
A-G: One third of the sleeve head depth. Rule a line from **G** to **H**.
A-I: Half of **A-C**. Rule a line down to **J**.
E-K: Half of **E-B** for the elbow position on this sleeve block.

STEP TWO

G: Measure **3 cm (1 ¼ in)** in. Mark.
E-O: Measure **2 cm (¾ in)** out and draw a line.
B-M: Measure **2 cm** up. Measure **2 cm** out from **M** to **N** and draw a line.

STEP THREE

Use the French curve to shape the sleeve head from **O**, up to **I**, and down to **H**.
Rule a curved line from **O**, down to **K** and **N**, as illustrated for the inner sleeve seam. Draw a line from **D** to **N** for the new hemline.
Measure between **1 and 3 cm (⅜ - 1 ¼ in)** out at **L**, depending on the amount of ease required. Use a hip curve or a large French curve to draw a curved line from **H** down to **D**. A vent can be added to the outer seam if so desired. Trace the upper sleeve pattern off and **blend all the curves**. Add a grain line, notches, hem, and seam allowance.

THE TAILORED SLEEVE

UPPER SLEEVE

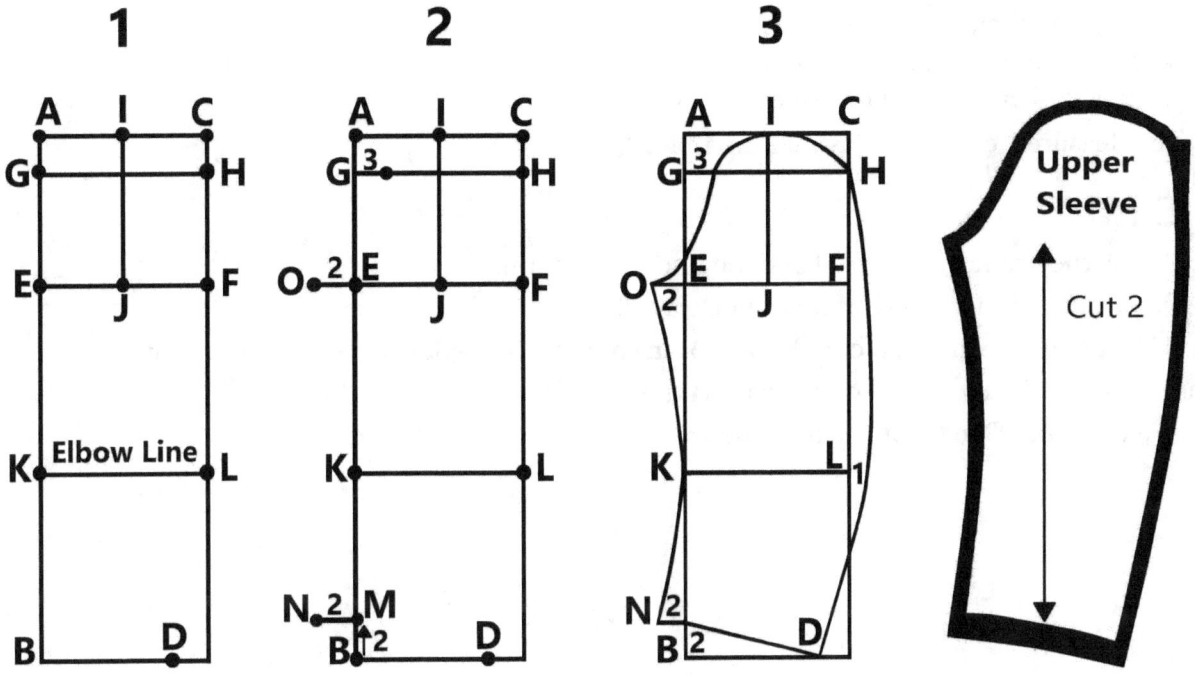

THE TAILORED SLEEVE

UNDER SLEEVE

Complete **step one** of the upper sleeve. Continue with the under sleeve as illustrated below. Trace the under sleeve pattern off and add a grain line, notches, hem, and seam allowances.

STEP FOUR

E-P: Measure **2 cm (¾ in)** in. Mark.
J: Measure **1 cm (⅜ in)** down. Mark.
K: Measure **4 cm (1 ½ in)** in. Mark.
B-M: Measure **2 cm** up. Measure **2 cm** in for **Q**.

STEP FIVE

H-P: Use the French curve to shape the underarm seam.
P-Q: Draw the inner sleeve seam as illustrated.
L: Measure between **1 to 3 cm (⅜ in - 1 ¼ in)** out at **L**, depending on the amount of ease required. Draw a curved line from **H** down to **D**.
Rule a line from **D** to **Q** for the hemline.

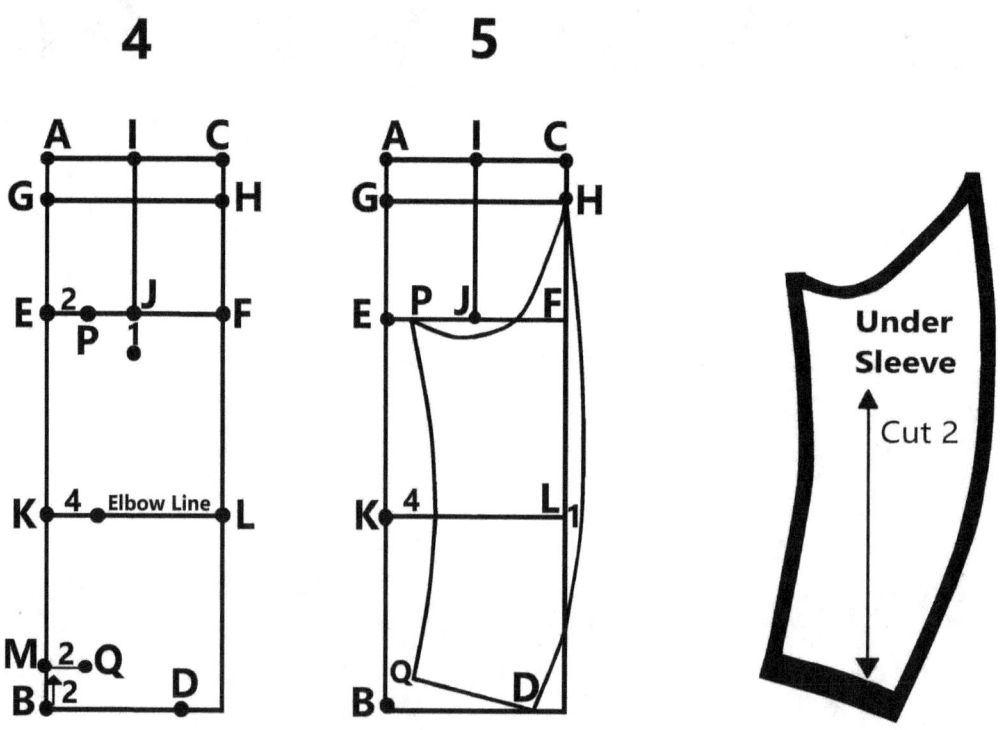

~118~

COLLARS

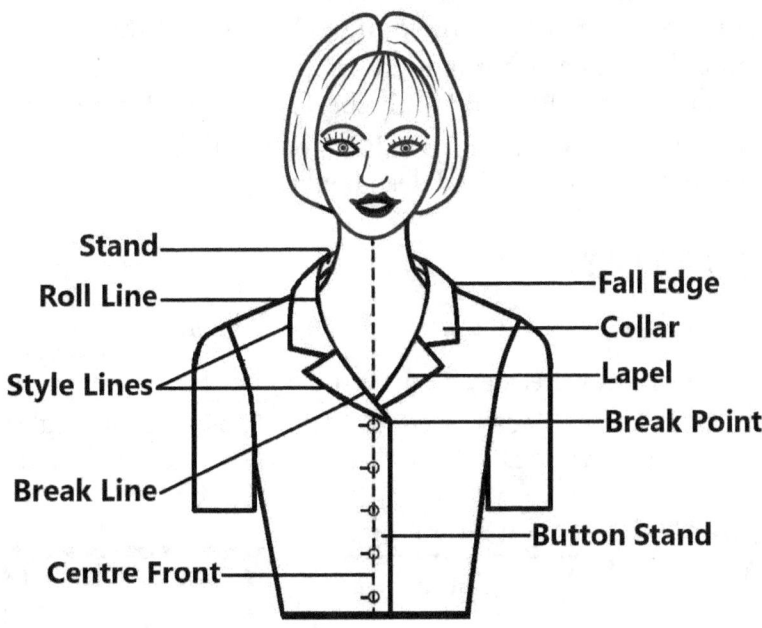

COLLAR CLASSIFICATION TERMS

Break Line: The line along which the lapel folds over.

Break Point: The point where the revere turns back to form the lapel.

Fall: The part that falls over the stand. It forms the depth of the collar from roll line to style line.

Roll Line: The line on which a collar or a lapel folds over.

Stand: The rise of the collar from the neckline to the roll line.

Style Lines: The shape of the outer edge of the collar and lapel (revere).

TYPES OF COLLARS

Collars come in a variety of shapes and sizes, but they are all part of three basic categories, which are **flat**, **rolled**, or **standing collars**.

Flat collars sit flat around the neckline, and the Peter Pan collar illustrates a flat collar.

Rolled collars stand up at a certain height, then roll over onto the garment. Examples of rolled collars are shawl collars, some shirt collars, and notched-tailored collars of jackets and coats.

Standing collars stand up straight around the neck, and the Mandarin collar is an example.

COLLARS

The basic collar is a rectangle with straight edges, but it can be converted into different collar styles by changing the style lines on the draft. The edges of the collar can be made to be round, straight, or pointed. The basic straight collar can be designed with a seam along the top edge, or it can be cut on the fold. The stand of the basic collar is **2.5 cm (1 in)** at the centre back and the collar depth can be **7 to 8 cm (2 ¾ - 3 ⅛ in)**. The grain line of the collar can be **straight**, **crosswise**, or **bias**, depending on the required design effect.

BASIC STRAIGHT COLLAR DRAFT

Draw a rectangle using half the front and back neck measurements.

A-B: Half the front and back neck measurement of the bodice block you are working with.
B-C: The collar depth at the centre back is **8 cm (3 ⅛ in)**. Close the rectangle. Measure **2 cm (¾ in)** out from **A** and rule a line down to **D**. Trace the collar off on the fold of paper.

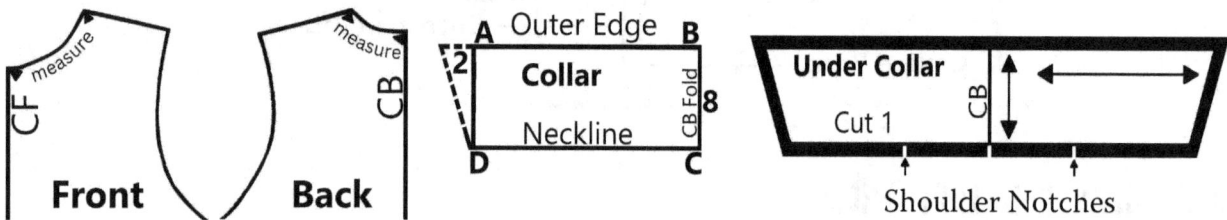

The upper collar is traced from the under collar, then made wider along the outer and front edges. This is done to prevent the collar seamline from being visible. Add **3 mm (⅛ in)** to the outer and front edges. Add **6 mm (¼ in)** to the outer edge when thick fabric is used. Apply these instructions to all upper collars.

STRAIGHT COLLAR VARIATION

Draft the basic straight collar. Measure **1 cm (⅜ in)** up at the centre back. Draw a curved line to the centre front. Measure **2 cm (¾ in)** out at the top edge. Complete the collar as illustrated.

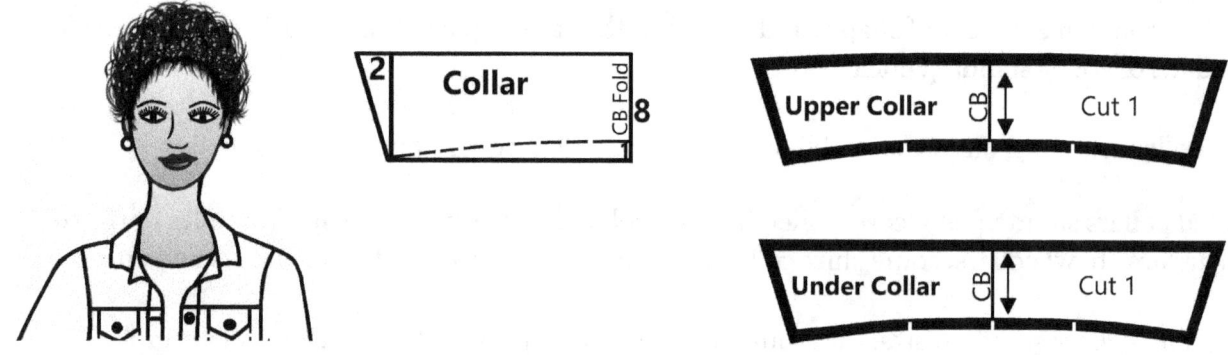

COLLARS

STRAIGHT COLLAR VARIATION

Draft the basic straight collar. Measure **4 cm (1 ½ in)** up from the neckline edge. Draw a curve from the centre back to the front. Measure **4 cm** up from the top edge of the rectangle and draw a curved line as illustrated. Trace an upper and an under collar on the fold of paper.

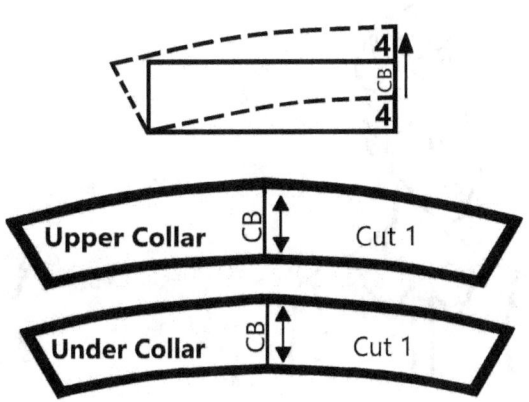

BASIC SHIRT COLLAR

Draft the basic straight collar. Measure **2.5 cm (1 in)** up from **C**. Measure **1 cm (⅜ in)** up from **D**. Rule a curved line from **E** as illustrated. Measure **3 cm (1 ¼ in)** out from **A**. Rule a line from **F** to **E**. Trace an upper and an under collar off. Add grain lines, notches, and seam allowances.

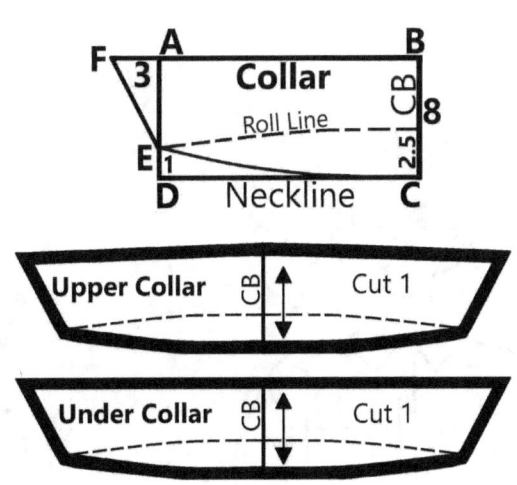

COLLARS

ALL-IN-ONE COLLAR AND STAND

Draft the basic straight collar. Measure **1 cm (⅜ in)** up and **2.5 cm (1 in)** out at the centre front. Shape the collar as illustrated. Trace the collar off as a single piece.

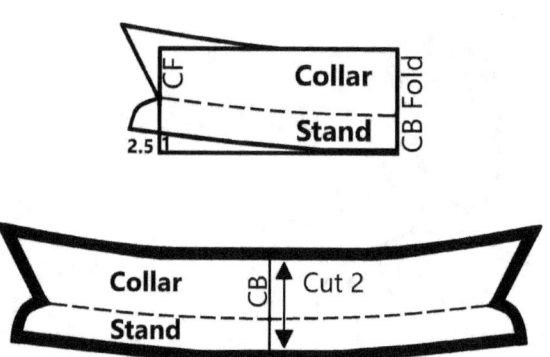

SHIRT COLLAR WITH A SEPARATE STAND

Draw a rectangle using half the front and back neck measurement and a depth of **10 cm (4 in)**. Draw the style lines as illustrated. Trace the collar and stand separately on the fold of paper.

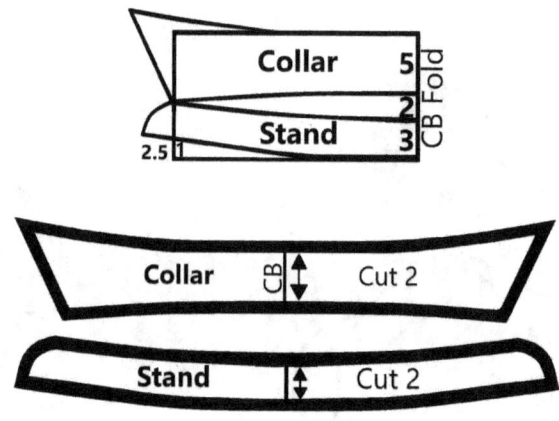

COLLARS

POLO COLLAR

The length of collar bands is determined by the amount of stretch in the fabric and the neckline measurement. A collar band cut from very stretchy fabric can be cut slightly shorter than the neck seamline. Bands cut from fabric with limited stretch such as **double knits** and **woven fabric** must be cut on the **true bias**. It is best to make a sample of this collar to check if it can pass over the head easily and to see if the fit around the neck is as desired.

Trace the basic front and back bodice blocks. Scoop the front and back neck when a wider neckline is desired. Measure the front and back neck. Draw a rectangle to the full length of the front and back neck measurement and twice the desired collar depth, plus seam allowance, when a single-folded collar band is required. Draw a rectangle to the full length of the front and back neckline measurement and four times the desired collar depth, plus seam allowance, when a double-folded collar band is required, as illustrated in the example below.

A-B: The full front and back bodice neckline measurement.
B-C: Four times the desired collar depth.

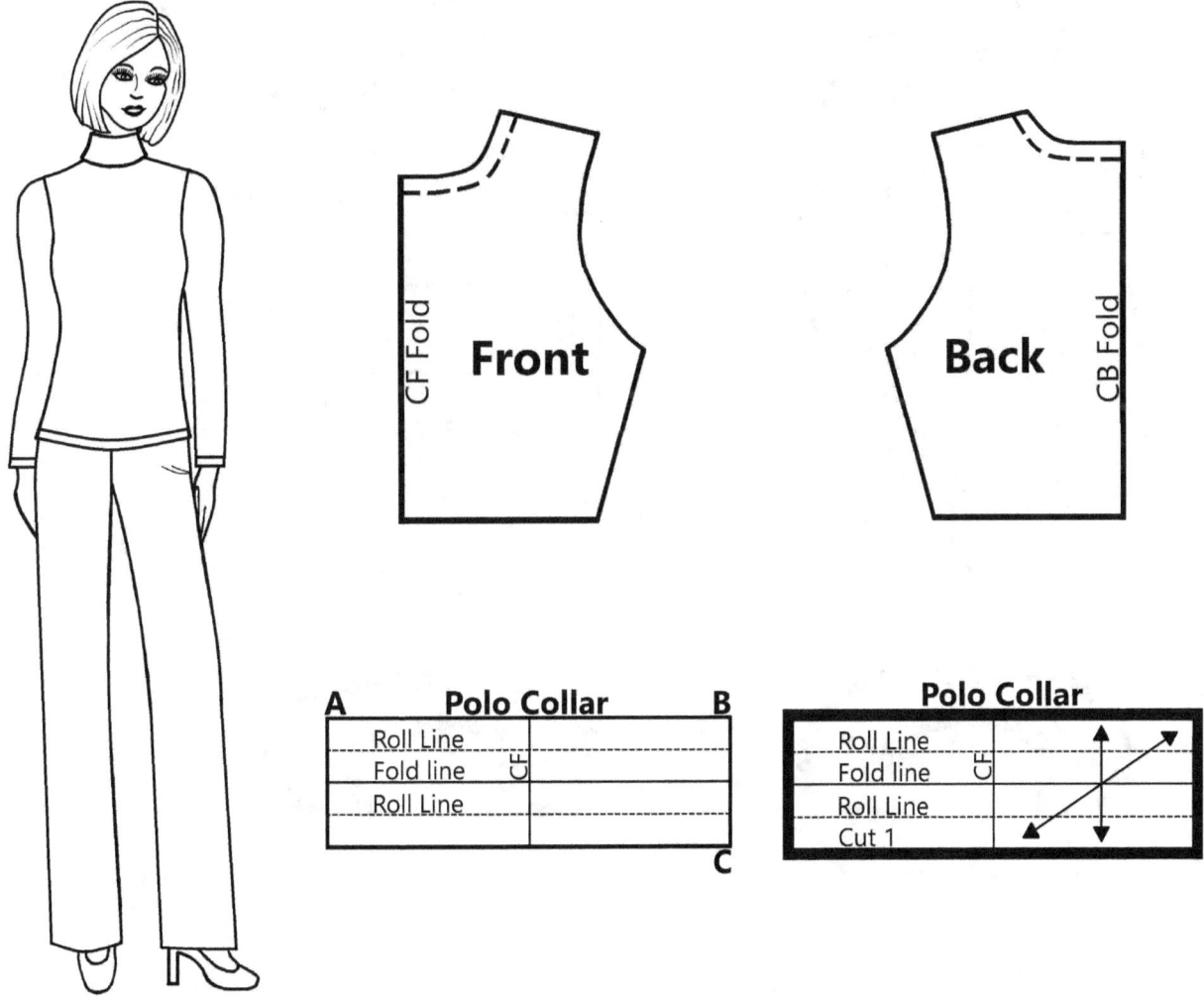

COLLARS

FLAT COLLARS

Flat collars are outlined on a front and back bodice pattern which are joined at the shoulder edges. The collars can be drawn to any shape desired.

BASIC PETER PAN COLLAR

Align a front and back bodice pattern on a sheet of paper. Pin the front and back at the shoulder line and overlap the armhole edge by **1.5 cm** (**⅝ in**) as illustrated. The amount of overlapping used at the shoulder will ensure that the collar will lie flat. Draw the collar to a desired depth and blend the curves. Trace the collar off.

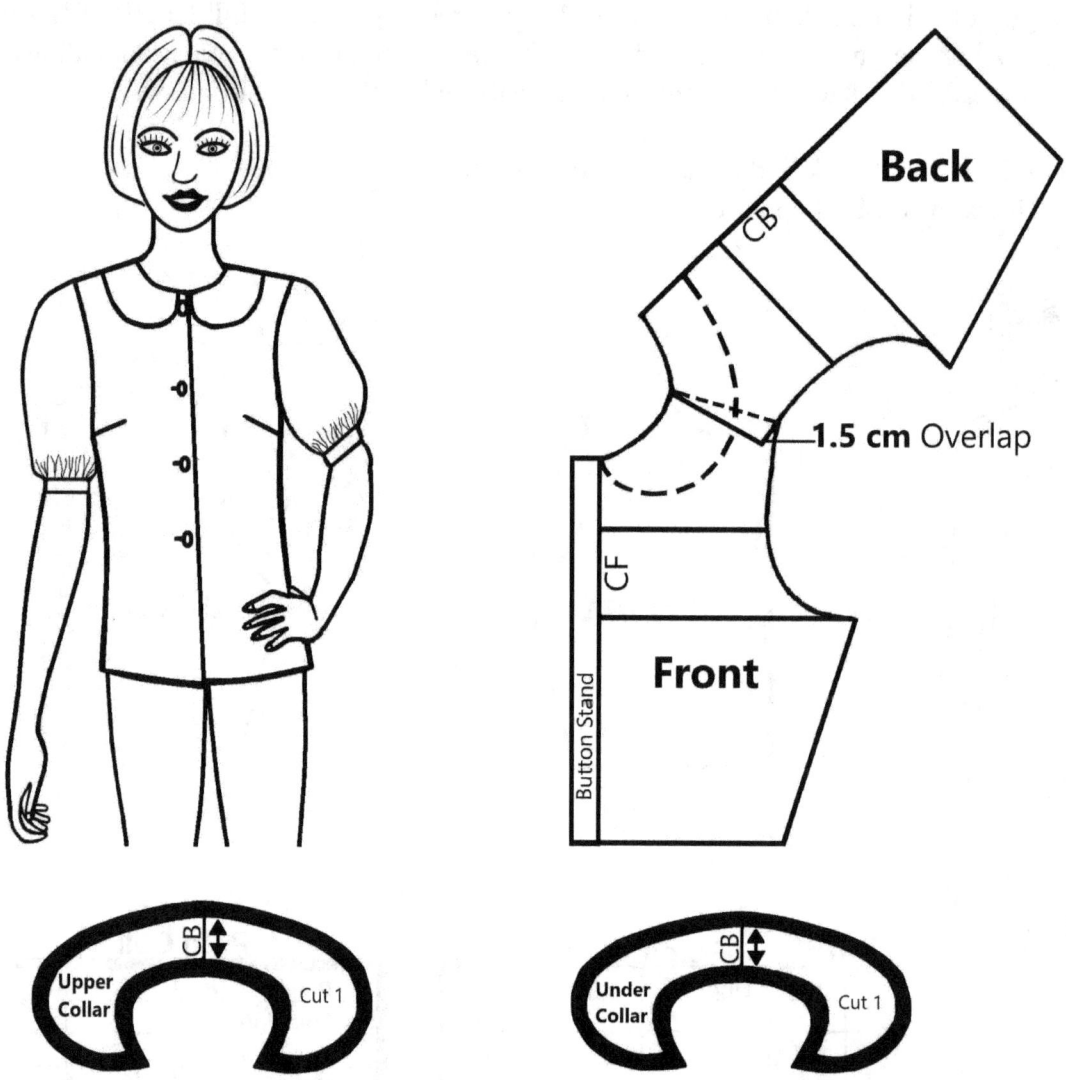

FLAT COLLARS

FRILLED COLLAR

Align the front and back bodice pattern at the shoulders without overlapping. Draw the collar as illustrated and to the required width. Trace the collar off and divide it into sections. Slash and spread the sections to the desired width on a sheet of paper. Secure in place with tape. Add a grain line, notches, hem, and seam allowances.

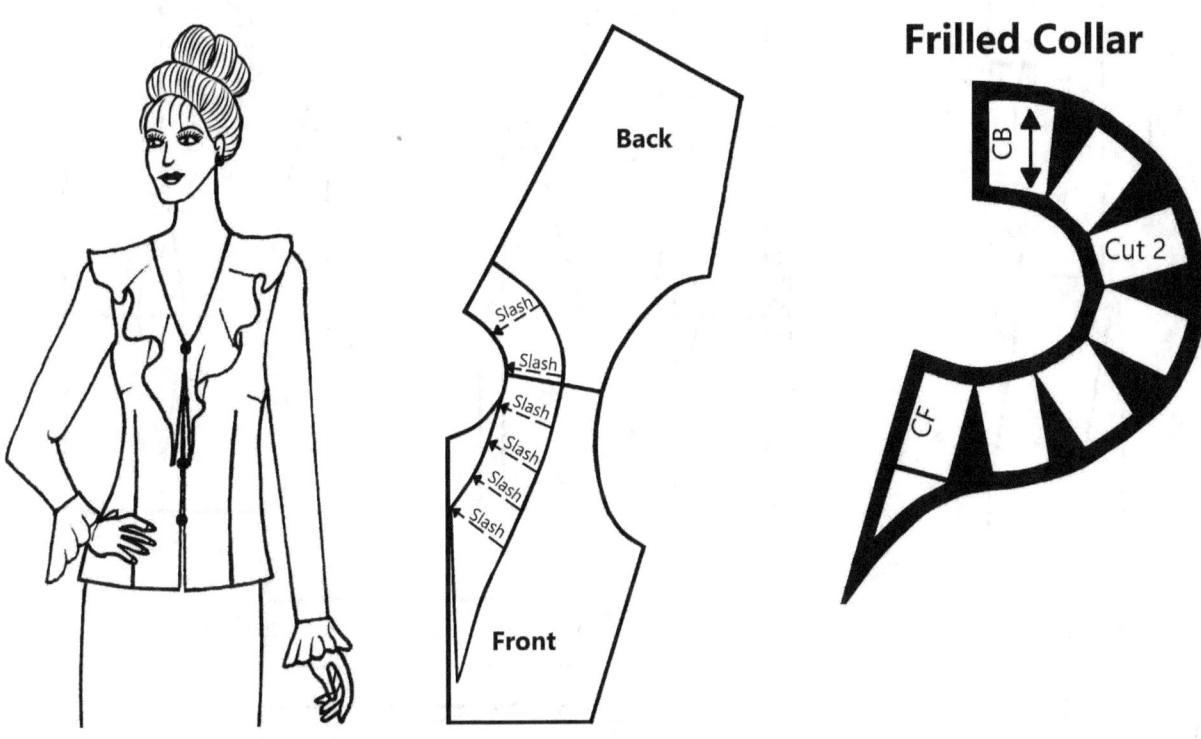

SLEEVE FLOUNCE

Draw a rectangle using the sleeve hemline circumference and the desired flounce depth. Draw slash lines. Cut the slash lines and spread them to half a circle on a sheet of paper. Secure the slashed sections with tape. Add a grain line, hem, and seam allowances.

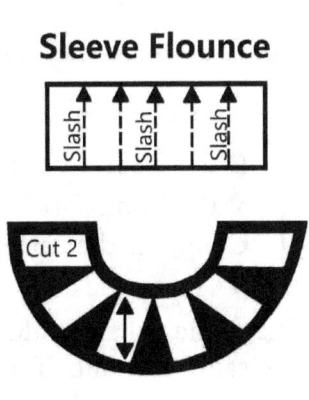

COLLARS

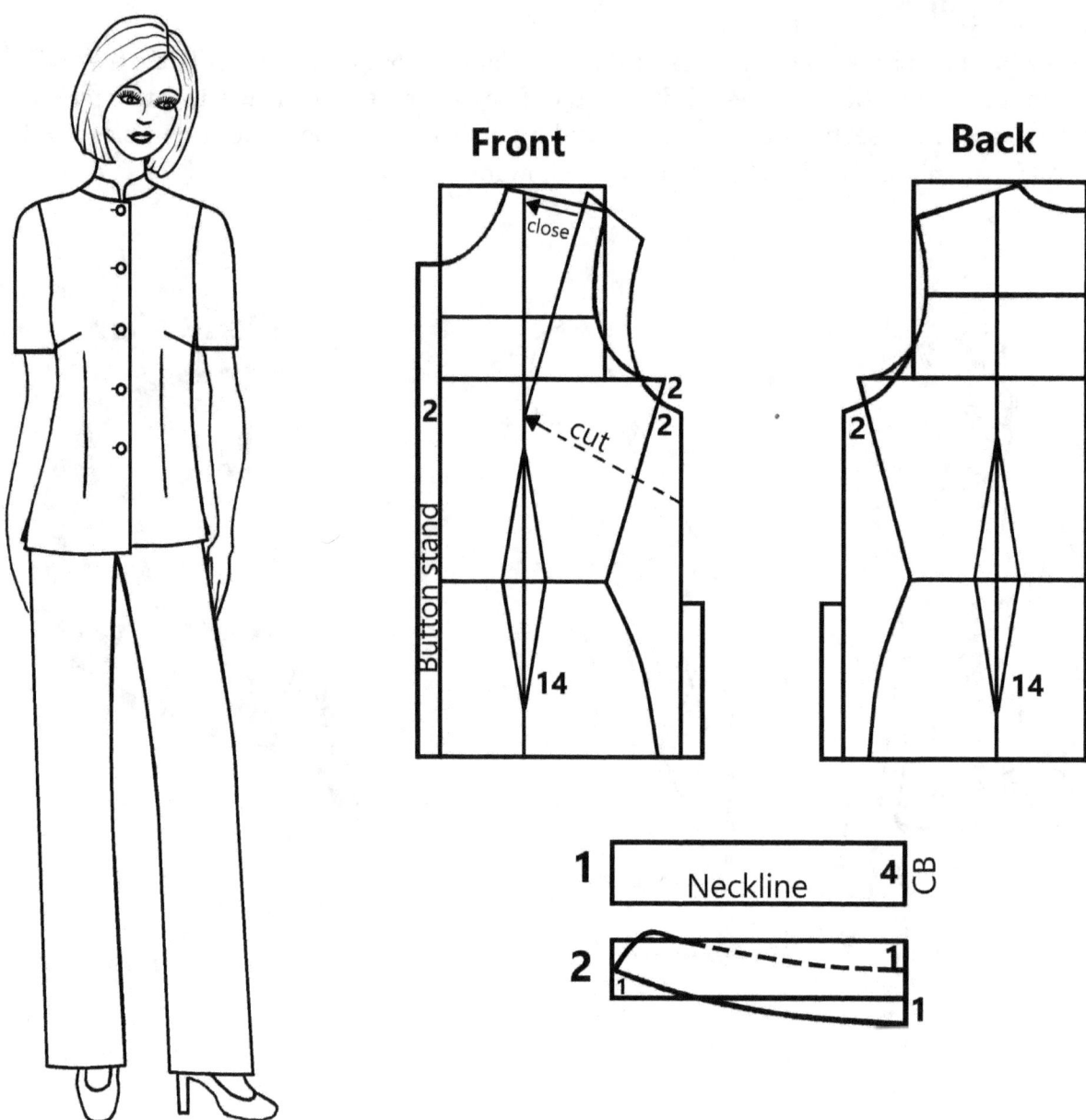

MANDARIN COLLAR

Draft the front and back bodice block and add the desired length. Add a button stand at the front. Drop **2 cm (¾ in)** along the side seam and measure **2 cm** out or as desired. Complete the pattern as illustrated. Complete the collar as follows:

1. Draw a rectangle using half the front and back neck measurement and **4 cm (1 ½ in)** wide.
2. Shape the collar by lifting the centre front by **1 cm (⅜ in)** and lowering the centre back by the same amount. Trace the collar off on the fold of paper. Open the pattern and add notches, a grain line, and seam allowance.

MANDARIN COLLAR

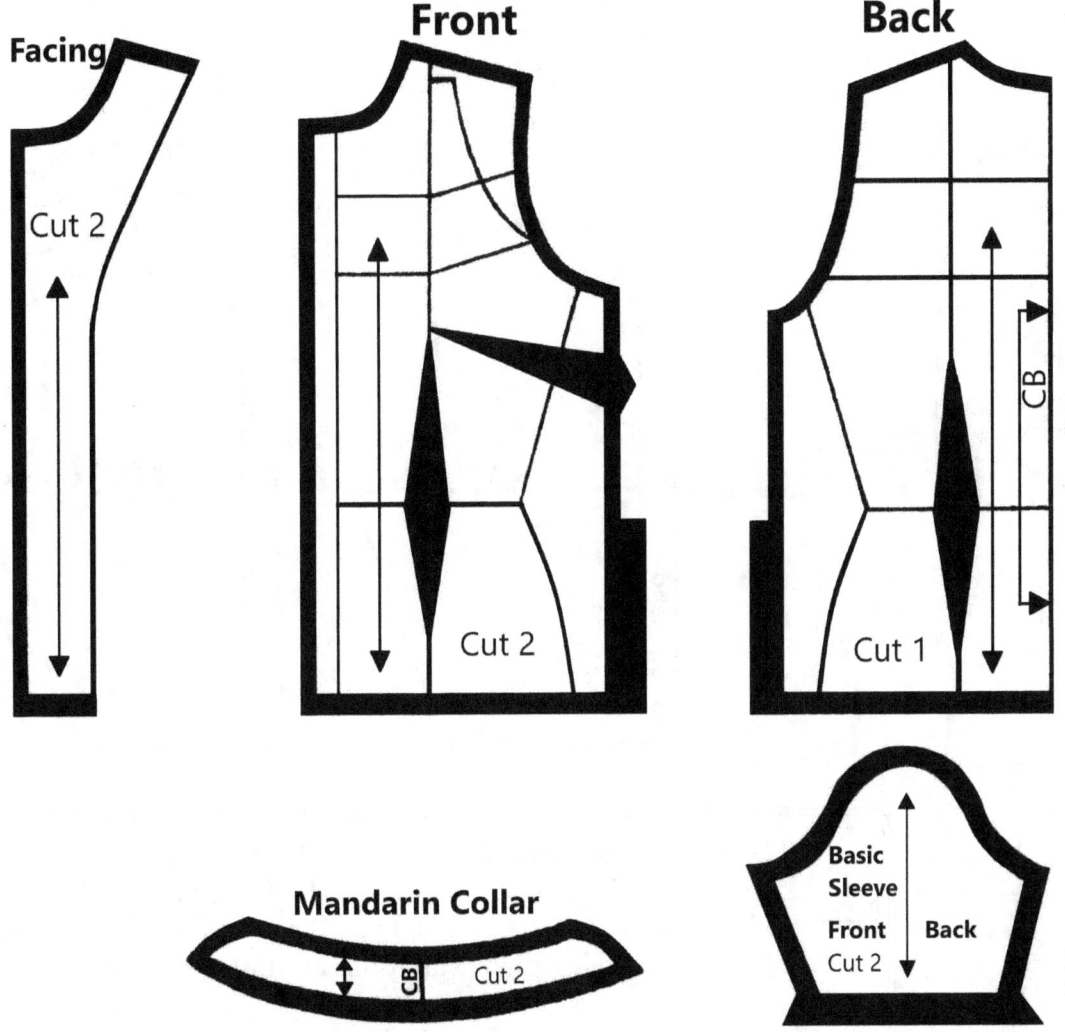

Stitch the darts in the front and back panels. Press. With right sides together, pin and stitch the front and back shoulders and sides seams. Press. Staystitch the neck edge. Interface the collar. Stitch the two collar sections, right sides together. Trim the seam allowance. Press the collar. Pin the collar to the neckline, right sides together, matching centre back and shoulder notches. Clip the upper layer of the collar at the shoulder edge. Unpin the upper layer of the collar between clips. Stitch the collar to the neck edge, keeping the upper layer free between clips. Clip into the neck seam allowances. Interface the facing and overlock the raw edges. Turn under the shoulder edges of the facing and press. Stitch the facing to the neck and front edges, right sides together. Grade the seam allowances and trim across the front corners. Clip seam allowances at the upper edge of facings. Press the neck seam allowance up toward the collar. Turn under the free edge of the collar and hand stitch in place. Slipstitch the folded edge of the facings to the shoulder seam allowances. Pin and sew the sleeves into the armholes and sew the hems. Sew the garment hem. Fold the side vent extensions and front facings to the inside and slipstitch the lower edges. Mark and sew buttonholes and buttons on. Press.

THE SHAWL COLLAR

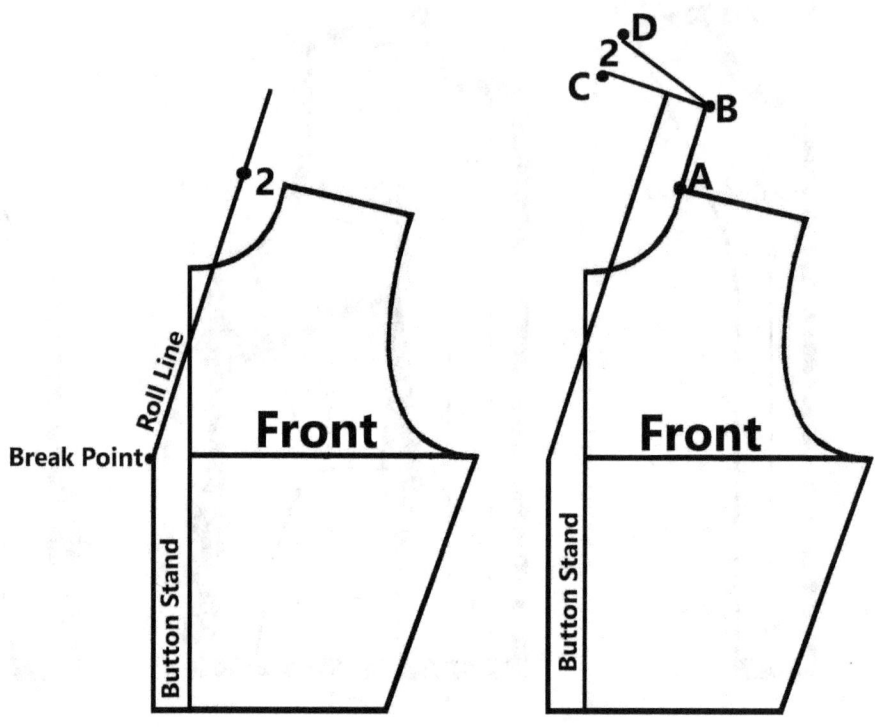

The basic shawl collar differs from all other collar types because the under collar is cut in one with the front bodice. The upper collar is cut in one with the facing. The shawl collar can be used in most garments and has many variations as illustrated in this book.

- Draft the basic front bodice block with the shoulder dart and the basic back bodice block. Lengthen or shorten the block as desired.
- Add a button stand to the front with a required width and length.
- Mark a point **2 cm (¾ in)** out from the neck edge.
- Rule the roll line (fold line) from the break point (turnover point) up and beyond the **2 cm** mark.
- Draw a second line parallel to the fold line at the neck edge, and equal to the back neck measurement marked **A-B** on the draft.
- Rule a line from **B** to **C** measuring **6 to 8 cm (2 ¼ - 3 ⅛ in)**, and measure **2 cm (¾ in)** up from **C**.
- Rule a line from **B** to **D** for the centre back neck seam, measuring the same as **B** to **C**.
- Shape the collar as desired and complete the pattern.
- Trace facing and the pattern sections off.
- Add grain lines, notches, hem, and seam allowances.
- Use the tailored, or basic set-in sleeve to complete the pattern.

THE SHAWL COLLAR

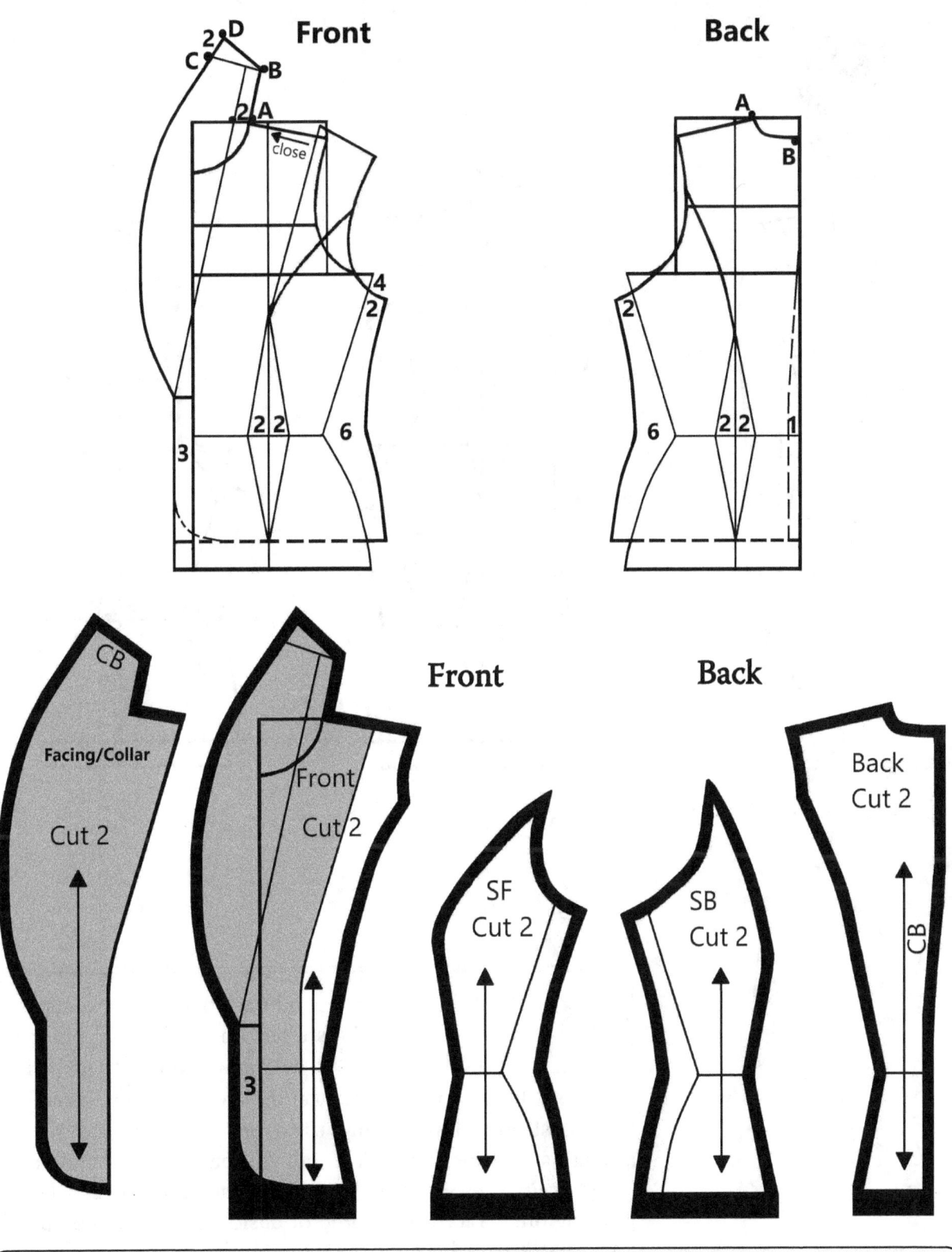

Sewing the shawl collar is illustrated on page **140**.

SHAWL COLLAR VARIATION

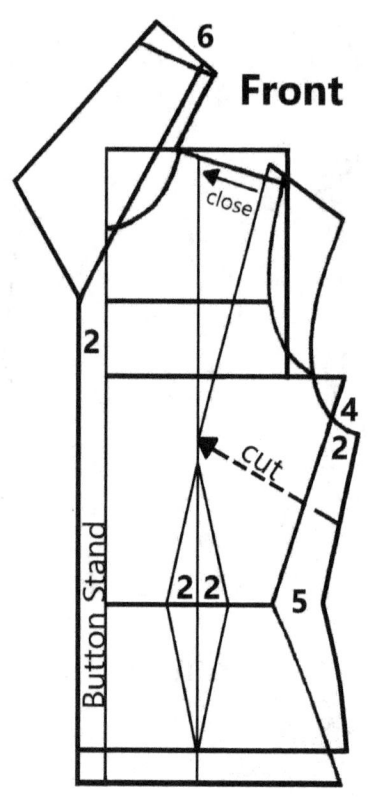
Front

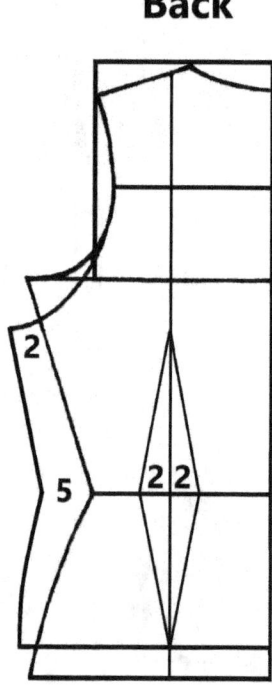
Back

Draft the basic front and back bodice blocks for the shawl collar, as illustrated on page **128**. Shorten the bodice block as desired. Add a **2 cm (¾ in)** button stand to the centre front. Draw the collar as illustrated. Ensure that the front and back side seam lengths are the same. Trace all the pattern pieces off and add grain lines, notches, hem, and seam allowances. Trace facing off. Trace the tailored or basic sleeve off to complete the pattern. Add **2.5 cm (1 in)** to the centre back lining panel for a pleat if the jacket is to be lined.

SHAWL COLLAR VARIATION

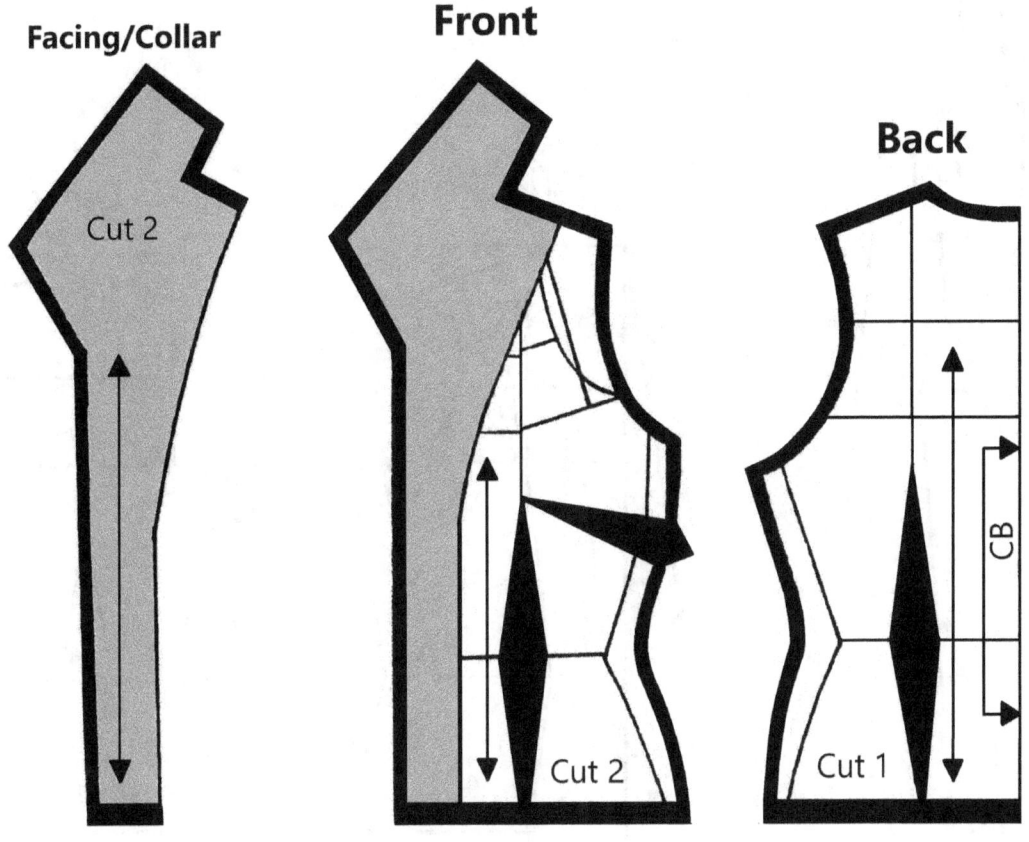

Mark and sew the darts on the front and back sections. Press the darts to one side. Neaten the front and back side seams with overlocking. Sew the shawl collar as illustrated on page **140**. Pin and stitch the garment's front and back side seams, right sides together. Press the seams open. Neaten the hem edges of the garment, the side seams, and the hem edges of both sleeves with overlocking. Sew the sleeves as described on page **73**. Turn up the garment and sleeve hem edges, tack, and hand stitch in place. Mark and sew buttonholes and buttons on. Press the garment.

SHAWL COLLAR VARIATION

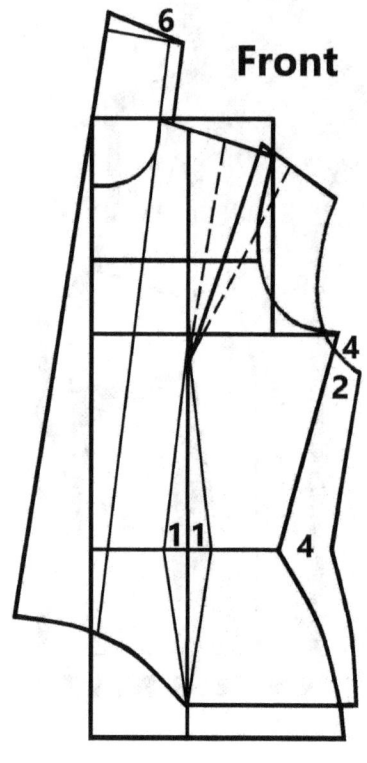
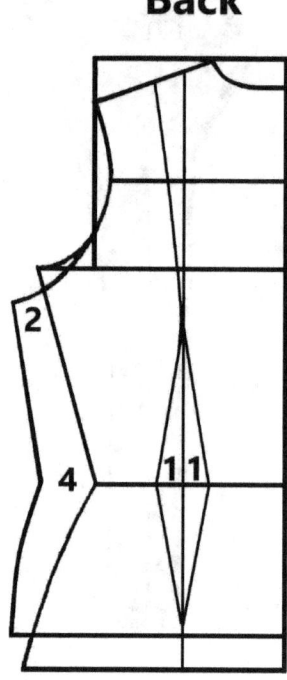

 Draw the shawl collar as illustrated. Shape the front to the required width and length. Draw a line from the centre of the back shoulder for a side and back panel. Move the shoulder dart on the front to correspond with the back shoulder line. Trace the pattern and facing off. Trace the tailored or basic set-in sleeve to complete the pattern. Add grain lines, notches, hem, and seam allowances.

SHAWL COLLAR VARIATION

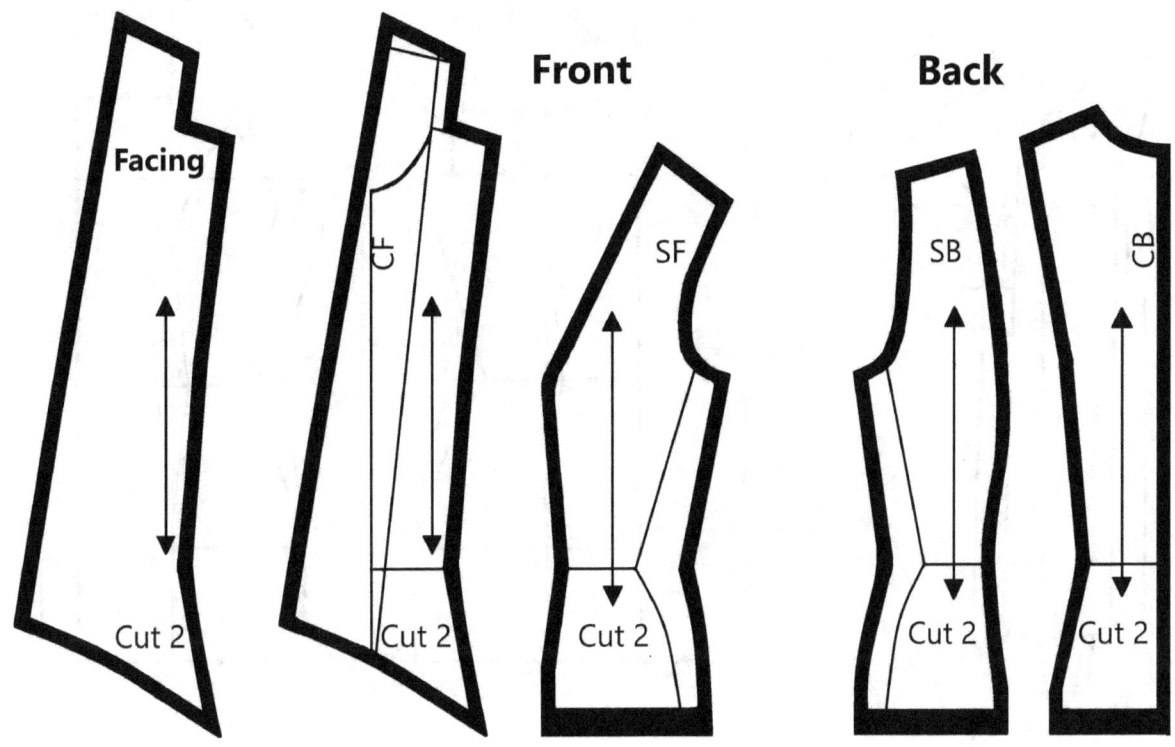

The front pattern can be used to cut facing, depending on the size of the panel. Sew the jacket panels together as described on page **95**. Interface the facing. Sew the lining panels and facing together separately and press. Add **2.5 cm (1 in)** along the centre back for the lining when lining is required. Fold the back lining panel right sides together to make a pleat. Stitch approximately **5 cm (2 in)** down along the centre back, starting from the top back neck edge, **2.5 cm (1 in)** from the folded edge. The pleat in the lining will ensure ease and comfort when the jacket is worn. Sew the collar in the manner described on page **140**. Complete the garment and press.

SHAWL COLLAR VARIATION

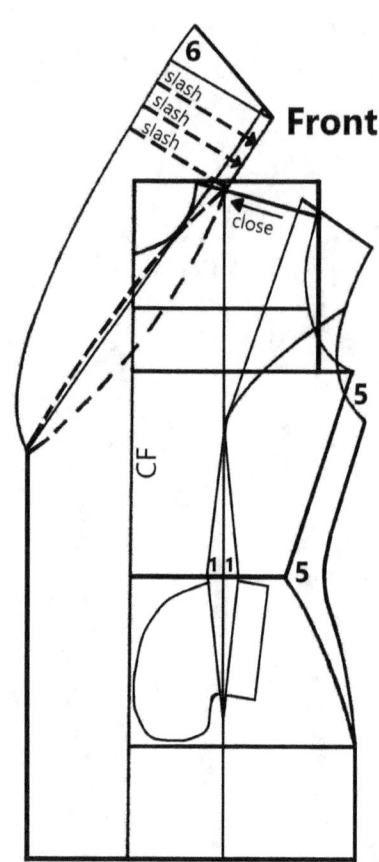
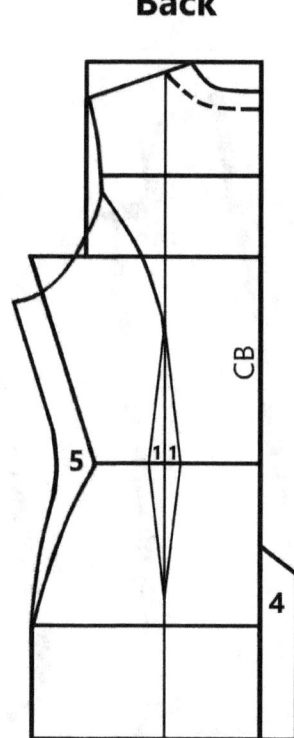

WIDE STAND AWAY SHAWL COLLAR
Draft the front bodice with the shoulder dart and the basic back bodice. Scoop the front and back necklines. Add the front button stand and draw the collar as illustrated. Draw a pocket and welt. Draw front and back facings. Trace all the pattern pieces off. Slash and spread the collar as required. Draft the tailored sleeve on page **116** to complete the pattern.

WIDE STAND AWAY SHAWL COLLAR

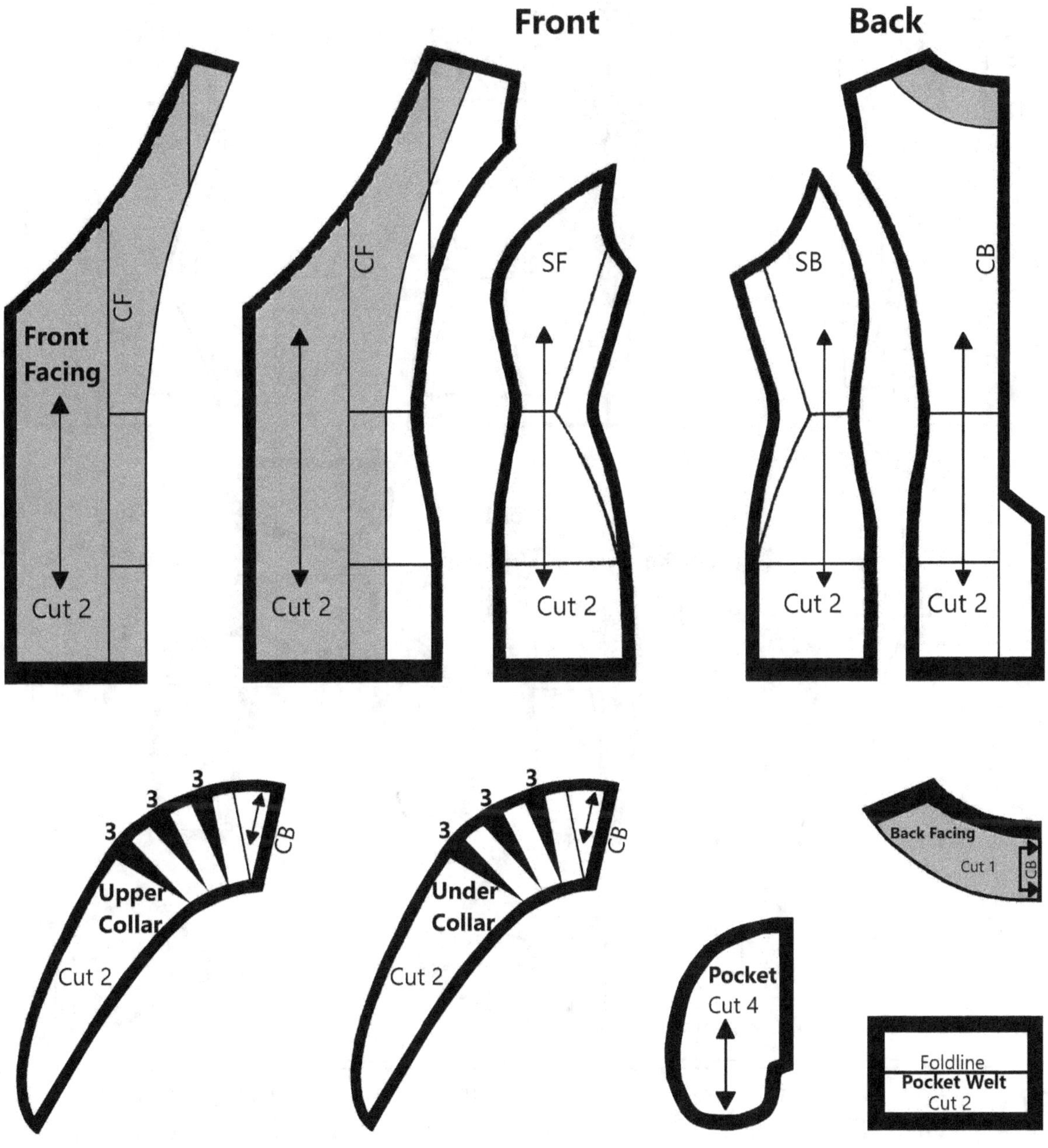

Front **Back**

Front Facing — CF — Cut 2

CF — Cut 2

SF — Cut 2

SB — Cut 2

CB — Cut 2

Upper Collar — CB — Cut 2 — 3 3 3 3

Under Collar — CB — Cut 2 — 3 3 3 3

Back Facing — CB — Cut 1

Pocket — Cut 4

Foldline
Pocket Welt
Cut 2

 Make a mock-up of the upper bodice and collar to achieve the desired collar effect. Stitch the front and back panels together as described on page **95**. Repeat the same for the lining panels if the garment is to be lined.

COLLARS

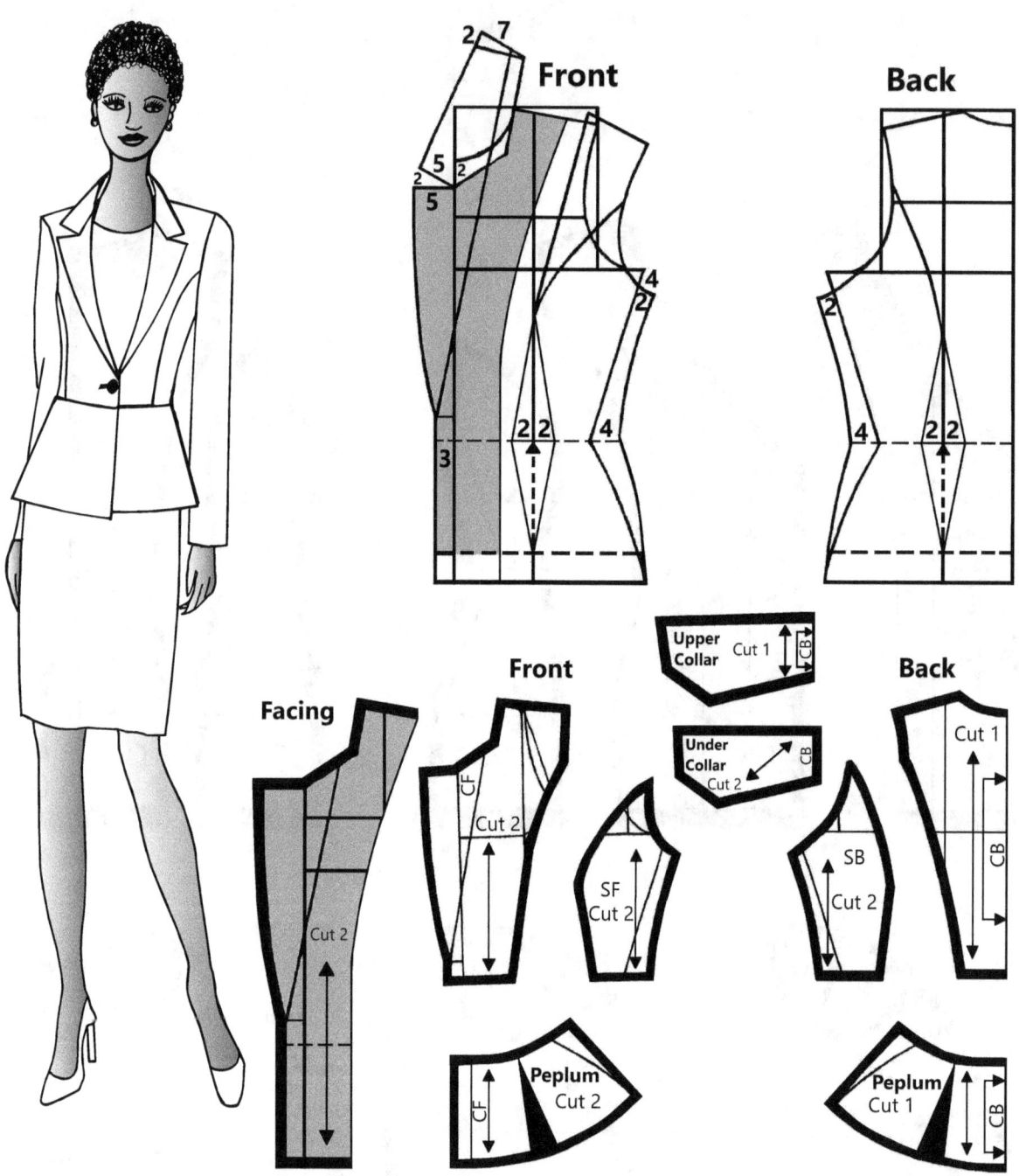

Draft the basic front and back as illustrated. Draw the collar and add the panels. Shape the front and back side seam lines as desired. Lift the hip line if desired. Trace the front and back peplum off. Cut up the centre of the peplum and close the dart. Place paper underneath and secure the cut sections with sticky tape. More flare can be added by slashing and spreading the peplum pattern as required. Trace the collar, facing, front, back, and side panels off. Trace the tailored or basic set-in sleeve to complete the pattern. Add hem and seam allowances, notches, and grain lines.

COLLARS

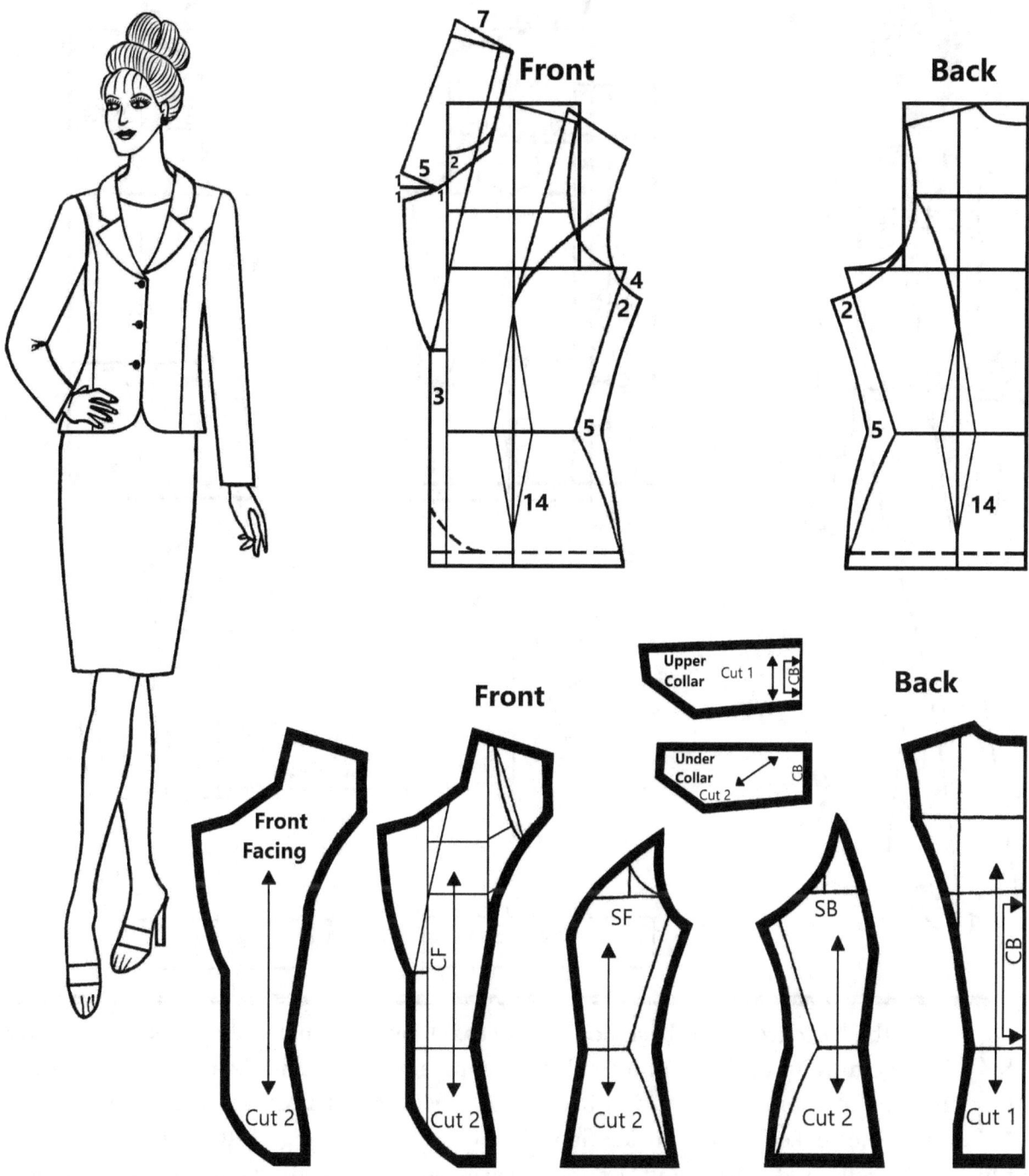

Draft the basic front block with the shoulder dart and the basic back block. Complete the pattern as illustrated. Add a **3 cm (1 ¼ in)** waist dart to the front and back bodice blocks. Shape the collar and the jacket hem line. Trace all the pattern pieces off. The front panel can be used to cut facing. Trace the tailored or basic sleeve off to complete this pattern. Add grain lines, notches, hem, and seam allowances.

COLLARS

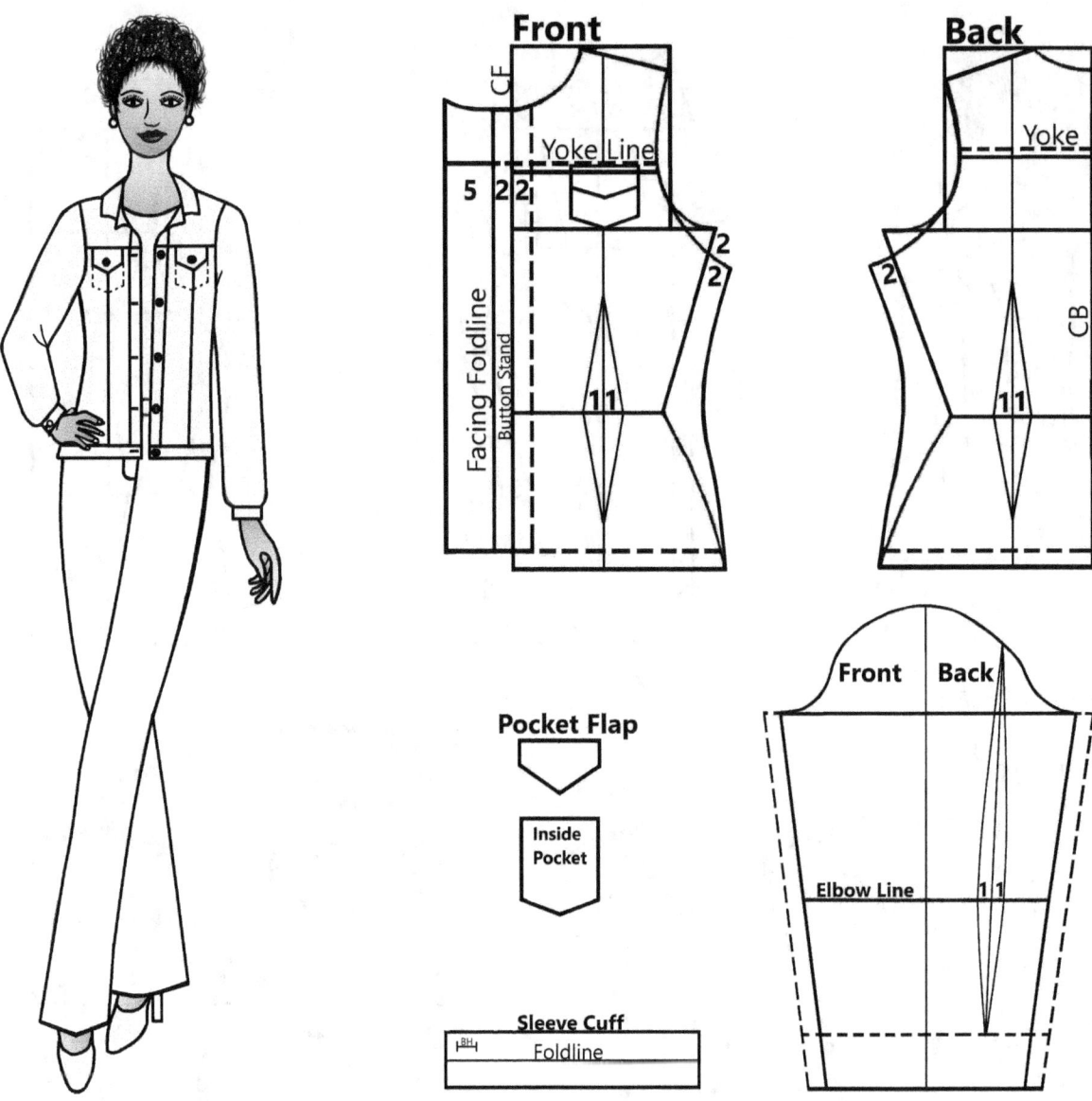

Draft the basic front and back bodice blocks. Draw the panels and yokes as illustrated. Add **2 cm (¾ in)** to the front for a button stand and **5 cm (2 in)** for facing. Use **2 cm (¾ in)** waist darts in the front and back. Add a front and back yoke at a desired height. Draw the pocket and the pocket flap. Draw the collar on page **120**. Extend the centre front line of the collar if desired. Draft the shirt sleeve and adjust the underarm seam if required. Shorten the sleeve length by the cuff depth and add **2 cm (¾ in)** to the sleeve length for ease. Rule a line down the back section of the sleeve. Measure **1 cm (⅜ in)** out on either side of the line and at elbow level. Rule curved lines to separate the front and back sleeve panels. Draw a rectangle for the cuff as demonstrated for the shirt cuff. Measure the lower edge of the jacket, including the **2 cm** for the button stand, and draw a waistband **8 cm (3 ⅛ in)** wide. Trace all the pattern pieces off and add grain lines, notches, hem, and seam allowances.

DENIM JACKET

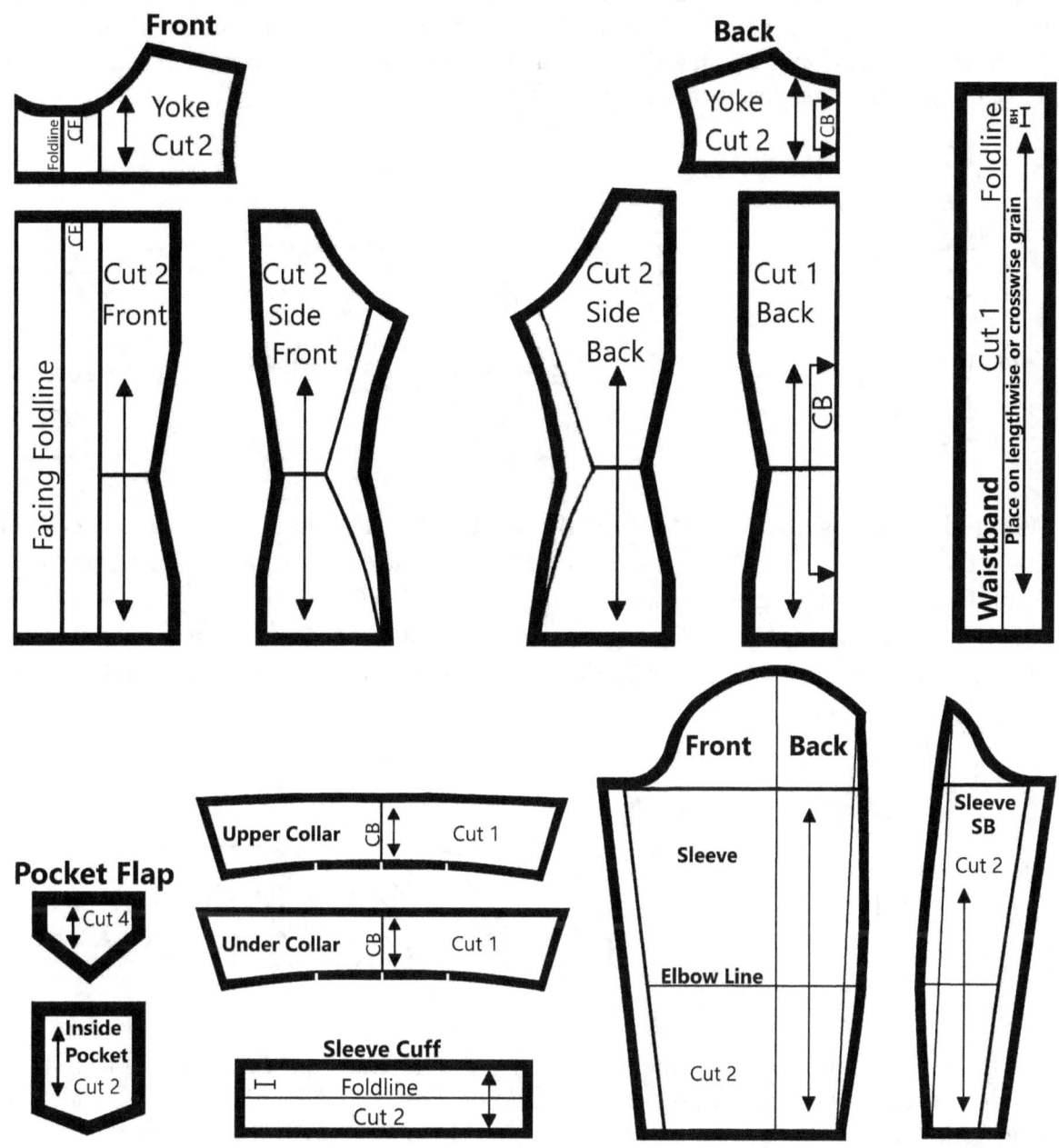

Wash the fabric first to preshrink it. Add a dash of white vinegar to the water to reduce fading. Press the fabric before cutting the panels out. Mark the fabric on the wrong side with tailor's chalk. Use flat fell or welt seams for a neater finish. Denim/Jeans needles or size **16/100** needles should be used when sewing denim. Use topstitching needles that have a bigger eye to accommodate the heavy topstitching thread. It is best to test topstitching with different stitch lengths. The ideal stitch length is **3.5 - 4.5 mm**. Use a walking foot or Hump Jumper presser foot for all the bulky seams. Use quality metal fasteners and buttons.

SEWING THE SHAWL COLLAR

1. With right sides together, pin and stitch the centre back seam of the garment's front panels and press it open. Staystitch the back neck and pivot on the shoulder and neckline corner. Continue staystitching on the shoulder seam about **2.5 cm** (**1 in**) in length. Clip into the corners as illustrated below.

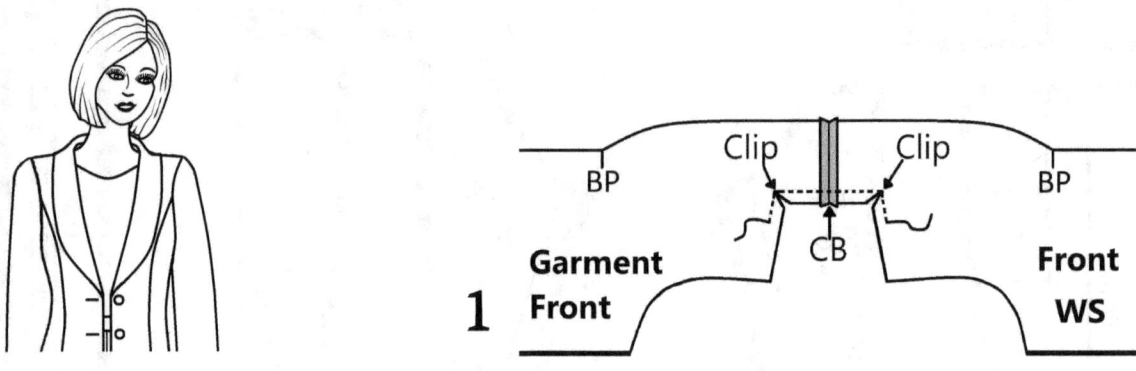

2. With right sides together, pin and stitch the front and back shoulder seams and back neck. Press the shoulder seams closed and neaten them with overlocking or a zigzag stitch.
3. Apply fusible interfacing to the wrong side of the collar/facings. Pin and stitch the two collar/facing sections, right sides together at the centre back and press the seam open. Staystitch around the back neck and clip into the reinforced corners. Neaten facing edges.

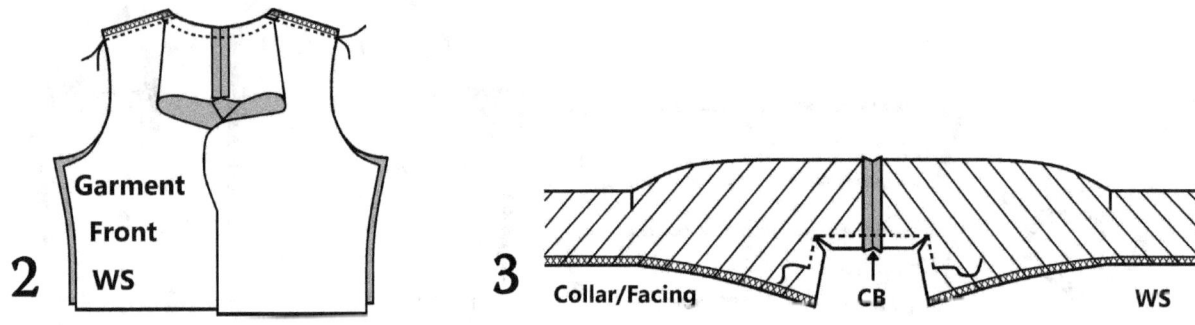

4. Pin the collar/facing to the garment, matching the notches up. Stitch it in place. Press. Grade the seam allowance. Clip into the breakpoint on both sides. Notch the collar seam. Understitch the collar and facing sections up to **4 cm** (**1 ½ in**) from the breakpoint.
5. Turn the collar/facing right side out and press. Clip the back neck seam allowance of the garment. Turn under the raw edge of the collar/facing at the back neck and slipstitch it in place. Turn under the facing edges and slipstitch it to the shoulder seams. Press.

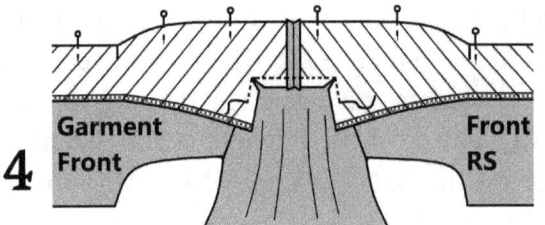 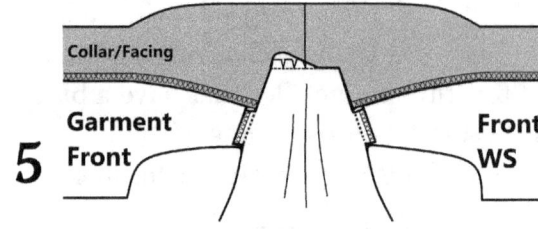

SHIRTS, BLOUSES, AND TOPS

Shirts and blouses are drafted with the same basic attributes. Both drafts have lowered armholes and ease added to the side seams. The draft can be dartless, or it can have waist darts, side bust darts (French darts), or darts that extend from the bust down to the hemline. The side seams and hemlines can be straight or curved as desired.

SHIRT AND BLOUSE SLEEVES

The basic set-in sleeve is modified to fit the armholes of shirts, blouses, and tops.

SHIRT AND BLOUSE COLLARS

Collars can be drafted as one-piece or two-piece. It can be cut on the straight grain, crosswise grain, or bias, depending on the desired design effect. The depth at the centre back varies from **6** to **8 cm** (**2 ½ - 3 ⅛ in**). The collar also has a **2.5 cm** (**1 in**) stand at the centre back.

SHIRTS, BLOUSES, AND TOPS

1

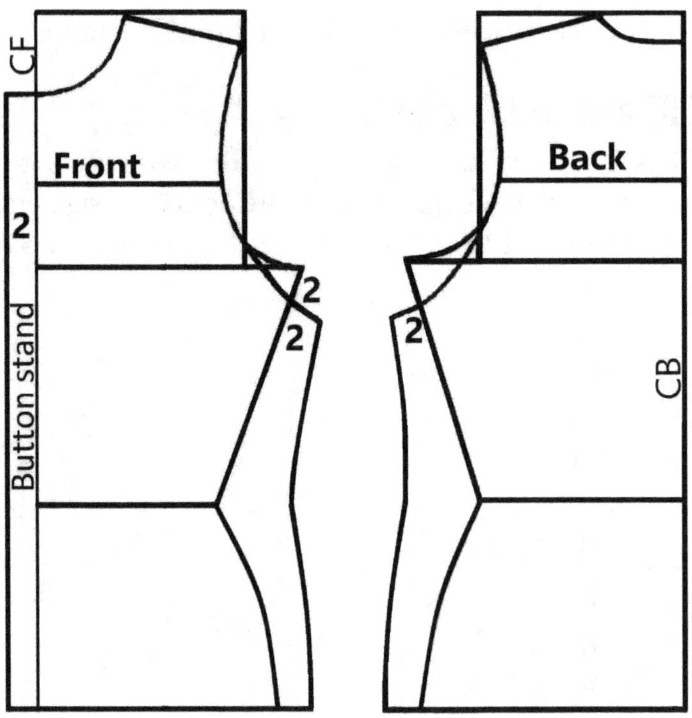

CASUAL SHIRT

1. Trace the front and back basic blocks. Add a button stand **2 cm (¾ in)** wide at the centre front. Drop the armhole by **2 cm (¾ in)** and measure **2 cm** out from the side seam. Redraw the armhole. Add a desired amount of ease to the front and back side seams. Shape the side seams if desired.

CASUAL SHIRT

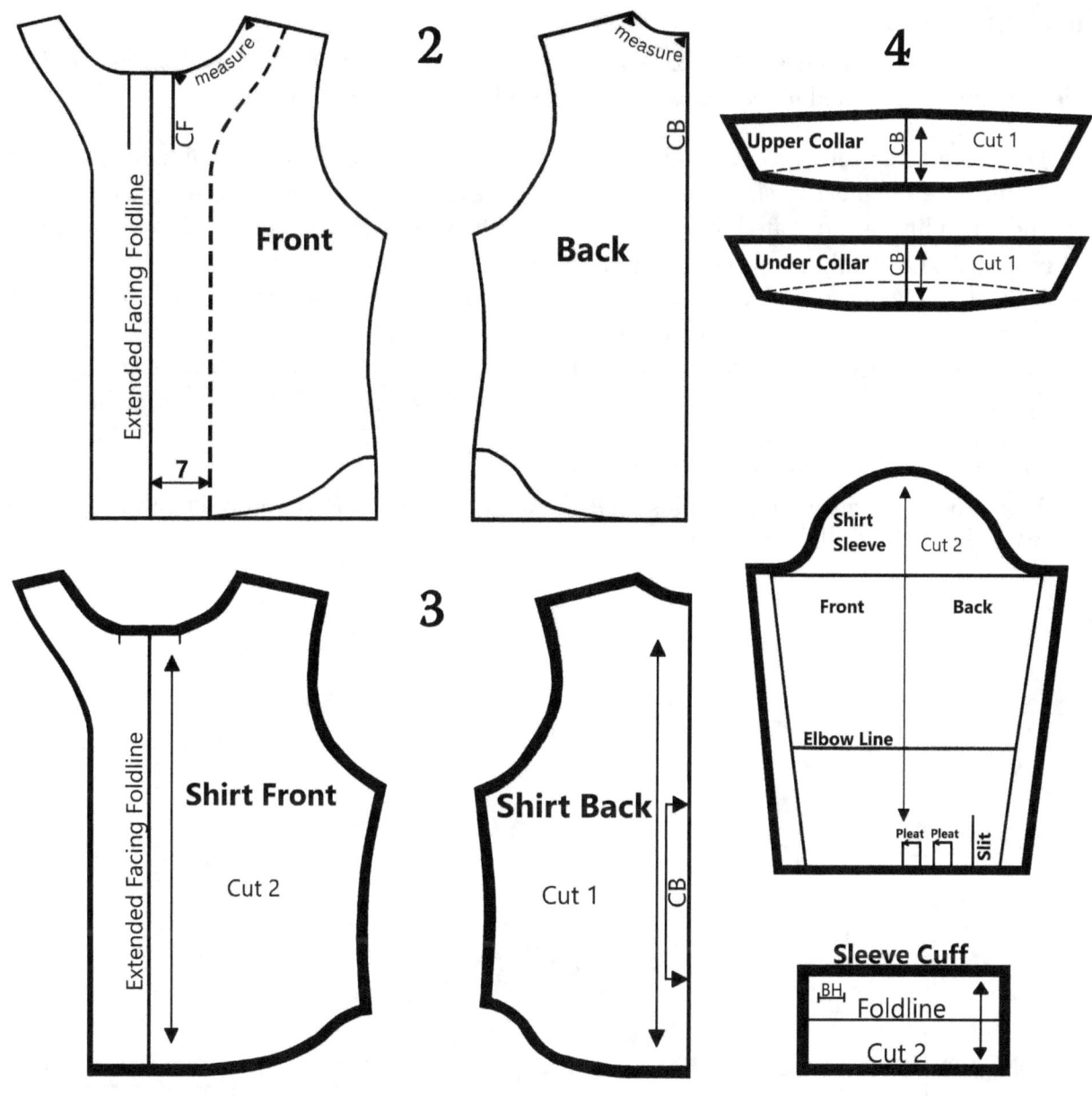

2. Draw facing **7 cm (2 ¾ in)** wide from the foldline as illustrated by the dotted line. Fold the paper on the foldline and under the draft. Trace the facing through on the dotted line. Notch the centre front neck as illustrated. Open the pattern and pencil the traced facing extension. Shape the front and back hemline if desired. Trace the shirt pattern off.
3. Add grain lines, notches, hem, and seam allowances.
4. Measure the front and back neck as indicated by the arrowheads. Draw the basic shirt collar as illustrated on page **121**. Add seam allowance. Use the **shirt sleeve draft** on page **144** to complete the pattern.

SHIRTS, BLOUSES, AND TOPS

THE SHIRT SLEEVE

This shirt sleeve is based on the basic set-in sleeve. The sleeve head is lowered and the underarm line is extended if needed, to fit the armhole of the shirt pattern.

1. Trace the basic set-in sleeve and lower the sleeve head **2 cm (¾ in)** as illustrated by the dotted line. Shape the sleeve head with the French curve. Extend or subtract from the underarm line as illustrated by the dotted line. The sleeve head should measure **1 cm (⅜ in)** more than the armhole measurement of the garment's pattern.
   A-B: Sleeve length minus the cuff depth, plus **2 cm (¾ in)** for ease. Rule a line across.
   C-D: The hemline width plus an amount for gathers or pleats if desired.
2. Trace the shirt sleeve pattern and draw a line **8 cm (3 ⅛ in)** long, from the bottom edge on the back section of the sleeve, when cuff plackets are required. Mark pleats or gathers. Add seam allowance to the pattern.
3. Draw a rectangle twice the desired cuff depth.
   A-B: The wrist measurement plus **7 cm (2 ¾ in)** for the overlap, underlap, and ease. Add seam allowance to the cuff pattern.

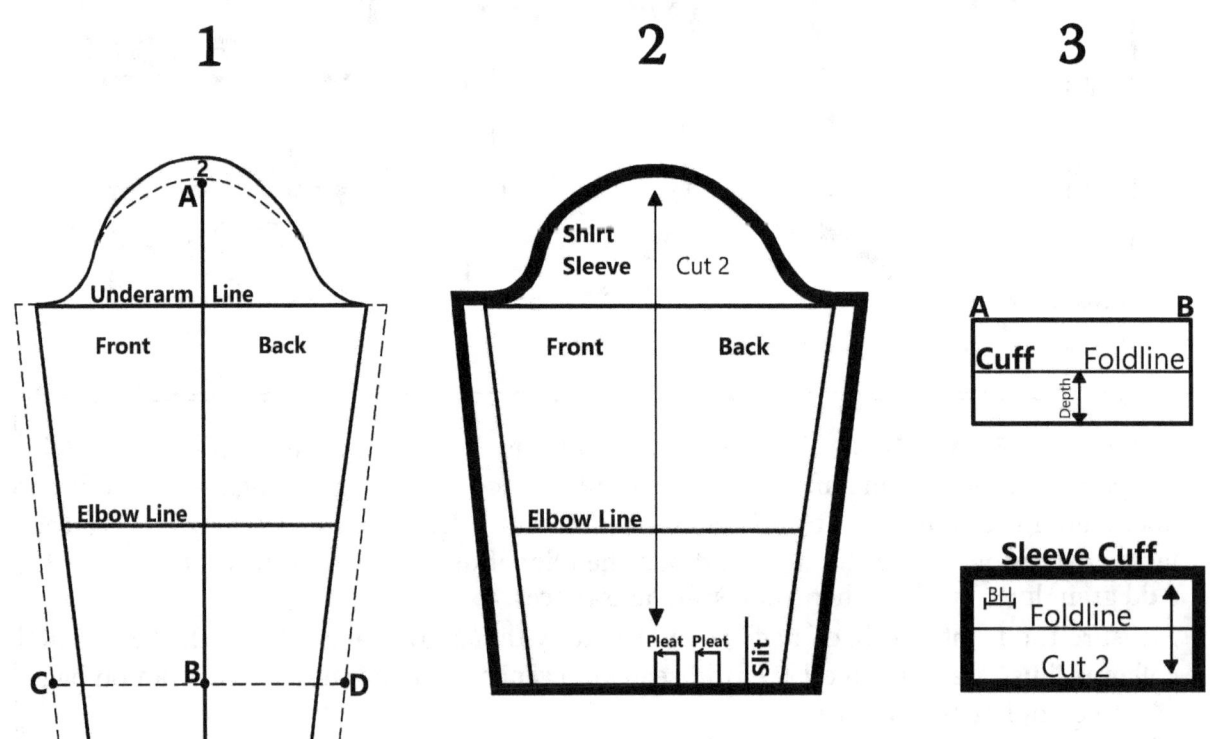

SHIRTS, BLOUSES, AND TOPS

SEWING CONTINUOUS BOUND CUFF PLACKETS

1. Mark an **8 cm (3 ⅛ in)** opening on the back section of the sleeve. Reinforce the stitching line of the placket opening with machine stitching. Start at the edge of the seam allowance, **6 mm (¼ in)** on both sides of the marked line, up to the point. Slash in the centre, up to the point.
2. Cut binding from self-fabric **3 cm (1 ¼ in)** wide and twice the length of the slashed opening. Press one long binding edge **6 mm (¼ in)** under.

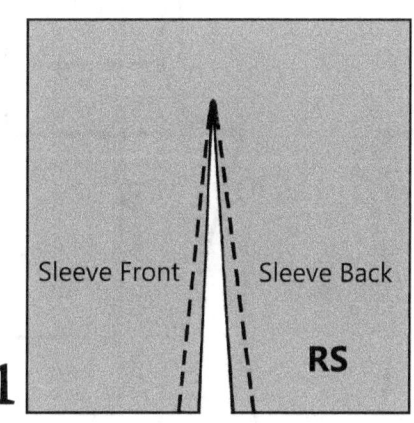

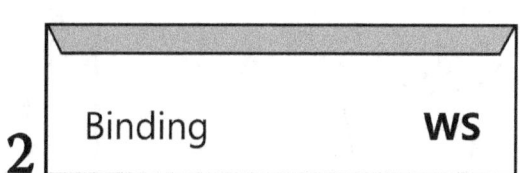

3. Spread the slashed opening and pin the right side of the unpressed binding edge to the wrong side of the sleeve. Machine stitch next to the slashed opening staystitching and within the binding's **6mm (¼in)** seam allowance. Press.
4. Bring the folded edge of the binding to the right side, encasing the raw edge. Pin or tack in place and secure with edgestitching. Press.

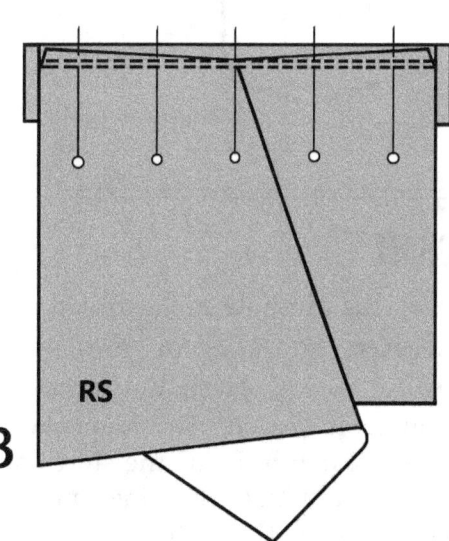

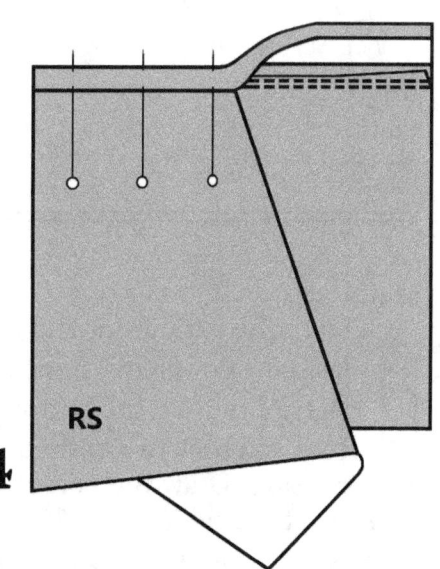

SHIRTS, BLOUSES, AND TOPS

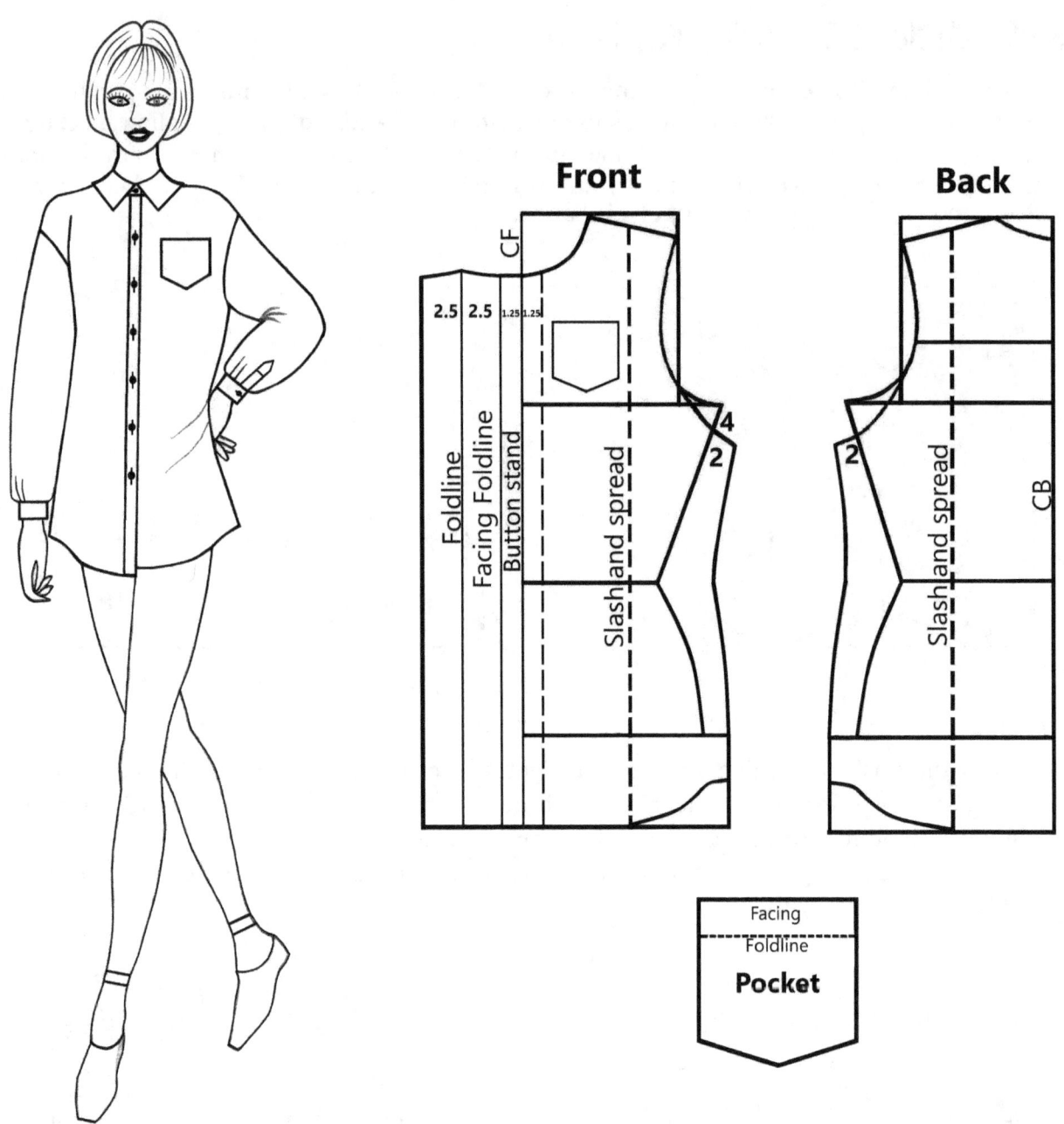

THE OVERSIZED SHIRT

Trace the basic front and back bodice blocks. Drop the armhole as illustrated or as desired. Lower the front and back hip line as desired. Add **1.25 cm (½ in)** to the centre front for the button stand and **5 cm (2 in)** for facing. Slash and spread the front and back to a desired amount. Curve the hemline if desired. Draw a pocket to the required size. Draw the pocket facing's foldline at a desired depth. Draw the shirt collar with a separate stand on page **122**. Trace all pattern pieces off and add grain lines, notches, hem, and seam allowances. Use the **oversized shirt sleeve** to complete the pattern.

THE OVERSIZED SHIRT

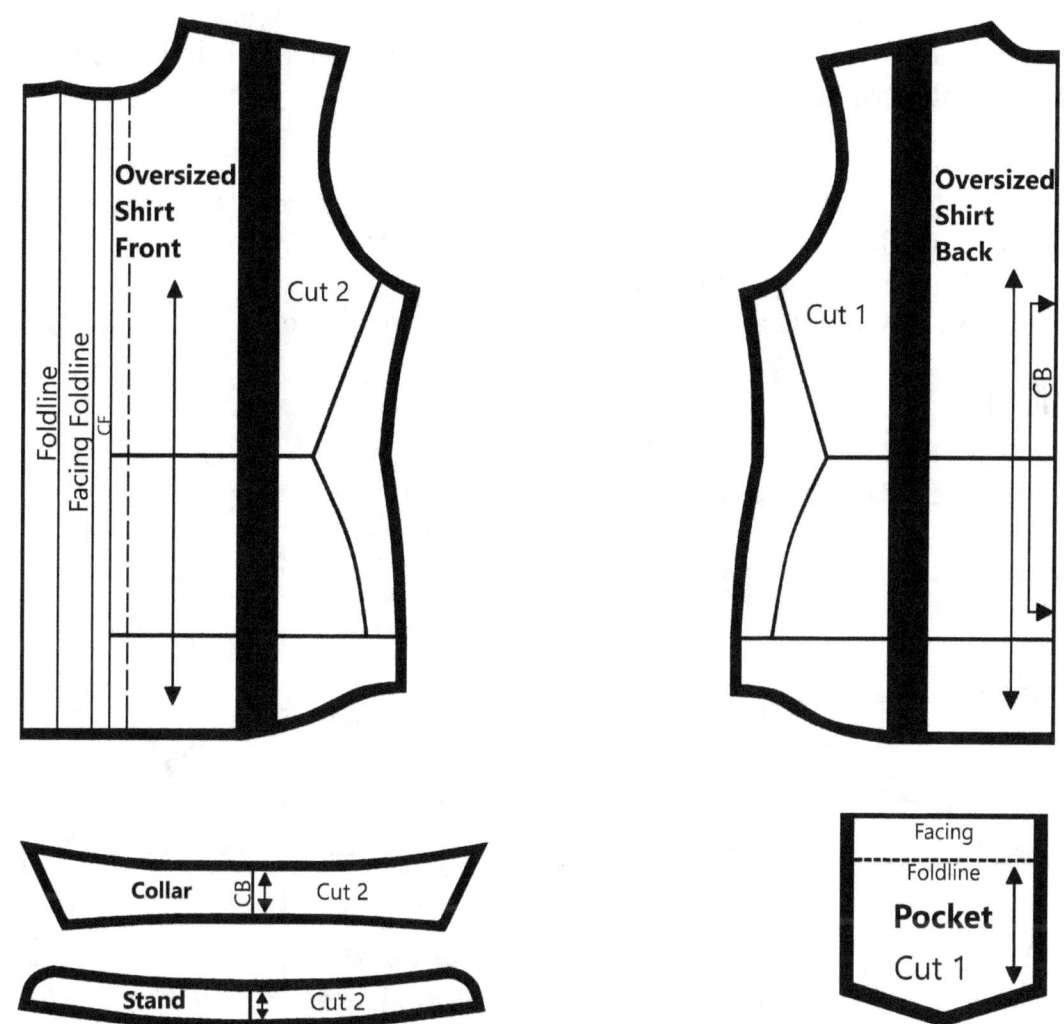

SEWING THE SHIRT FRONT EDGES AND POCKET

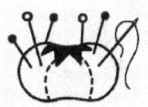 **Shirt front edges**: Fold the front edges to the inside along the marked foldline. Press and tack. Fold the edges to the inside along the facing line. Press and tack. Edgestitch the front edges. Topstitch **2.5 cm (1 in)** from the front edges.
Pocket: The wrong side of the pocket can be interfaced if desired. Overlock the pocket top raw edge. Turn the pocket facing to the right side along the foldline. Stitch along each side of the facing, using a **1 cm (⅜ in)** seam allowance. Trim the top corners. Turn the facing to the wrong side. Fold the bottom and side seam allowances to the wrong side and press. Pin the pocket onto the marked placement line of the garment's left front and edgestitch in place. Complete the shirt as described on page **155**.

SHIRTS, BLOUSES, AND TOPS

THE OVERSIZED SHIRT SLEEVE

The **oversized shirt sleeve** draft can be used for oversized shirts, Tracksuits, sports tops, fleece jackets, and more. Draft the sleeve on the fold of a sheet of paper as illustrated below. The sleeve head should measure **1 cm (⅜ in)** more than the armhole measurement of the garment pattern. Extend the underarm line if needed. **Adjust the hemline when cuffs and plackets are required as illustrated in the shirt sleeve.**

A-B: Sleeve length.
A-C: Half the sleeve head depth measurement plus **2.5 cm (1 in)**. Rule a line across.
A-D: The front armhole measurement. Rule a line from **A** to **D**.
D-F: One third the measurement of **A** to **D**.
B-E: Half the desired wrist measurement. Rule a line from **D** down to **E**.

SLEEVE HEAD

Hollow the curve **6 mm (¼ in)** between **D** and **F**.
Raise the curve **1 cm (⅜ in)** between **A** and **F**.

Trace the sleeve pattern off and add a grain line, notches, and seam allowances.

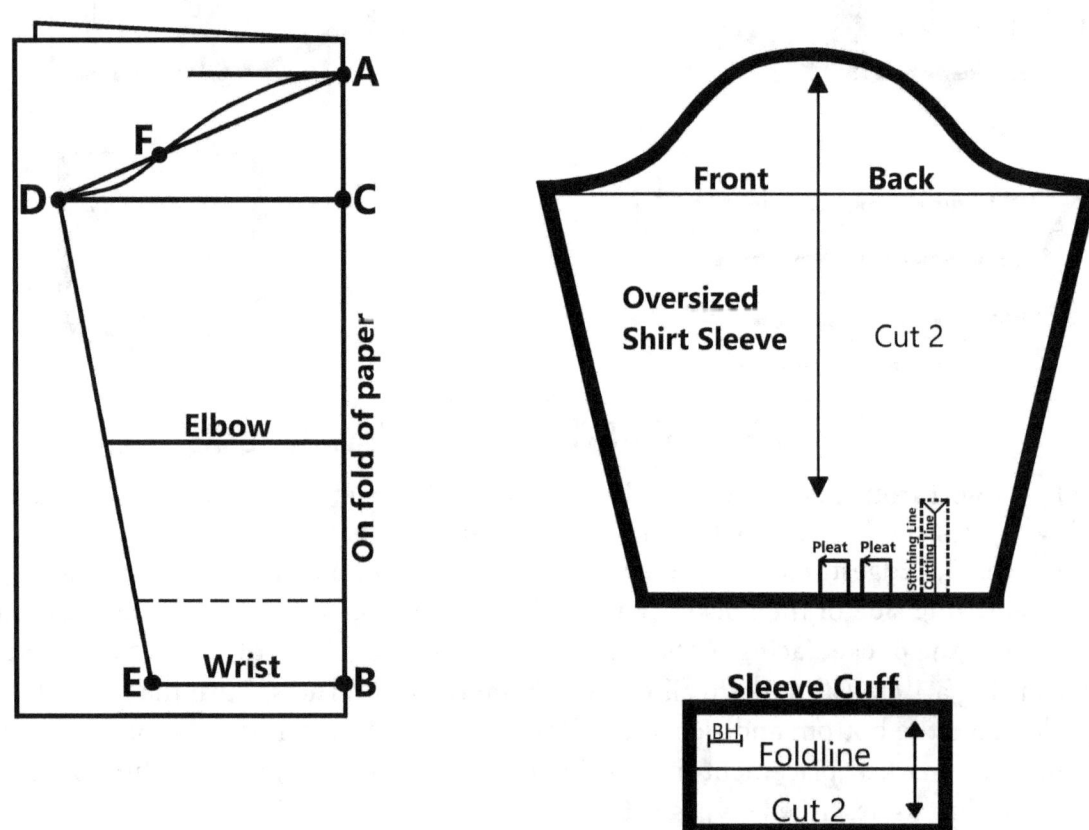

APPLYING A TWO-PIECE ROLLED COLLAR

1. Interface both collar pieces with lightweight fusible interfacing.
2. Pin and stitch the upper and under collar, right sides together. Understitch the under collar if desired. Trim and grade the seam allowances. Trim across both corners. Press. Turn the collar to the right side and use a point turner to neaten both corners. Press the collar.

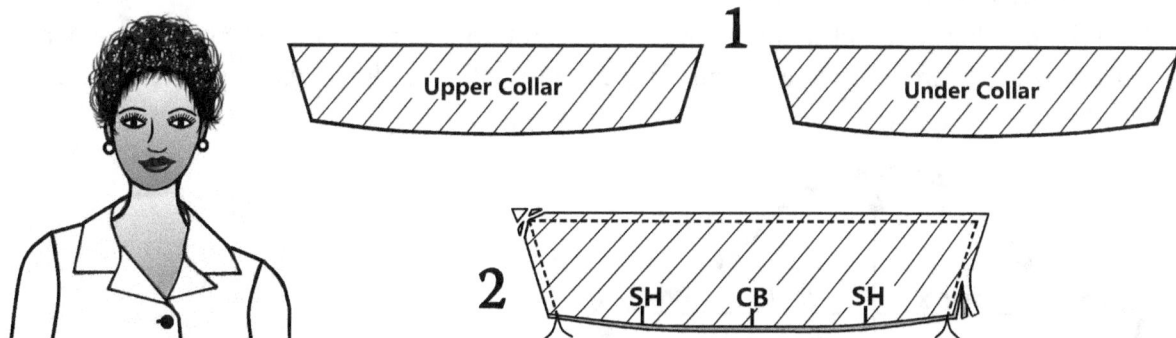

3. Apply lightweight fusible interfacing to the front facings. Pin and stitch the garment's front and back shoulder seams, right sides together. Press the seams open. Staystitch the garment neckline and front facings just inside the seamline. Clip the neckline seam allowance.
4. Pin the under collar to the garment neckline, while keeping the upper collar out of the way, and matching the centre back and shoulder notches up. Stitch the under collar to the neckline from one shoulder notch, across the back neck, to the other shoulder notch.

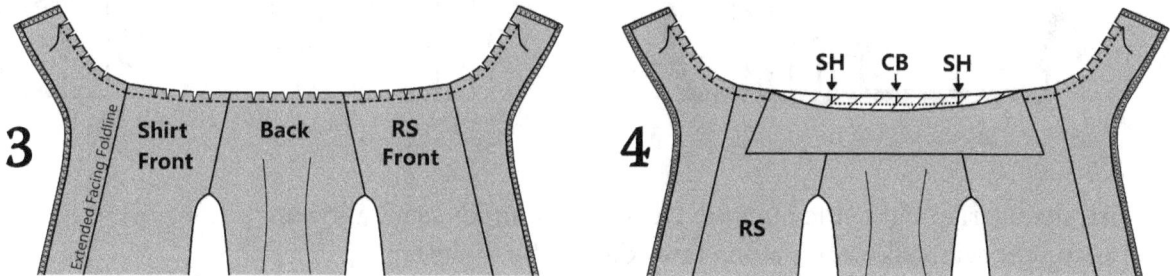

5. Press the shoulder seam allowance of the facing to the wrong side. Fold the facings over the collar and stitch up to the shoulder seamlines. Clip into the upper collar and seam allowances at both shoulders. Trim and grade the seam allowances. Trim the front corners.
6. Turn the facing to the wrong side. Place the seam allowance foldline of the upper collar and facing ends slightly over the seamlines and tack in place. From the right side of the garment, stitch in the ditch to secure the collar and facing edges in place, or use a slipstitch. Press.

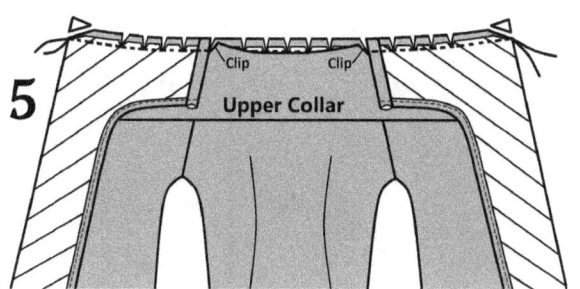 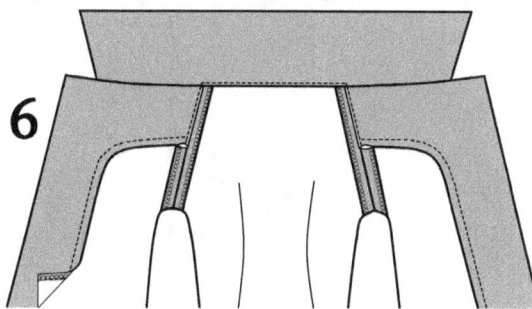

~ 149 ~

SHIRTS, BLOUSES, AND TOPS

SEWING SHIRT CUFF PLACKETS

1. Mark the opening for the plackets onto the wrong side of the sleeve.
2. Draw the placket pattern and add seam allowance. Cut the overlap and transfer the markings onto the wrong side of the fabric.
3. Fold the overlap right sides together and stitch the top section up to the marked side edge. Clip into the seam allowance. Trim and grade the seam allowance. Taper the corners and point.

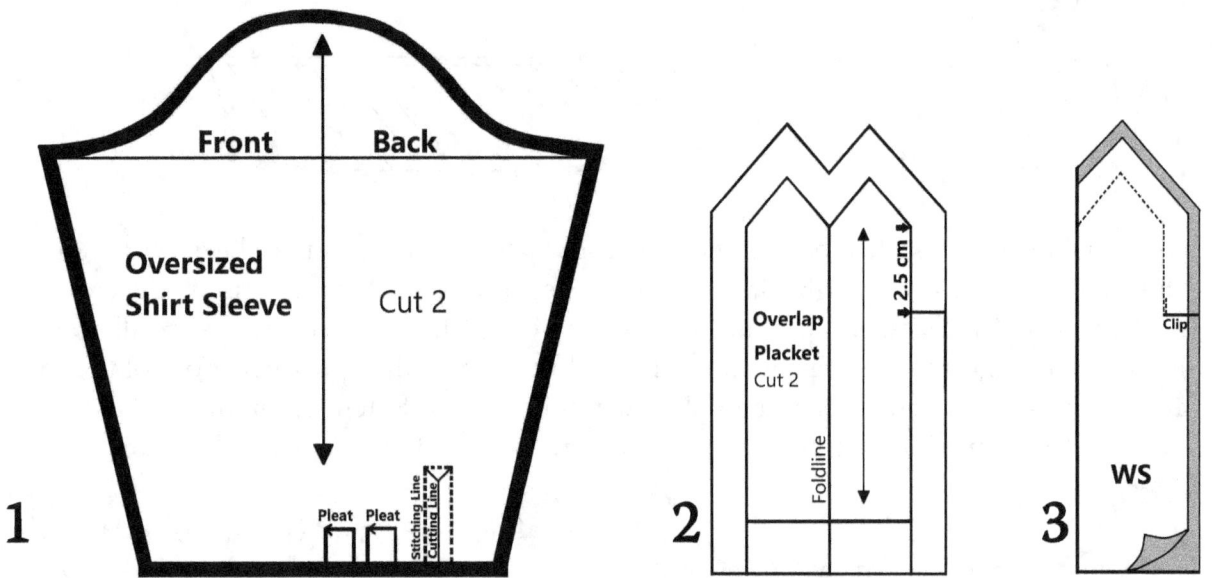

4. Turn the overlap right side out and press. Press under seam allowance along one edge.
5. Press under seam allowance along one edge of the underlap.

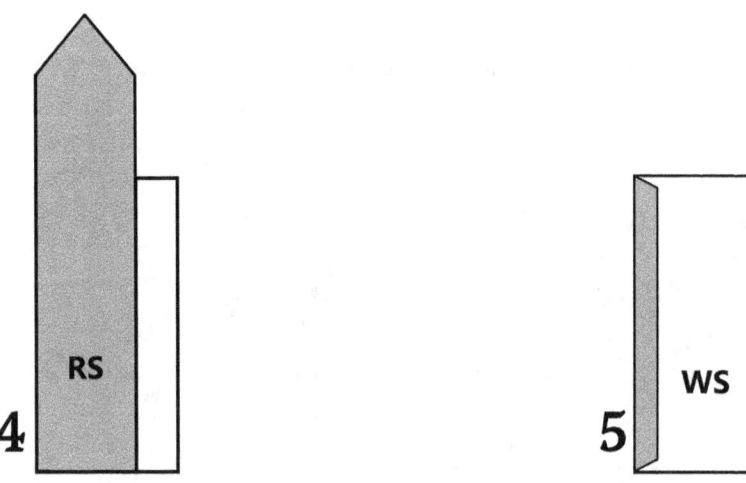

SHIRTS, BLOUSES, AND TOPS

6. Sew reinforcing stitches within the marked placket seamline. Slash to within **1 cm (⅜ in)** of the placket top and into the corners.
7. Pin and stitch the right side of the underlap to the wrong side of the back placket edge. Press the seam allowance toward the underlap. Bring the underlap to the right side. Pin and tack the folded edge over the stitching line. Edgestitch it in place.

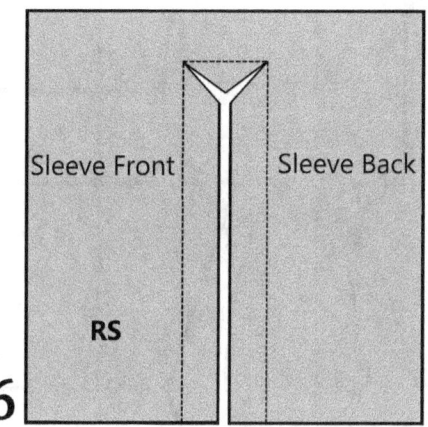
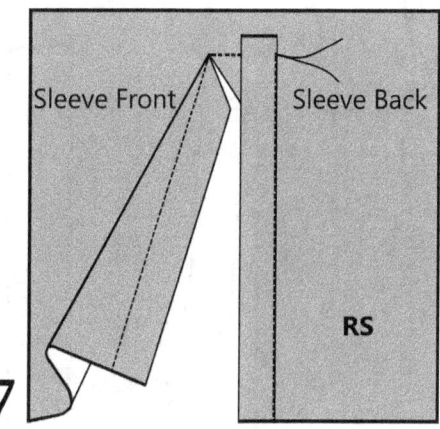

8. Pin the right side of the overlap edge to the wrong side of the front placket edge. Stitch in place and trim the seam allowance. Press the seam allowance flat. Place the folded edge of the overlap over the stitching line and pin it in place. Pin the top section of the overlap to the sleeve, covering the top portion of the underlap. Tack in place.
9. Topstitch, starting from the lower edge, up around the point, and across the placket.

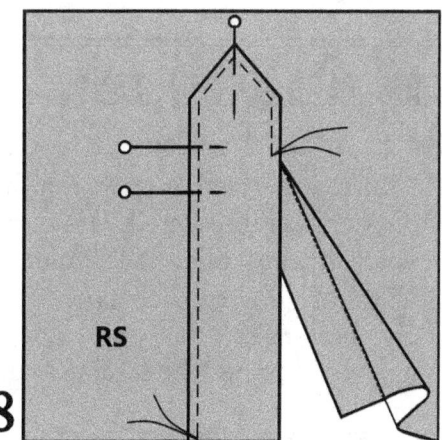
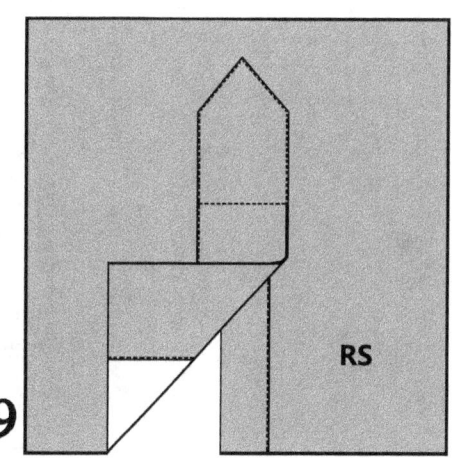

SHIRTS, BLOUSES, AND TOPS

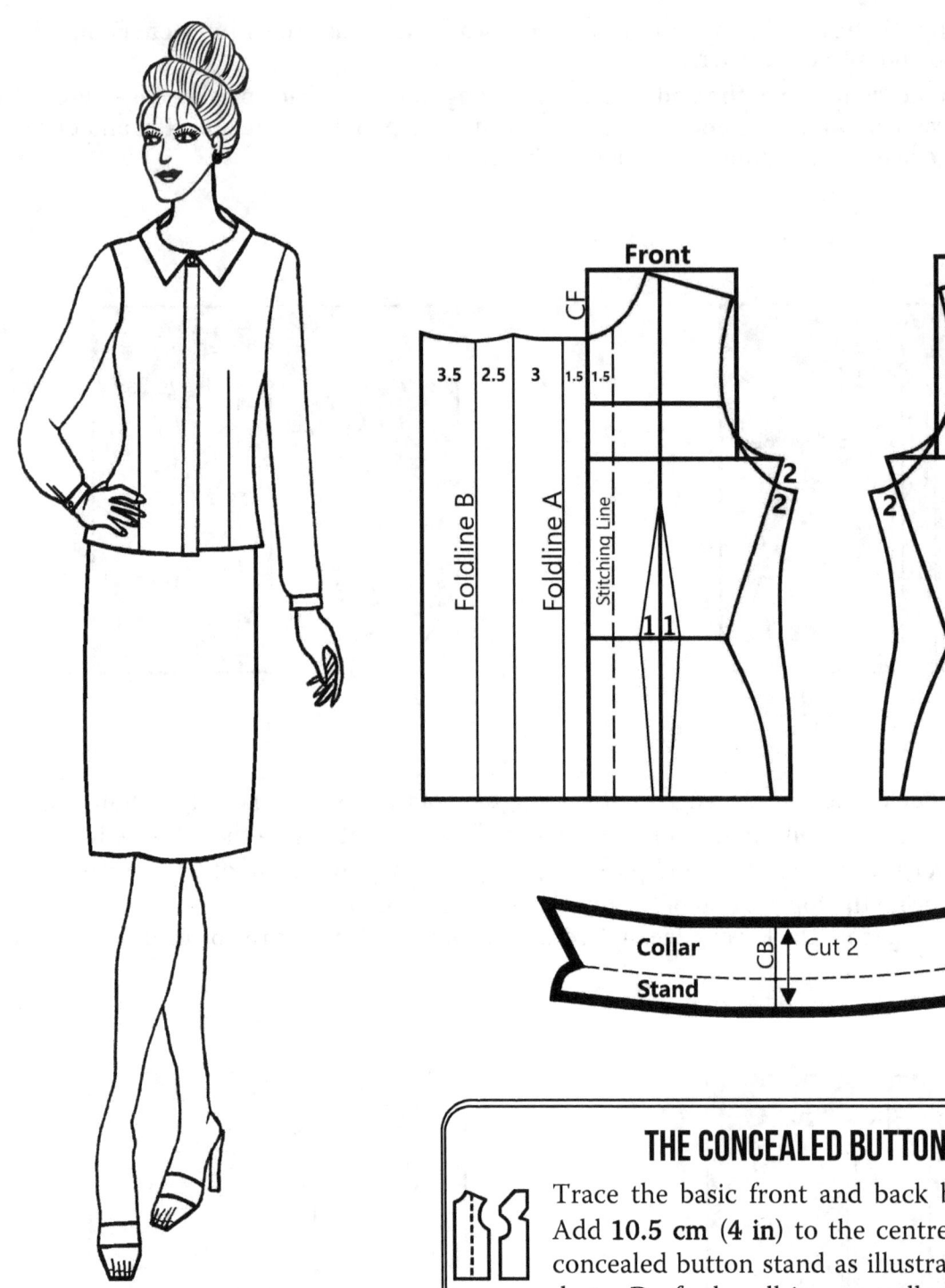

THE CONCEALED BUTTON STAND

Trace the basic front and back bodice blocks. Add **10.5 cm** (**4 in**) to the centre front for the concealed button stand as illustrated. Draw the darts. Draft the all-in-one collar and stand as illustrated on page **122**. Draft the shirt sleeve pattern on page **144** to complete the pattern. Trace the pattern pieces off. Add grain lines, notches, hem, and seam allowances.

THE CONCEALED BUTTON STAND

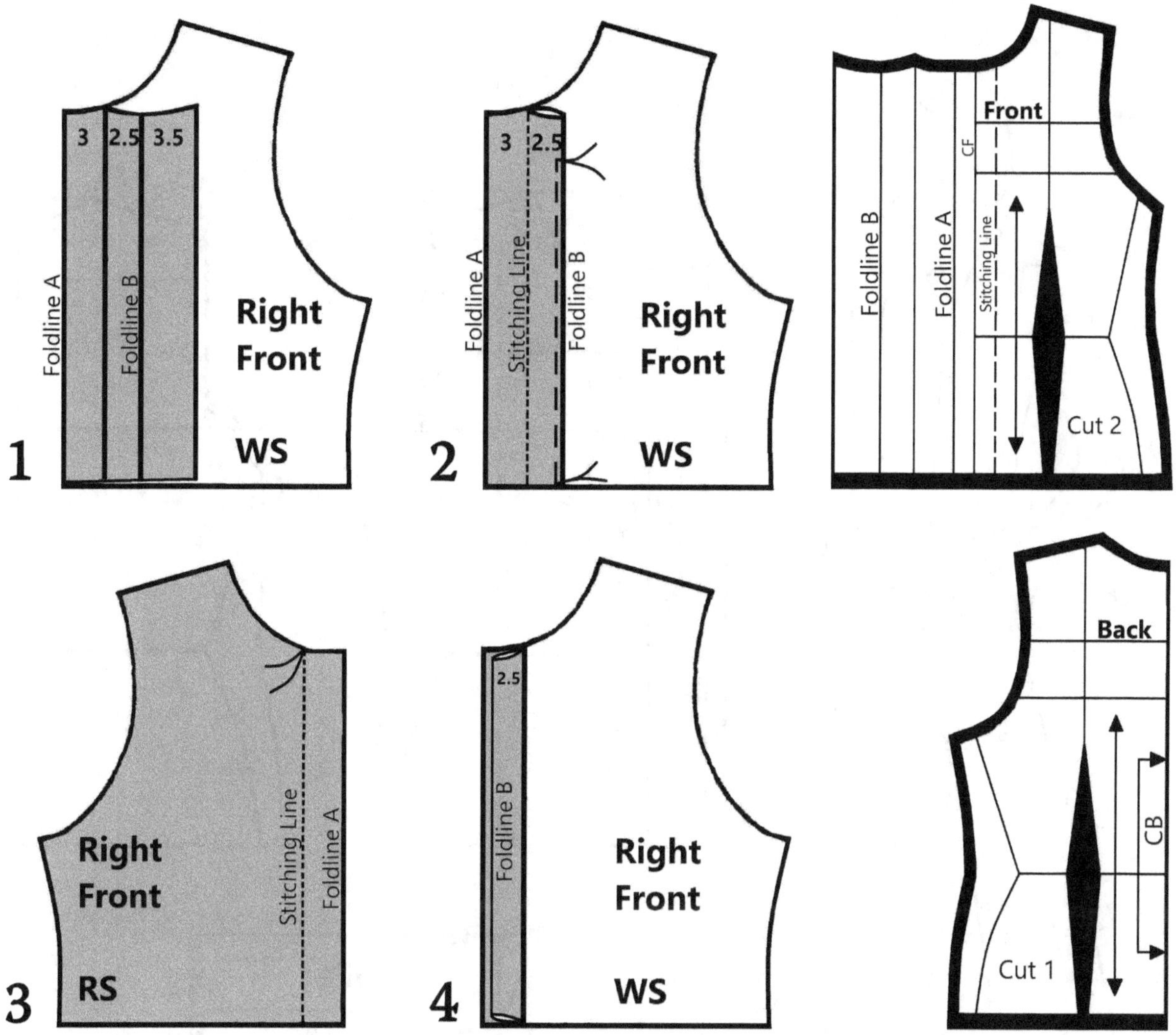

SEWING THE CONCEALED BUTTON STAND

1. Notch the foldlines and stitching lines at the top and bottom edges of the front panels. Fold **9 cm** (**3 ½ in**) of the right front panel along foldline **A** to the wrong side and press.
2. Fold **3.5 cm** (**1 ½ in**) along foldline **B** under. Press and tack through all layers.
3. On the garment's right side, stitch on the marked stitching line.
4. On the garment's wrong side, press foldline **B** (button stand) to the left.

Complete the left front by trimming **6 cm** (**2 ¼ in**) from the **10.5 cm** (**4 in**) extension. Fold the raw edge of the shirt left front **1 cm** (**⅜ in**) to the wrong side and press. Fold **2.5 cm** (**1 in**) to the wrong side for the button stand. Press and tack. Edgestitch it in place. Stitch the front and back shoulders, right sides together. Neaten the raw edges. Press. Staystitch the front and back neck. Clip the neckline. Complete the collar and attach it to the neckline. Sew bound cuff plackets on the sleeves if desired. Complete the shirt as described on page **155**.

SHIRTS, BLOUSES, AND TOPS

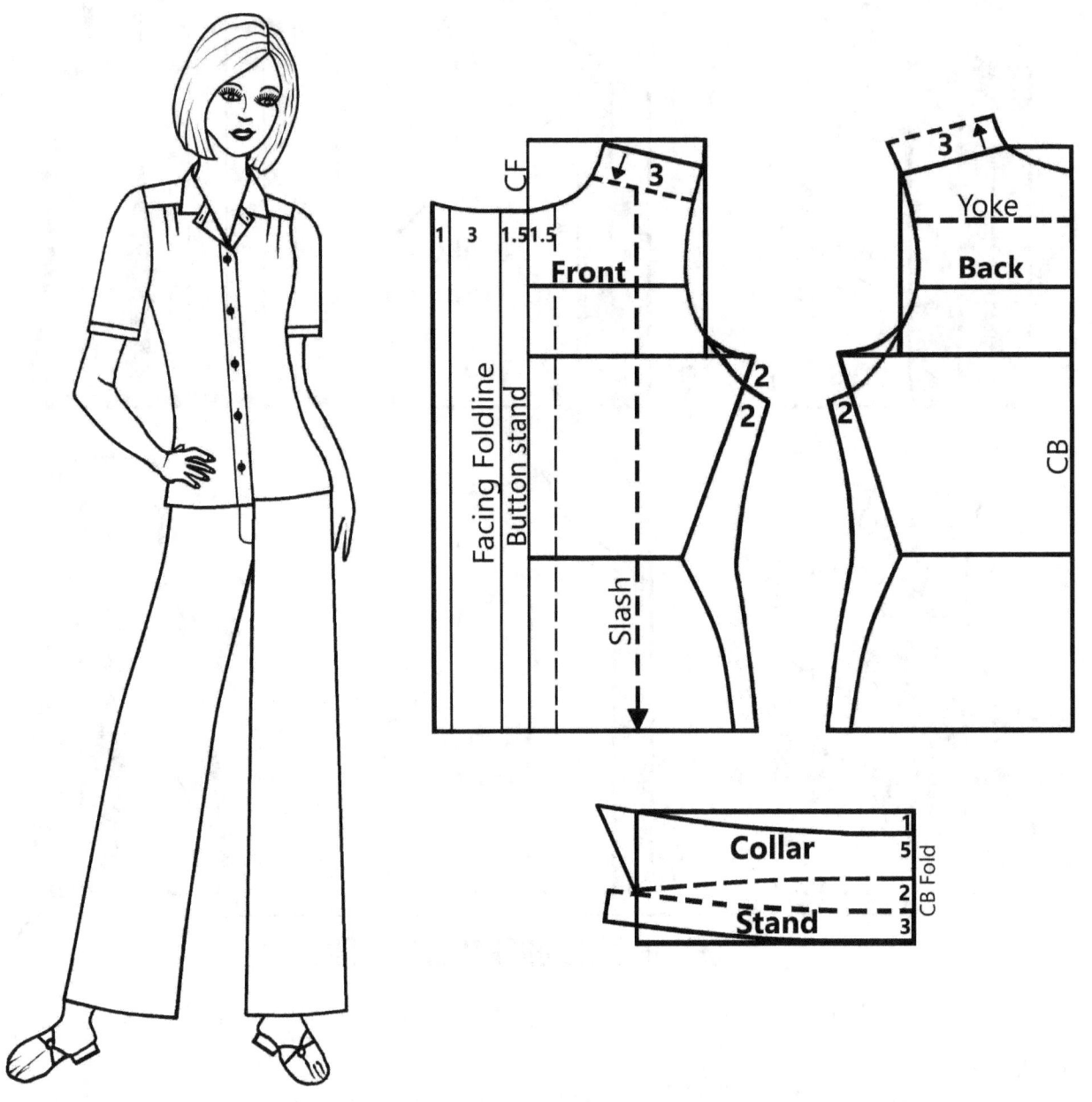

YOKE SHIRT

Draft the basic front and back bodice blocks. Drop the front shoulder by **3 cm (1 ¼ in)**. Lift the back shoulder **3 cm** as illustrated. Draw the yoke line on the back pattern at a required height. Add **1.5 cm (⅝ in)** to the centre front for the button stand and **4 cm (1½ in)** for facing. Draw a rectangle for the collar with a depth of **11 cm (4 ¼ in)** and the neck measurement of the pattern. Complete the pattern as illustrated. Trace all the pattern pieces off. Slash the front pattern and spread it to a desired amount for pleats or gathers. Add grain lines, notches, hem, and seam allowances.

YOKE SHIRT

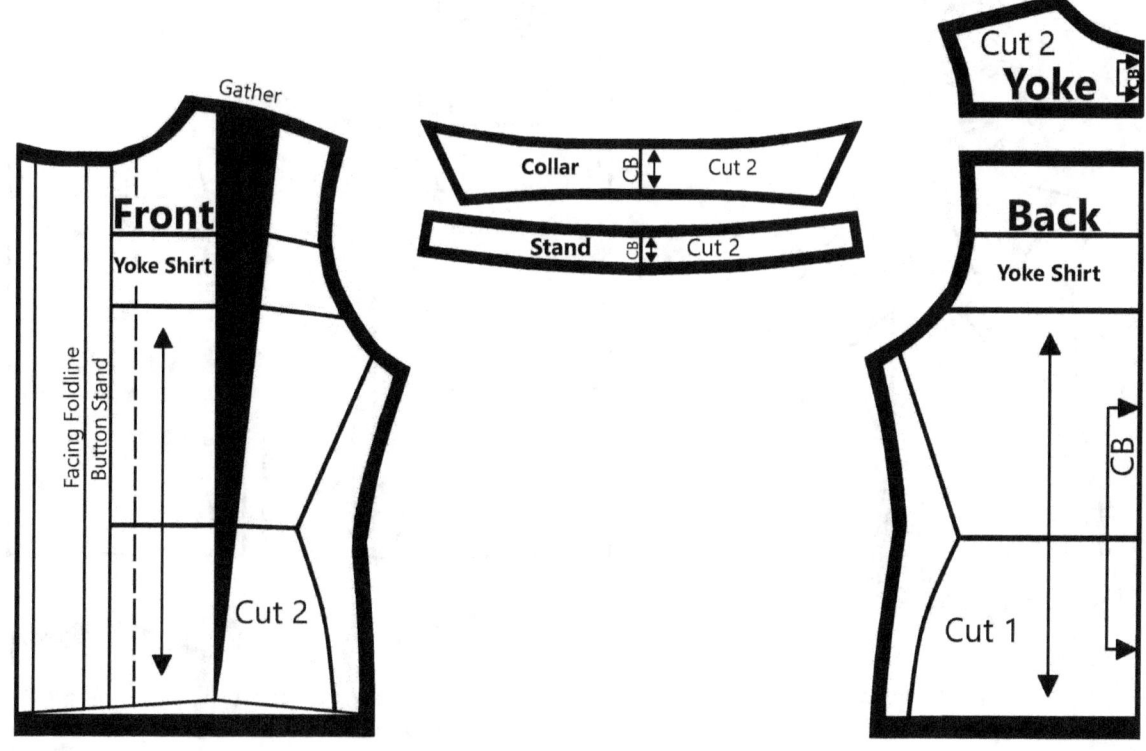

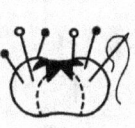
Iron lightweight interfacing on the wrong side of the shirt front facing, collar, and collar stand. Sew gathers or pleats on the front panels. Press **1 cm (⅜ in)** on the centre front edges under. Fold the facing to the inside along the facing foldline and press. Tack and edgestitch the front edges. Tack the yoke to the shirt back, right sides together. Tack the right side of the yoke facing to the wrong side of the shirt back. Stitch through all three layers. Grade the seam allowances. Press the yoke and facing upward. Tack the wrong side of the shirt's front panels to the right side of the yoke-facing shoulder seams. Place the shirt between yoke and yoke facing. Pin shoulder seams of yoke and shirt fronts right sides together. Stitch through all three layers. Turn shirt to right side and press. Sew the collar panels right sides together. Trim the corners and grade the seam allowance. Turn the collar to the right side. Press. Topstitch outer edges of collar if desired. Pin the collar stand to the collar, right sides together. Repeat for the stand facing. Stitch and grade the seam. Turn right side out. Staystitch and clip garment neck seamline. Pin the right side of the stand facing to the wrong side of the shirt neckline and stitch. Press the seam towards the stand facing. Turn the seam allowance of the collar stand **1 cm (⅜ in)** under and press. Pin the pressed edge to the right side of the shirt, over the neckline seam. Topstitch along the folded edge. With right sides together, pin the sleeve into the armhole and stitch. Repeat for the other sleeve. Stitch the side seams, starting at the hemline, up to the end of the sleeve seam. Sew the sleeve hems. Press under **1 cm (⅜ in)** of the shirt hem allowance. Fold the hem another **1 cm**, press, and stitch in place. Make buttonholes and sew buttons on.

SHIRTS, BLOUSES, AND TOPS

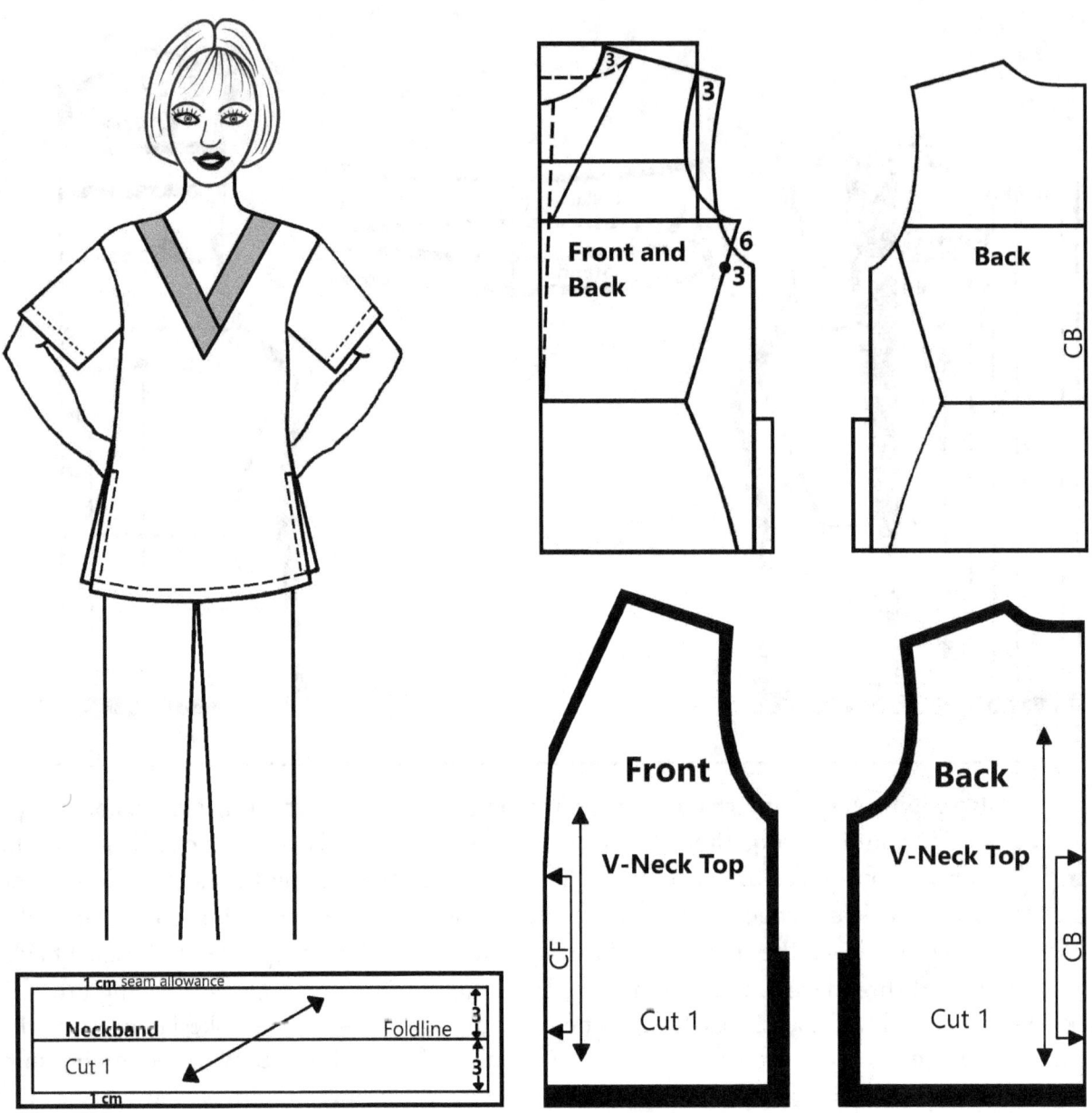

OVERSIZED TOP WITH OVERLAPPED V-NECK

Draft the basic front bodice block. Adjust the front gape as illustrated. Scoop the front neck by **3 cm (1 ¼ in)**. Draw the V-neck to a desired depth. The V-neck can be a straight line or drawn with a slight curve. Draw the back neck at the front. Extend the shoulder line by **3 cm (1 ¼ in)** or to a desired amount. Drop the armhole by **6 cm (2 ¼ in)** and measure **3 cm (1 ¼ in)** out or to a desired amount. Redraw the armhole as illustrated. Draw a line down and across to the hip line. Draw the side vents to the required width. Trace the back pattern from the front. Measure the neckline and draw the neckband pattern **5 cm (2 in)** longer. Draft the oversized shirt sleeve on page **148**.

SEWING THE OVERLAPPED V-NECK

1. Mark the centre front of the garment on the wrong side with a water-soluble pen. Mark the **1 cm (⅜ in)** seam allowance on either side of the centre front.
2. With right sides together, pin and stitch the front and back shoulder seams. Neaten the raw edges with overlocking or a zigzag stitch. Staystitch the neckline and snip into the V up to the stitching line.
3. Cut the neckband longer than the neckline measurement and on the **bias** when using fabric without stretch. Cut lightweight interfacing on the **bias** and interface the neckband. Fold the neckband in half, wrong sides together and press. Pin the band to the neckline. From the wrong side, start stitching from the centre front, up and around the neckline, ending **4 cm (1½ in)** from the centre front. Stretch the band slightly as you sew around the back neck.

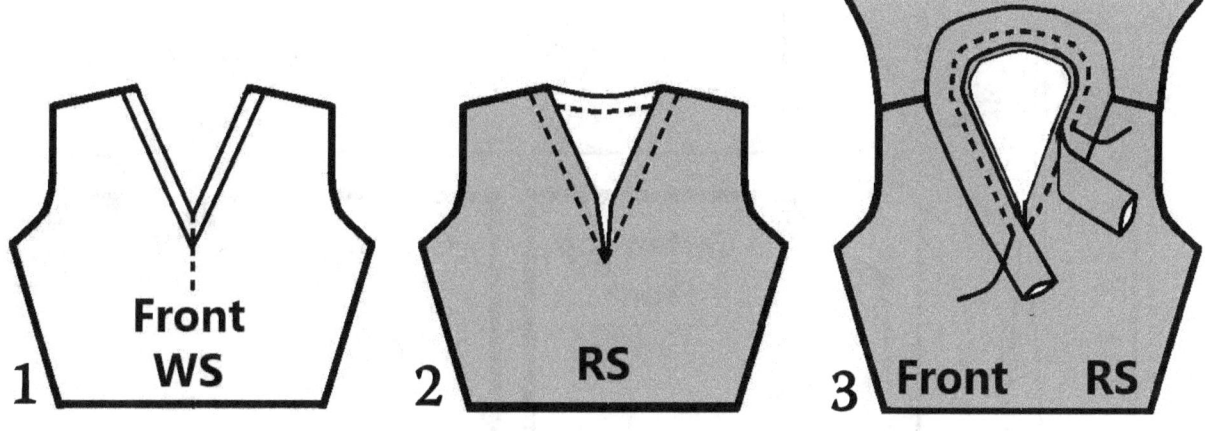

4. Lay the garment flat with the right side up. Tuck the extensions inside the seam opening. Overlap the right-hand side over the left for women. Press the seam flat. Secure the band with a pin at the centre front.
5. Flap the garment out of the way to expose the seam allowance. Stitch the opening close from the wrong side and pivot at the V.
6. Stitch the free end of the band to the seam allowance. Trim the band's extensions up to the seam allowance. Overlock the raw ends.

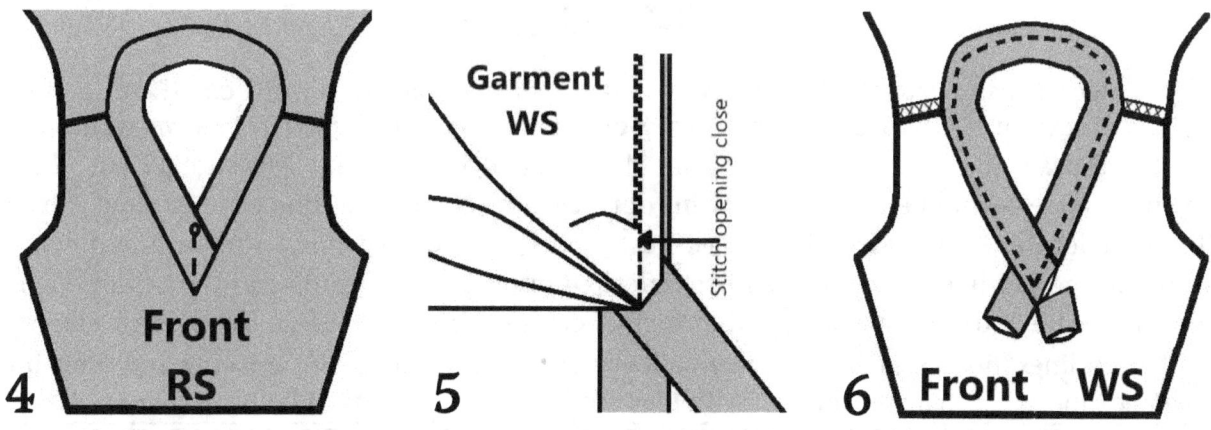

SHIRTS, BLOUSES, AND TOPS

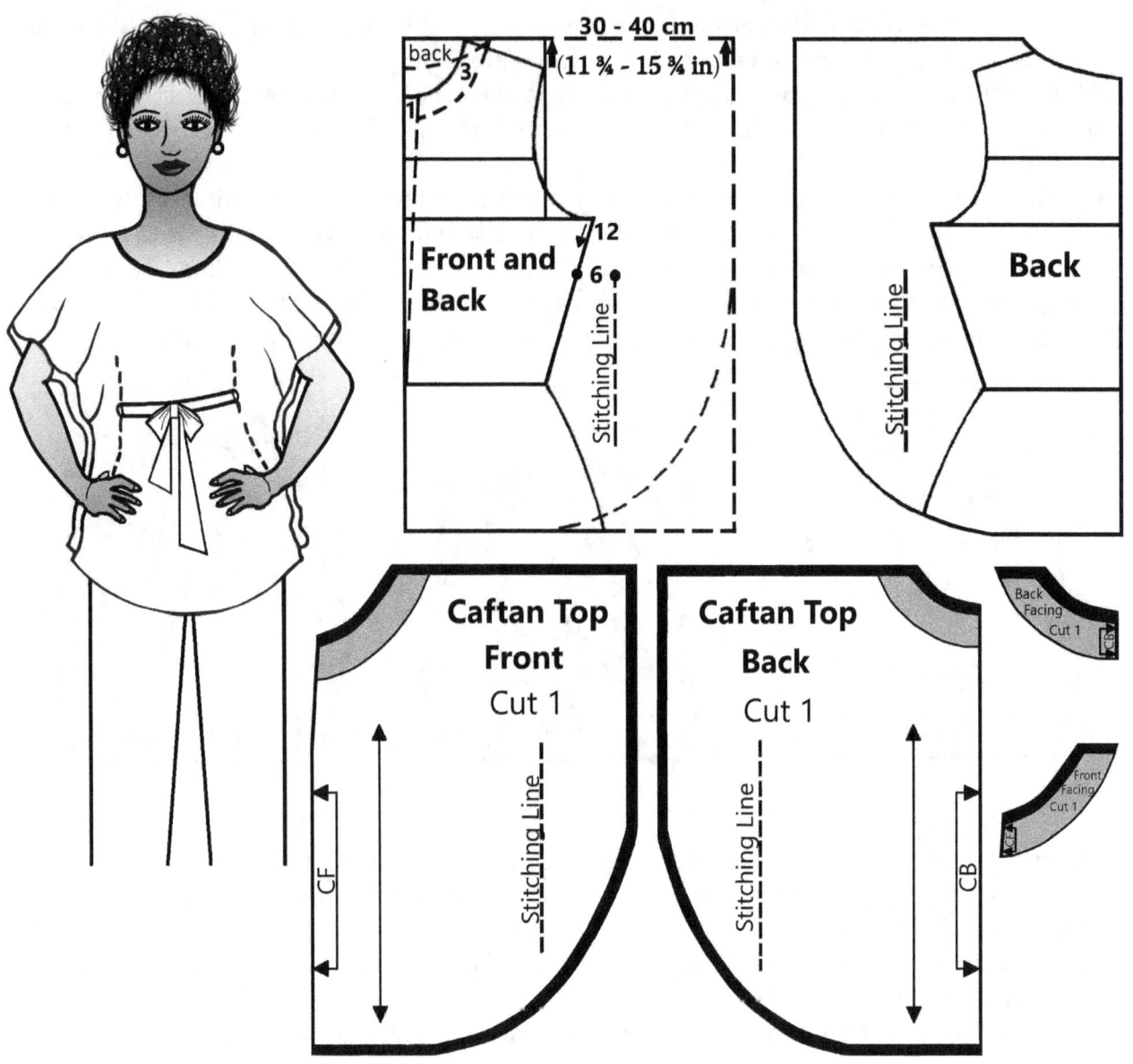

CAFTAN STYLE TOP

Trace the basic front bodice block on a large sheet of paper. Trim **1 cm (⅜ in)** from the centre front neck. Scoop the neck by **3 cm (1¼ in)** or as desired. Drop **3 cm** at the centre front and draw the back neck curve from the scooped front neck. Measure **12 cm (4¾ in)** down the side seam line and **6 cm (2¼ in)** out. Draw the stitching line as illustrated. Extend the shoulder line to a desired length as illustrated by the dotted line. Rule a line down and across to the hip line. Curve the hemline if desired or use the straight line as the hemline. Trace the back pattern from the front, on the original centre front line. Trace the pattern pieces off. Add grain lines, notches, hem, and seam allowances. Draw the neckline facing and trace it off. The neckline can also be finished off with bias binding. Draw a belt if a belt is required.

BATWING SLEEVE TOP

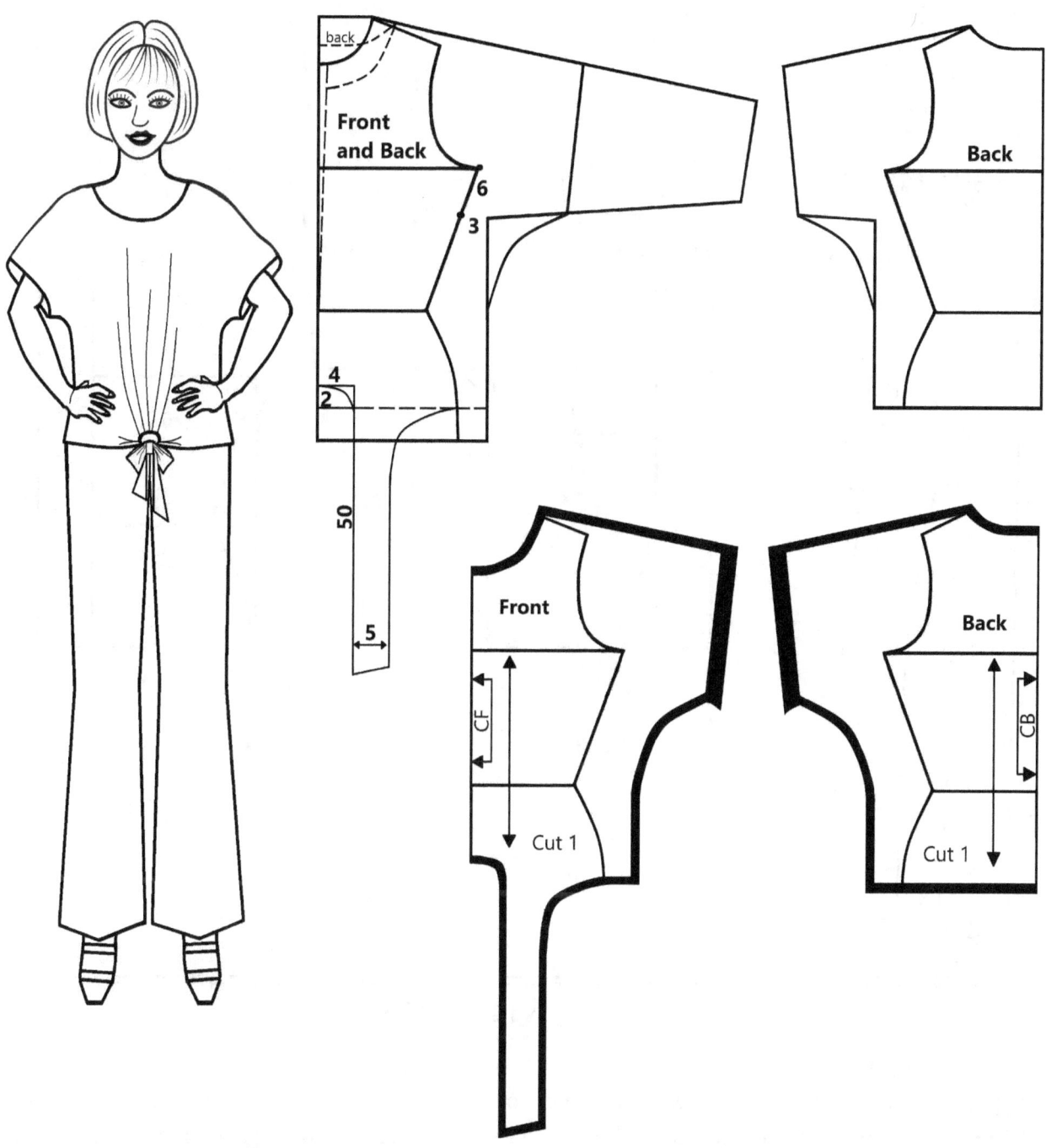

Draft the basic front kimono block and draw the batwing sleeve style lines. Shorten the bodice as desired. Draw the desired sleeve length. Scoop the front neck by **3 cm** (**1 ¼ in**) or as desired. Draw the back neck. Measure **2 cm** (**¾ in**) up and **4 cm** (**1 ½ in**) in at the centre front. Measure **50 cm** (**19 ¾ in**) down from the **4 cm** mark for the tie. Use the French curve to draw the curves at the centre front and the hip line to complete the front. Trace the pattern sections off. Add grain lines, notches, hem, and seam allowances.

SHIRTS, BLOUSES, AND TOPS

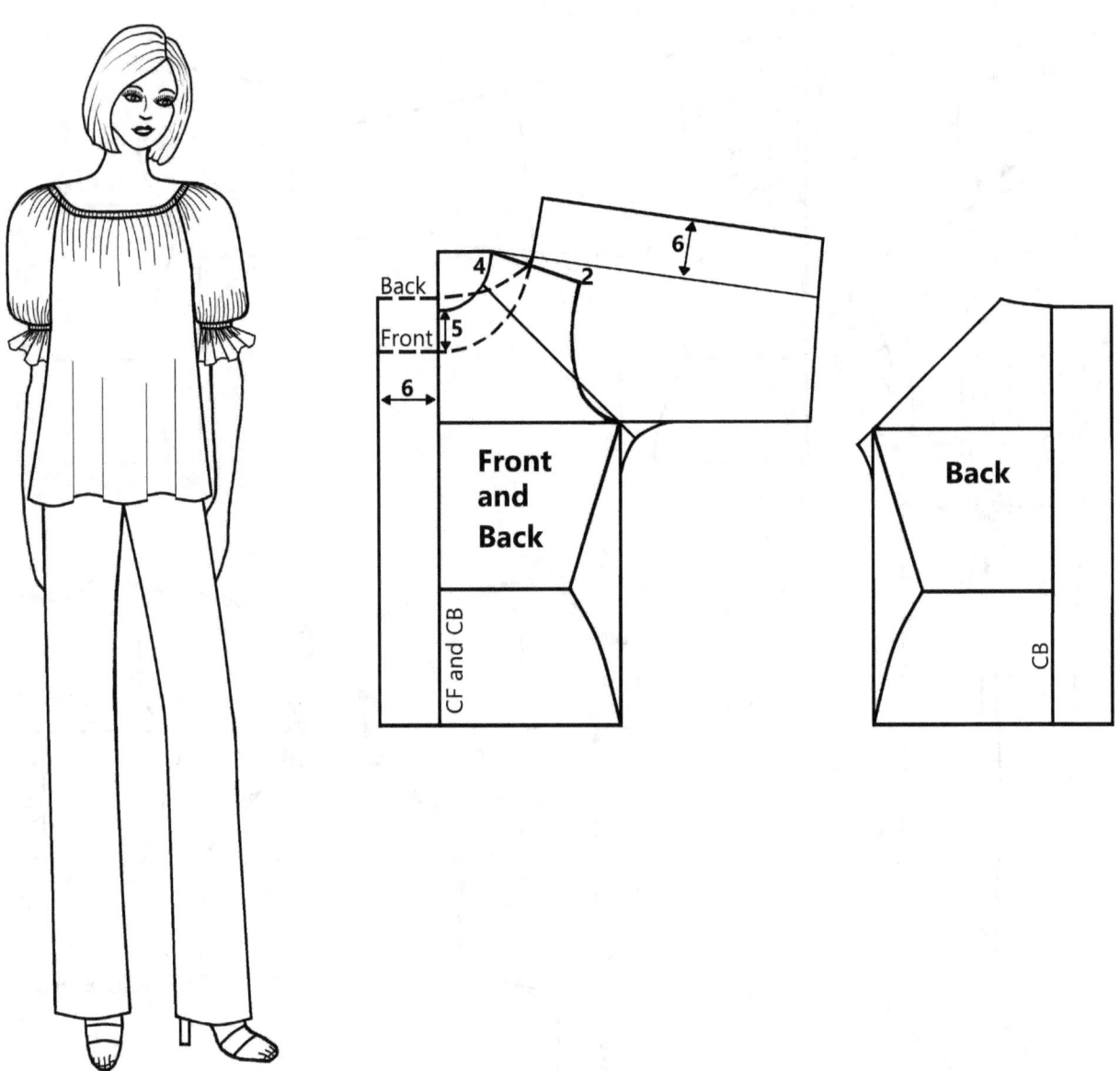

PEASANT BLOUSE

Trace the basic front bodice block. Shorten or lengthen the bodice as required. Rule a line from the underarm down to the hip line. Measure **2 cm (¾ in)** up from the tip of the shoulder. Rule a line from the neck edge to the required length, touching the **2 cm** mark. Rule a line down for the sleeve width and across towards the bust line. Draw a curve for the underarm seam. Measure **4 cm (1 ½ in)** down from the neck edge and rule a line from this point to the underarm curve as illustrated. Scoop the front neck **5 cm (2 in)** or as desired. Draw the back neck from the new neckline as illustrated. Add **6 cm (2 ¼ in)** at the centre front and above the new shoulder line for gathers. Trace a front and a back bodice from the front draft. Trace the back and front sleeve sections off and align them next to each other on paper. Secure in place with tape. Add grain lines, notches, hem, and seam allowances.

PEASANT BLOUSE

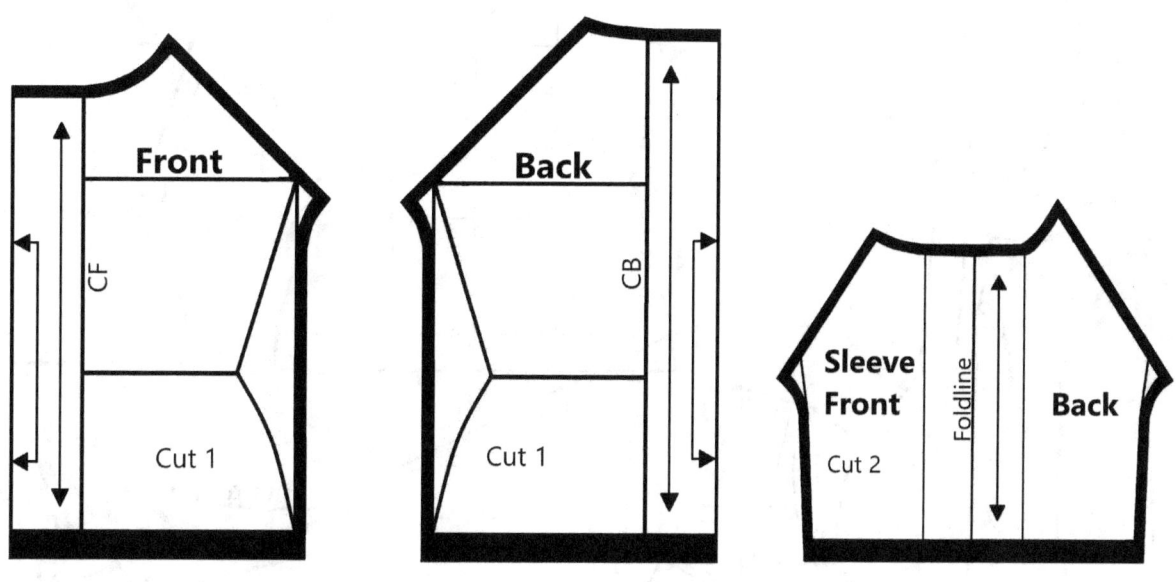

The scooped neckline and sleeve hem of the peasant blouse can have a casing with elastic or drawstring, or it can be finished off with bias binding. Elastic was used for this sample. Pin and stitch the front section of each sleeve to the blouse front, right sides together. Pin and stitch the back section of each sleeve to the blouse back. Overlock the armhole seams. Pin the front and back of the blouse, right sides together and stitch down the sleeve and side seams. Overlock or zigzag the seams. Starting at the centre back, pin bias tape to the neckline, right sides together. Fold **6 mm (¼ in)** of each end of the binding to the wrong side. Stitch the binding to the neckline inside the pressed fold. Turn the binding over to the wrong side of the garment and press. Stitch in place, leaving each end of the binding open to insert elastic. Cut elastic to the required length and thread it through the casing. Secure the elastic in place. Neaten the raw edges of the blouse and sleeve hem. Turn **6 mm (¼ in)** of the blouse and sleeve hem under twice. Press and stitch in place. Rule a line with a washable fabric marker **3 cm (1 ¼ in)** from the sleeve hem edge. Stitch thin elastic to the line, using a small zigzag stitch. Press the garment.

SHIRTS, BLOUSES, AND TOPS

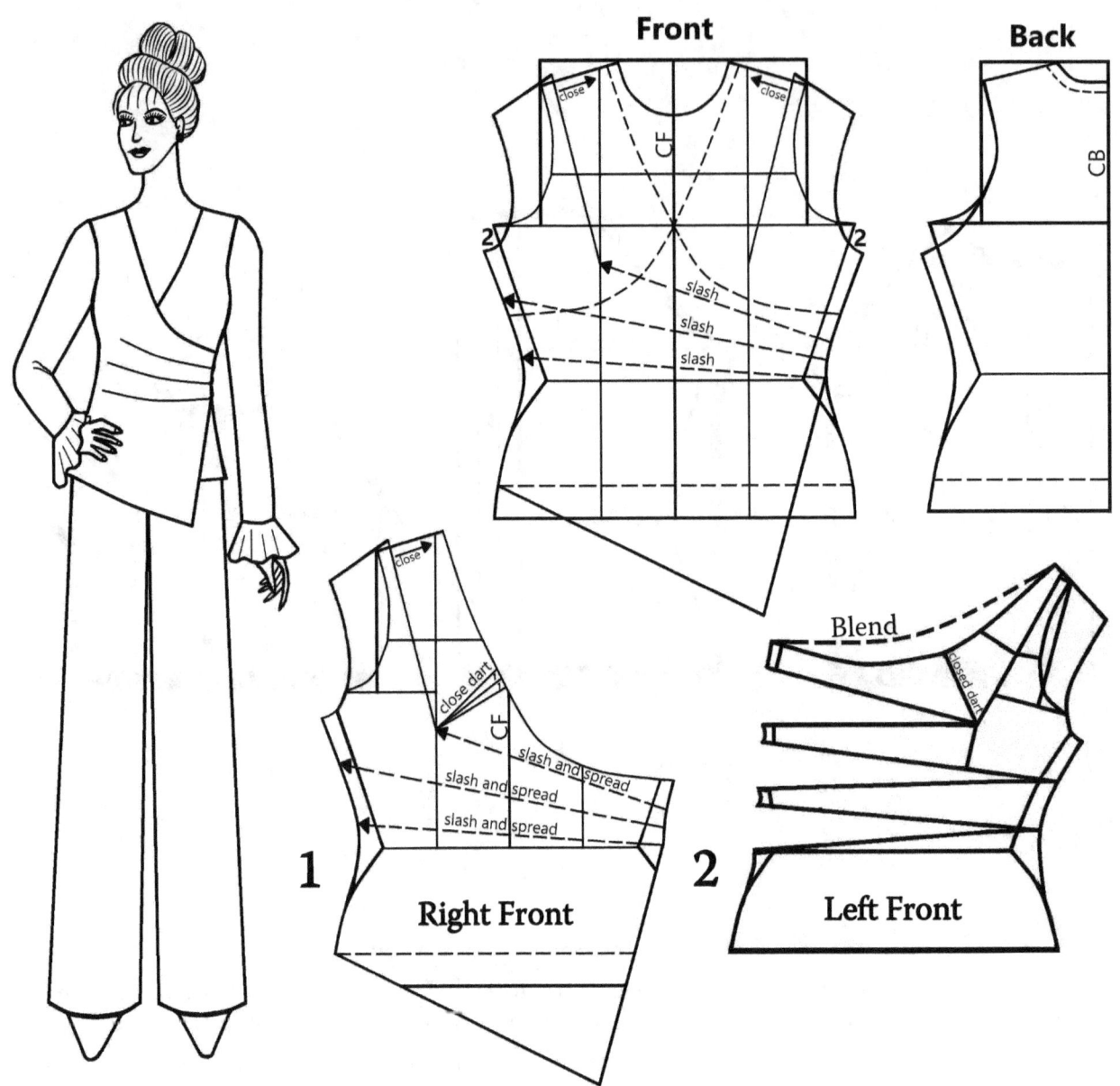

ASYMMETRICAL WRAP BLOUSE

Draft the front bodice block with the shoulder dart on the fold of a sheet of paper. Draft the basic back bodice block. Scoop the neckline by **1 cm (⅜in)** if desired. Adjust the front and back bodice length as required. Open the sheet and draw the style lines for one front panel. Fold the sheet along the centre front and trace the style lines through. Open the sheet and outline the right and left front sections with two different colour pencils.

1. Trace the right and left front panels off. Draw a **2 cm (¾ in)** dart on the front neckline.
2. Slash the marked drape lines. Close the shoulder dart and secure it with tape. Close the dart on the neck and redraw the neckline. Place the slashed sections on paper and spread the two lower drape lines **6 cm (2 ¼ in)** wide. Repeat for the right front panel.

ASYMMETRICAL WRAP BLOUSE

Right Front

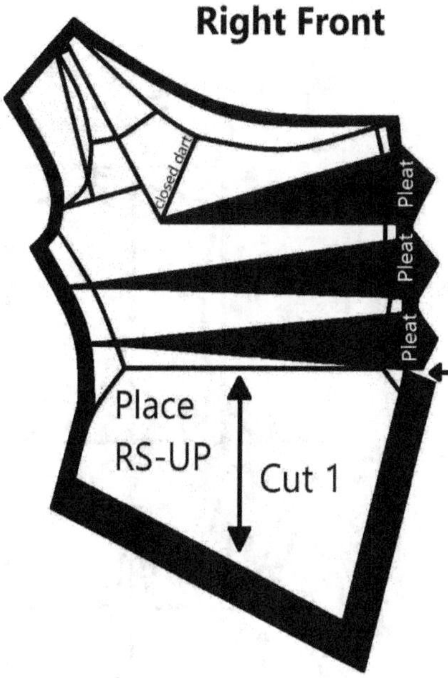

Left Front

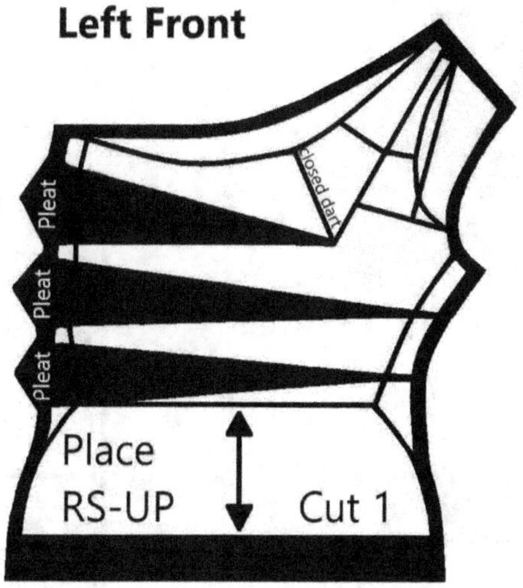

Back

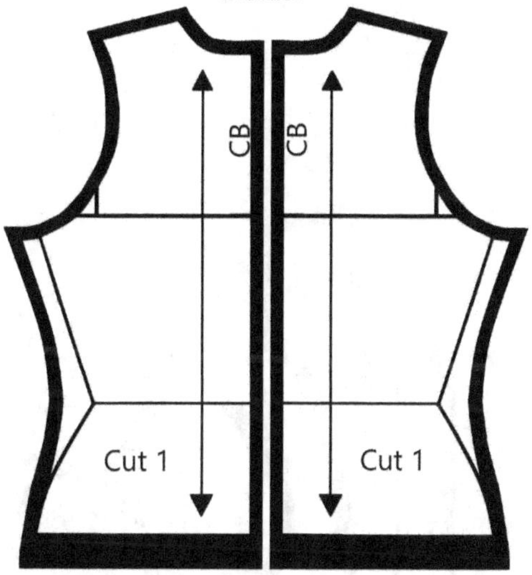

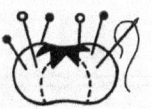

Insert a side or back zipper when using fabric with little or no stretch. The back can be cut on the fold of fabric when using stretch fabric. The pattern pieces should all be placed right side up and on the right side of the fabric.

Fold the marked pleats of the front panels and machine baste in place. Fold the bottom hemline of the right front panel over twice, press and machine stitch in place. Clip into the seam allowance as illustrated above. Fold the right front vertical hemline over twice and machine stitch in place. The back neck can be finished off with a facing and the front panels with binding made from self-fabric, or the entire neckline can be finished off with binding. Draft the desired sleeve pattern.

SHIRTS, BLOUSES, AND TOPS

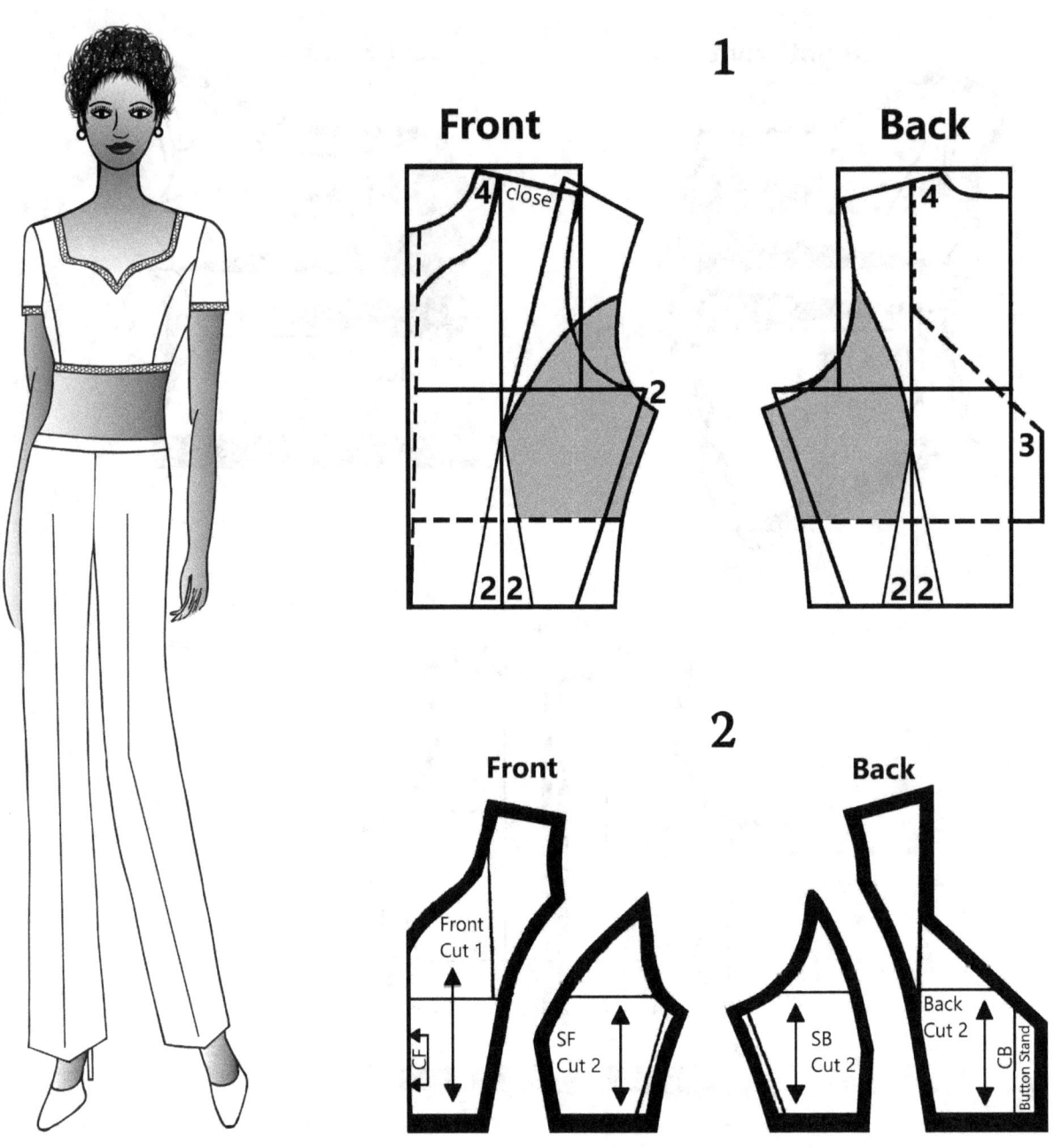

CROPPED TOP

Trace the front block with the shoulder dart and the basic back block. Scoop the front and back necklines and draw the style lines as illustrated. Shorten the bodice as desired. Trace the front and back panels off. Trace facings off. Add grain lines, notches, hem, and seam allowances. Add the basic sleeve or a sleeve of your choice to complete the pattern.

THE BASIC SKIRT

The basic skirt block is the basis from which all other skirt styles derive. Draft half the basic front and back skirt blocks as follows:

1. **Front:** Draw a vertical line from **A** to **B** for the skirt length.
2. Draw a horizontal line from **A** to **C** measuring a quarter of the waist circumference.
3. Measure **18 cm (7 in)** from **A** to **E** for the hip depth or length.
4. Rule a horizontal line from **E** to **F** measuring a quarter of the hip circumference.
5. Use the hip curve or a large French curve to draw a curve from **C** to **F**.
6. Rule lines from **F** to **D** and **B** to **D**. Repeat the above steps for the back skirt block.
7. Add **3 cm (1 ¼ in)** to the side front waist for a dart. Draw a curved line from the waist to the hip.
8. Drop **2 cm (¾ in)** at the centre front waist and mark. Draw the new waist with the hip curve or a large French curve.
9. Construct a **3 cm (1 ¼ in)** wide dart in the centre of the front waistline, placing **1.5 cm (⅝ in)** on either side of the centre dart line. Draw the front dart **10 cm (4 in)** long.
10. **Back:** Add **4 cm (1 ½ in)** to the side of the back waist for a dart. Draw a curved line from the waist to the hip.
11. Drop **2 cm (¾ in)** at the centre back waist and draw the new waistline.
12. Construct a **4 cm (1 ½ in)** wide dart in the centre of the back waistline, placing **2 cm (¾ in)** on either side of the centre dart line. Draw the back dart **14 cm (5 ½ in)** long.

The basic skirt block draft continues on the next page.

THE BASIC SKIRT

Draft half the basic front and back skirt blocks as follows:

A-B: The front skirt length.
A-C: Quarter of the waist circumference.
A-E: Hip depth or length is **18 cm (7 in)**.
E-F: Quarter of the hip circumference.
C-F: Draw a curve with the hip curve.
B-D: Quarter of the hip circumference.
Repeat the same steps for the back block.

G-H: The back skirt length.
G-I: Quarter of the waist circumference.
G-L: The hip depth is **18 cm (7 in)**.
K-L: Quarter of the hip circumference.
I-K: Draw a curve with the hip curve.
H-J: Quarter of the hip circumference.

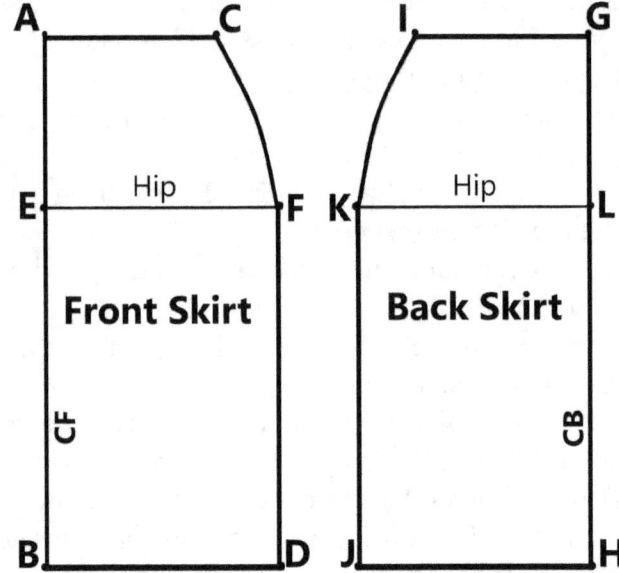

FRONT

Add **3 cm (1 ¼ in)** to the front waist for a dart. Rule a curved line from the side of the waist to the hip line. Drop **2 cm (¾ in)** at the centre front waist (**A**) and draw the new waistline with the hip curve, as illustrated by the dotted line. Construct a dart in the centre of the new waistline measuring **3 cm (1 ¼ in)** wide and **10 cm (4 in)** long.

BACK

Add **4 cm (1 ½ in)** to the side of the back waist for a dart. Rule a curved line from the waist to the hip line. Drop **2 cm (¾ in)** at the centre back waist (**G**) and draw the new waistline as illustrated. Construct a dart in the centre of the waistline measuring **4 cm (1 ½ in)** wide and **14 cm (5 ½ in)** long.

This is a fitted skirt block. Add a desired amount to the side seams for a looser fit.

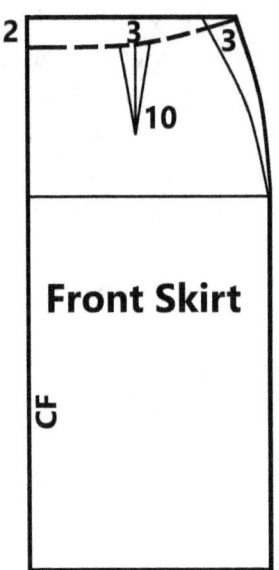
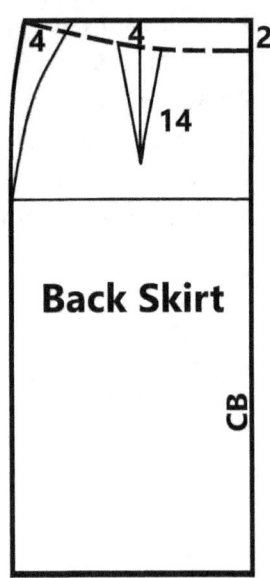

THE BASIC SKIRT

1. Draft the basic skirt on a sheet of paper. Add **4 cm (1 ½ in)** at a required height, at the centre back for a slit or vent. Trace the skirt pattern off. Close the darts and secure them with pins. Trace facing off or measure the waist and draw a waistband **10 cm (4 in)** longer than the waist measurement and twice the desired width. The extra amount added to the waistband length is for ease, seam allowances, an underlap, or overlap.
2. Add **2 cm (¾ in)** side seam allowances. Add **1.5 cm (⅝ in)** seam allowances at the waist and centre back seam. Add **4 cm (1½ in)** hem allowance. Add notches.

Mark the darts on the front and back skirt panels. Sew the darts and press it to one side. Overlock the centre back and side seams. Pin and sew the centre back seam from the marked zipper opening, to the marked vent opening. Press. Stitch the zipper into the centre back seam. Pin and stitch the front and back side seams together. Staystitch the waistline. Press the seams. Interface the waistband and overlock one long edge. Pin and stitch the long raw edge of the waistband to the waistline, matching notches. Grade the seam allowances. Fold the waistband along the foldline, right sides together. Stitch the ends and extension of the waistband. Trim the seam allowance and corners, and turn it to the right side. Press the waistband to the inside along the foldline. Pin and tack the free edge of the waistband in place. From the right side of the garment, stitch inside the waist seam. This is known as "stitching in the ditch." Sew your choice of fasteners on. Neaten the skirt hemline. Sew the skirt hem and vent in place. Press the garment.

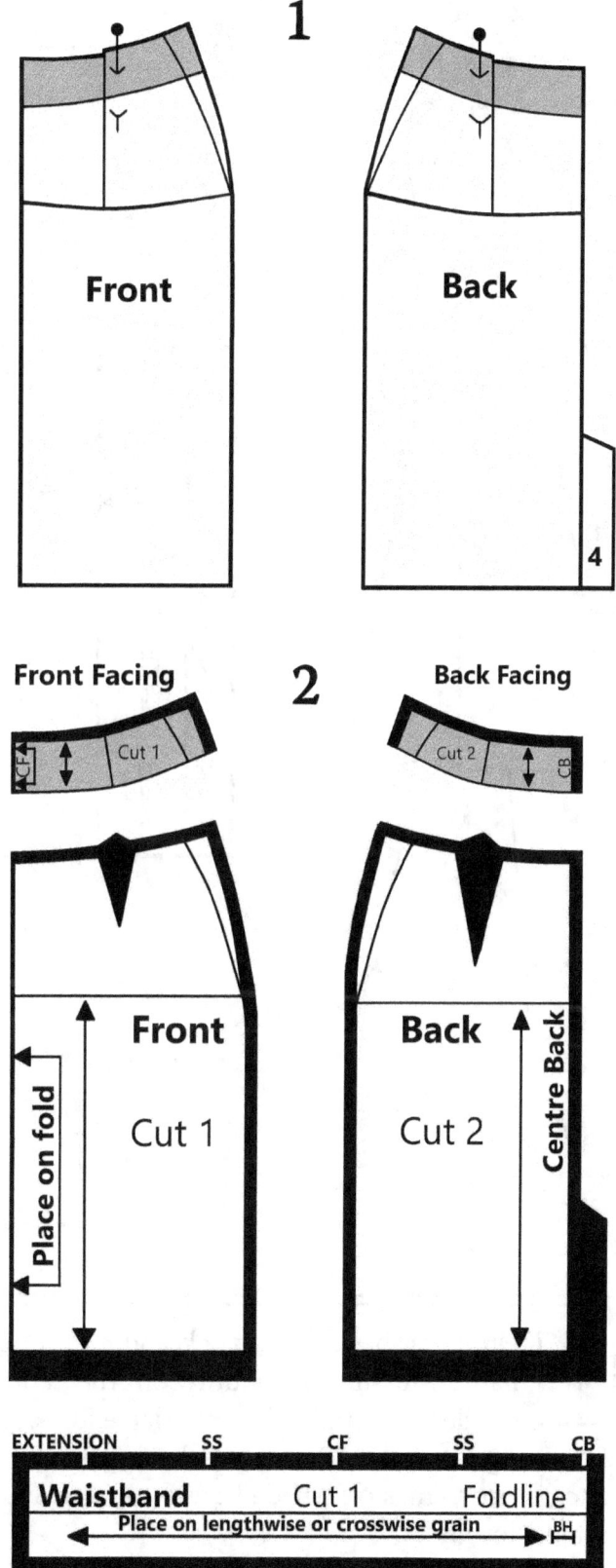

FLARED WRAP SKIRT

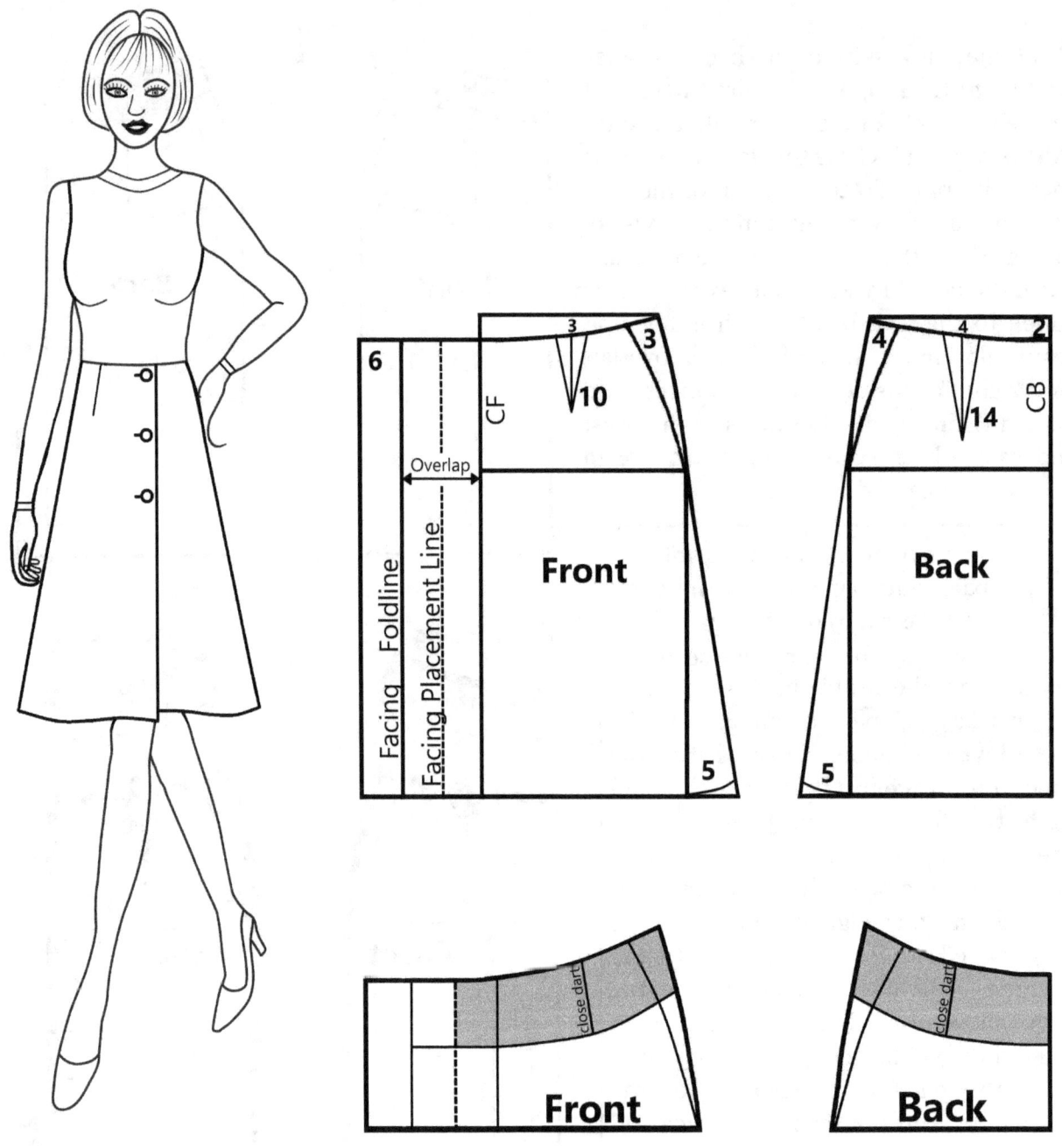

Draft the basic skirt block and add a desired amount to the side front and back for flare. Measure the width from the centre front to the dart point or beyond to obtain the desired width of the overlap extension. Add a **6 cm (2 ¼ in)** extension to the overlap for facing. Trace the front and back patterns off. Close the darts and trace the front and back waist facings off (shaded areas), as illustrated above. Add grain lines, notches, hem, and seam allowances.

FLARED WRAP SKIRT

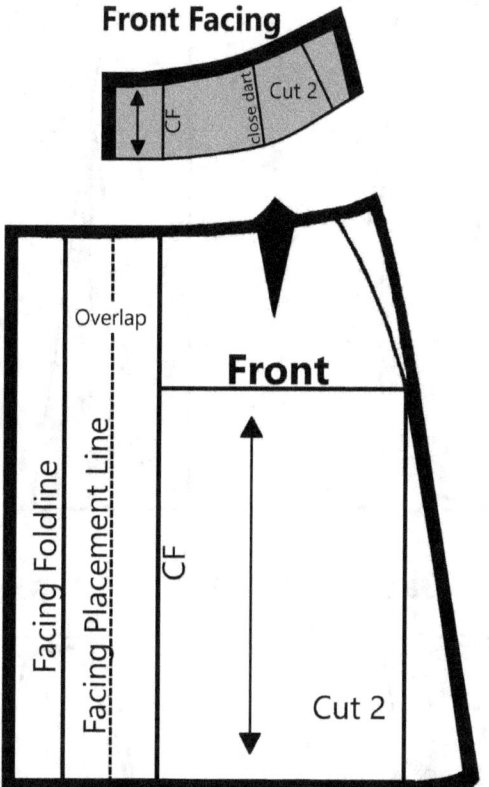

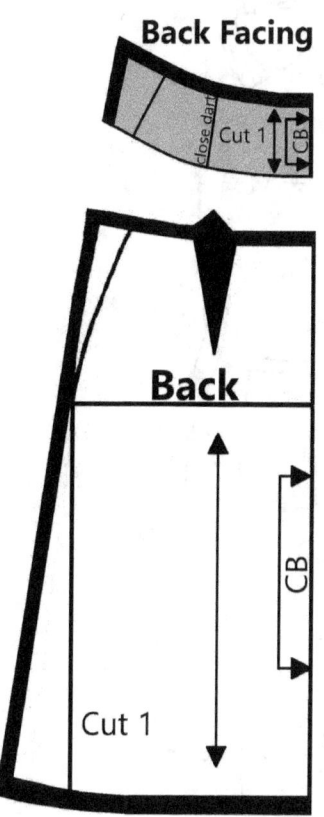

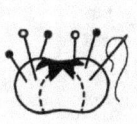

Sew the darts on the front and back skirt panels. Interface the front facing extensions. Neaten the front and side seams with overlocking. With right sides together, stitch the back and front side seams. Press. Interface the wrong side of the front and back waist facing pieces. Neaten the sides seams. Pin and stitch the sides of each front facing to the back facing. Press the seams and overlock or zigzag the bottom edge of the facing. Pin and stitch the front edges of the waist facing to the front edges of the facing extensions. Press the seam allowance towards the extensions. Stitch the facing extension seam allowances from the top to the hemline. With right sides together, pin and stitch the facing to the garment waist. Trim, grade, and clip the seam allowances. Press the waist seam allowances towards the facing. Understitch the facing or topstitch the waist edge. Tack the front facing extensions in place and press. Mark and sew buttonholes and buttons on. Attach a suitable fastener on the inside, to hold the underlap in place. Turn the hem up and hand stitch in place. Press the garment.

FLARED SKIRTS

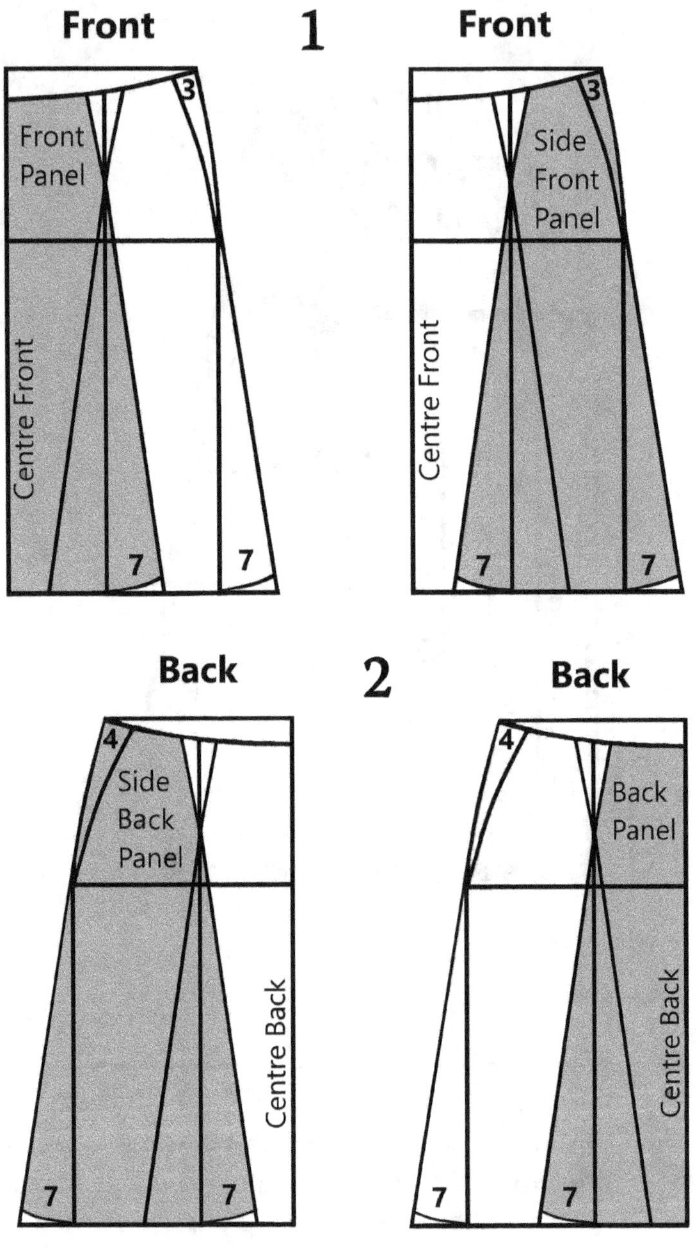

1. Draft the basic front and back skirt block. Draw in the style lines as illustrated. Add a desired amount of flare to the side of each panel as illustrated. The side seam lines must measure the same length as they were before the flare was added. Trace the front and side front panels off. See the shaded areas on the pattern.
2. Repeat the same for the back pattern. Add the same amount of flare to the back panels that was added to the front panels. Measure the waistline and draw a waistband. Add grain lines, notches, hem, and seam allowances.

FLARED SKIRTS

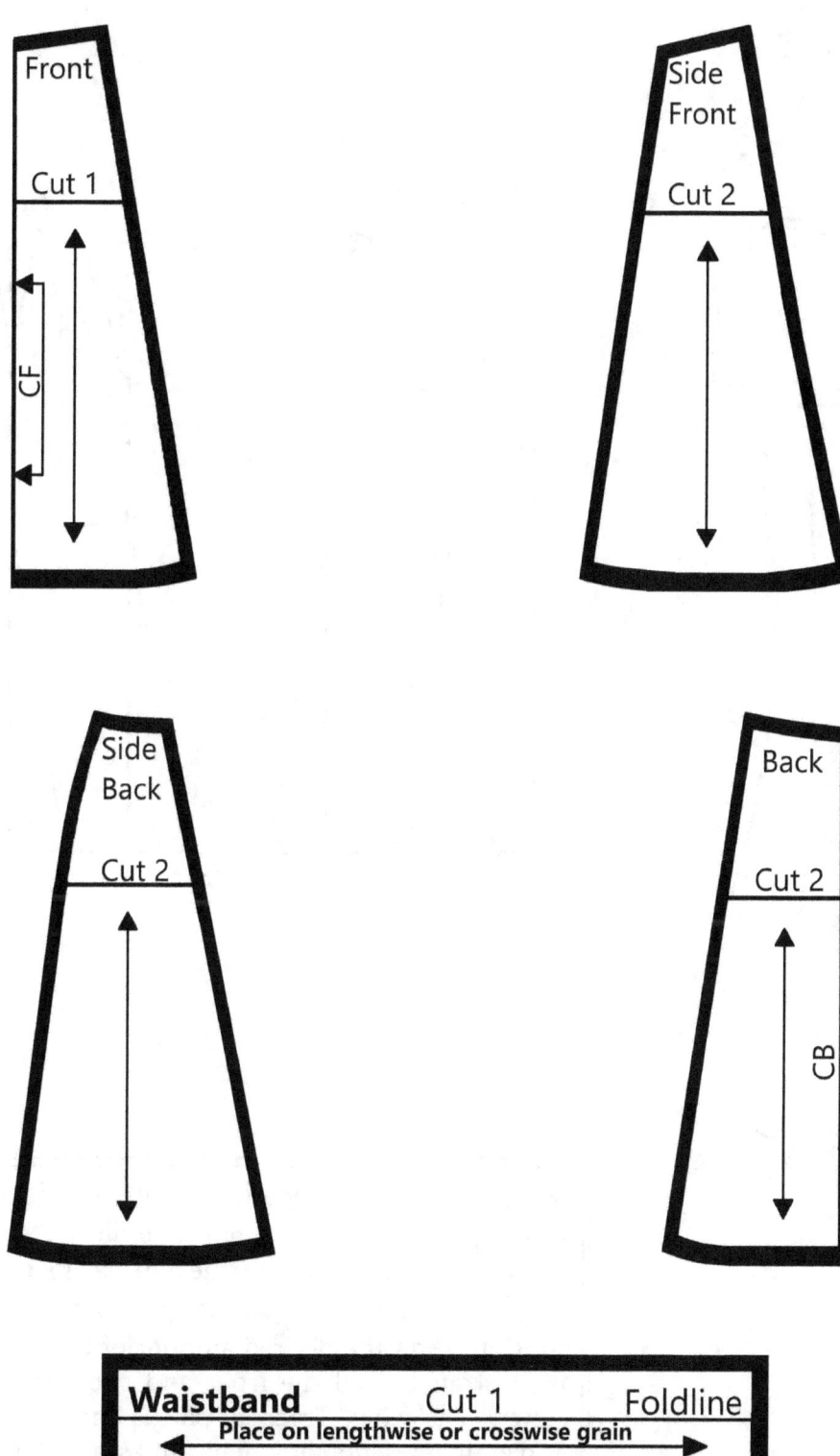

FLARED SKIRTS

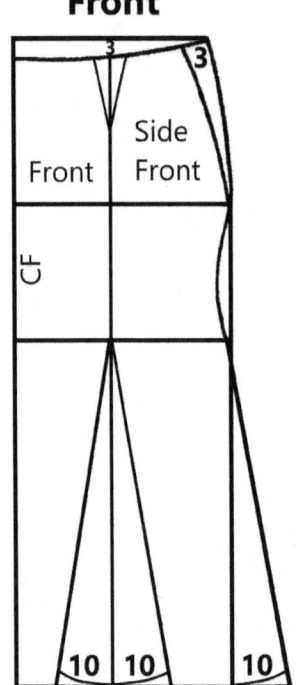
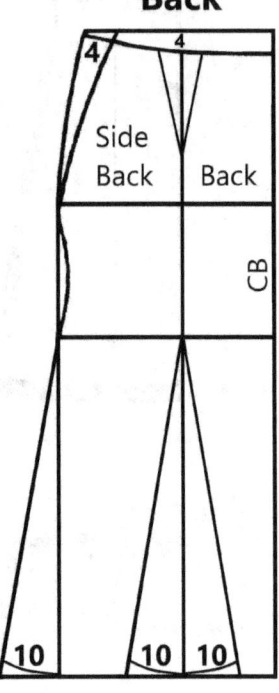

Add the required length to the basic front and back skirt block as illustrated. Drop the hip line by a further **20 cm (8 in)** and rule a line across. Start the panels from this new hip position. Add the desired amount of flare to the panels as illustrated. Fold the front and back darts close and draw waist facing. Trace all panels and waist facing off. Add grain lines, notches, hem, and seam allowances.

FLARED SKIRTS

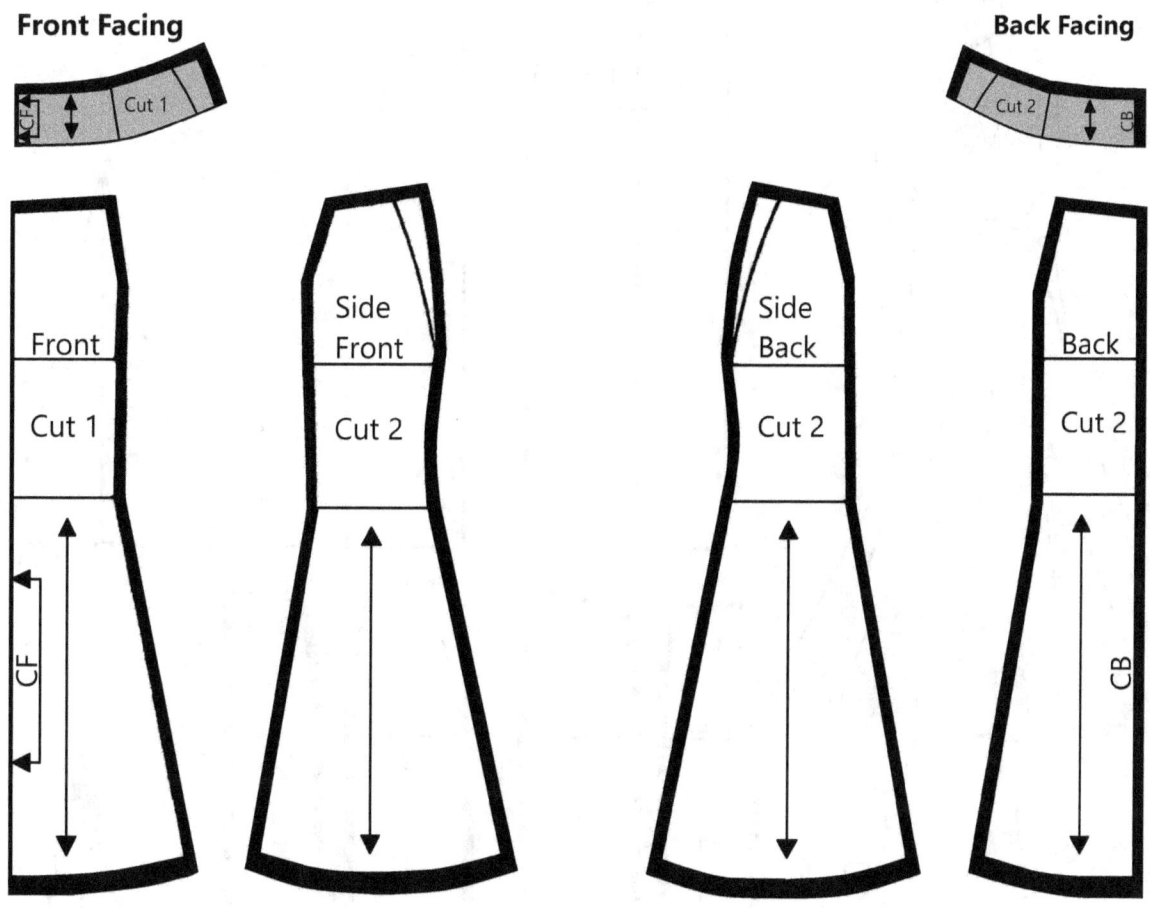

Iron fusible interfacing on the waist facing. Overlock the skirt side and centre back seams. With right sides together, pin the front and side front skirt panels, starting at the waist and bottom edge first, then the middle section. Stitch in place. Repeat the same for the back and side back panels. Pin and stitch the centre back seam up to the marked zipper opening. Insert a zipper of your choice in the centre back seam. Pin and stitch the skirt back and front side seams, right sides together. Press the seams open. Neaten the facing side seams. Pin and stitch the facing side seams, right sides together. Neaten the facing bottom edge. Attach the facing to the waistline. Trim, grade, and clip the waist seam allowances. Press the seam allowances towards the facing. From the right side of the garment, understitch the facing to the seam allowances. Turn the facing to the inside of the garment and press the waistline. Turn the facing ends under and slipstitch it to the zipper tape. Attach a hook and eye above the zipper. Slipstitch the facing side seam allowances to the skirt side seam allowances. Sew the hem and press the garment.

FLARED SKIRTS

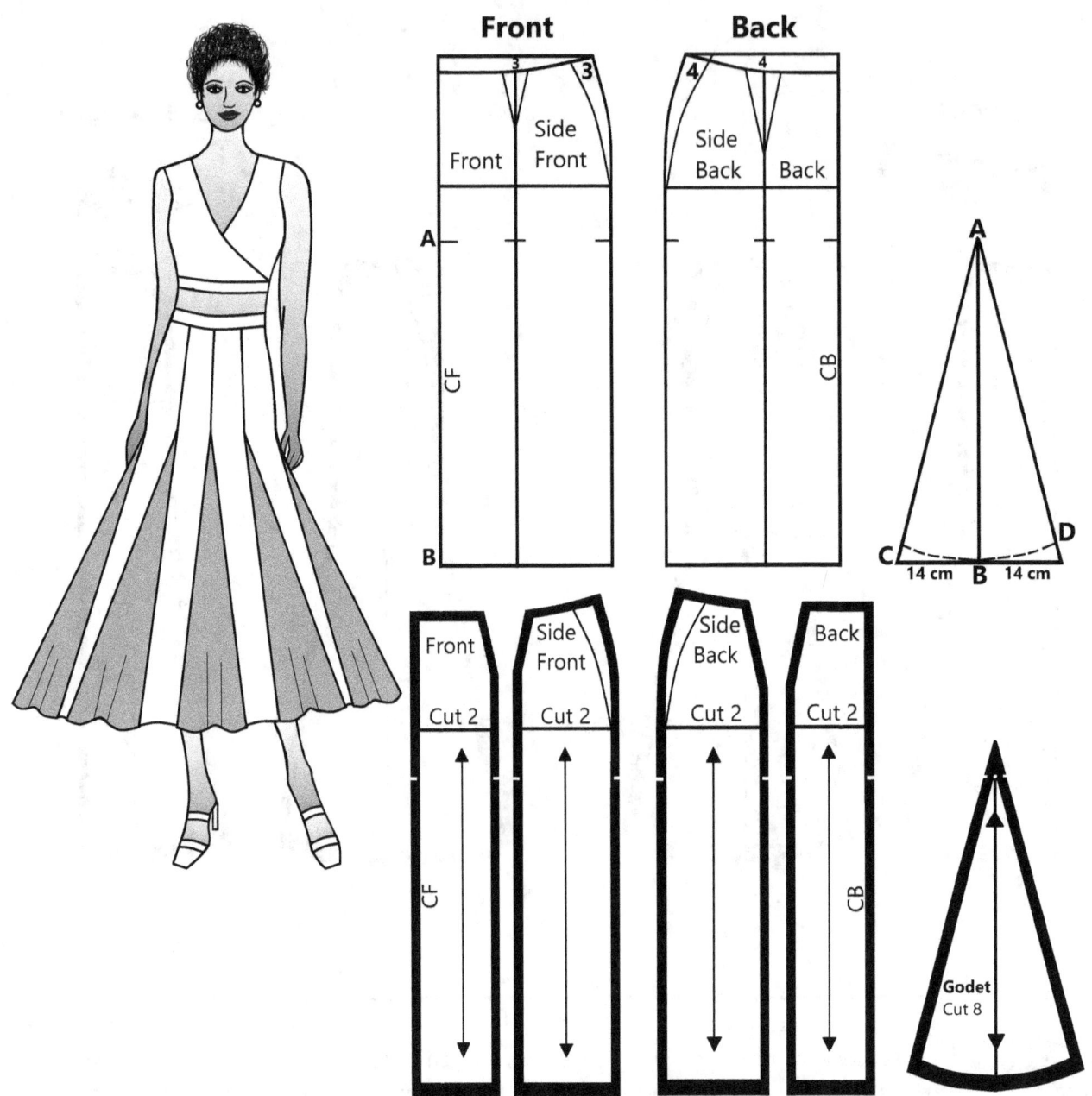

SKIRT WITH GODETS

Skirt: Trace the basic skirt block and draw the panels on the front and back as illustrated. Mark the desired height of the godets on each panel. Trace the panels off.

Godets:

A-B: Godet length.

B-C: Half the desired godet width. An amount of **14 cm (5 ½ in)** was used for this example.

A-D: The same length as **A** to **B**. Draw a curved hemline as illustrated. Repeat for the opposite side. Add grain lines, notches, hem, and seam allowances to all pattern pieces.

INSERTING IN-SEAM GODETS

1. Mark the desired length of the godets on the skirt panels. Overlock the seams of the skirt panels and the sides of the godets. With right sides together, using a **1.5 cm (⅝ in)** seam allowance, pin and stitch the skirt panels up to the marked notches. Press the seams open.
2. Mark match points on the godets. Pin a godet to one seam, right sides together, matching notches up. Start stitching from the top of the godet match points, down to the hemline.

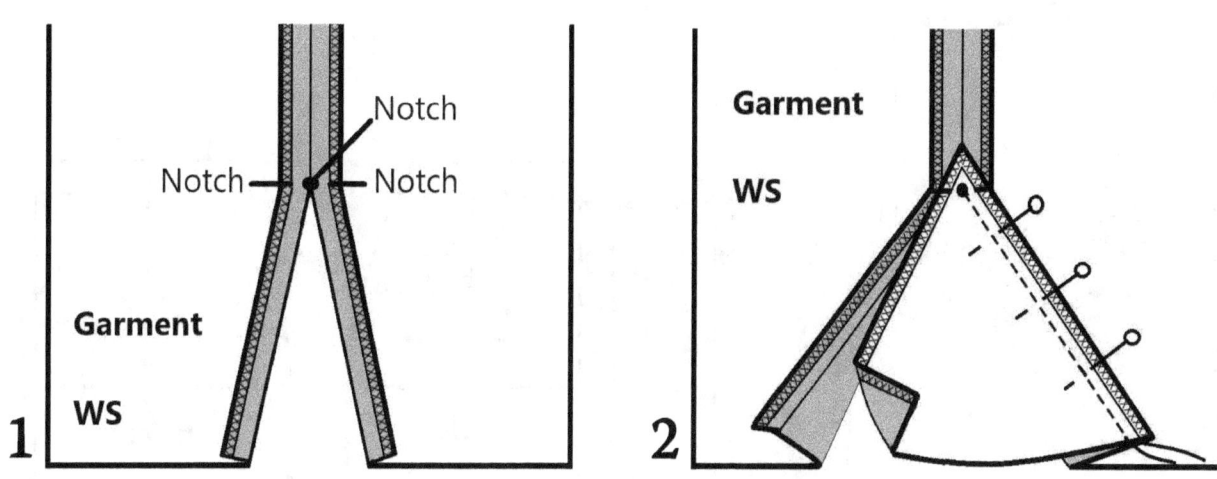

3. With right sides together, pin and stitch the godet to the other seam, matching notches up. Repeat the same sewing instructions for the remaining godets.
4. Press the godets and seams in the same direction as illustrated below.

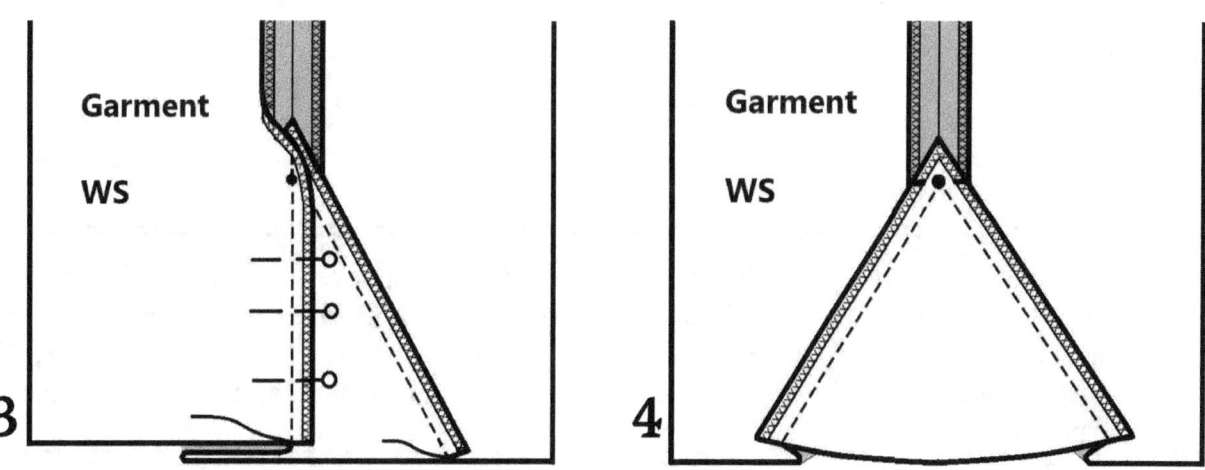

~ 175 ~

SKIRTS

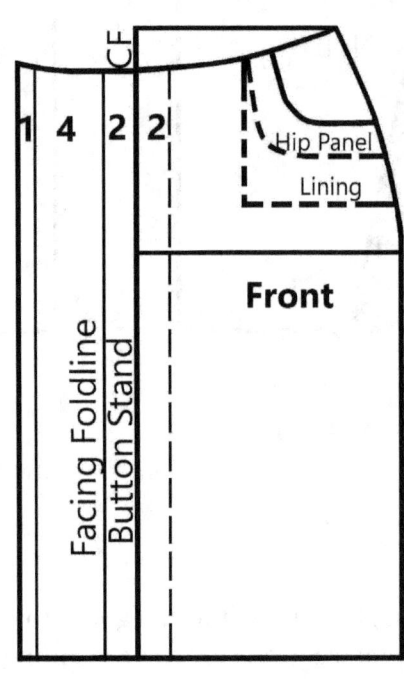
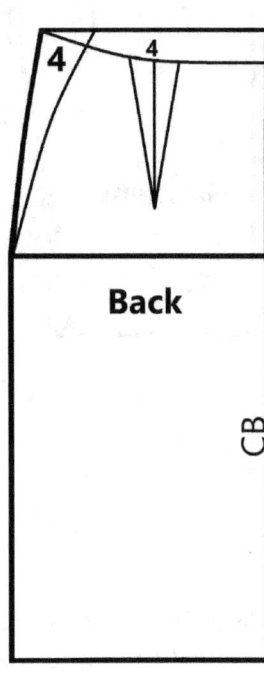

 Draft the basic skirt without the front dart and draw the pockets as illustrated. Add **2 cm** (**¾ in**) to the centre front for the button stand and **5 cm** (**2 in**) for the facing. Trace the hip panel and pocket lining patterns off. Trace the skirt pattern off. Measure the waistline and draw a waistband. Add grain lines, notches, hem, and seam allowances to all pattern pieces.

SKIRTS

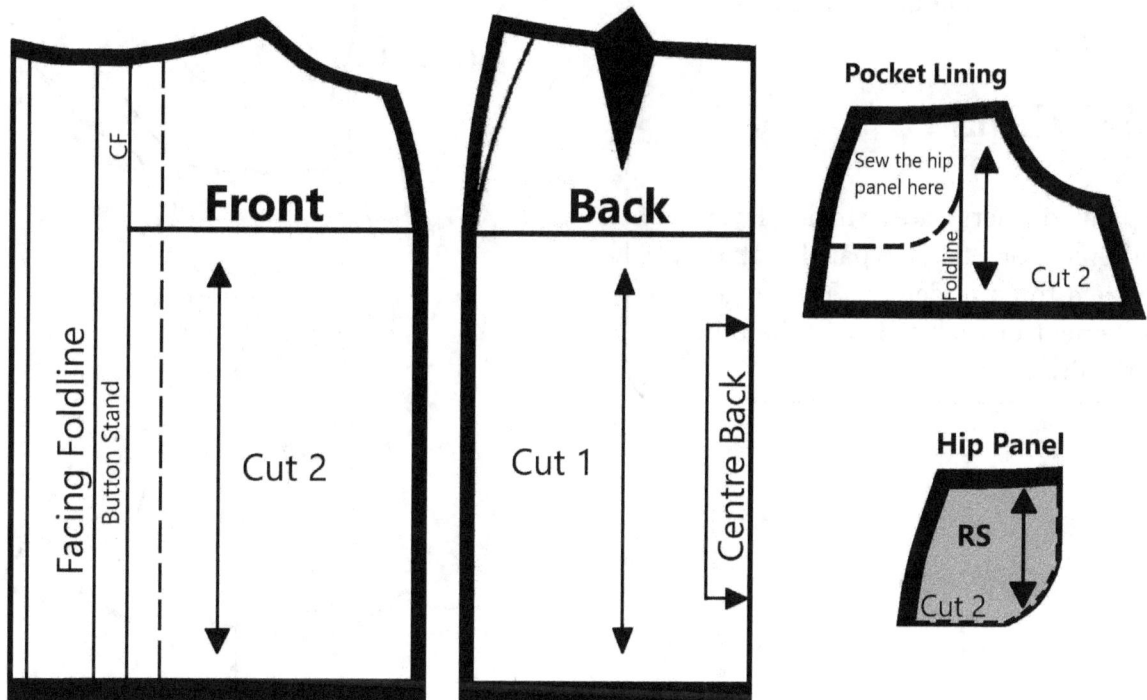

 Follow the sewing instructions for the Jeans front pockets on page **209**. Complete the remaining sections of the skirt. Press the garment.

SKIRTS

TIERS

Tiers are rows of fabric that are attached, or separate fabric layers that are attached to an underlay. The width of each tier may be **1 ½** to **2** times more than the previous tier. The amounts used depend largely on the amount of fullness that is required.

SEPARATED TIERS

Separated tiers are single layers of gathered or flared panels that are stitched to an underlay. The length and placement of each tier must be outlined in the draft.

SKIRT WITH GATHERED TIERS

Trace the basic skirt without the darts. Add a desired amount to the sides for flare. Decide on the skirt and yoke length. Divide the sections below the hip into two equal parts and rule a line across. Measure **5 cm** (**2 in**) up from this line. Mark the stitching and placement lines for the first and second tiers. Trace the yoke and underlay off. Repeat the same for the back pattern. Draw a rectangle using the first tier length and a quarter of the hip measurement times **1 ½** or **2** for the width. In the example below the first tier width is **¼** of the hip times **2** and the second tier width is **¼** of the hip times **2.5**. Repeat the same for the back.

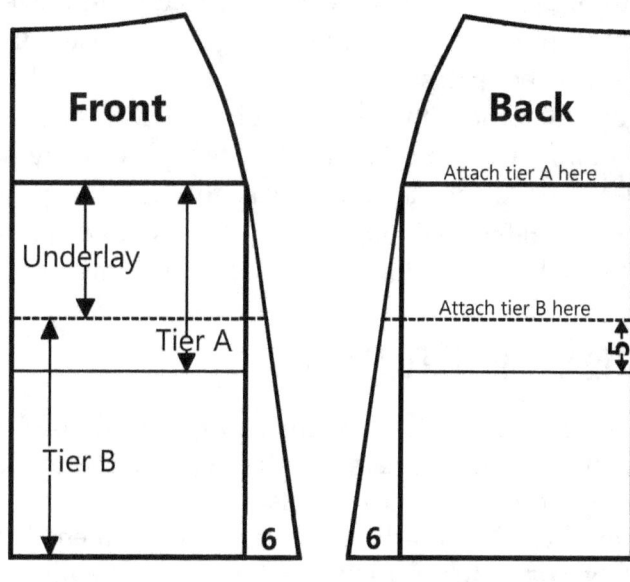

Front
Underlay
Tier A
Tier B
6
Back
Attach tier A here
Attach tier B here
5
6

CF
Front Yoke
Cut 1
Back Yoke
Cut 2
CB
CF
Front
Underlay
Cut 1
Back
Underlay
Cut 1
CB
Gather
CF
Tier A
1/4 Hip x 2
Cut 1
Gather
Tier A
1/4 Hip x 2
Cut 1
CB
Gather
CF
Tier B
1/4 Hip x 2.5
Cut 1
Gather
Tier B
1/4 Hip x 2.5
Cut 1
CB

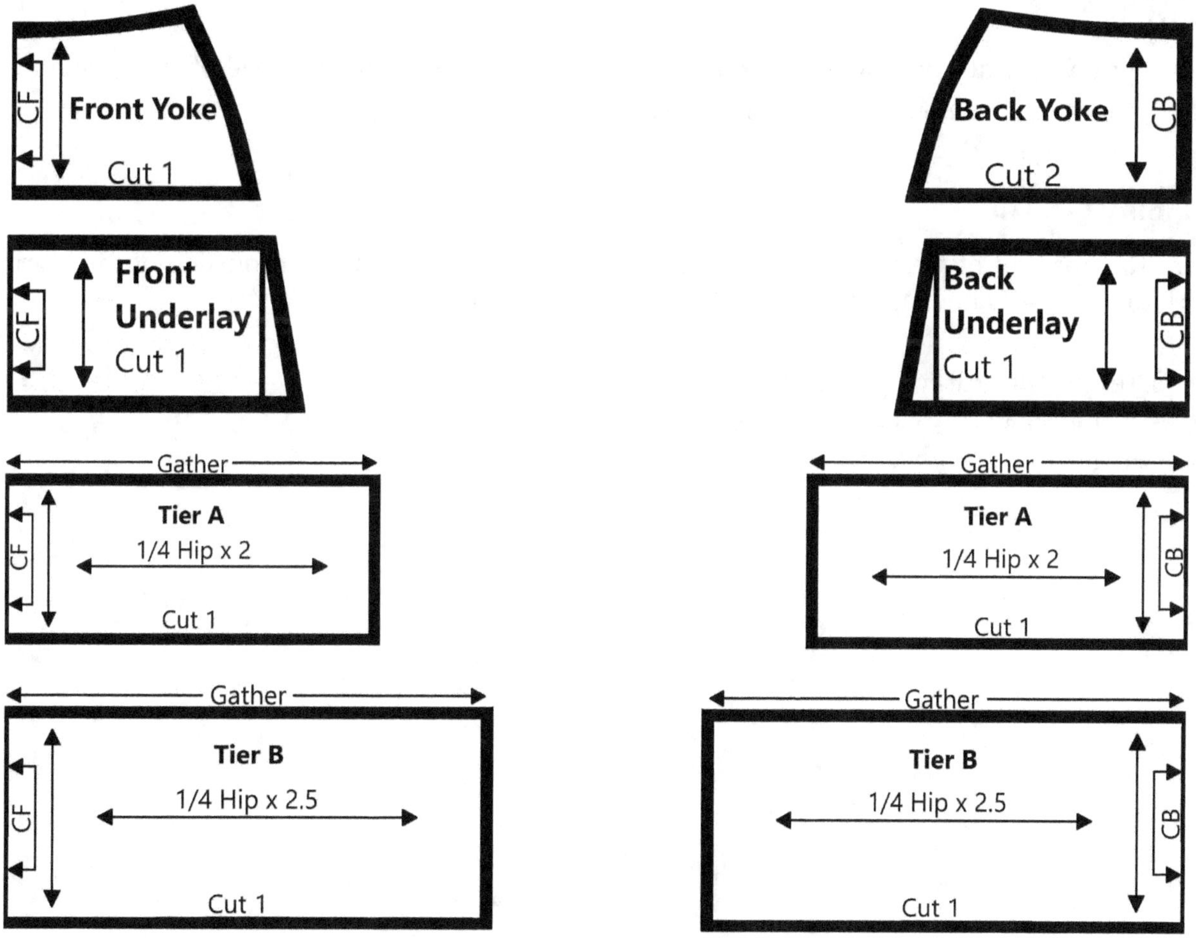

PLEATS

Pleats are formed when the fabric is folded onto itself. It can be found on a variety of garments and you will most often see them on skirts. Pleats are a way of adding extra fullness to a garment. They can be pressed or un-pressed pleats. The amount of fabric used for pleats depends largely on the silhouette required. Pleats can be folded in different styles, but the most commonly used pleats are the **box pleat, knife pleat,** and **inverted pleat.** The **accordion pleat** is best made by a commercial pleater. A pleat has 3 layers which consist of an **outer layer, middle,** and **inner layer.** Pleats may be full depth (the same amount of fold inside and outside), or shallow pleats where the inner folds are not touching.

SUITABLE FABRIC FOR PLEATS

Most light to medium-weight fabric can be used to make pleats. Decide whether your pleated garment will be laundered or dry-cleaned before choosing the fabric for the garment. Laundering can remove some pleats unless you are willing to reform them while pressing the garment. Other alternatives are to have your garment or fabric **professionally pleated**, or each fold can be **edgestitched** from the top to the hemline. The pleat can also be **topstitched** up to the required length, for example from the waist, down to the hip.

PLEAT SIZE

The depth and width of a pleat depend on personal preference and the style of the garment. The same applies to the amount of fullness required in a garment.

MARKING PLEATS

Mark the position of pleats on your pattern. Place the pattern on the wrong side of the fabric and mark the pleat fold lines and placement lines with one of the following methods:

- Dressmaker's carbon paper and tracing wheel
- Cutting small snips into the fabric
- Making marks with fabric pencils or chalk

PLEATS

BOX PLEAT

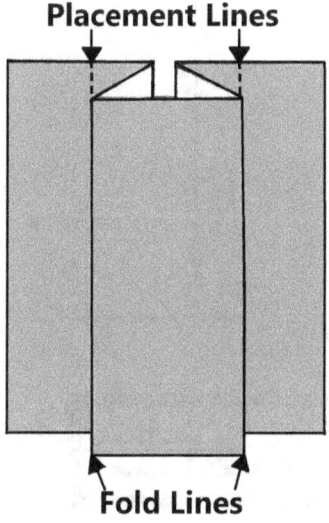

INVERTED PLEATS

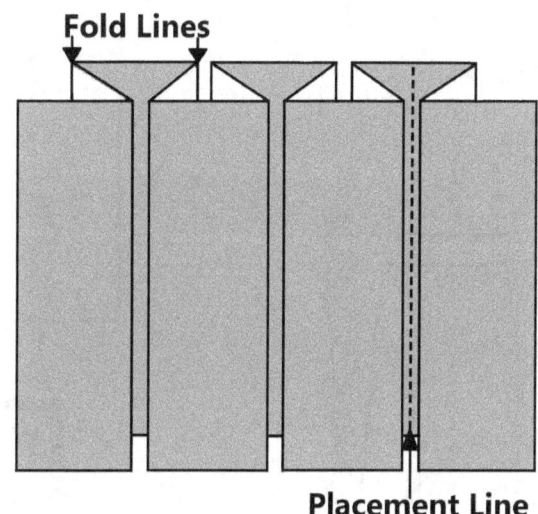

KNIFE PLEATS

ACCORDION PLEATS

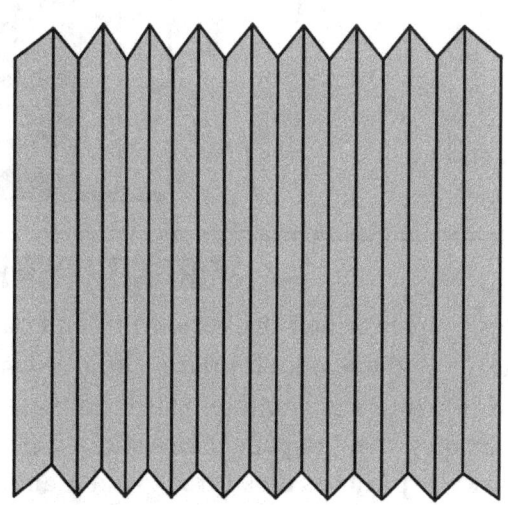

PLEATED SKIRTS

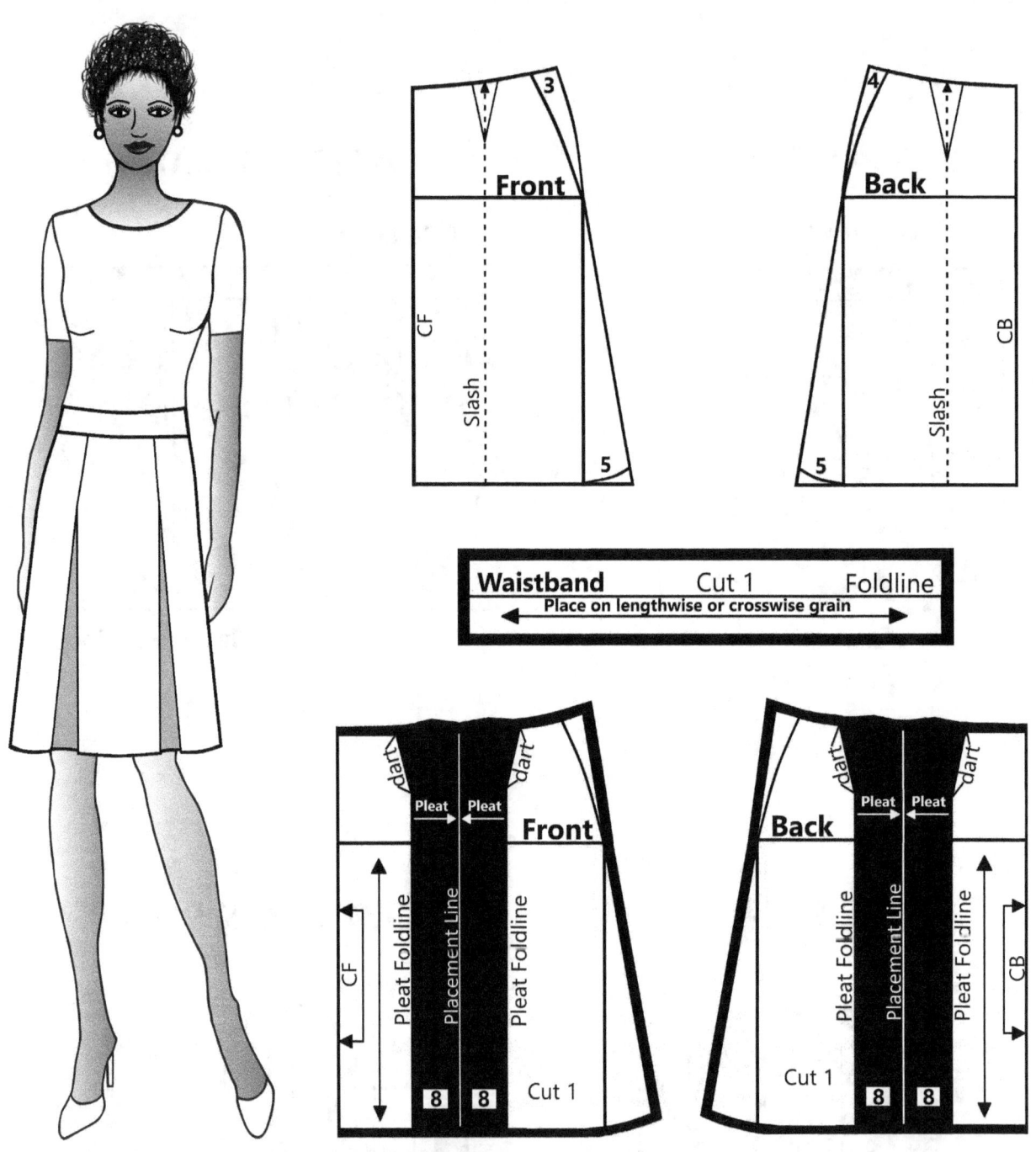

SKIRT WITH TWO FRONT AND BACK INVERTED PLEATS

Trace half the basic front and back skirt block with the darts. Add a desired amount to the sides for flare. Rule a slash line from the waist through the centre of the dart and down to the hemline. Slash the pattern and space the front and side front **16 cm (6 ¼ in)** apart on a sheet of paper. Use sticky tape to secure them in place. Repeat for the back pattern. Mark the pleats as illustrated. Add grain lines, notches, hem, and seam allowances.

PLEATED SKIRTS

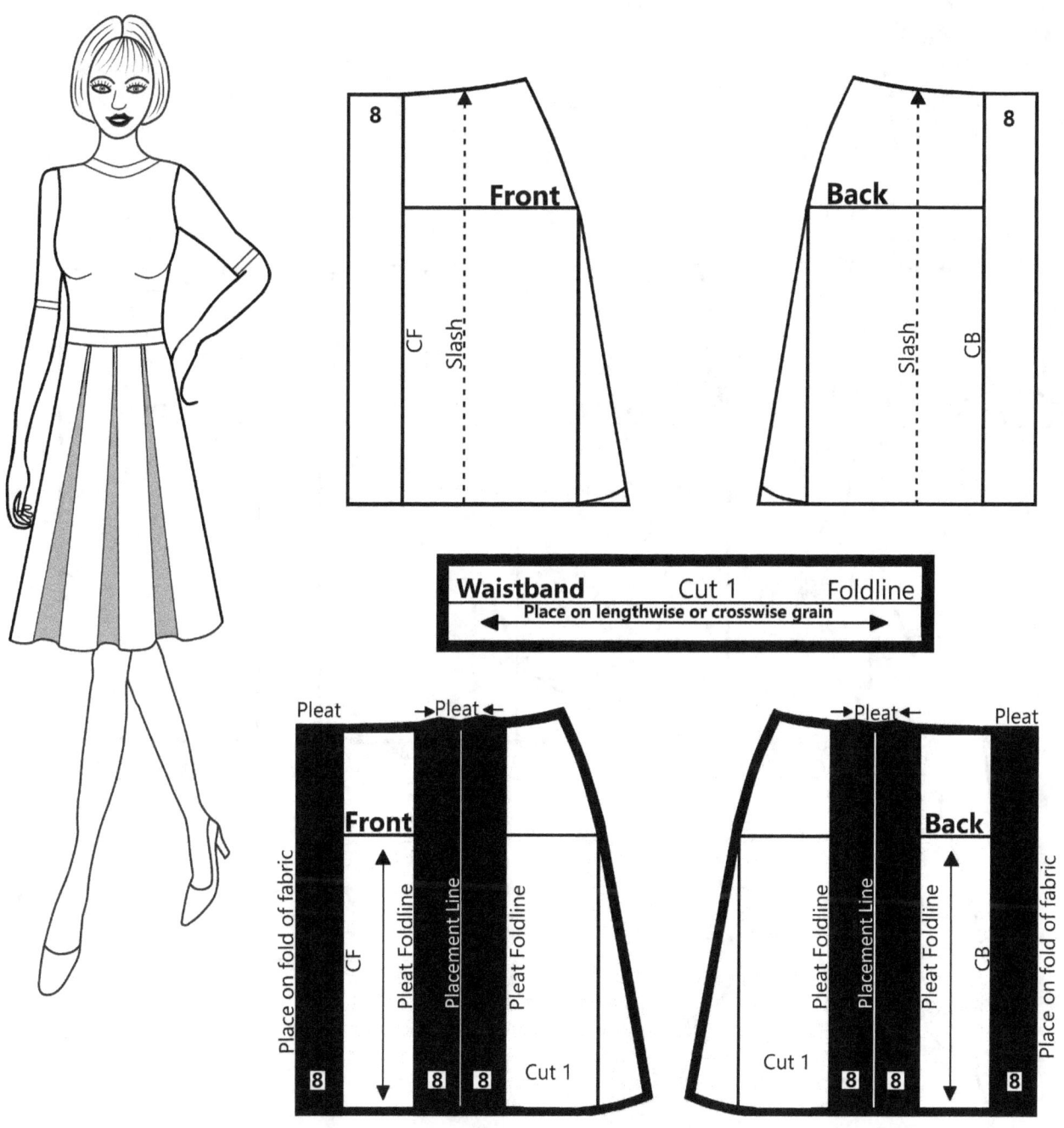

SKIRT WITH THREE FRONT AND BACK INVERTED PLEATS

Trace half the basic front and back skirt block without the darts. Add a desired amount to the side for flare. Mark a slash line from the centre of the front and back waistline. Add **8 cm (3 ⅛ in)** at the centre front and centre back for a pleat. Slash the pattern and space the front and side front **16 cm (6 ¼ in)** apart on a sheet of paper. Secure them in place with sticky tape. Repeat for the back pattern. Mark the pleats as illustrated. Add grain lines, notches, hem, and seam allowances.

ASYMMETRICAL PLEATED SKIRT

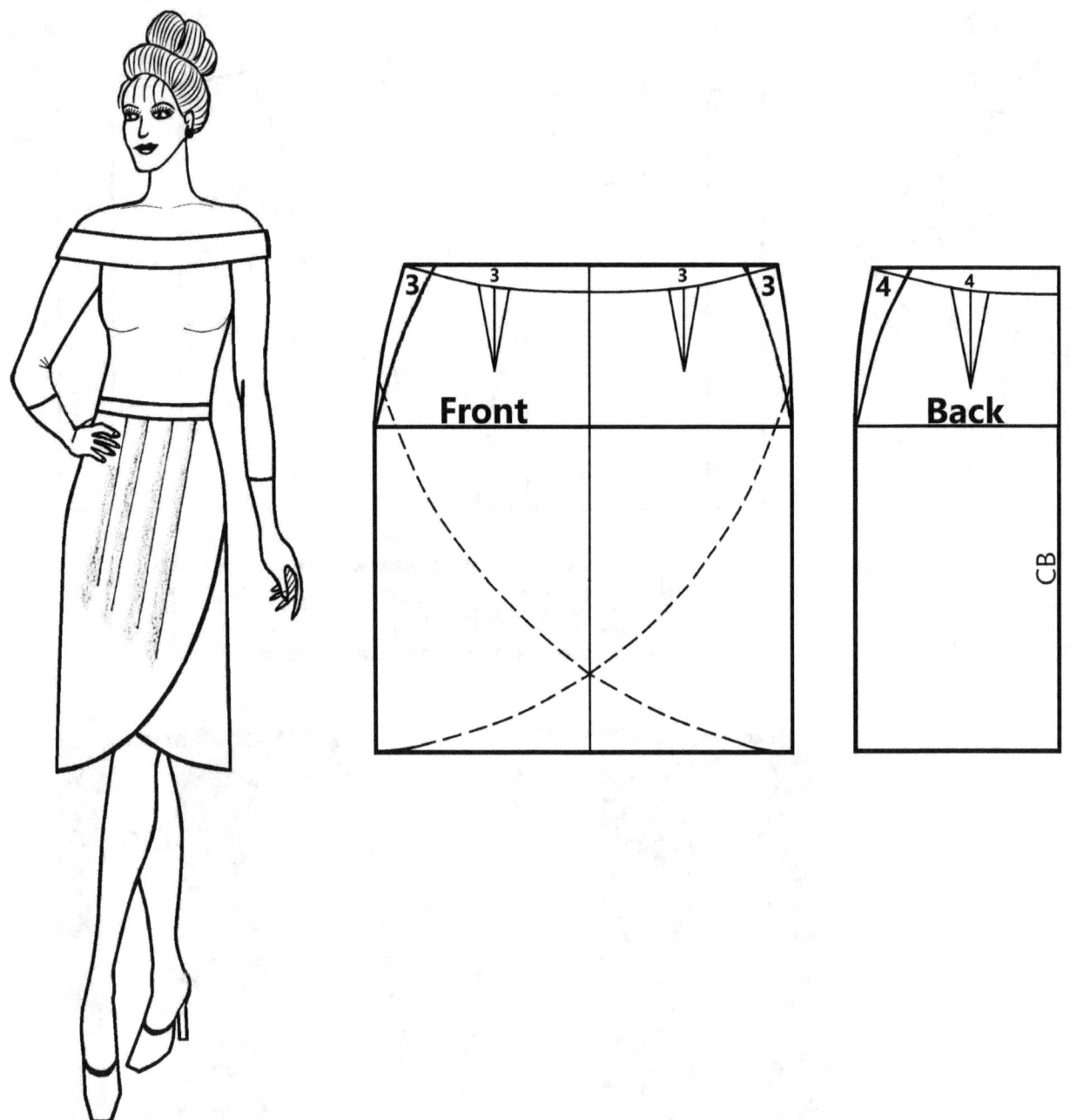

Draft the basic skirt on the fold of a sheet of paper. Trace the lines through. Open the sheet and draw the style lines as illustrated. Trace the right front panel without the darts and left the front panel with the darts. Draw slash lines on the right front panel as illustrated. Slash the lines up to the hemline and spread them to a desired amount on a a sheet of paper for pleated drapes. Fold the pleats in place on the pattern and secure them with pins. Add the hem and seam allowances before cutting the pattern out. Measure the waist and draw a waistband.

ASYMMETRICAL PLEATED SKIRT

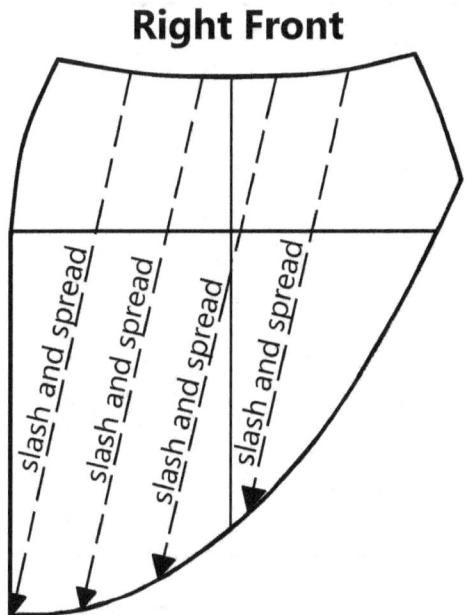
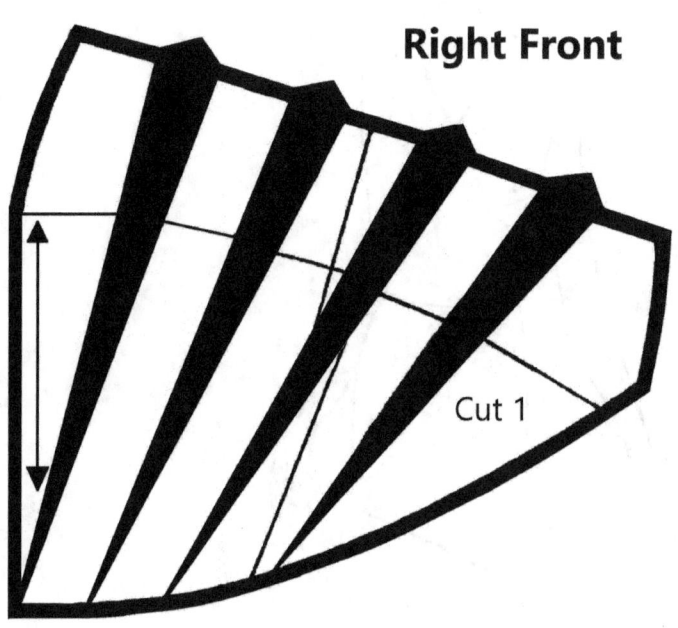
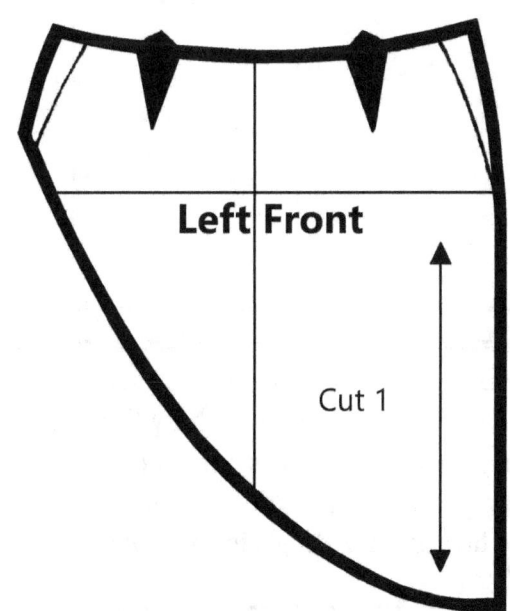
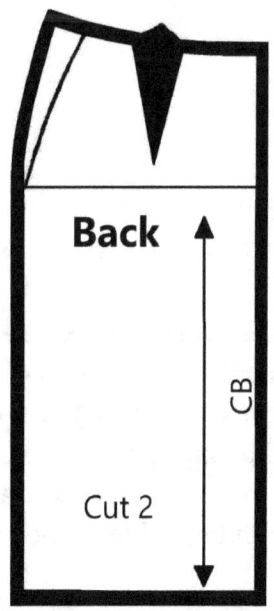

ASYMMETRICAL SKIRT VARIATION

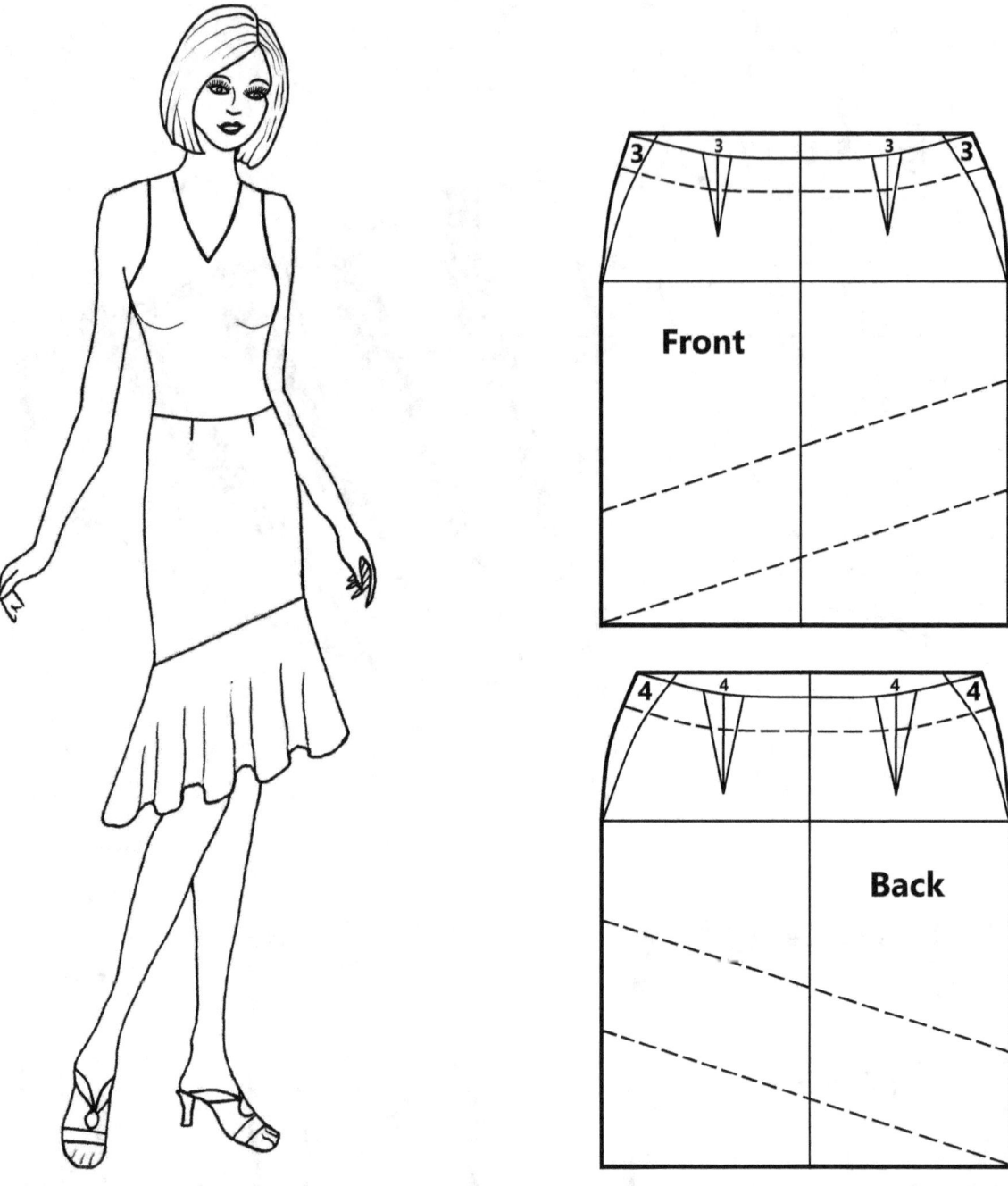

Draft the basic skirt on the fold of a sheet of paper. Lower the waistline if desired. Trace the lines through with a tracing wheel. Open the sheet of paper and draw the flounce in at the desired height as illustrated. Trace the front and back skirt sections off. Slash the flounce pattern and open the sections approximately **5 cm** (**2 in**) wide on a sheet of paper. Secure the sections with tape. Blend the curves. Trace facing off. Add grain lines, notches, hem, and seam allowances.

ASYMMETRICAL SKIRT VARIATION

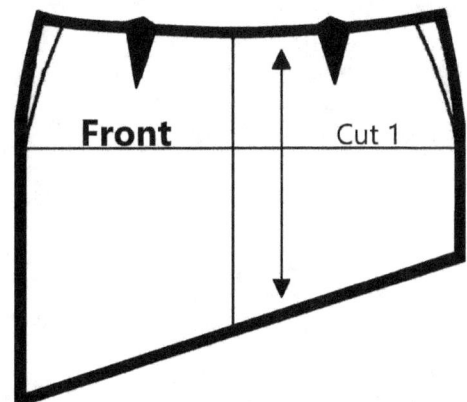 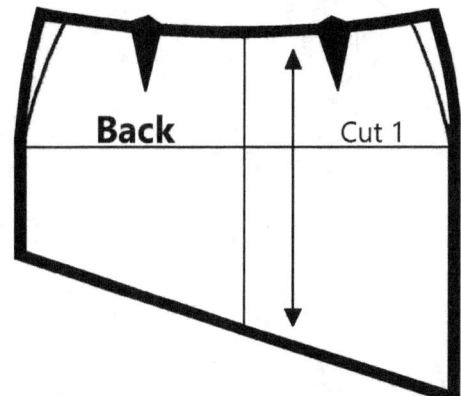

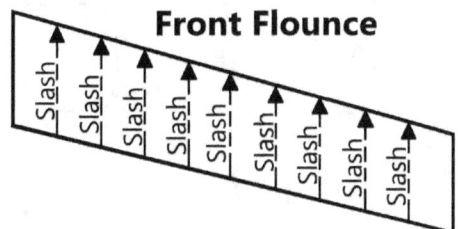 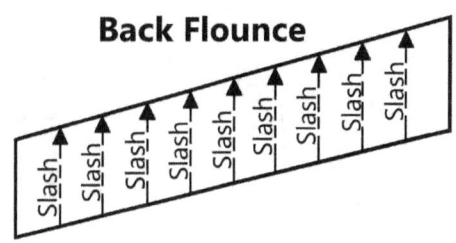

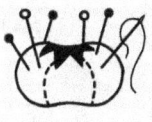 Mark the wrong side of the fabric with tailor's chalk. Place all the pattern pieces on the **right** side of the fabric. Pin and cut all the sections out. Sew all the darts on the skirt panels and the lining if the skirt is to be lined. Overlock the side seams of the skirt and flounce panels. Pin and sew the front flounce to the skirt front. Repeat for the back skirt panel. Neaten the seams. With right sides together, pin and sew one side of the skirt from the marked zipper opening, down to the hemline. Stitch a zipper of your choice in the side seam. Pin and sew the other side seam of the skirt, right sides together. Apply interfacing to the facing pieces. Neaten the facing side seams, pin and sew them together. Press the seams open. Pin and sew the facing to the waistline, right sides together. Trim, grade, and clip the seam allowances. Turn the facing to the inside of the garment and press the waistline. Understitch the facing to the seam allowances. Turn the facing ends under and slipstitch it to the zipper tape. Complete the facing side seams as described before. Sew the hem and press the garment.

ASYMMETRICAL SKIRT VARIATION

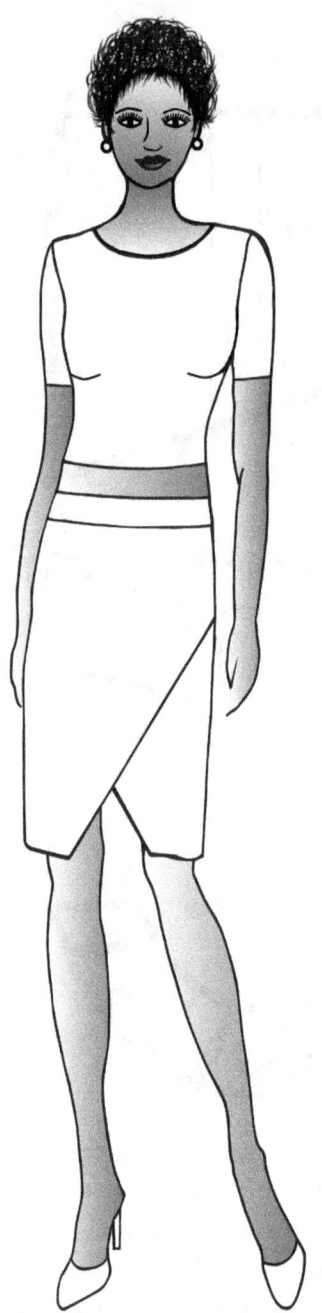
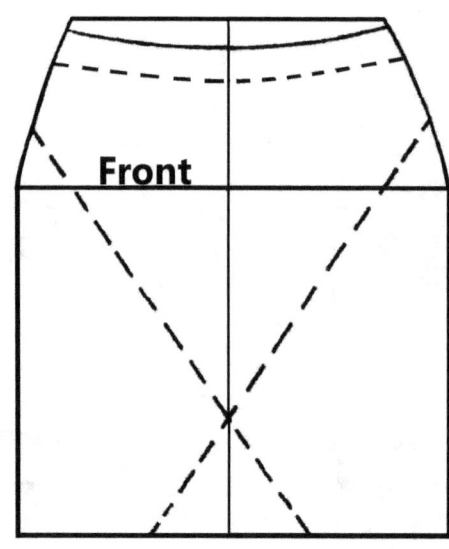
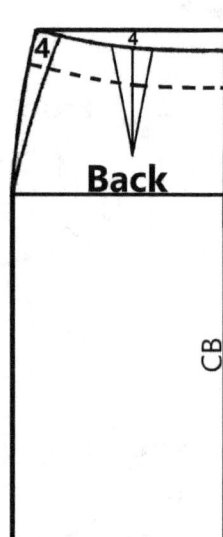

Draft the basic skirt on the fold of a sheet of paper. Trace the lines through. Open the sheet and draw the style lines as illustrated. Lower the waistline if desired. Measure the waistline and draw a waistband longer than the waist measurement. Trace the skirt panels off. Add grain lines, notches, hem, and seam allowances.

ASYMMETRICAL SKIRT VARIATION

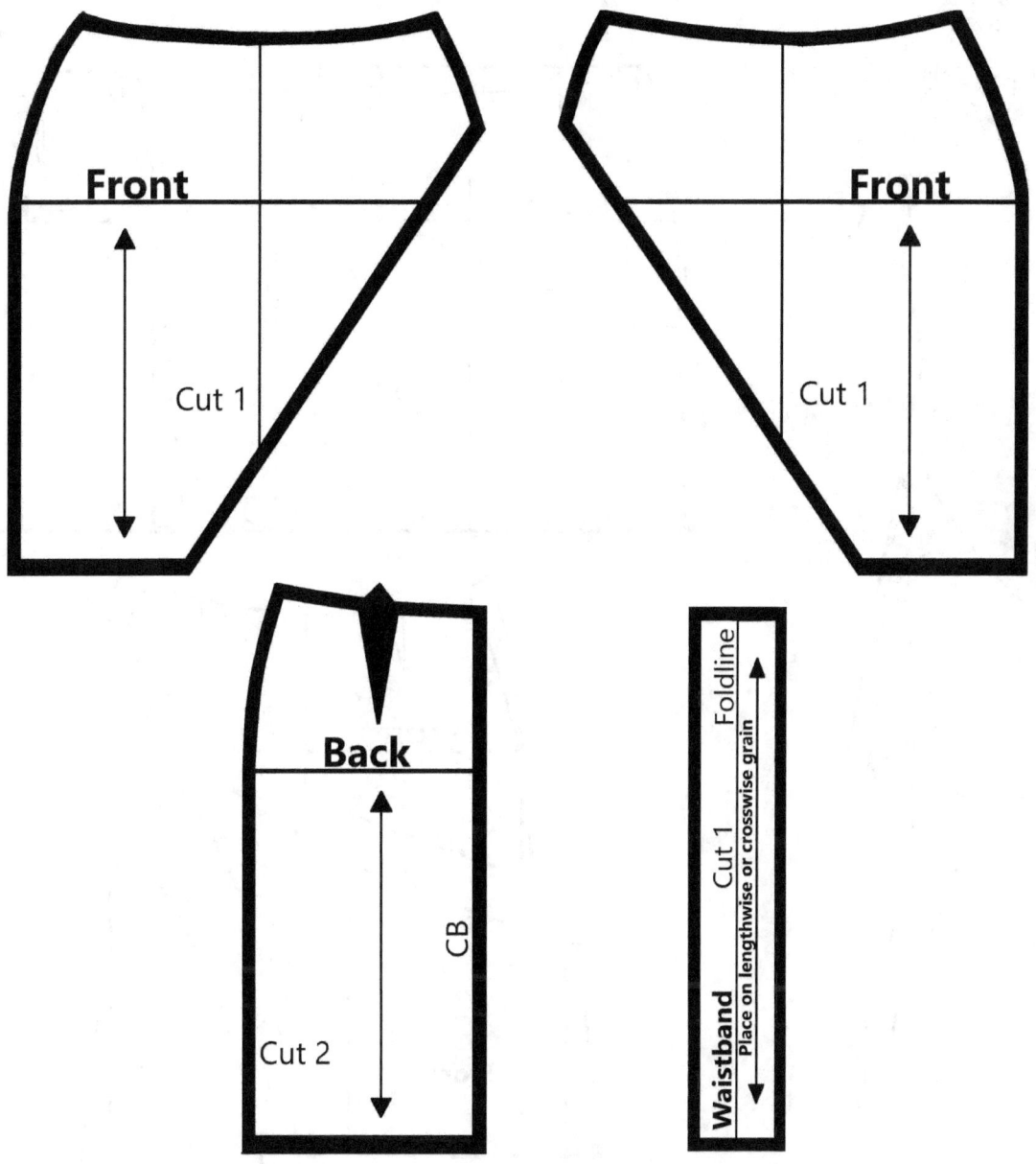

Place all the pattern pieces on the right side of the fabric and cut the panels out. Neaten the side seams with overlocking. Press the seam allowances of the long slanted edges on the skirt fronts to the inside. Stitch the long slanted edges and press. Place the right front panel on the left front and machine baste the short side seams to each long side seam. Baste the front waste edges of the skirt together. Sew the darts on the back panels and press. Sew the centre back seam, right sides together, up to the marked zipper opening. Sew a zipper in the centre back seam. Sew the front and back skirt panels, right sides together. Press the side seams open. Complete the skirt with a waistband. Sew the hem.

ASYMMETRICAL SKIRT VARIATION

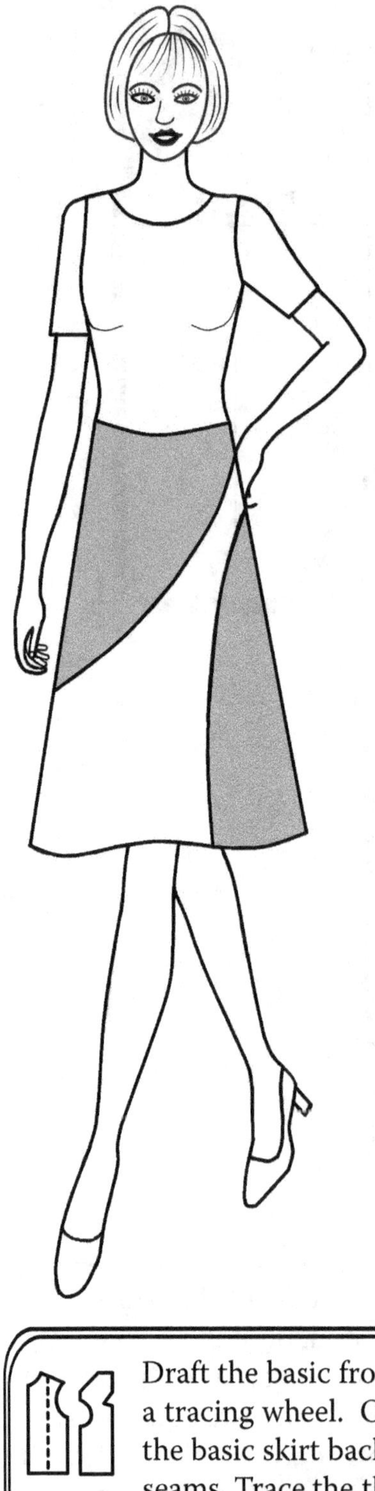

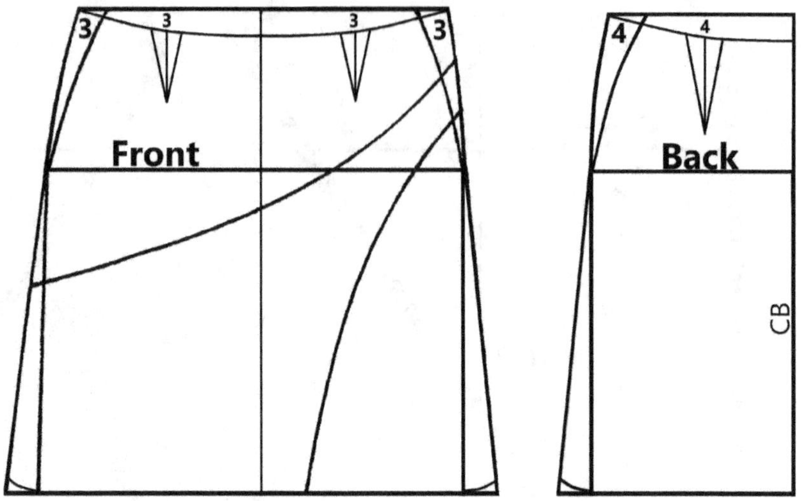

 Draft the basic front skirt on the fold of a sheet of paper. Trace the lines through with a tracing wheel. Open the sheet of paper and draw all the style lines as illustrated. Draft the basic skirt back separately. Add a desired amount of flare to the front and back side seams. Trace the three front pattern sections off separately. Fold the darts close on the first front panel and secure it with sticky tape. Trace the skirt back off. Trace front and back facings off. Add grain lines, notches, hem, and seam allowances to all the pattern pieces.

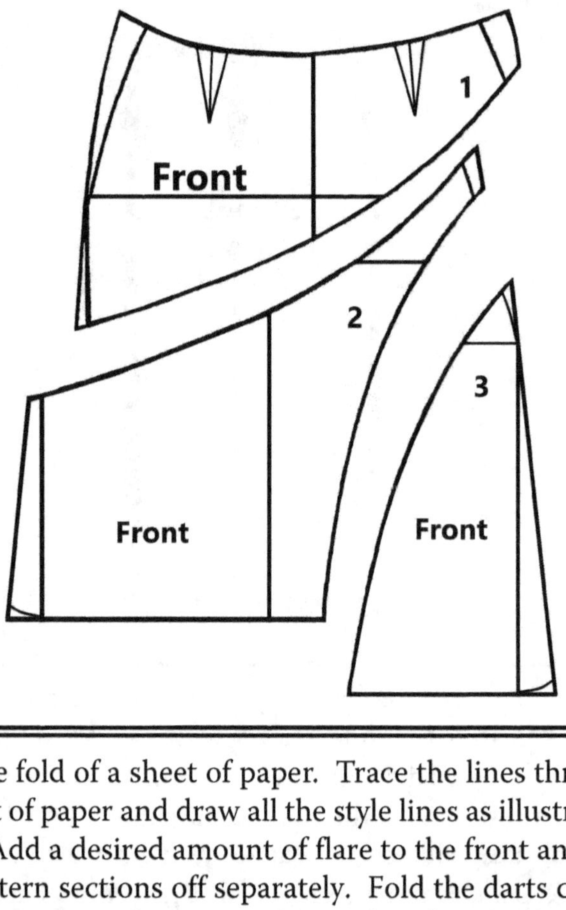

ASYMMETRICAL SKIRT VARIATION

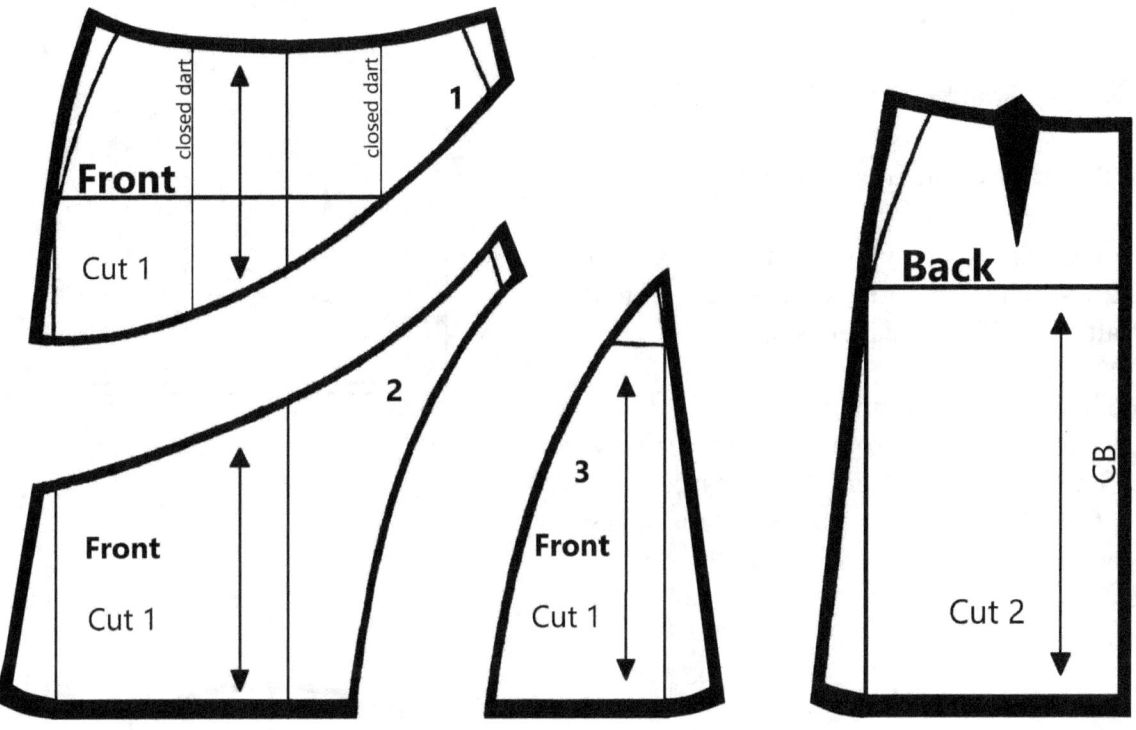

The skirt can be cut on the bias for a softer draping effect. Lay all the pattern pieces on the right side of the fabric. Mark the wrong side of the fabric with tailor's chalk before removing the pattern pieces from the fabric. Pin the two lower front sections, right sides together, and sew a narrow single seam. Pin and sew the top front panel to the lower skirt panel. Neaten the raw edges. With right sides together, pin and sew the back panels up to the marked zipper opening. Sew the zipper in the centre back seam. Neaten the front and back side seams with overlocking. With right sides together, pin and sew the front and back side seams. Finish the waist off with facing. Trim, grade, and clip the seam allowances. Understitch the facing and complete the waist as described on page 173. Turn the hem up and hand stitch it in place. Press the garment.

CIRCULAR SKIRTS

FULL-CIRCLE SKIRT

The equation for determining the radius of this skirt is as follows:

The waist measurement minus **3 cm (1 ¼ in)**, then multiplied by **1/6** or divided by **6**.
A waist measurement of **75 cm (29 ½ in)** was used for this skirt. Subtract **3 cm (1 ¼ in)** and divide by **6**.
The radius measurement is **12 cm (4¾ in)**.

Fold a large sheet of paper in half and rule right angle lines longer than the skirt length. Complete the draft on the fold of paper as follows:
A-B: The radius.
A-C: The same measurement as **A-B**.
Measure the radius out from **A** and draw the waist.
B-D: The desired skirt length. Measure the skirt length from the waist line, using a tape measure. Cut two copies from the draft to complete the circle.

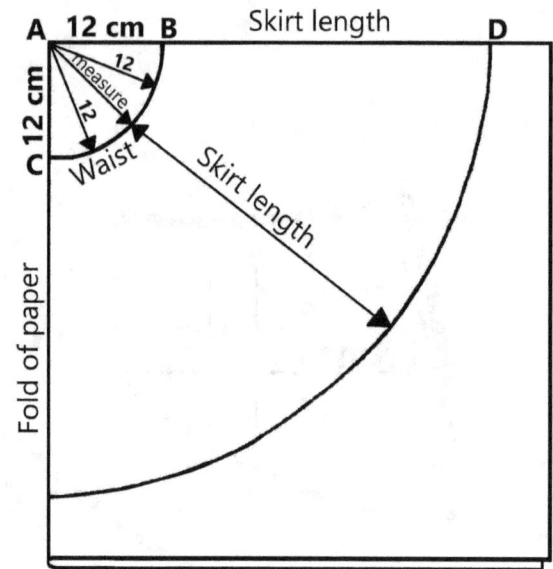

A side zipper can be inserted in the side seam, or fold the back pattern in half and cut two back panels. This will result in a centre back seam. Staystitch the waist **1.5 cm (⅝ in)** from the waist edge to prevent it from stretching out of shape. A waistband, or facing can be used to finish the waist off. Hang all circular skirts for at least **24 hours** before sewing the hem.

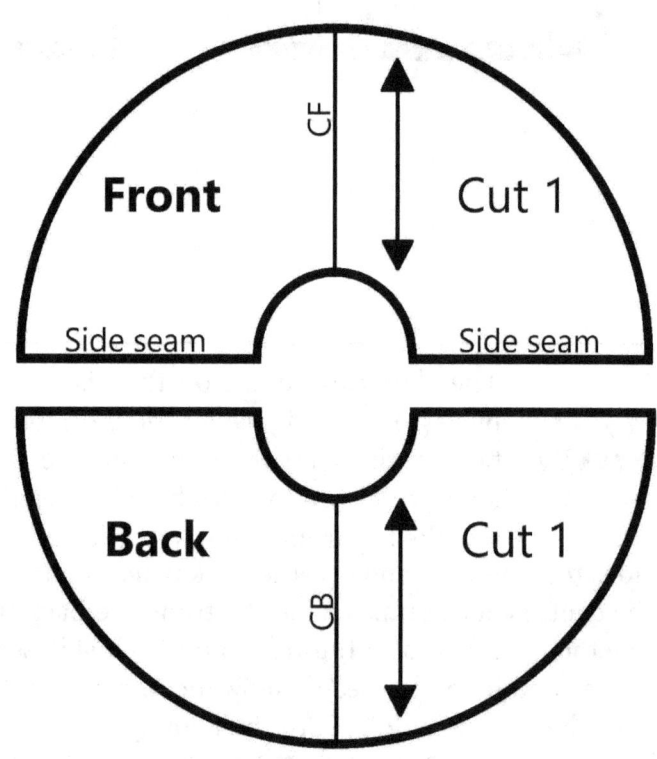

~ 192 ~

CIRCULAR SKIRTS

HALF-CIRCLE SKIRT

The equation for determining the radius of this skirt is as follows:

The waist measurement minus **3 cm (1 ¼ in)**, then multiplied by **1/3** or divided by **3**.

A waist measurement of **75 cm (29 ½ in)** was used for this skirt. Subtract **3 cm (1 ¼ in)** and divide by **3**.

The radius measurement is **24 cm (9 ½ in)**.

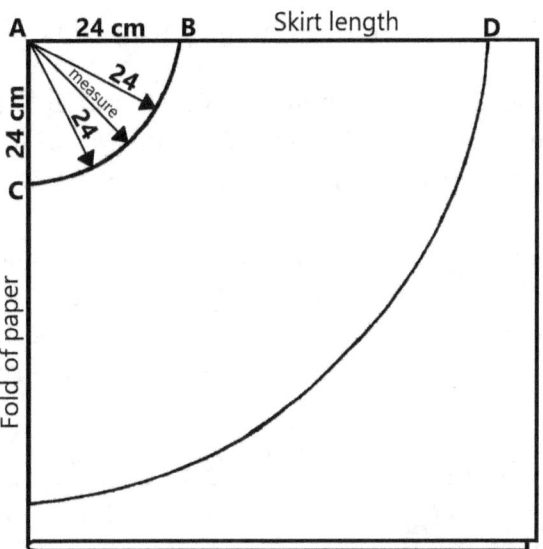

Fold a sheet of paper in half and rule right angle lines. Complete the draft on the fold of paper as described for the full circle skirt. Cut the pattern once when only one centre back seam is required or cut up the centre front of the pattern when two separate panels with side seams are required.

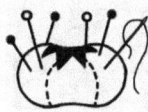 Cut the pattern once on fabric and staystitch the waist as described for the full circle skirt. The skirt will only have a centre back seam. A waistband, or facing can be used to finish the waist off.

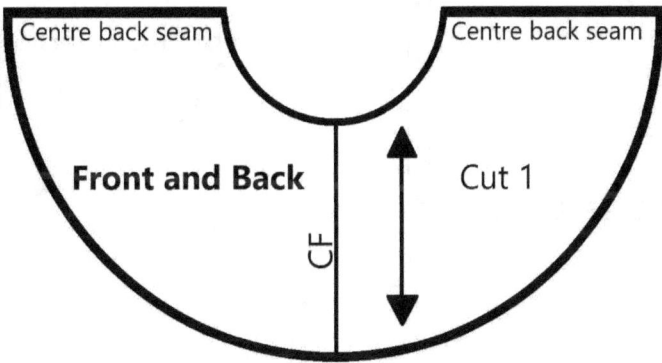

Cut the original half circle skirt pattern in half to obtain a separate front and back panel with two side seams. Cut the pattern into four equal sections when four seams are required.

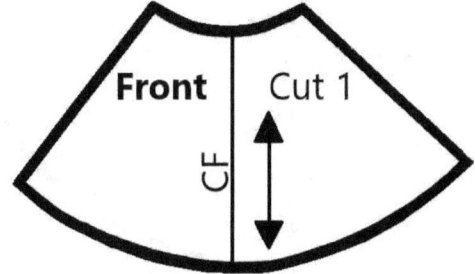 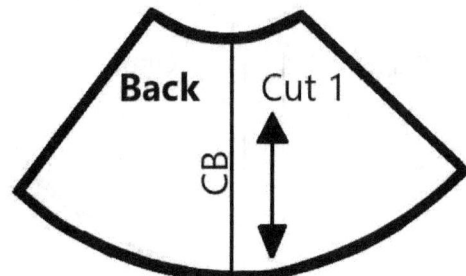

CIRCULAR SKIRTS

THREE-QUARTER CIRCLE SKIRT

The equation for determining the radius of this skirt is as follows:

The waist measurement **plus 4 cm (1 ½ in)**, then multiplied by **1/5** or divided by **5**. A waist measurement of **75 cm (29 ½ in)** was used for this skirt. Add **4 cm (1 ½ in)** and divide by **5**. The radius measurement is **15.8 cm (6 ¼ in)**.

Fold a large sheet of paper in half **twice** and complete the draft as illustrated. The result will be a full circle with a much larger waist. One-quarter section of the circle skirt must be removed. The remainder section (shaded area), can be used as is when one seam is required. Cut the pattern (shaded area) in half when two seams are required as illustrated below.

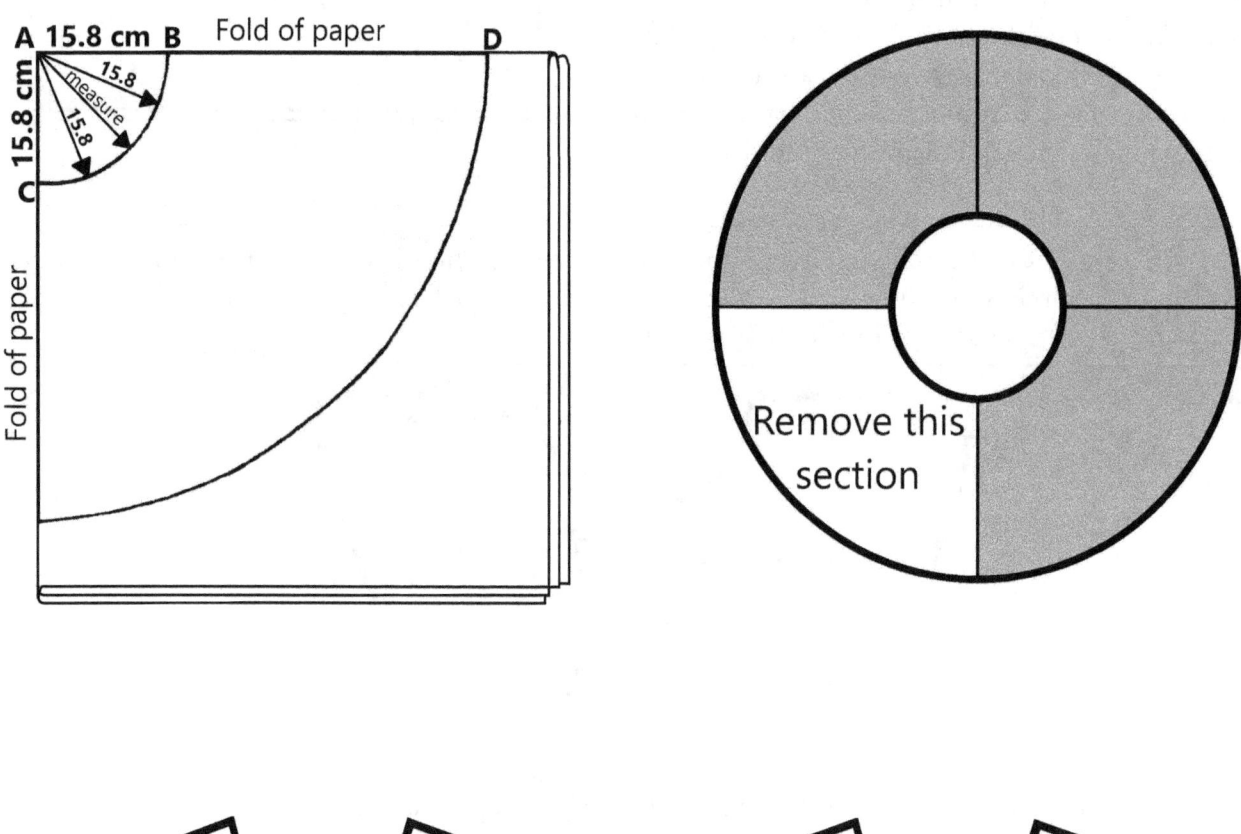

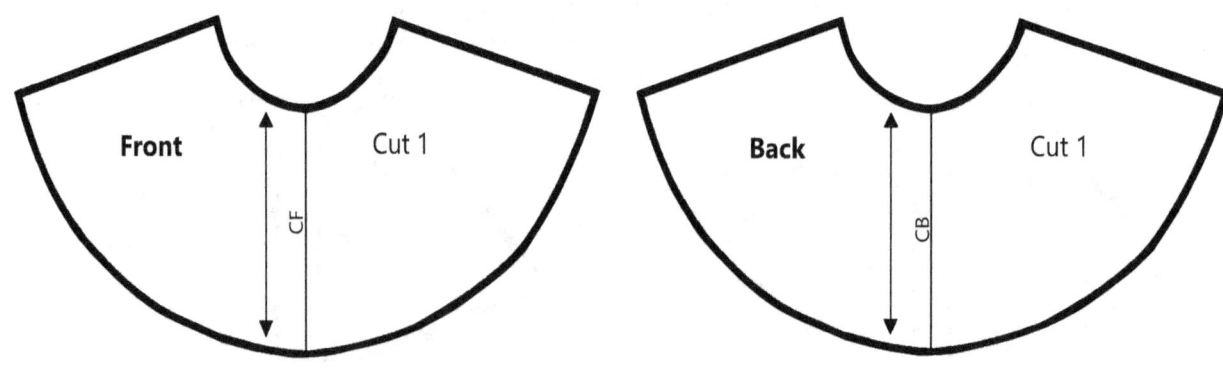

WORKING WITH BIAS FABRIC

PREPARING FABRIC FOR CUTTING

The true bias refers to the **45-degree angle** that intersects the lengthwise grain and the crosswise grain of the fabric. Both the back and the front of a garment can be cut on the bias, depending on the style of the garment and personal preference. If both front and back are cut on the bias, then the seams are sewn where the fabric has the most give. Care must be taken not to stretch the fabric out of shape while sewing.

JOINING TWO BIAS EDGES

With right sides together, pin the seam edges together, starting at the top and bottom edges first, then the section in between. Pin the seam at **4 cm (1½ in)** intervals. The fabric will be very flexible, but the length should match exactly.

JOINING A BIAS EDGE TO A STRAIGHT EDGE

Place the straight edge of the fabric on top of the bias edge. Place the bias edge face down in the machine. Feed the fabric through the machine, while holding the straight edge firmly. If the bias edge is on top, the lower straight edge will strengthen the seam and will allow you to feed the bias edge evenly through the machine.

CUTTING AND JOINING BIAS STRIPS

Strips cut on the true bias are used in a variety of ways, ranging from neckline facings, bound edges on garments, piping, ultra-thin spaghetti shoulder straps and so much more. Joining bias strips must be done on the straight grain of the fabric. Use narrow seams when joining the end of bias strips. Include **6 mm (¼ in)** seam allowance when you cut bias strips.

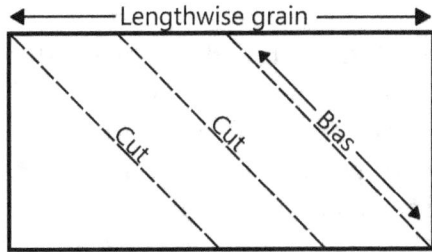

Mark parallel lines with even spacing on the true bias of the fabric.

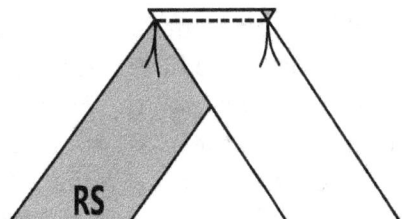

Cut two strips on the marked lines. Pin and stitch the strips right sides together.

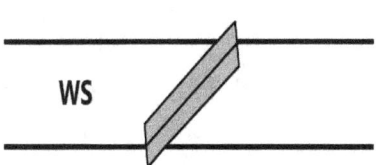

Press the **6 mm (¼ in)** seam allowance open and trim the corners.

TROUSERS

BASIC TROUSER DRAFT

Trousers produced by the following instructions are fitted in the waist and over the hips and fall straight from thigh to ankle. **A desired amount of ease can be added to the side of the waist and hip lines.** The basic trouser block is used as a base for other trouser derivatives that are illustrated in this book.

FRONT

1. **A-B:** Quarter of the waist circumference.
   A-C: Measure **18 cm (7 in)** down from the waist to the hip line.
   C-D: Quarter of the hip circumference.
   Draw a curved line from **B** to **D** with the hip curve.
   A-E: Crotch depth plus **1.5 cm (⅝ in)** ease.
2. **E-F:** One twelfth of the hip circumference minus **2 cm (¾ in)**.
   Draw a curve from **C** to **F** to complete the front crotch. Rule a line from **F** to **G** and **D**.
3. Add **3 cm (1¼ in)** to the side of the waistline for a dart, if a dart is required. Draw a curve from the **3 cm** mark to **D**. Drop **2 cm (¾ in)** from **A** and draw a new waistline as illustrated. Construct a dart in the centre of the curved waistline measuring **3 cm (1¼ in)** wide and **10 cm (4 in)** long.
   B-L: The required trouser length.
   Mark the centre of the crotch line and rule a line down to the required trouser length.
   H-I: Half the measurement of **H** to **J**.
   J-K: Half the measurement of **K** to **L** (required trouser hemline width).
   M-N: The knee position.
   Draw the inside leg seam from **F** to **K** and the side seam from **G** to **L**.

BACK

4. Repeat step one of the front trouser block.
5. **E-F:** One twelfth of the hip circumference plus **2 cm (¾ in)**.
   Draw a curve from **C** to **F**. Rule a line from **F** to **G** and **D**.
6. Measure **2 cm (¾ in)** in and **2 cm** up from **A**. Add the **2 cm (¾ in)** to the side of the waist and draw a curved line down to the hip line. Add **4 cm (1½ in)** to the side of the waistline for a dart and rule a line down to the hip line as illustrated. Rule a line from the raised centre back to the side of the waist, touching the original waistline. Rule another line from the raised centre back down to **C**. Construct a dart at a right angle and in the centre of the new waistline, measuring **4 cm (1½ in)** wide and **14 cm (5½ in)** long. Complete the trouser length as described for the front.
   K-L: The back hemline is **2 cm (¾ in)** wider than the front hemline.

Always add or subtract equal amounts to each side of each trouser leg when legline shaping is desired.

TROUSERS

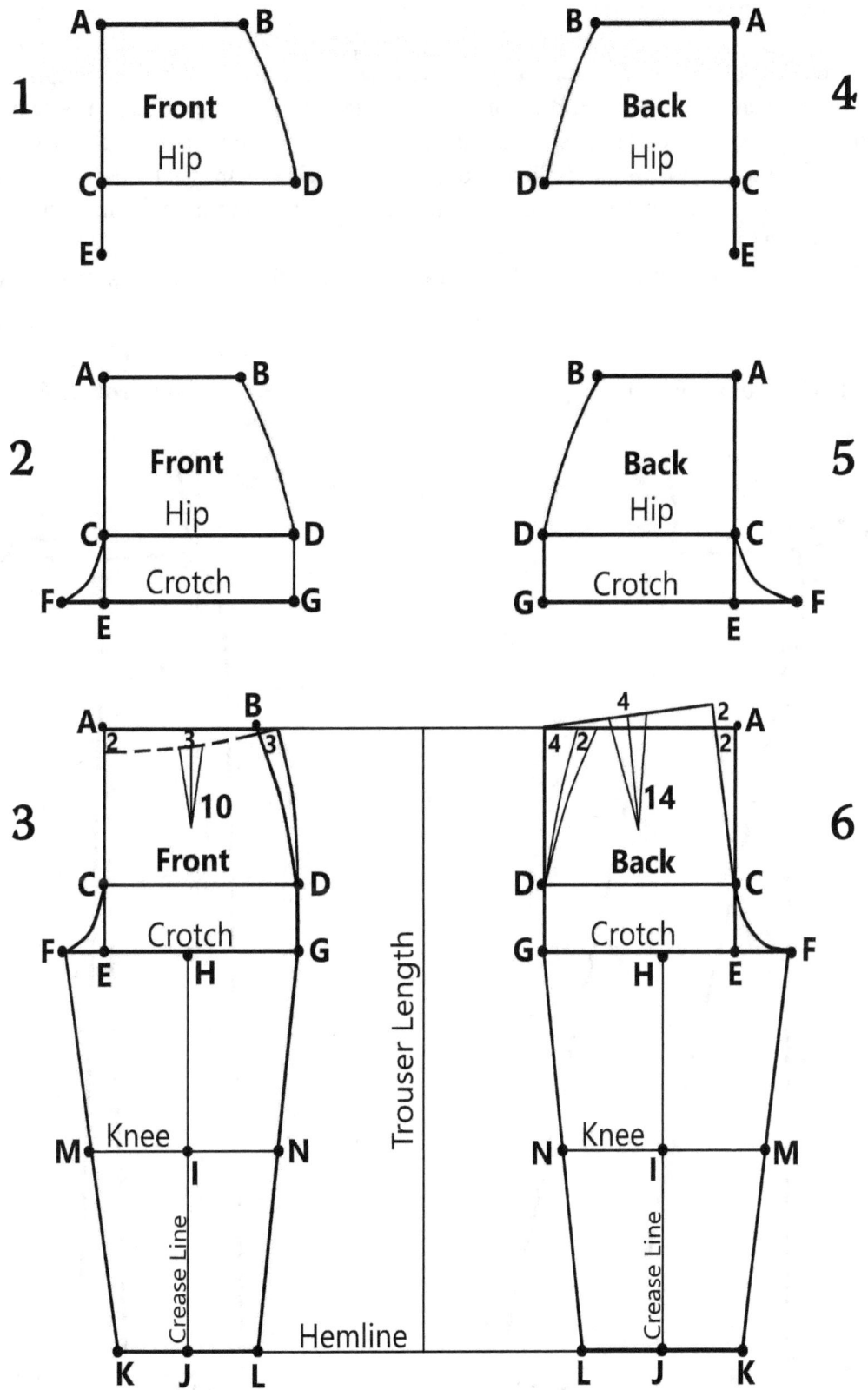

TROUSERS

FRONT

7. Draw a fly at the centre front **4 cm (1 ½ in)** wide and to the required length. Draw a fly shield **10 cm (4 in)** wide and **2 cm (¾ in)** longer than the fly. Shape the front and back trouser legs as desired, using a hip curve and a ruler. Scoop the front and back waistline when a lower waistline is desired. Always ensure that the front and back side seams are the same length. Draw a waistband or facing as described on page **167** to complete the pattern.
8. Trace the pattern pieces off and add grain lines, notches, hem, and seam allowances.

Basic Trouser Front

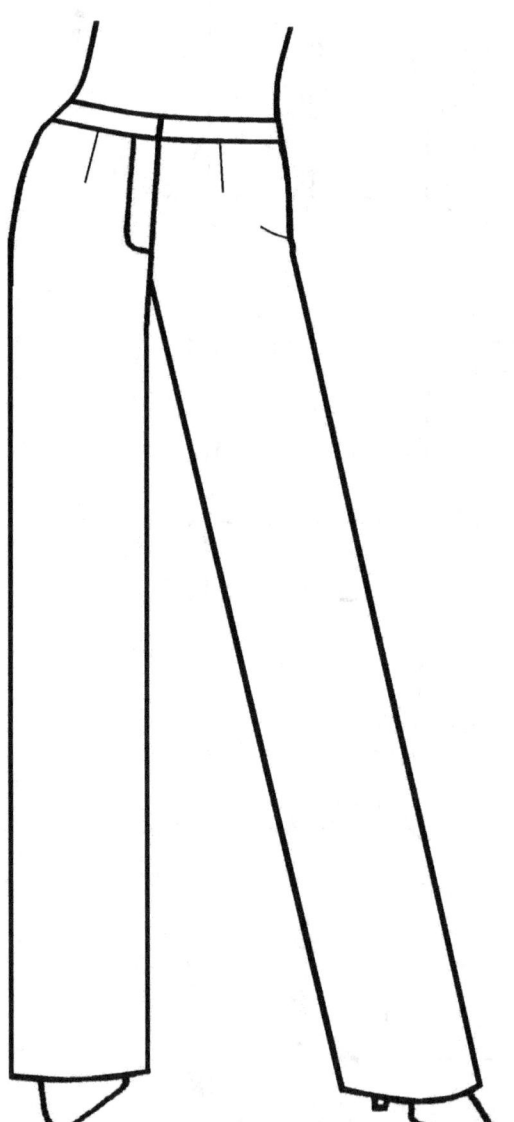

Basic Trouser Back

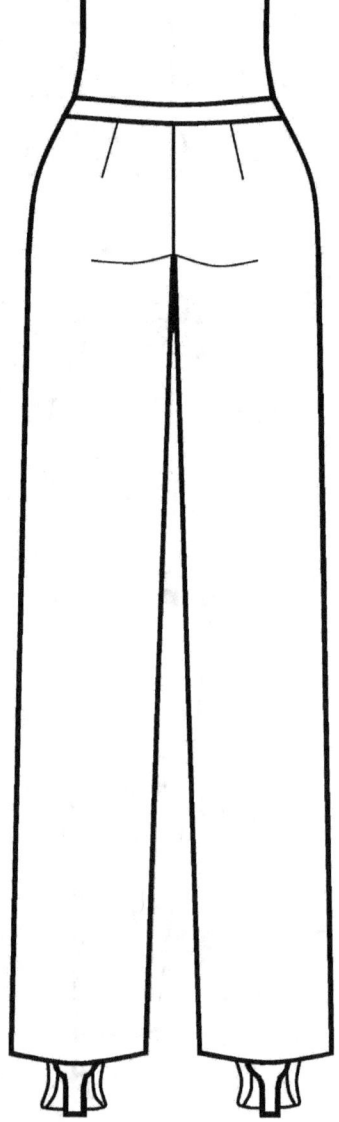

BASIC TROUSER

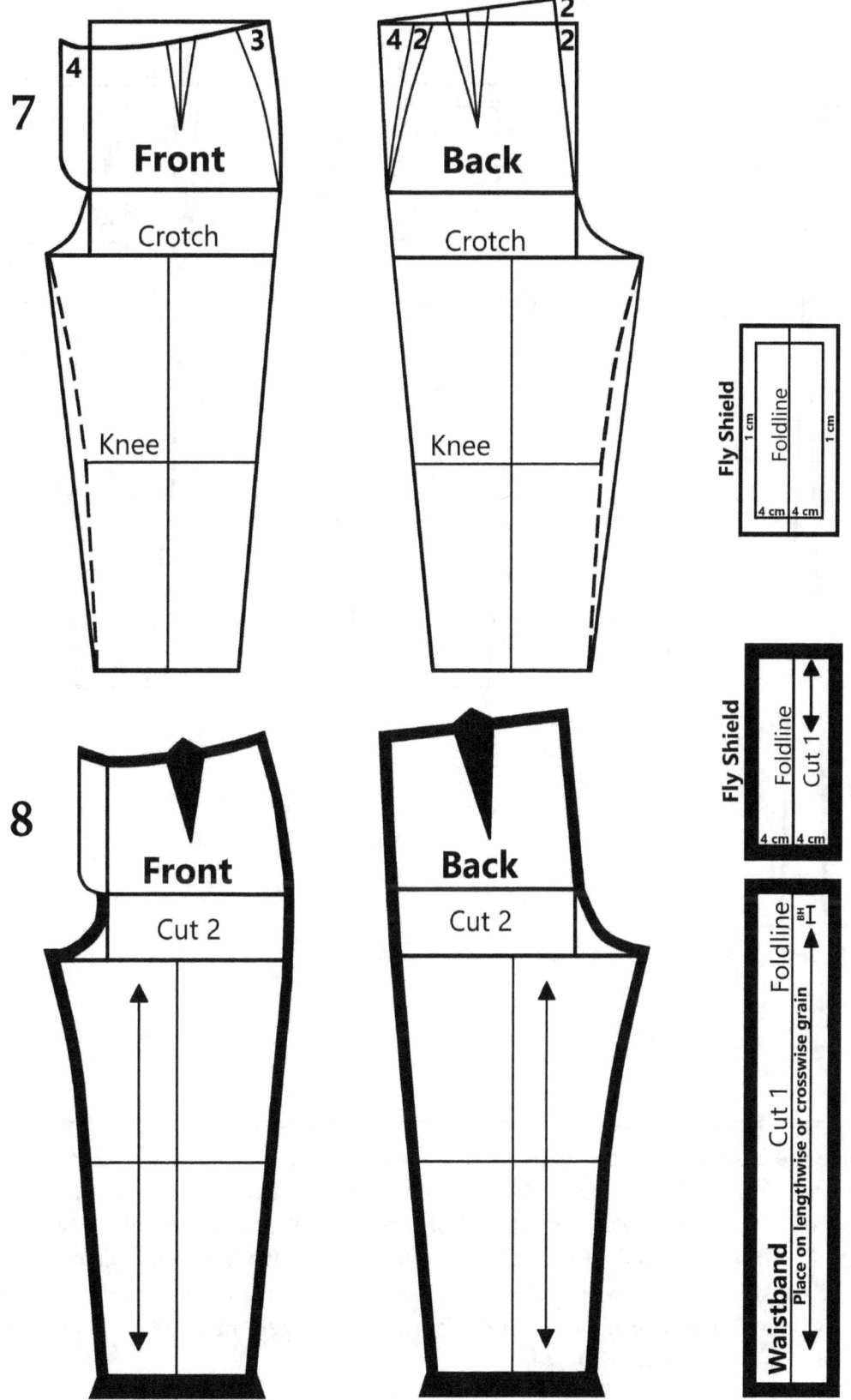

PLEATED TROUSER

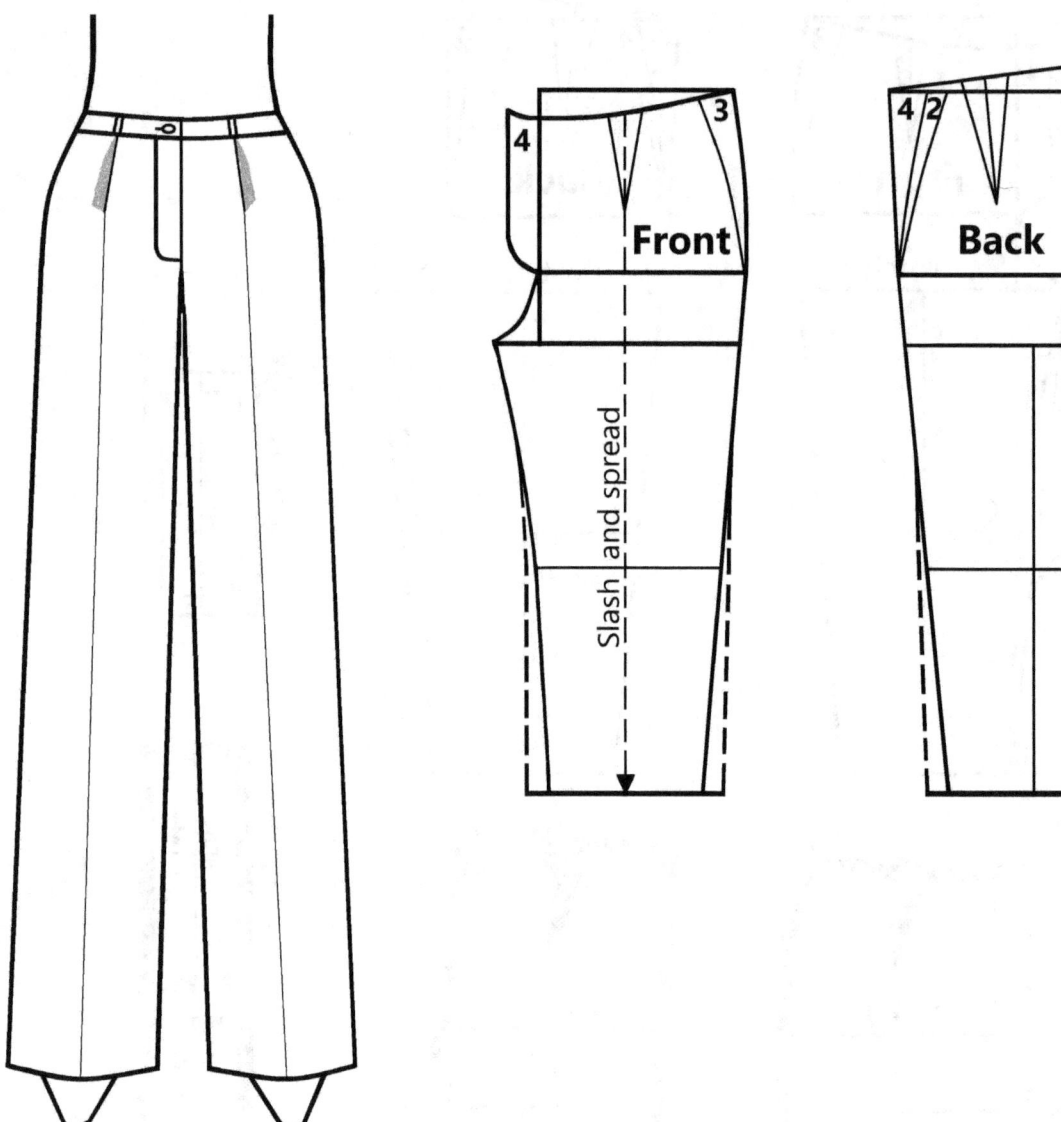

Trace the basic front and back trouser blocks. Shape the legline as desired. Slash down the front up to the arrowhead and open **2 cm** (¾ **in**) at the waistline. The dart allowance at the side, plus the amount of spread at the waistline will give a pleat depth of **2.5 cm** (**1 in**) once folded. Open the waistline further when deeper pleats are desired. Measure the waistline and draw the waistband to the desired width as described on page **167**. Draw the fly shield **10 cm** (**4 in**) wide and **2 cm** (¾ **in**) longer than the fly. Add grain lines, notches, hem, and seam allowances.

PLEATED TROUSER

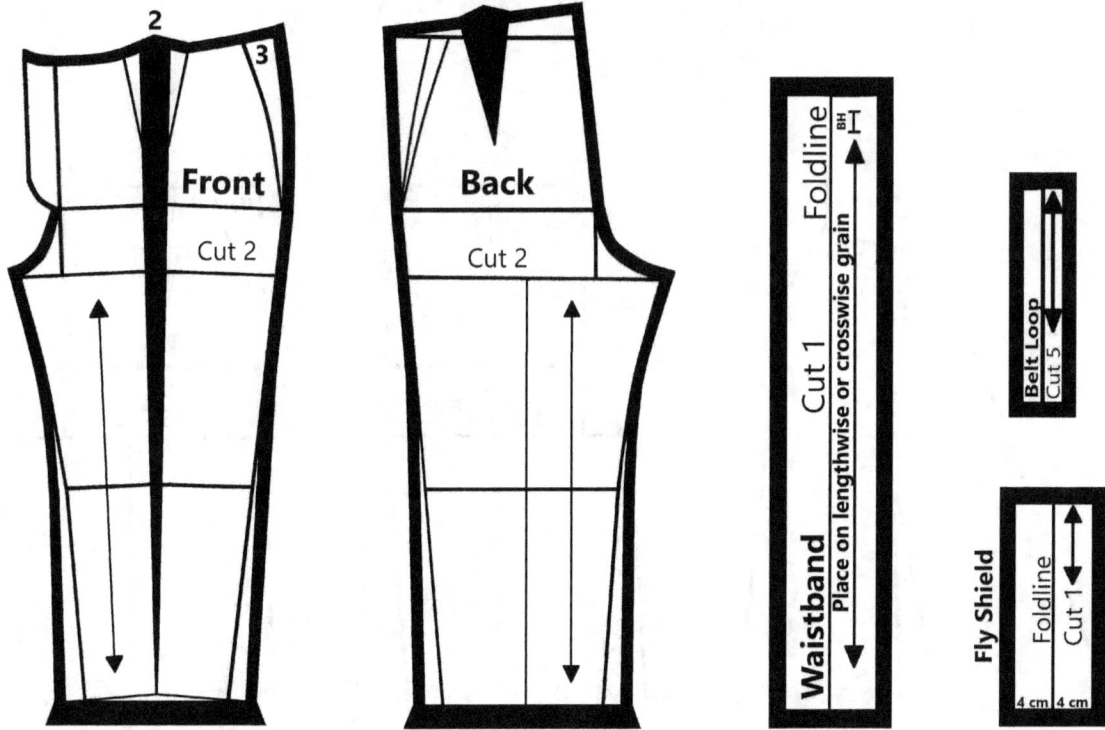

Cut the trouser panels out and trim the left front fly extension to measure **1.5 cm** (⅝ in) from the centre front. Mark the darts, pleats, and centre front line of the fly. Overlock the crotch, side, and inside leg seams of the trouser panels. Fold the pleats on the trouser front and baste in place along the top edge of the waistline. Sew the darts on the back panels. Stitch the front crotch seam from the marked zipper opening, down to about **4 cm** (1 ½ in) from the edge of the inside leg. Fold the left front edge under and move **6 mm** (¼ in) beyond the centre front seamline. Press. Place the fold next to the zipper teeth, pin, and baste in place using a zipper foot. Fold the right front fly extension along the foldline, press, and place it over the closed zipper. Pin the zipper tape to the fly extension on the inside. Stitch along the centre of the zipper tape. Mark the stitching line on the right side of the trouser and topstitch, ending with a curve. Press the fly shield in half and overlock the raw edges. Pin and stitch the fly shield to the left front, close to the foldline. Remove basting. Stitch a bar tack across the lower seamline. Join the front legs to the back legs at the inside leg seams. Join the front and back crotch seams. Sew the front and back side seams. Neaten the edges of the belt loop strip. Fold the edges of the strip to the centre and press. Topstitch both edges. Cut the strip into five pieces. Pin and stitch a belt loop edge to each pleat, back darts, and to the centre back seam. Interface the waistband. Neaten one long end with overlocking. Fold the waistband lengthwise and press. Attach the raw edge of the waistband to the waist. Trim and grade the seam allowances. Fold the waistband right sides together and stitch across both front ends. Trim the seam allowances and corners. Pin the free edge of the waistband to the waistline. Working on the right side, stitch in the ditch through all layers. Turn the raw edge of each belt loop under and topstitch in place. Sew a hook and bar on the waistband, or sew a buttonhole and button on. Neaten the raw edges of the hemline and hand stitch in place. Press.

PALAZZO PANTS

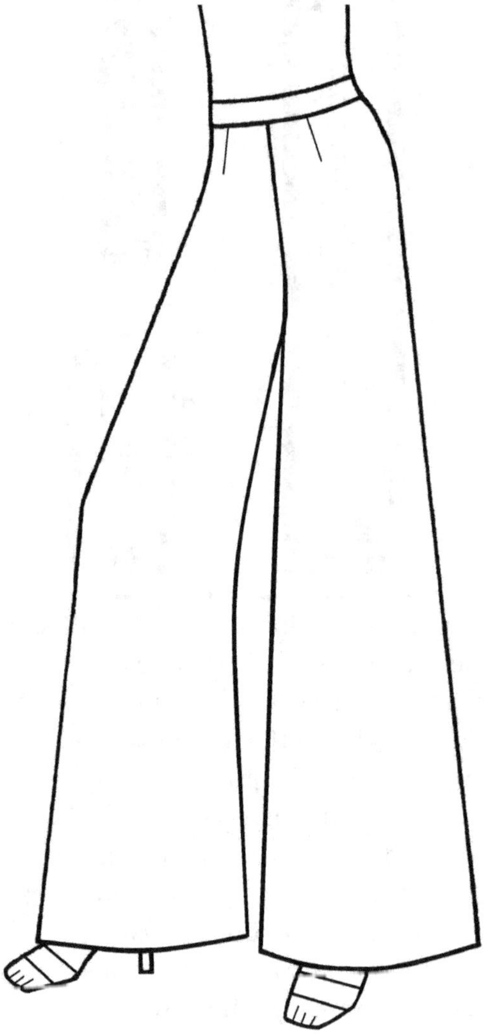

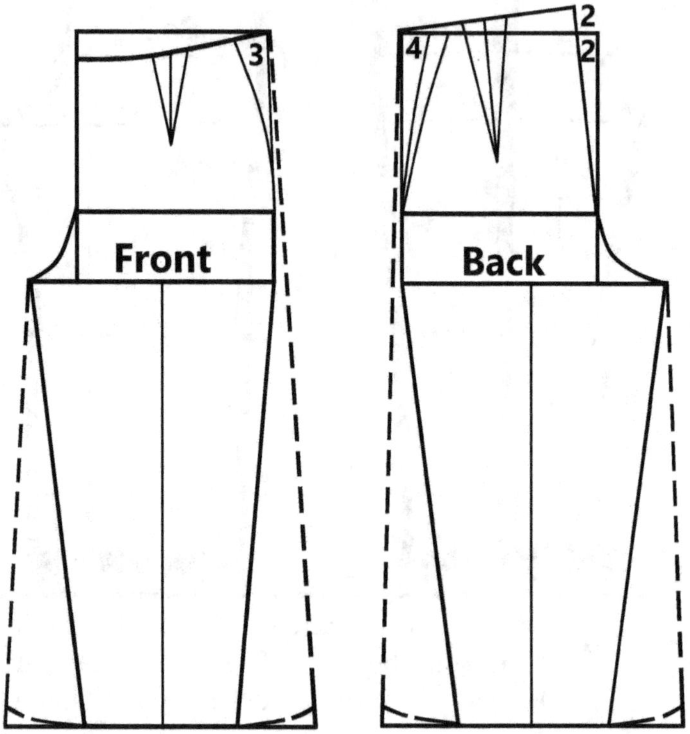

 Draft the basic trouser block without the front fly. Lower the front and back waistlines if so desired. Rule lines to add the desired amount of flare as illustrated by the dotted lines. Draw a waistband or trace front and back facing as described on page 167. Add grain lines, notches, hem, and seam allowances.

PALAZZO PANTS

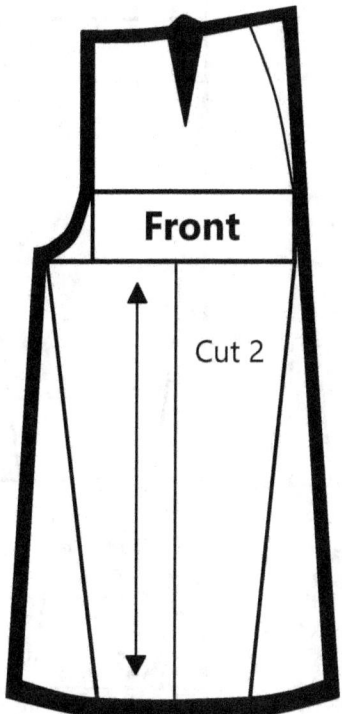
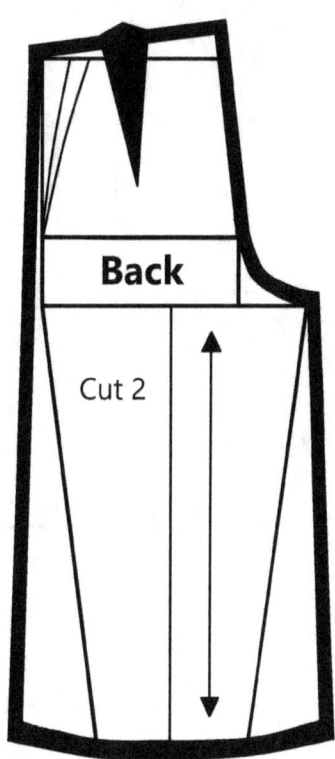

Neaten the crotch, side, and inner leg seams of the front and back panels with overlocking. Sew the darts on the front and back panels. Pin and sew one front leg to one back leg at the side and inner leg seams, right sides together. Press the seams open. Place one leg inside the other, right sides together. Pin and stitch the front and back crotch seams, leaving an opening for a back zipper. Apply fusible interfacing to the waistband. Fold the waistband in half lengthwise and press. Pin and stitch the waistband to the garment, right sides together. Trim and grade the waist seam allowances. Stitch a zipper of your choice in the centre back seam. Stitch the free edge of the waistband to the waistline as described before. Sew the hem and press the garment.

WRAP PANTS

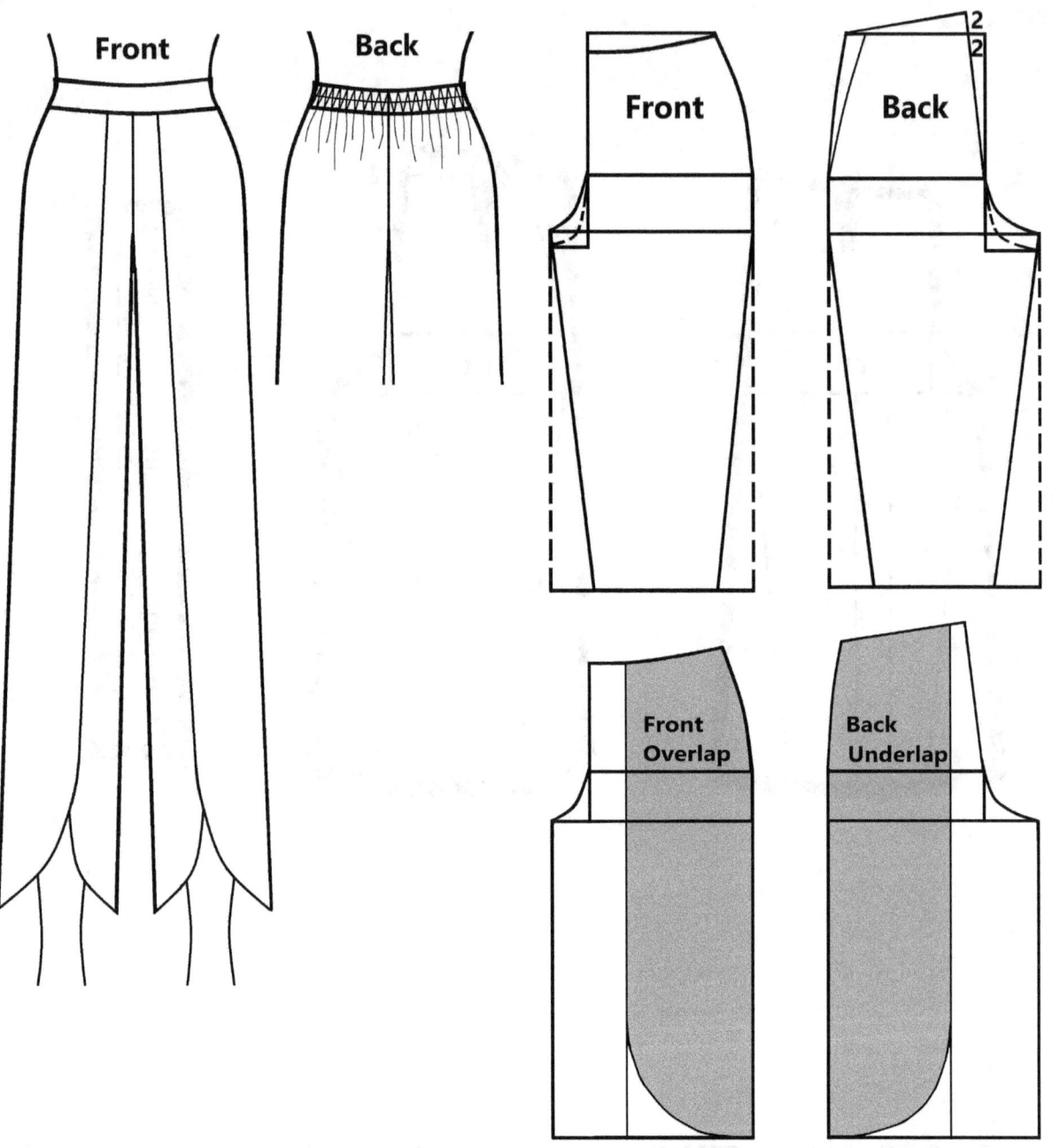

Draft the basic front trouser without the dart. Lower the waistline if so desired. Lower the crotch line by **2 cm (¾ in)** for a looser fit. Rule vertical lines from the crotch and the side seams for flare. Rule a vertical line from the waist down to the hemline and as close to the centre front as desired. The hemline can be curved as illustrated or straight. Repeat the same steps for the back on a separate sheet of paper. Trace the front overlap and back underlap (shaded sections) off. Attach the front overlap to the side of the back pattern and the back underlap to the side of the front pattern as illustrated on page **205**. Draw a front and back waistband to a desired width. Add notches, grain lines, hem, and seam allowances.

WRAP PANTS

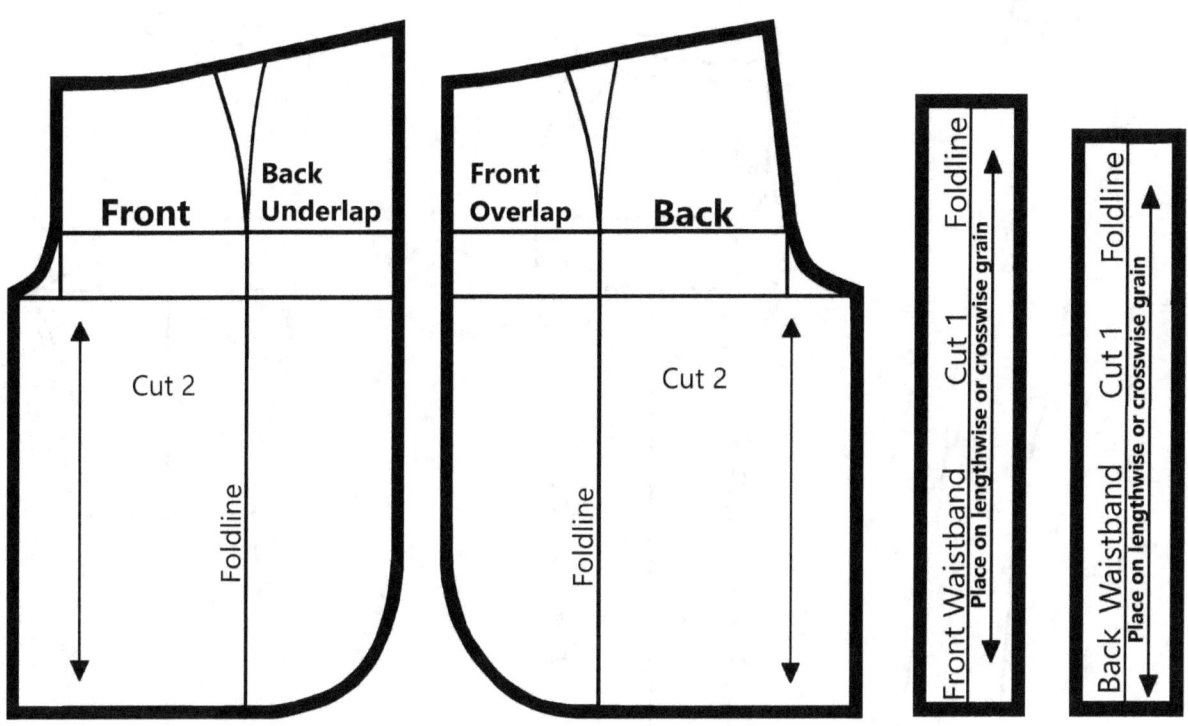

Pin and stitch the front and back inseam of each leg, right sides together. Neaten the seams with overlocking or a zigzag stitch. Pin and stitch the front and back crotch seams, right sides together. Overlock the crotch. Overlock the hemline and vertical edges. Fold and press the vertical edges and hemline to the wrong side. Stitch in place. Overlap the wrap sections on the front and back waistline to correspond with the notches. Pin and machine baste in place. Interface the front waistband. Pin and stitch the side seams of the front and back waistbands, right sides together. Fold and press the waistband in half lengthwise, wrong sides together. Pin the waistband to the waistline, right sides together, matching notches. Stitch the waistband to the waistline, leaving an opening on each side of the back waistband. Insert elastic into the back waistband with a safety pin or bodkin. Secure both ends of the elastic to the waistband side seams with safety pins. Stitch the elastic down vertically on the waistband side seams to secure it in place. Stitch the side openings closed and overlock the waistline raw edge.

TROUSER WITH FRONT HIP POCKETS

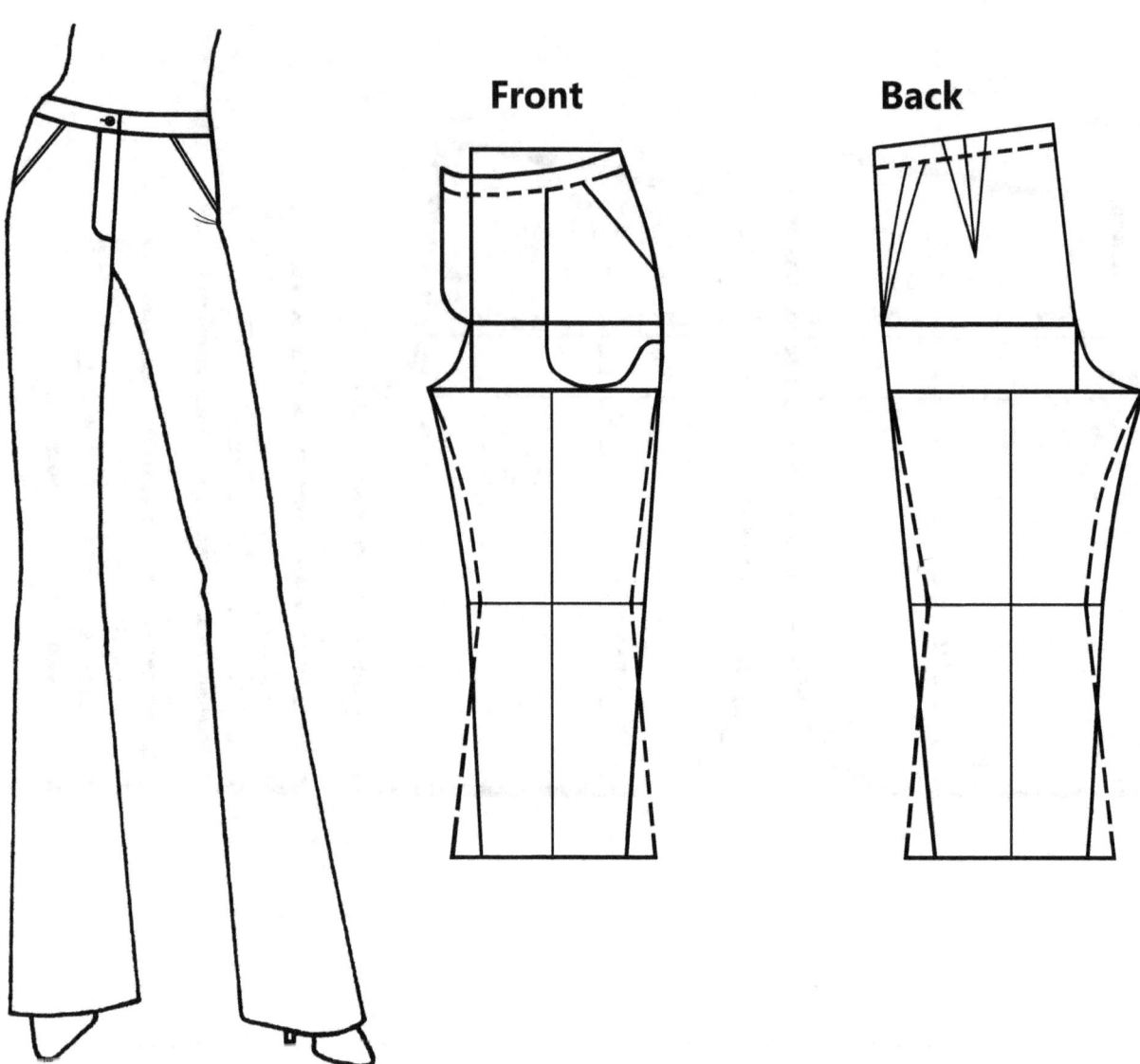

Trace the basic trouser block without the front dart. Lower the waistline as desired. Draw the front hip pocket and lining panel as illustrated. Shape the side and inside leg seams as desired. Measure the waistline and draw a waistband to the desired width. Draw a fly shield **10 cm (4 in)** wide and **2 cm (¾ in)** longer than the fly. Trace the trouser, hip panel, and pocket lining sections off. Add grain lines, notches, hem, and seam allowances.

SEWING SLANTED FRONT HIP POCKETS

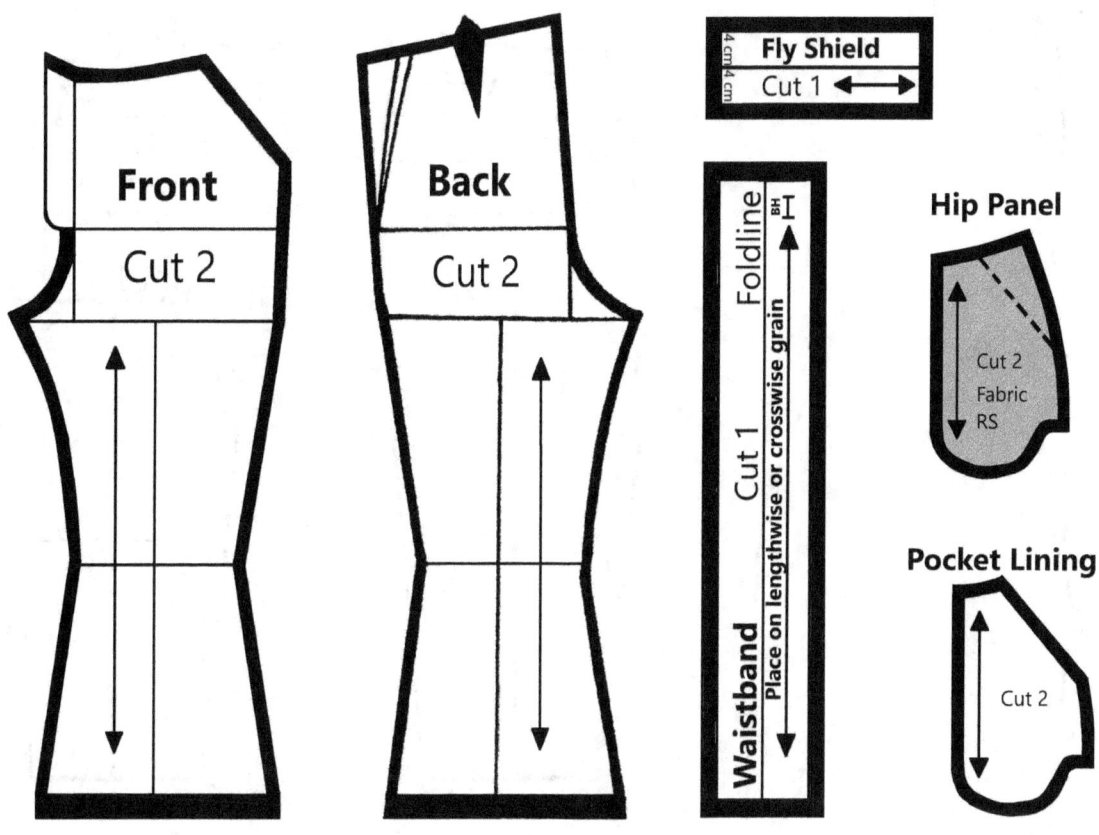

Apply a strip of fusible tape or interfacing on the wrong side of the garment along the pocket opening. Cut the pocket lining from cotton and the hip panel, which forms part of the pocket, from self-fabric. Pin the pocket lining to the pocket opening, right sides together, and stitch in place, using a **1 cm (⅜ in)** seam allowance. Trim the lining seam allowance to half its width. Press the seam allowance towards the lining. Turn the pocket lining to the wrong side and press the pocket opening, ensuring that the edge of the lining is **3 mm (⅛ in)** from the pocket opening edge. On the right side of the garment, topstitch **6 mm (¼ in)** from the pocket opening edge. Pin the hip panel that forms part of the pocket bag, to the pocket lining, right sides together. Stitch the pocket bag together, using a **1 cm (⅜ in)** seam allowance. Press. Neaten the raw edge around the pocket with overlocking. Turn the pocket to the inside and secure it with pins. Machine baste the pocket to the waistline and side seam. Repeat the above steps for the opposite side. Overlock the trouser side seams and complete the remainder of the trouser as described before.

BASIC JEANS

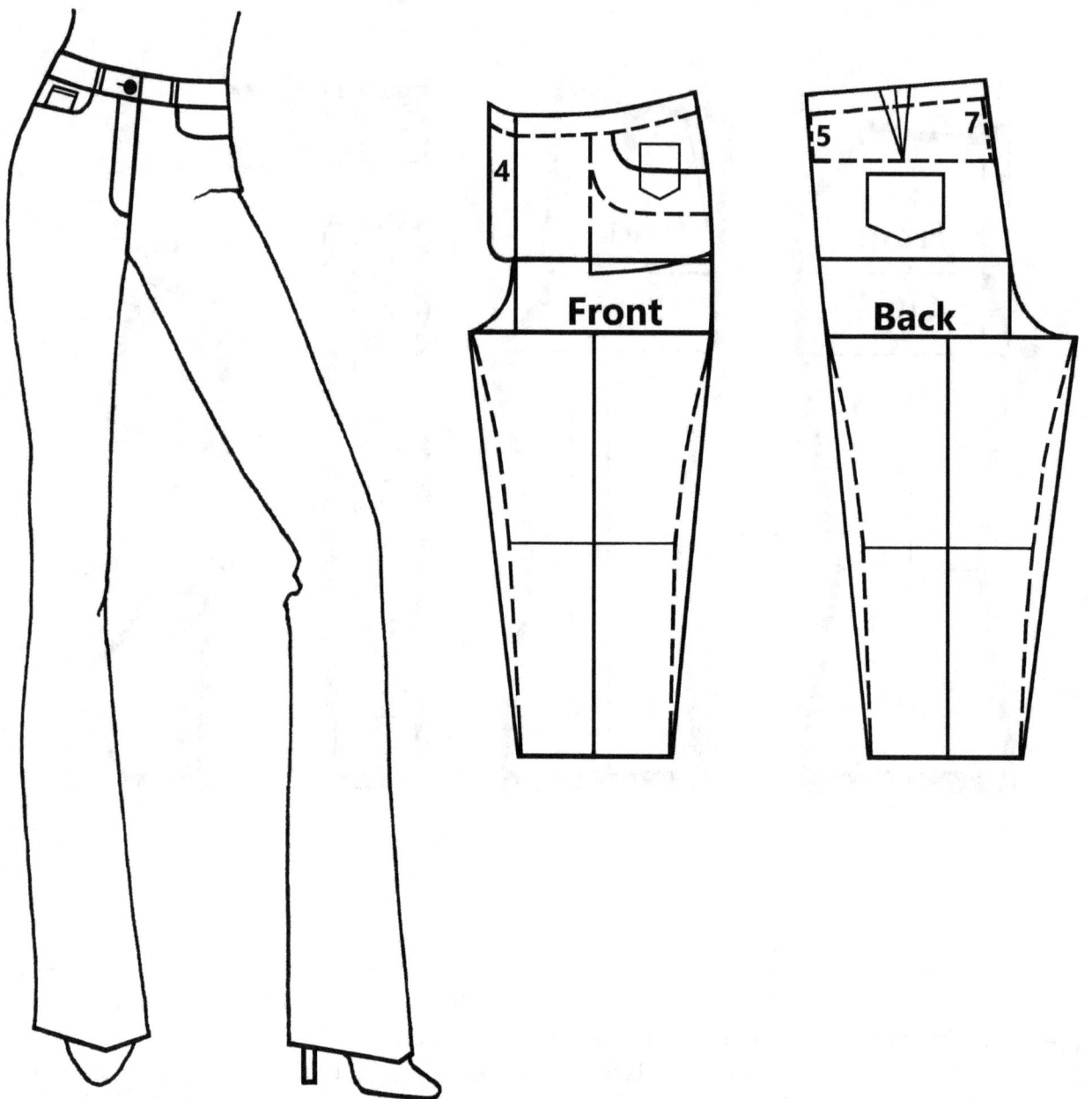

Trace the basic trousers without the front dart. Lower the front and back waistline if so desired. Draw the pockets on the front as illustrated. Draw a dart **2 cm** (**¾ in**) wide and **7 cm** (**2 ¾ in**) long on the back. Draw the back yoke **7 cm** (**2 ¾ in**) wide at the centre back, or to a desired width. Draw the side of the yoke **5 cm** (**2 in**) wide, or as desired. Trace the back yoke off and fold the dart close. Secure the dart with sticky tape. Trace the remaining pattern pieces off. Draw a waistband **10 cm** (**4 in**) longer than the waist measurement and double the required width. Add grain lines, notches, hem, and seam allowances.

SEWING JEANS FRONT HIP POCKETS

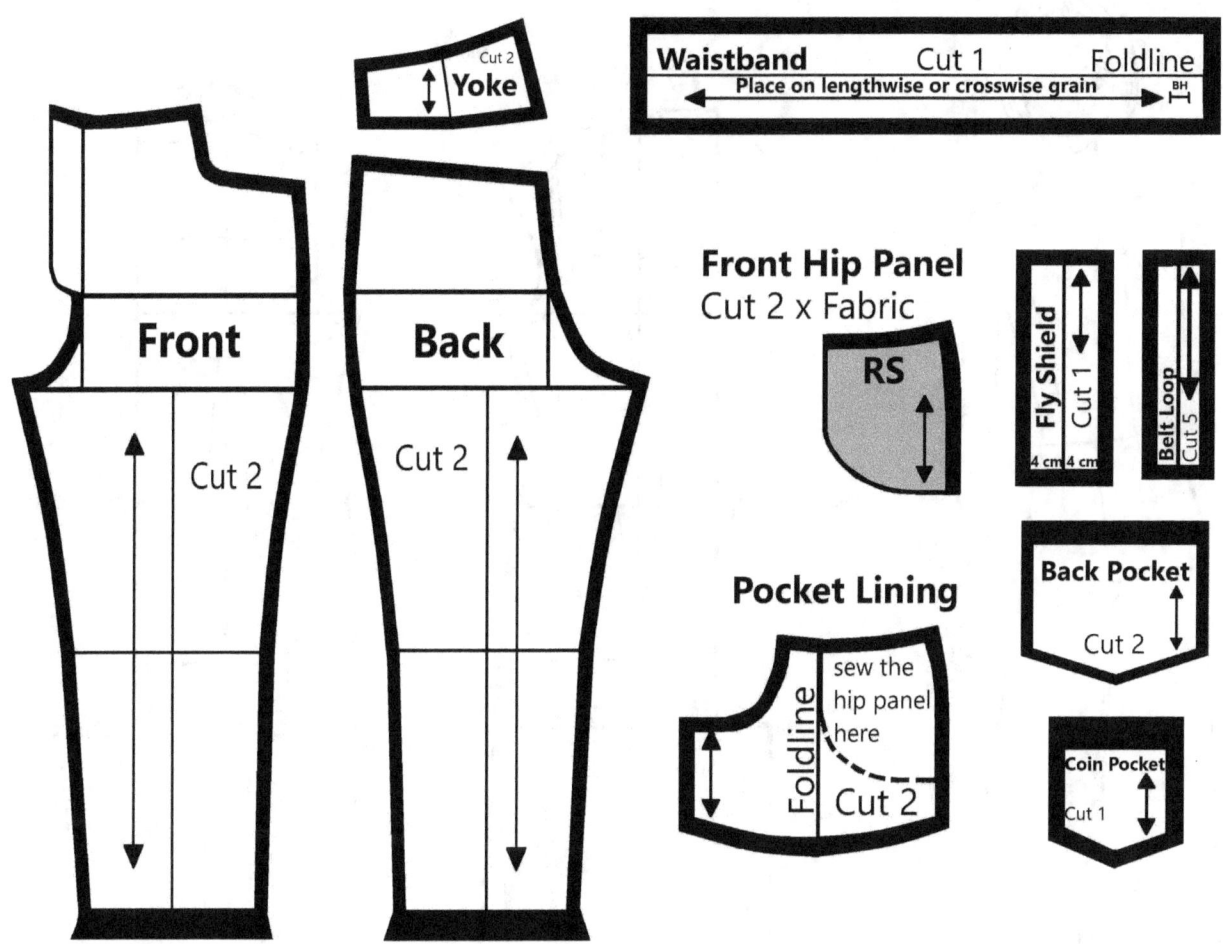

Wash the denim to pre-shrink it before cutting it. Always use denim needles, or the appropriate size machine needle to sew denim fabric. Overlock the hip panel that forms part of the pocket. Fold the pocket lining in half and press. Pin and stitch the hip panel to the pocket lining, facing right side up. Overlock the edges of the coin pocket. Fold the side seam allowances to the wrong side. Press. Fold the top hem down. Press and sew two rows of topstitching. Pin the coin pocket to the hip panel and stitch it in place. Pin and sew the pocket lining to the pocket opening, right sides together. Trim, grade, and clip the seam allowances. Fold the pocket lining to the wrong side and press. Topstitch the pocket opening. Fold the lining side seams, right sides together, and pin and sew the bottom edge. Overlock the bottom edge. Pin the pocket to the waistline and side seam and baste it in place. Repeat for the other side. Pin and stitch the front crotch, right sides together, up to the marked zipper opening. Apply the zip to the front crotch. Sew the back yokes to the back leg panels. Overlock. Press and topstitch the seam. Prepare the back pockets. Pin and sew the back pockets in place. Pin and sew the back crotch seams, right sides together. Topstitch the crotch seams. Pin and sew the front and back inseams, right sides together. Topstitch the inseam if desired. Pin and sew the side seams together. Attach a waistband and belt loops. Sew the hem. Press the garment.

JUMPSUIT

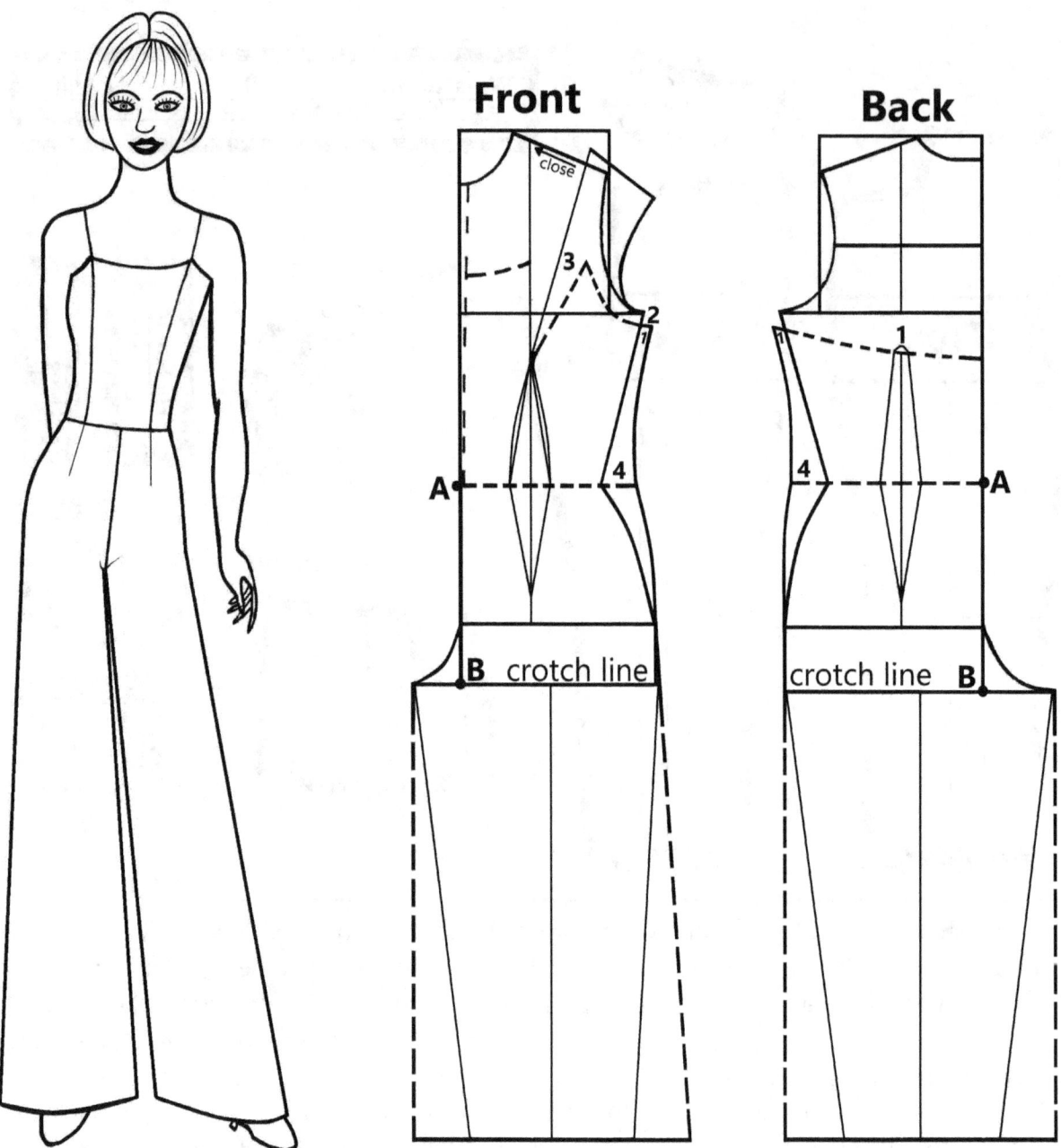

Draft the basic front and back bodice blocks. Draw the front and back necklines as illustrated. Increase the shoulder dart by **3 cm (1¼ in)**. Drop **2 cm (¾ in)** along the side seam. Add the basic trouser block to the front and back bodice: **Measure the crotch depth plus 5 cm (2 in) from A to B** for the front and back as illustrated. This will allow extra ease at the crotch of the jumpsuit. Add flare to the front and back leg seams. Measure your torso and compare it with the draft. Fold the front and back darts close and trace facing off. Trace the remaining pattern pieces off. Add grain lines, notches, hem, and seam allowances.

JUMPSUIT

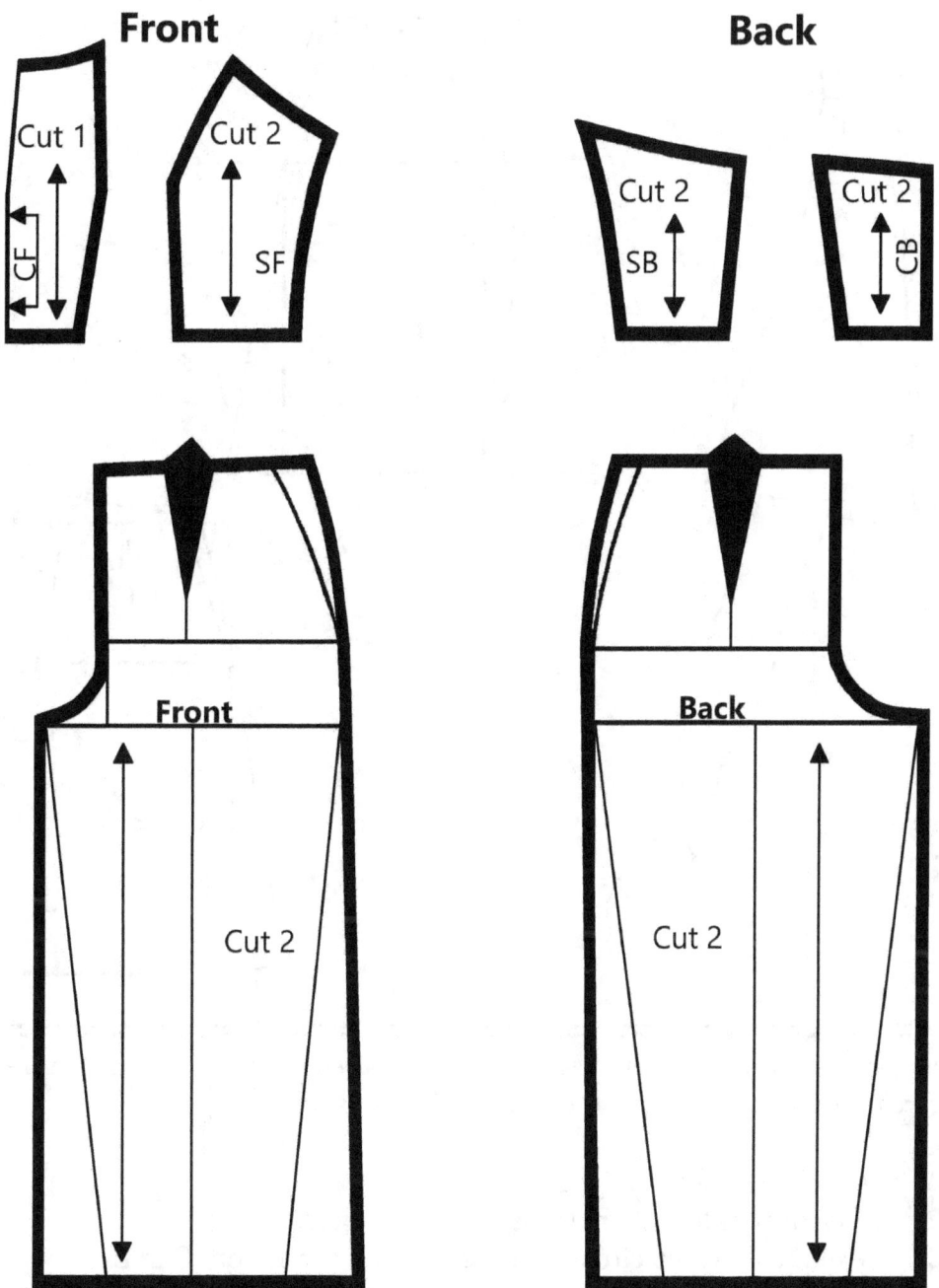

BASIC CULOTTES

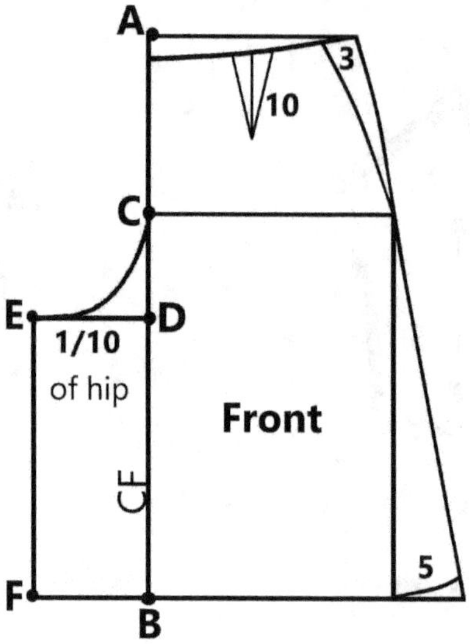

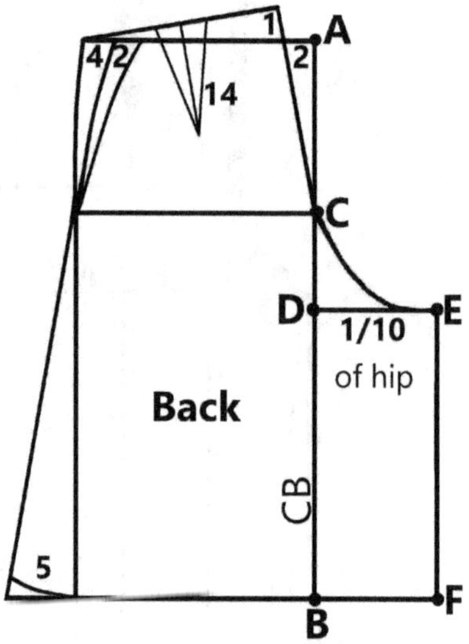

Draft half the basic front and back skirt to a desired length and add a desired amount of flare to the side. Complete the front and back as follows:

Front

A-B: The desired culottes length.

A-D: Crotch depth plus **1.5 cm (⅝ in)** or more for ease.

D-E: One tenth of the hip circumference. Draw a curve from **C** to **E**.

Rule a line from **E** down to **F** and across to **B**. Repeat the above steps for the back.

Back

Measure **2 cm (¾ in)** in from **A**. Raise the centre back waistline by **1 cm (⅜ in)** and rule a line down to **C**. Rule a line from the raised waistline to the side of the original waistline. Draft a waistband, or trace facing from the front and back pattern while the darts are folded close. Trace the pattern pieces off. Add grain lines, notches, hem, and seam allowances.

BASIC CULOTTES

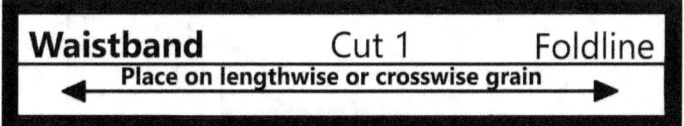

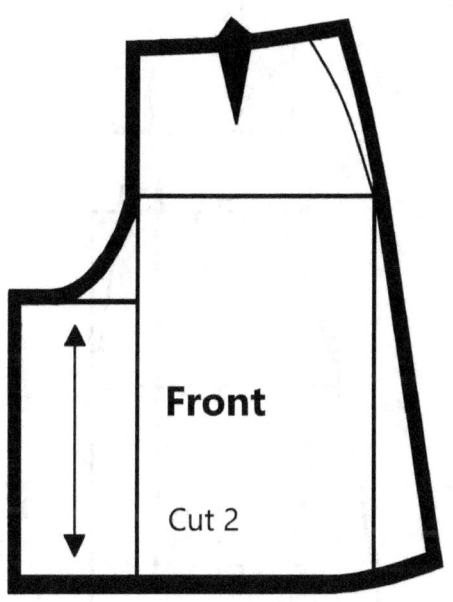

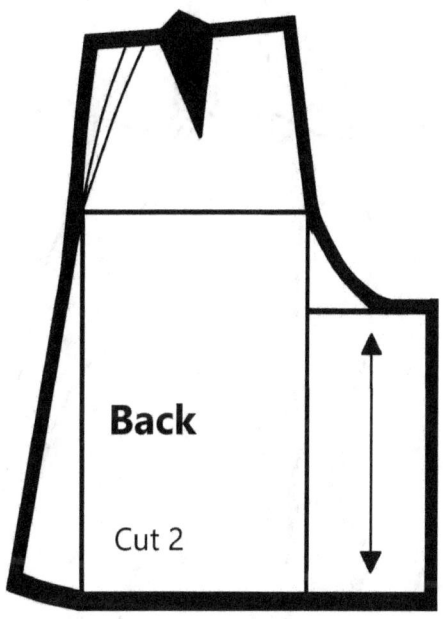

Neaten the crotch, side seams, and inner leg seams of the front and back panels. Stitch the darts on the front and back panels. Stitch the front and back inner leg seams, right sides together. Stitch the front and back crotch seams together up to the marked zipper opening in the back seam. With right sides together, pin and stitch the front and back side seams. Interface the waistband. Fold the waistband lengthwise, wrong sides together, and press. Pin and stitch the waistband to the waistline, right sides together. Grade the seam allowances. Insert a zipper of your choice in the centre back seam. Complete the waistband as described before. Sew the hems and press the garment.

FLARE CULOTTES

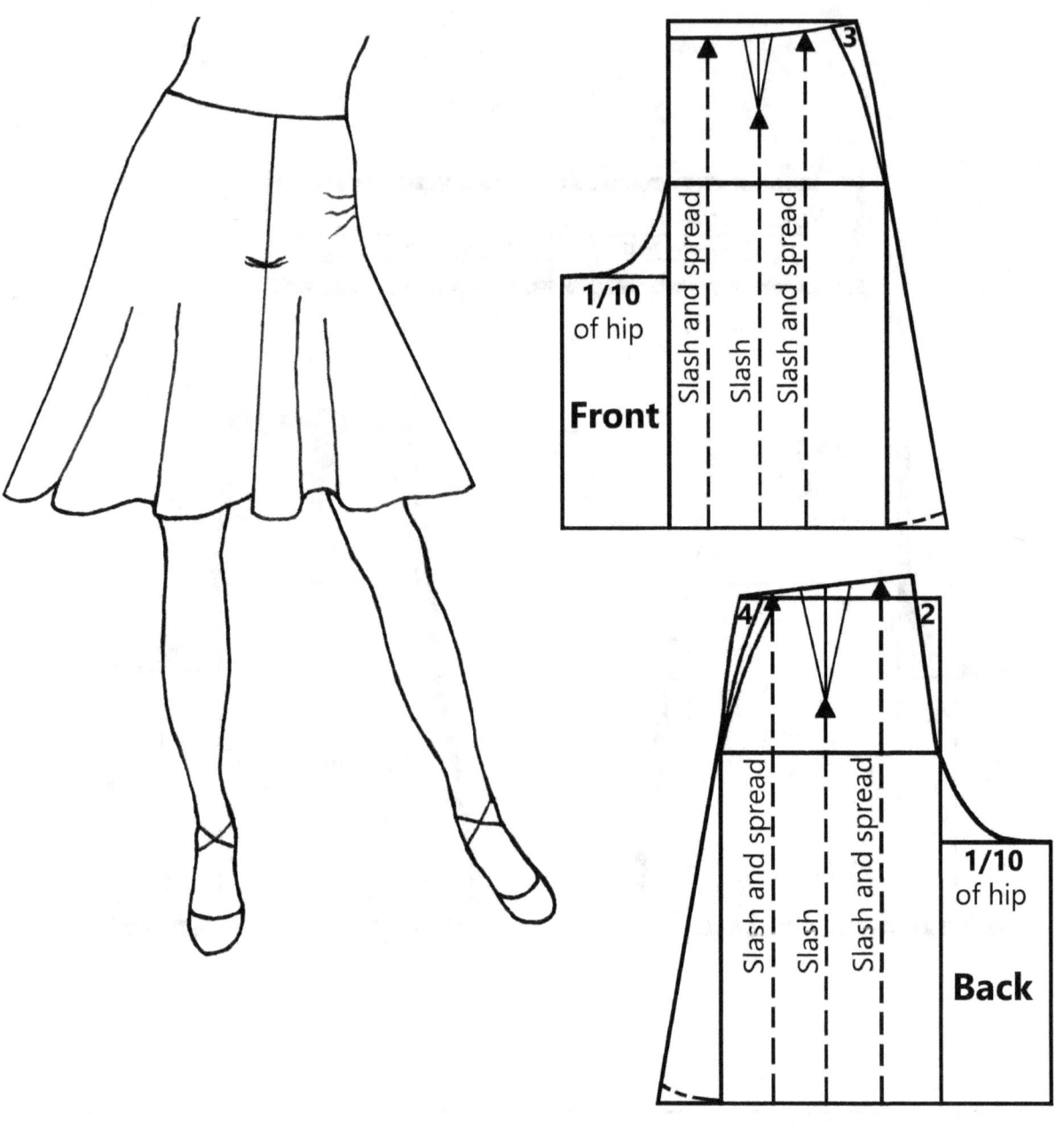

Draft the basic Culottes pattern as illustrated. Trace the front and back patterns off. Draw a vertical line from the front dart down to the hemline and a line on either side of the dart. Slash into the dart line up to the arrowhead and fold the dart close for flare at the hemline. Slash and spread the other two vertical lines to add the same amount of flare. Place paper under the slashed sections and secure them with tape. Repeat the same for the back pattern. Draw a waistband, or trace front and back waist facings off. Add grain lines, notches, hem, and seam allowances.

FLARE CULOTTES

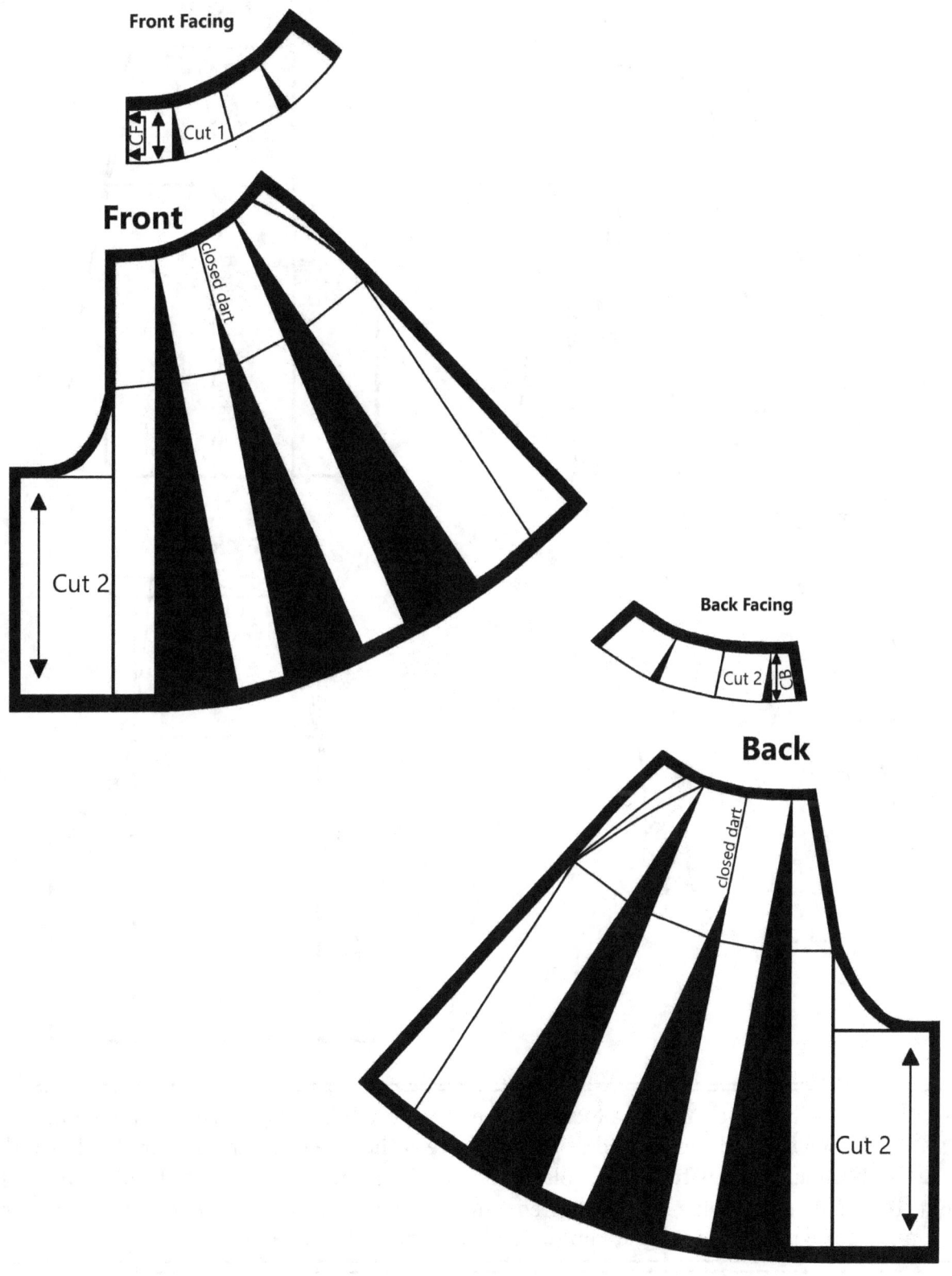

PLEATED CULOTTES

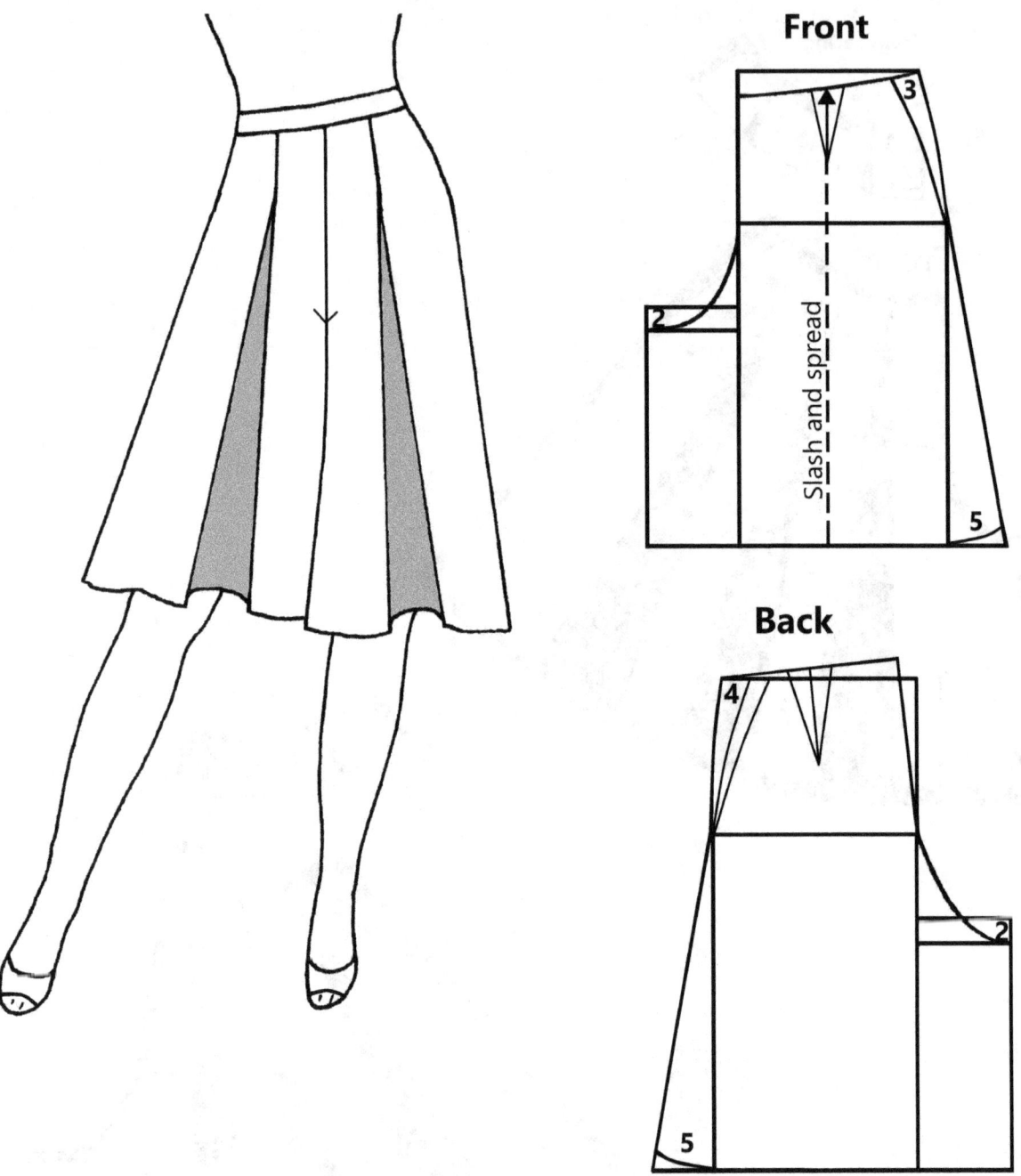

Draft the basic Culottes block and drop the crotch line by a further **2 cm (¾ in)** for a looser fit. Add the desired amount of flare at the side front and side back. Trace the front and back patterns off. Slash the front pattern up to the arrowhead. Spread the front **16 cm (6 ¼ in)** wide, or as desired. Measure the waistline and draw a waistband to complete the pattern. Add grain lines, notches, hem, and seam allowances.

PLEATED CULOTTES

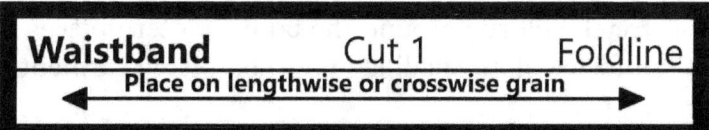

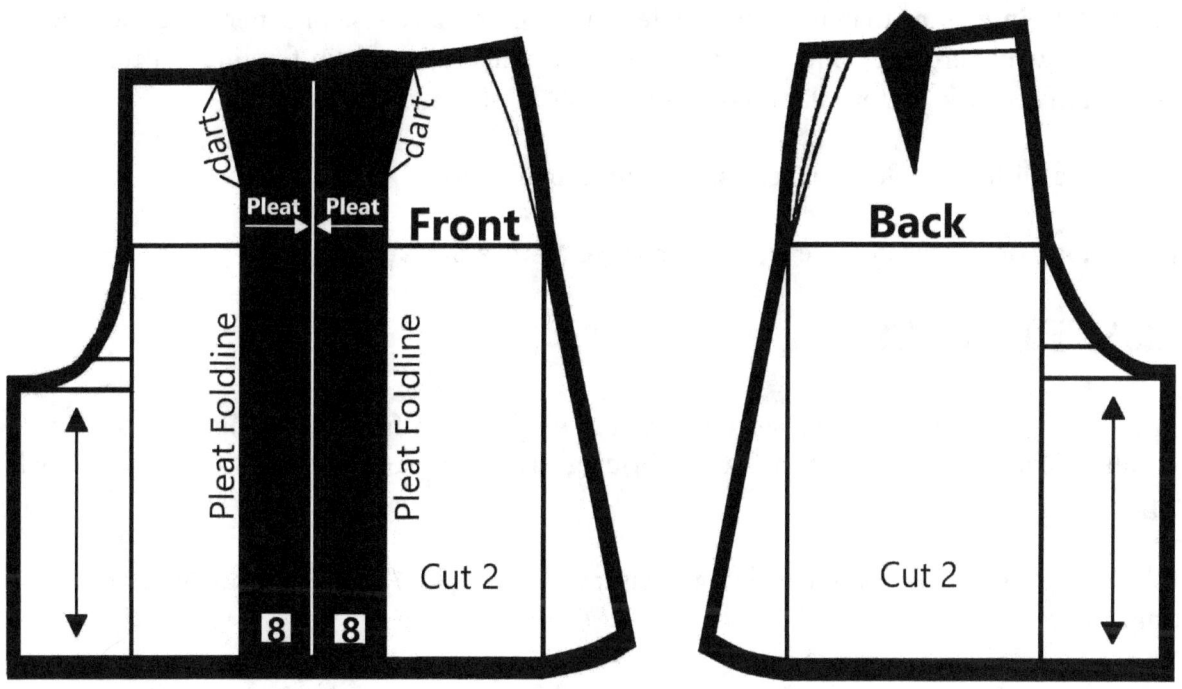

Neaten the crotch, side seams, and inner leg seams of the front and back panels. Pin and stitch the front crotch panels, right sides together. Mark and fold the pleats on the right side of the front panels. Machine stitch a section of the pleats close, up to a desired length to form inverted pleats. Stitch the back crotch seam up to the marked zipper opening. Stitch the front and back inner legs and side seams, right sides together. Interface the waistband. Pin and stitch the waistband to the waistline, right sides together. Grade the seam allowances. Insert a zipper in the centre back seam. Complete the waistband as described before. Sew the hems and press the garment.

WORKING WITH STRETCH FABRICS

PREPARING STRETCH FABRIC FOR CUTTING

Preshrink stretch fabric before cutting. Press the fabric with an iron on a low setting. Determine which direction of the fabric has the greatest amount of stretch before placing the pattern on the fabric for cutting. To ensure a comfortable fit, it is best to position the pattern on the fabric so that a greater amount of stretch will run around the body. Pattern pieces must be placed in the same direction to ensure uniform colour shading in the completed garment.

Support the fabric on the work surface while pinning and cutting out, to prevent the fabric from stretching out of shape.

Pin with ball-pointed pins that are specially designed for knits. These pins penetrate between the knitted loops, while ordinary pins break the fibres, which will result in fraying. Pattern weights can be used to keep the pattern flat on the fabric instead of pins.

Cut the fabric with sharp dressmaker's shears, or a rotary cutter.

Mark the fabric on the wrong side with tailor's chalk or dressmaker's pens.

SEWING STRETCH FABRICS

It is important to use the correct needles when sewing stretch fabrics. Using incorrect needles will result in skipped stitches. Stretch the fabric lightly at the front and back of the needle while sewing.

Stretch needles and ball-point needles are suitable for Nylon/Spandex, Cotton/Spandex, T-shirting, and more.

Twin stretch needles are used for finishing hems and for decorative stitching.

SEWING THREAD

Polyester and Nylon sewing thread have some stretch and are best for sewing knits.

STITCHES

Zigzag stitch: A small zigzag stitch works well on stretch fabrics.

Stretch stitch: Some modern sewing machines have a built-in stretch stitch to sew stretch fabric.

Straight stitch: This stitch may be used on some stretch fabrics, even though a zigzag stitch or stretch stitch is preferred.

SPORTSWEAR

SPORTS BRA

Draft the basic front and back bodice blocks. Scoop the necklines and armholes as illustrated. Shorten the front and back as desired. Make allowance for a **6 cm (2 ¼ in)** wide casing at the bottom of the front and back draft as illustrated. Trace the front, back, and casing sections off. Slash the front up to the arrowheads. Spread the sections to a desired width for gathers. Add grain lines, notches, and seam allowances.

SPORTSWEAR

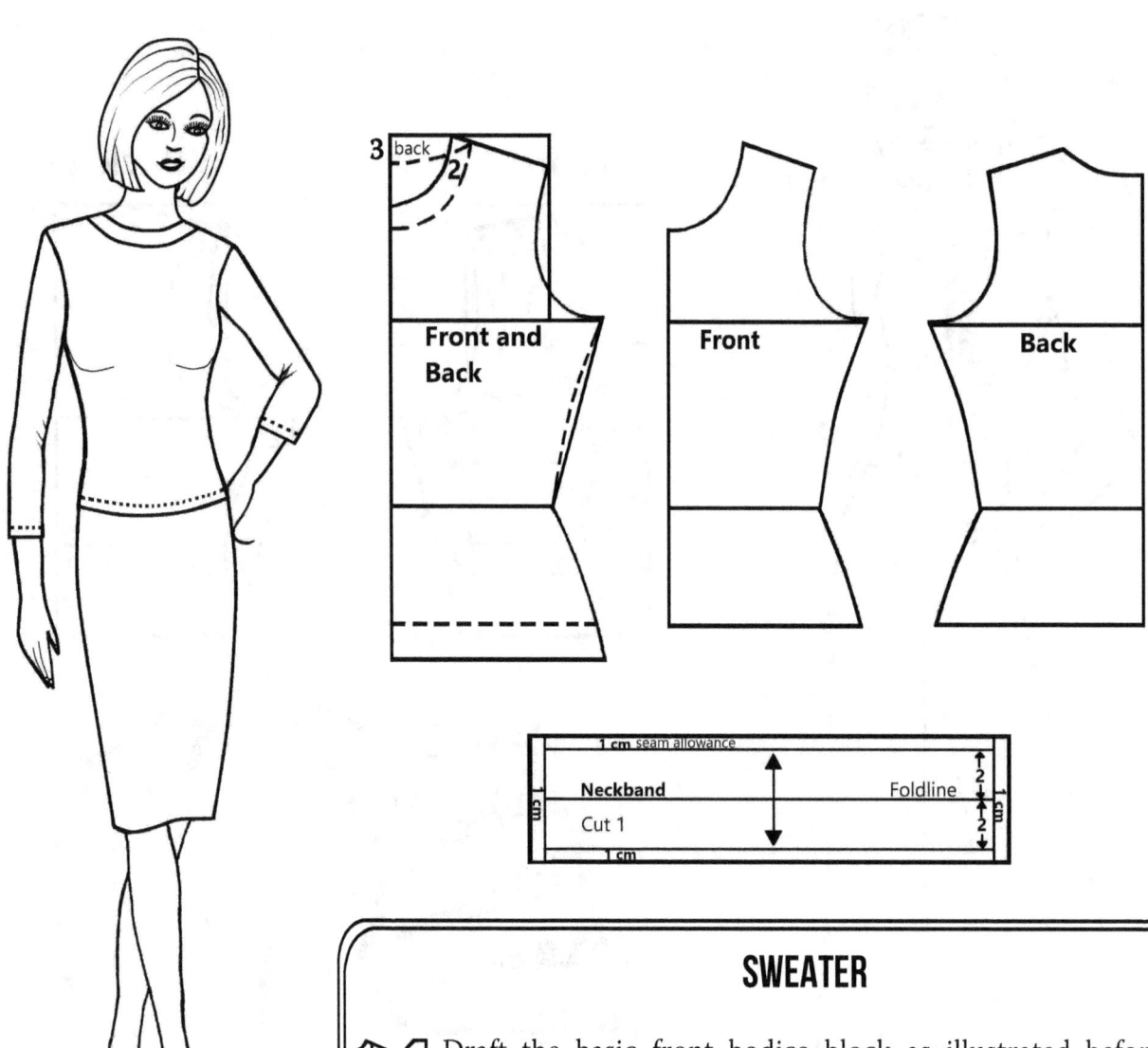

SWEATER

Draft the basic front bodice block as illustrated before. Scoop the neckline by **2 cm** (¾ in), or by a desired amount. Drop **3 cm** (1 ¼ in) at the centre front and draw the back neck as illustrated by the dotted line. Shorten the bodice length as desired. Fold the paper under the draft and trace the back from the front. Trace the front and back patterns on a new sheet of paper. Measure the scooped neckline. Draft the length of the neckband for a crew neckline finished with self-fabric at **80%** of the neckline circumference and at **75%** when using rib trim. Draft the width of the neckband twice the desired finished width. Add **1 cm** (⅜ in) seam allowances to all pattern pieces and **2 cm** hem allowances. Use the knit sleeve draft on page **222** to complete the pattern.

SWEATER

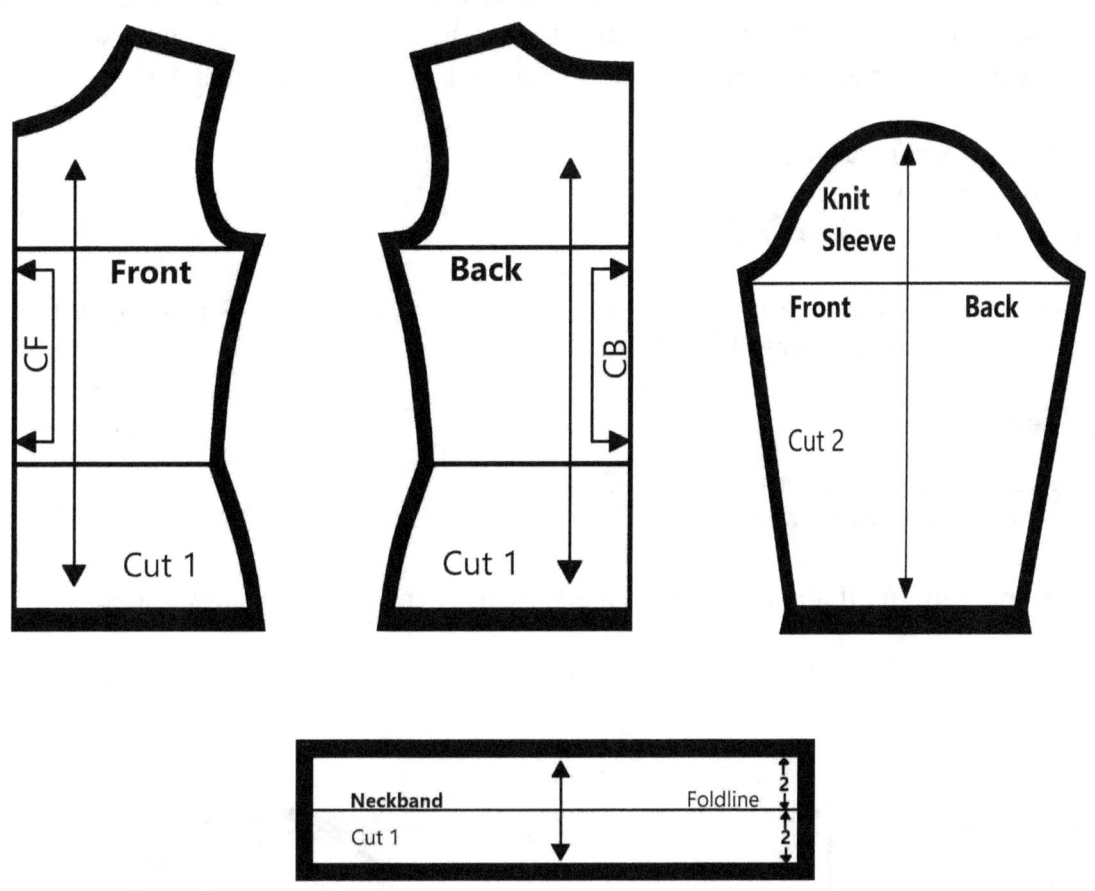

Use good-quality sweater knits, stretch needles, and matching sewing thread. It's best to reinforce the shoulder seams of knit (stretchy) garments to prevent them from losing shape. The shoulder seams of knits can be reinforced with preshrunk cotton tape, fusible bias tape, self-fabric, or clear elastic, and more. Choose a method that is suitable for your fabric. With the shoulder seams right sides together, pin or tack the reinforcement strips on the back shoulder seamlines. Stitch them in place using a zigzag stitch or overlocking. Press the shoulder seams towards the back bodice. Cut the neckband from self-fabric or rib trim. Pin and stitch the ends of the neckband, right sides together. Press the seam open. Fold the neckband in half lengthwise, wrong sides together, and press. Quarter pin mark the neckline and the neckband and complete the neckline as described on page **225**. With right sides together, pin the sleeve into the armhole, matching notches and the underarm seam. Stitch the sleeve in place. Repeat for the other sleeve. Pin and stitch the side seams and sleeve seams, right sides together, starting at the bottom edge of the garment, up to the sleeve hem. Finish the hems off with a twin stretch needle.

SPORTSWEAR

KNIT SLEEVE

Draw a rectangle on the fold of a sheet of paper for the **knit sleeve** block as illustrated below. Measure the sleeve head and compare it with the armhole measurement of the pattern. **Reduce** or **extend** the underarm line when adjustments are needed and **blend** the sleeve curves.

A-B: Half the top arm measurement.
B-C: The sleeve length. Close the rectangle.
C-D: Half the desired hemline width.
B-E: Depth of sleeve head.
Rule a line from **E** across to **F** for the underarm line. Rule a line from **D** to **F** and from **B** to **F**.
F-G: One third the measurement of **B** to **F**.

SLEEVE HEAD

Hollow the curve **1 cm (⅜ in)** between **F** and **G**.
Raise the curve **2 cm (¾ in)** between **B** and **G**.

Trace the sleeve pattern off and add a grain line, notches, hem, and seam allowances.

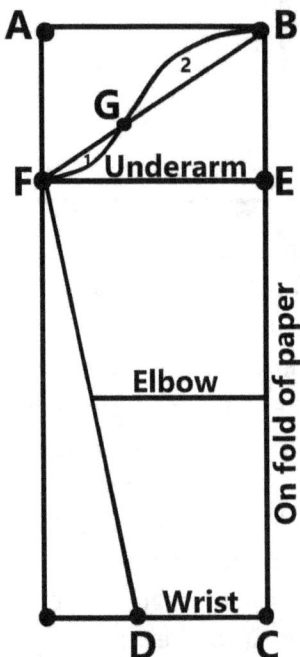
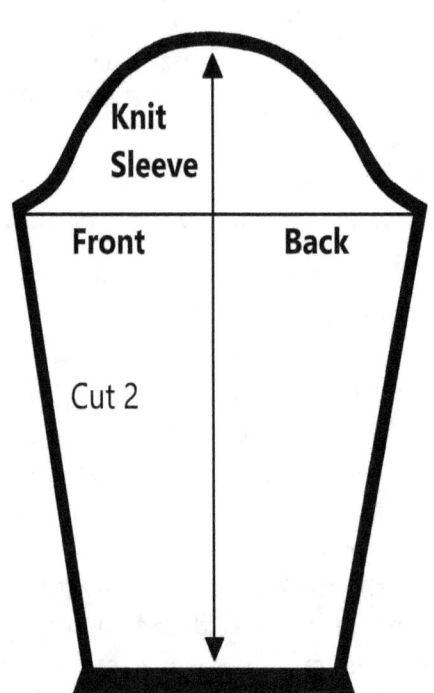

SPORTSWEAR

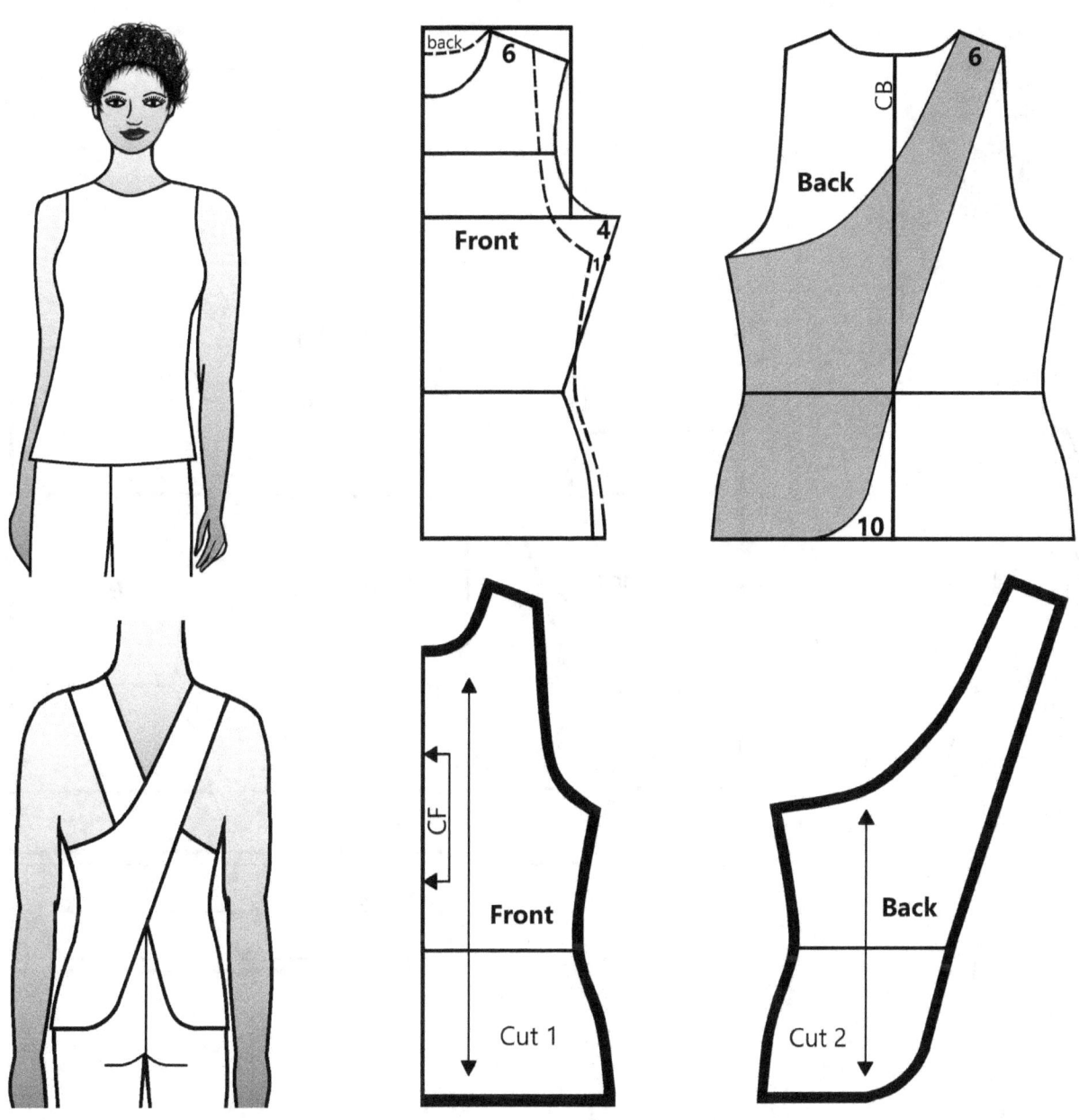

YOGA TOP

Trace the basic front bodice block. Measure **6 cm** (**2 ¼ in**) from the base of the neck for the shoulder width or a desired amount. Drop **4 cm** (**1 ½ in**) along the side seam and measure **1 cm** (**⅜ in**) in. Redraw the armhole as illustrated by the dotted line. Measure **1.5 cm** (**⅝ in**) out at the waist and hip lines, or a desired amount. Redraw the waist and hip as illustrated. Draw the back neck at the centre front. Trace the back from the front on the fold of paper. Open the sheet and draw the style lines as illustrated by the shaded section. Trace the pattern pieces off and add grain lines, notches, hem, and seam allowances.

SPORTSWEAR

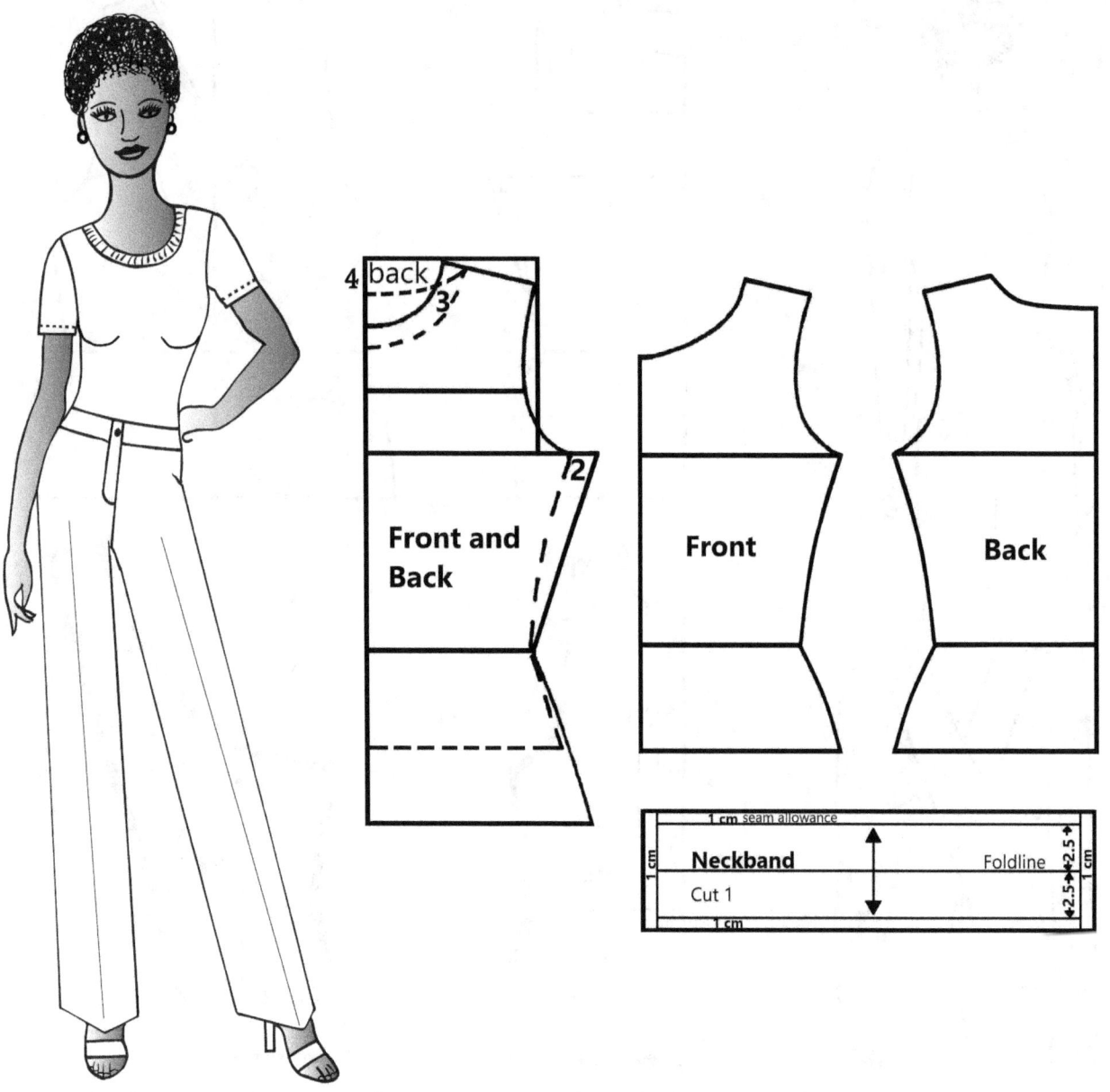

FITTED T-SHIRT

Draft the basic front bodice block. Shorten the bodice as desired. Scoop the neckline. Drop **4 cm** (**1 ½ in**) at the centre front and draw the back neck as illustrated. Trace the back from the front draft. Trace the front and back patterns on a new sheet of paper and measure the neckline. Draft the neckband pattern to the required width and length as described on page **220**. Add grain lines, notches, hem, and seam allowances. Use the knit sleeve draft on page **222** to complete the pattern.

FITTED T-SHIRT

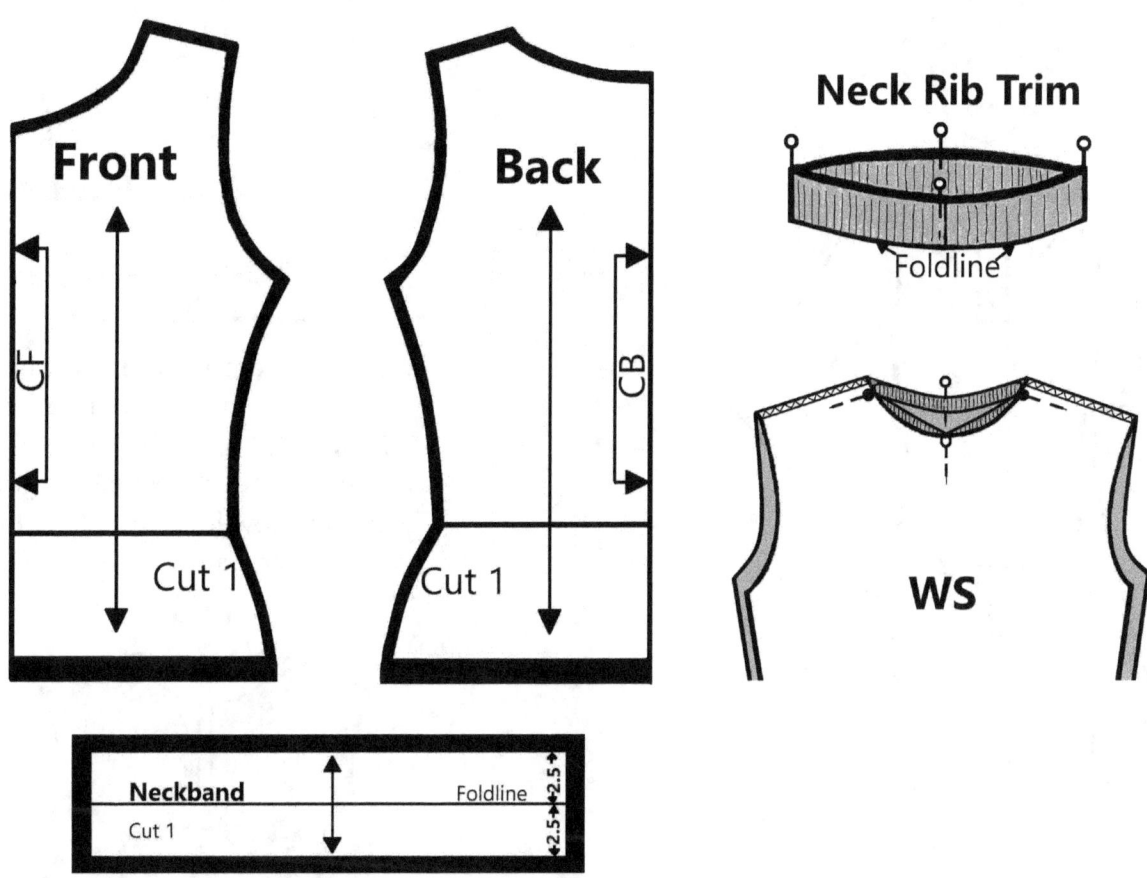

Stitch and reinforce the shoulder seams as described on page **221**. Press the shoulder seams towards the back. Cut rib trim to three quarters of the T-shirt neck circumference. Stitch the rib trim ends, right sides together. Fold the rib trim in half lengthwise, wrong sides together. Quarter pin mark the rib trim as illustrated above. Quarter pin mark the neckline by placing the shoulder seams together and mark the centre front and centre back neck with a pin. Put the centre front and centre back markings on top of each other and mark the side quarters. Turn the top with right side inside. Place the rib trim inside the garment, right sides together, matching the quarter pin marks. Stitch the rib trim to the neckline, using overlocking or a narrow zigzag stitch while stretching the rib trim to fit the neckline. Topstitch the neckline with a twin stretch needle if desired. With right sides together, pin the sleeve into the armhole, matching notches and the underarm seam. Stitch the sleeve in place. Repeat for the other sleeve. Pin and stitch the side seams and sleeve seams, right sides together. Finish the hems off with a twin stretch needle.

SPORTSWEAR

GOLF SHIRT WITH PLACKET OPENING

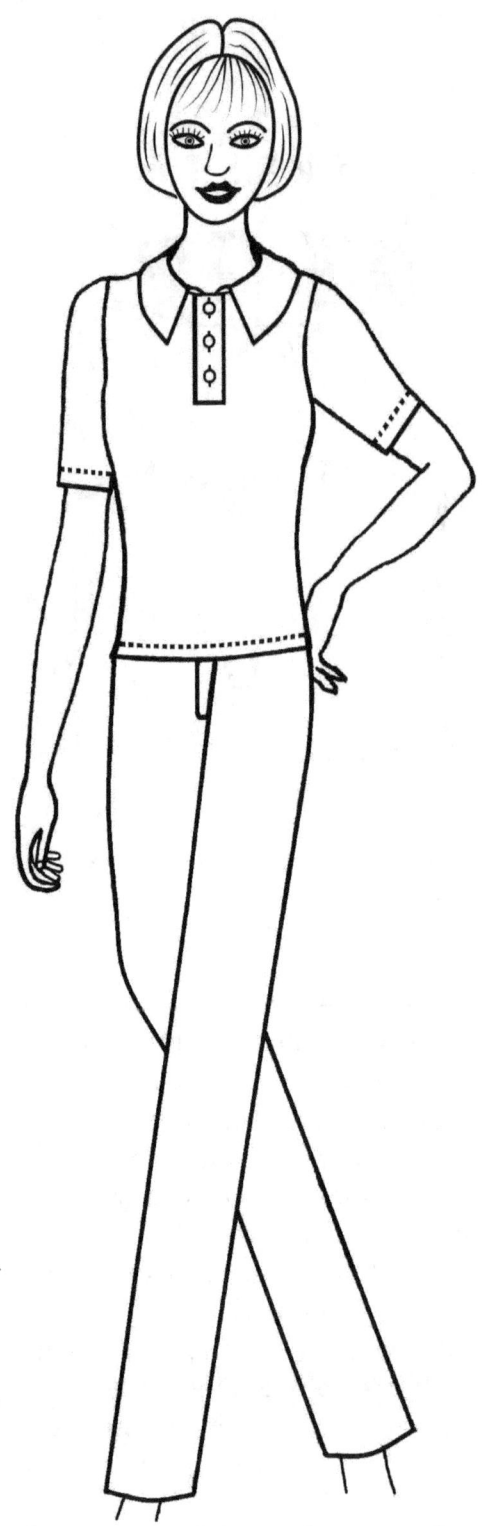

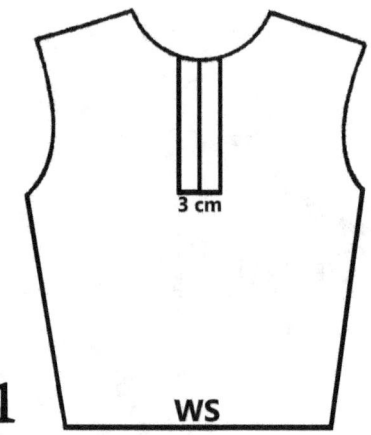

Mark the centre of the T-Shirt with a fabric marker. Mark a line **1.5 cm (⅝ in)** on both sides of the centre line to a desired length. This will allow for a **3 cm (1 ¼ in)** wide placket band.

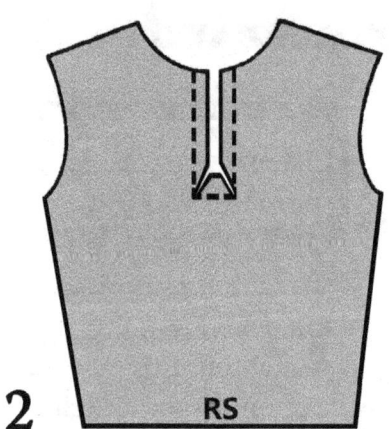

Stitch on the marked lines. Use a shorter stitch to reinforce both corners. Cut down the centre line up to **2 cm (¾ in)** from the bottom stitches. Cut into the corners. Trim the seam allowance so that **1 cm (⅜ in)** remain on both sides of the centre front.

SPORTSWEAR

GOLF SHIRT WITH PLACKET OPENING

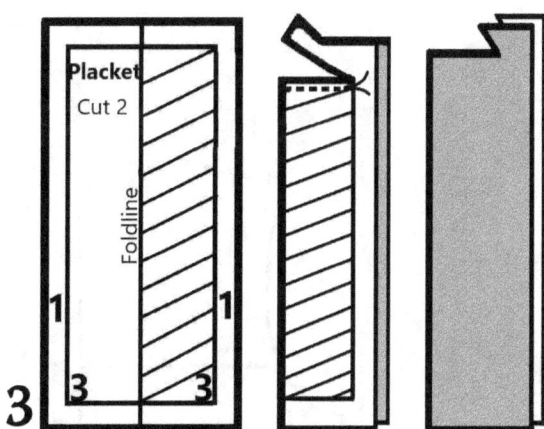

Cut two plackets measuring **8 cm (3 ⅛ in)** wide and to the required length. Iron interfacing on one side of each placket. Fold the plackets right sides together and stitch the top edge closed for **2 cm (¾ in)**. Trim the seam allowances. Turn it to the right side and press.

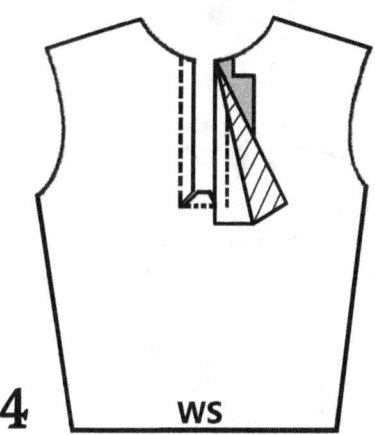

Pin the right side of the plackets to the wrong side of the front opening. Sew up to the corners on each side. Trim the seam allowances and press it towards the plackets. Fold the seam allowance of each placket's free edge under and press.

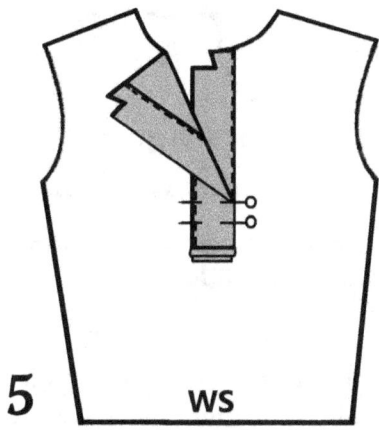

Fold the plackets to the right side of the garment and place the pressed edges over the stitching lines. Pin and tack them in place. Edgestitch them in place. Push the plackets to the wrong side. Overlap it right over left for ladies. Neaten the triangular wedge. Pin and tack the plackets in position.

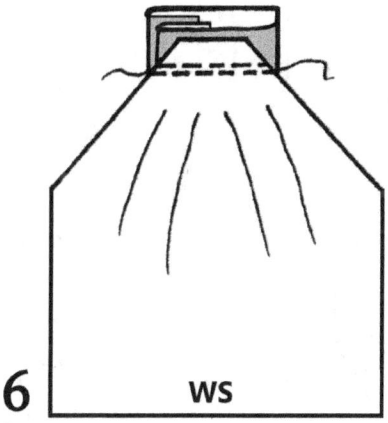

With right sides together, stitch the bottom edge of the plackets as illustrated above. Grade the seam allowance and neaten the bottom edge with overlocking. Stitch a reinforcing line or cross-stitching on the right side, at the bottom of the placket, if desired.

SPORTSWEAR

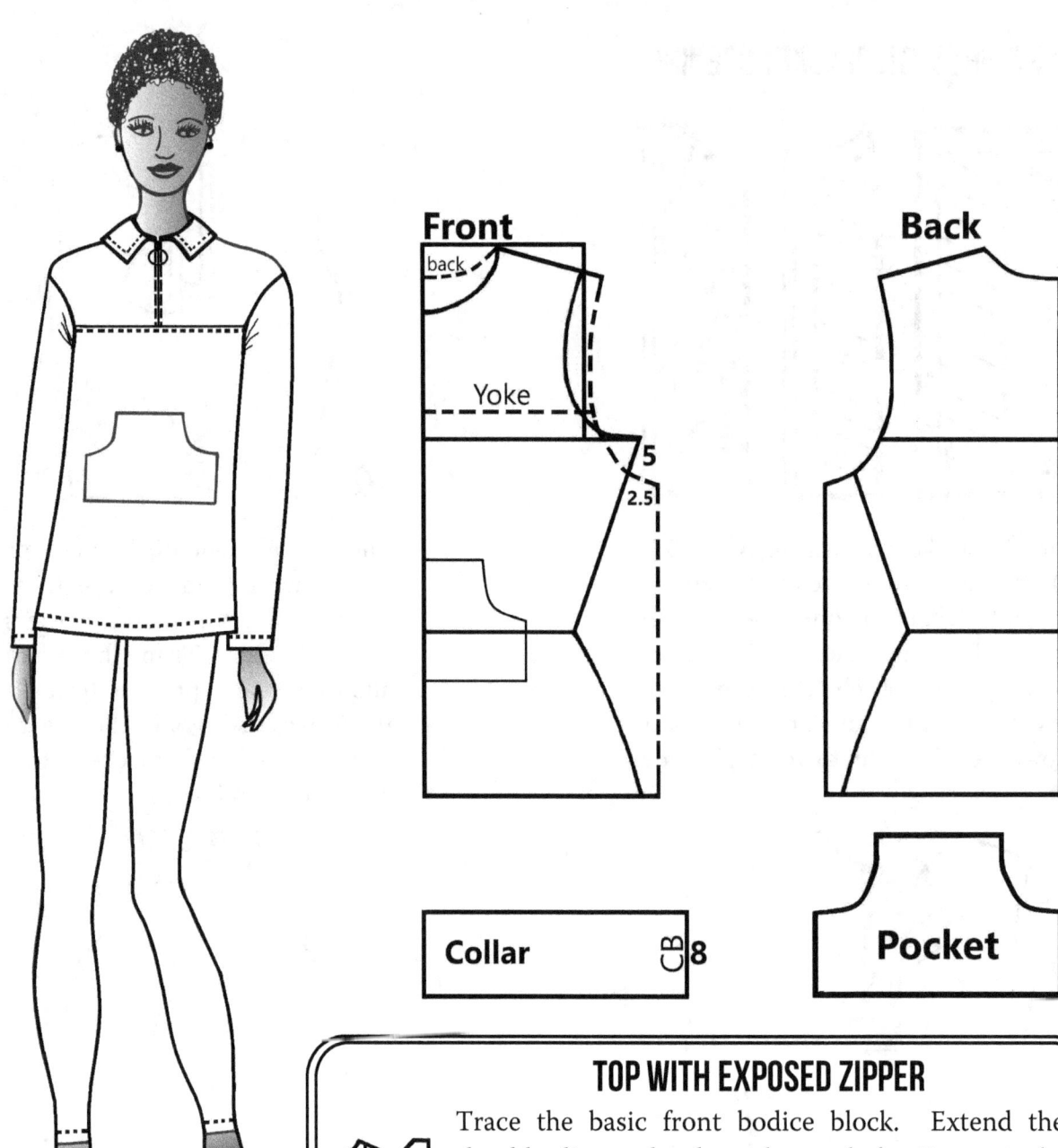

TOP WITH EXPOSED ZIPPER

Trace the basic front bodice block. Extend the shoulder line and redraw the armhole. Draw a yoke on the front at a desired height. Draw the back neck and trace the back pattern from the front. Draw the pocket on the front. Draw the basic straight collar on page **120** with or without the pointed style line. Subtract the amount that will be used for the front opening, from the collar draft. Trace the yoke, front, back, pocket, and collar off. Use the **oversized shirt sleeve** draft on page **148** to complete the pattern. Adjust the sleeve hemline. Add grain lines, notches, hem, and seam allowances.

TOP WITH EXPOSED ZIPPER

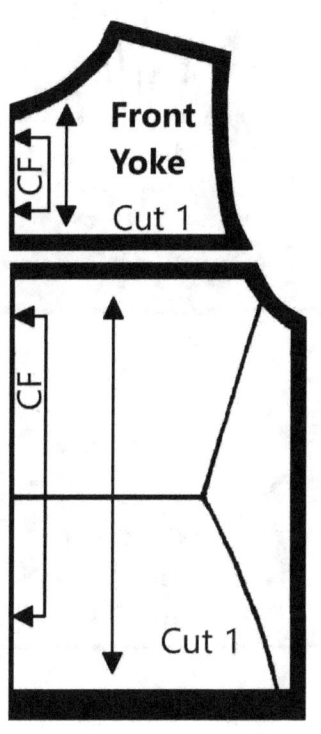
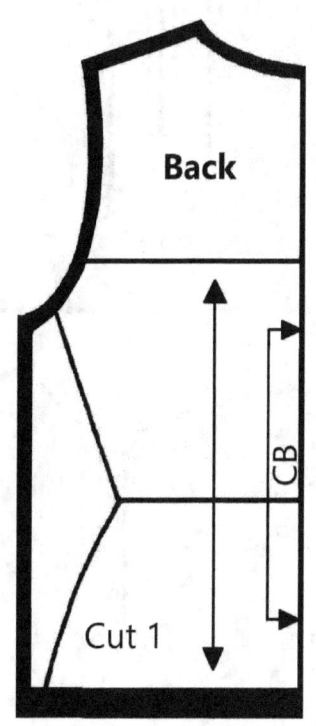
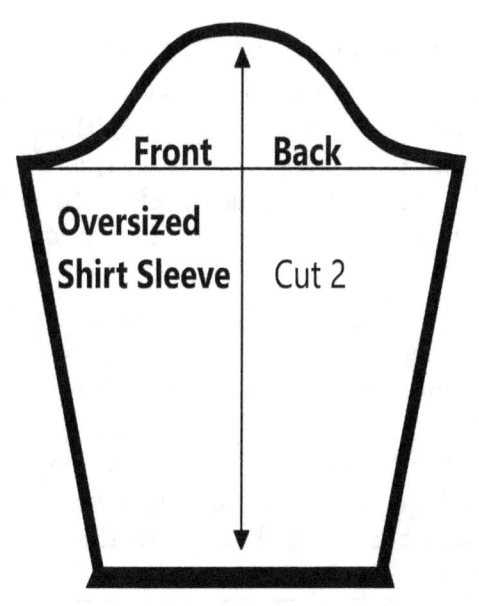
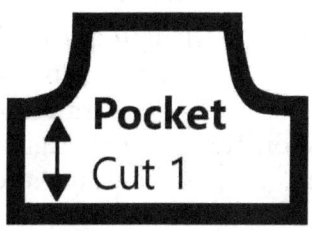
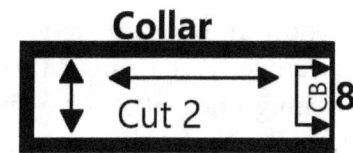

SPORTSWEAR

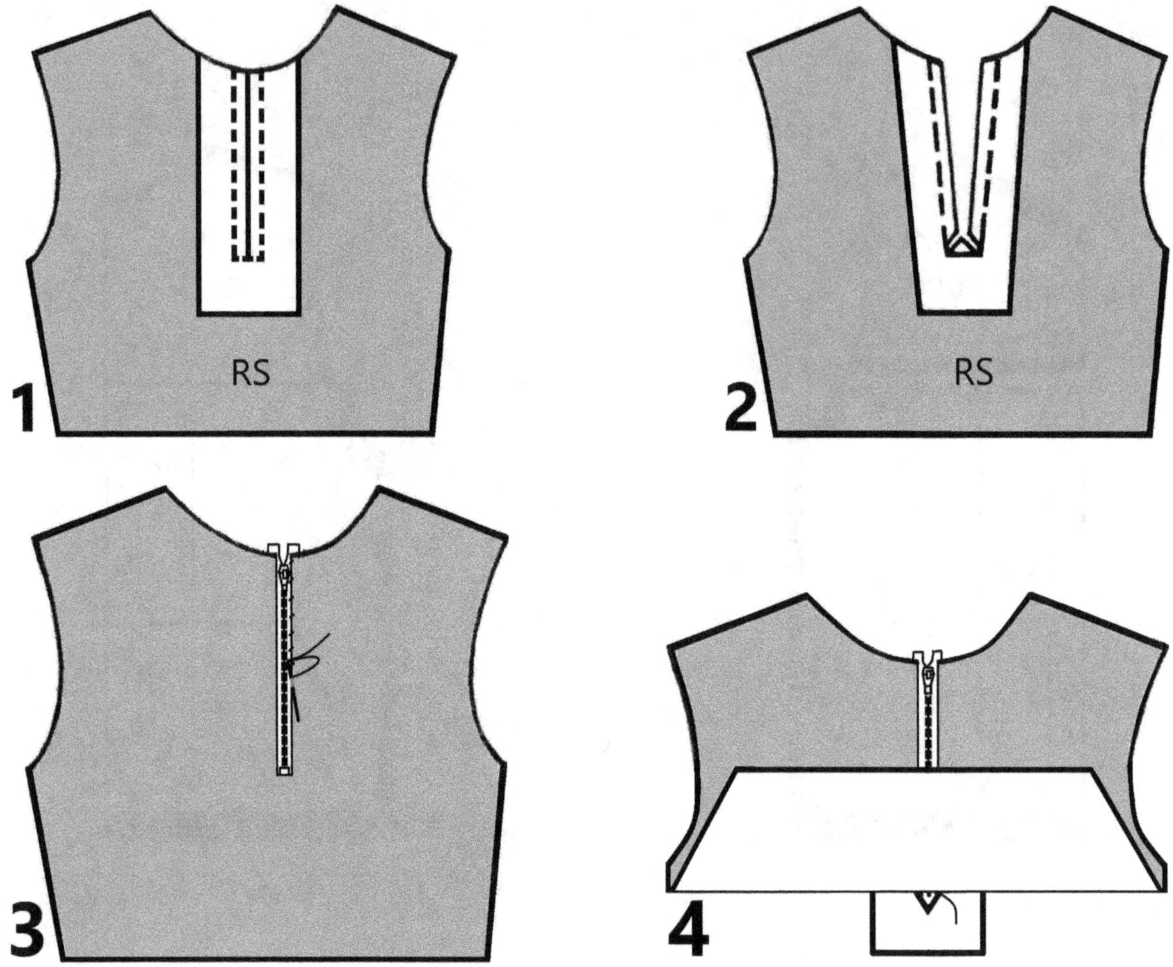

EXPOSED ZIPPER APPLICATION

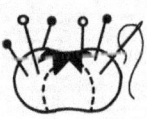

1. Lightly press a crease on the centre front of the garment and mark the desired length of the placket. Cut a stay facing **8 cm** (**3 ⅛ in**) wide and **4 cm** (**1 ½ in**) longer than the marked placket opening. Draw a line down the centre of the stay. Draw lines **5 mm** (**¼ in**) from the centre line. Place the stay over the marked line on the garment, right sides together. Pin and tack the stay in place. Sew the stay to the garment by stitching on the lines on both sides of the centre line and across the bottom of the placket as illustrated.

2. Slash through the centre of the stay and down to within **1 cm** (**⅜ in**) of bottom stitching. Clip into the lower corners.

3. Turn the stay to the wrong side of the garment and press. Place the zipper underneath the opening and hand-tack the garment to the zipper tape.

4. Lift the bottom edge of the garment upwards to expose the triangular section of the stay. Stitch the triangle to the zipper tapes with a zipper foot. Flap the garment over to expose the original stitching line. Stitch the zipper to the garment from the bottom to the top, along the stitching line. Repeat for the opposite side. Remove the tacking stitches.

SPORTSWEAR

THE HOOD

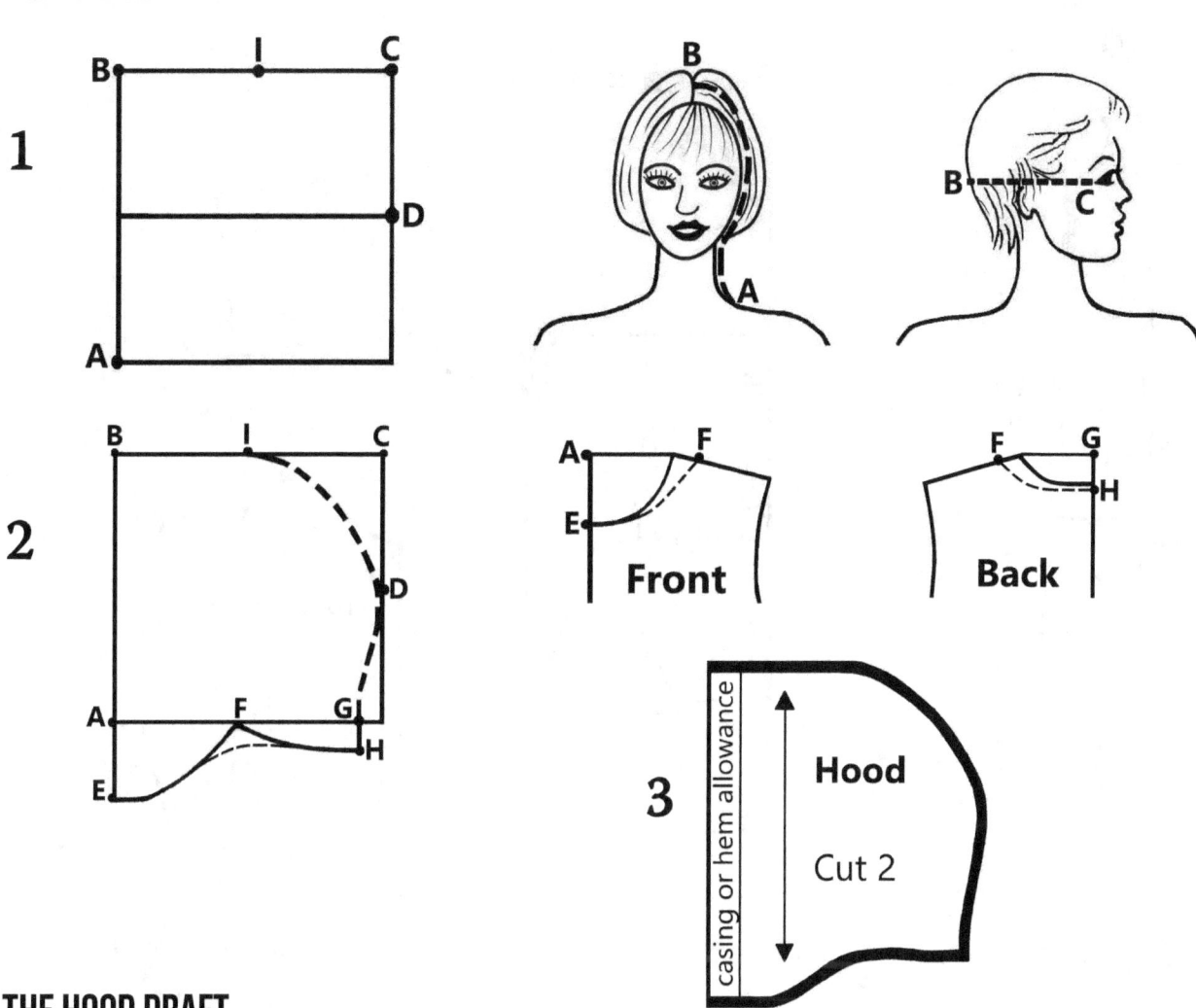

THE HOOD DRAFT

1. **A-B:** The measurement from the base of the neck to the middle of the head.
   B-C: Half the measurement from the outer corner of one eye, around the back head, to the outer corner of the other eye. B to I is half the measurement of **B** to **C**. Mark.
   C-D: Half the measurement of **A** to **B**. Close the grid.
2. **A-E:** The measurement of the front neck depth in the final draft.
   A-F: Measure the distance from **A** to **F** after adjustments have been made in the final draft of the garment's pattern and add **1 cm (⅜ in)** to that amount. Draw a curved line from **E** to **F**.
   F-G: Measure the distance from **F** to **G** in the final draft and add **1 cm** to that amount.
   G-H: The amount that was dropped at the centre back neck of the garment's pattern after adjustments have been made. Draw a curved line from **F** to **H**. Shape the hood with the French curve as illustrated and blend all curves.
3. Trace the pattern off. Add an allowance at the centre front for a casing or a hem. Add a grain line, notches, and seam allowances.

SPORTSWEAR

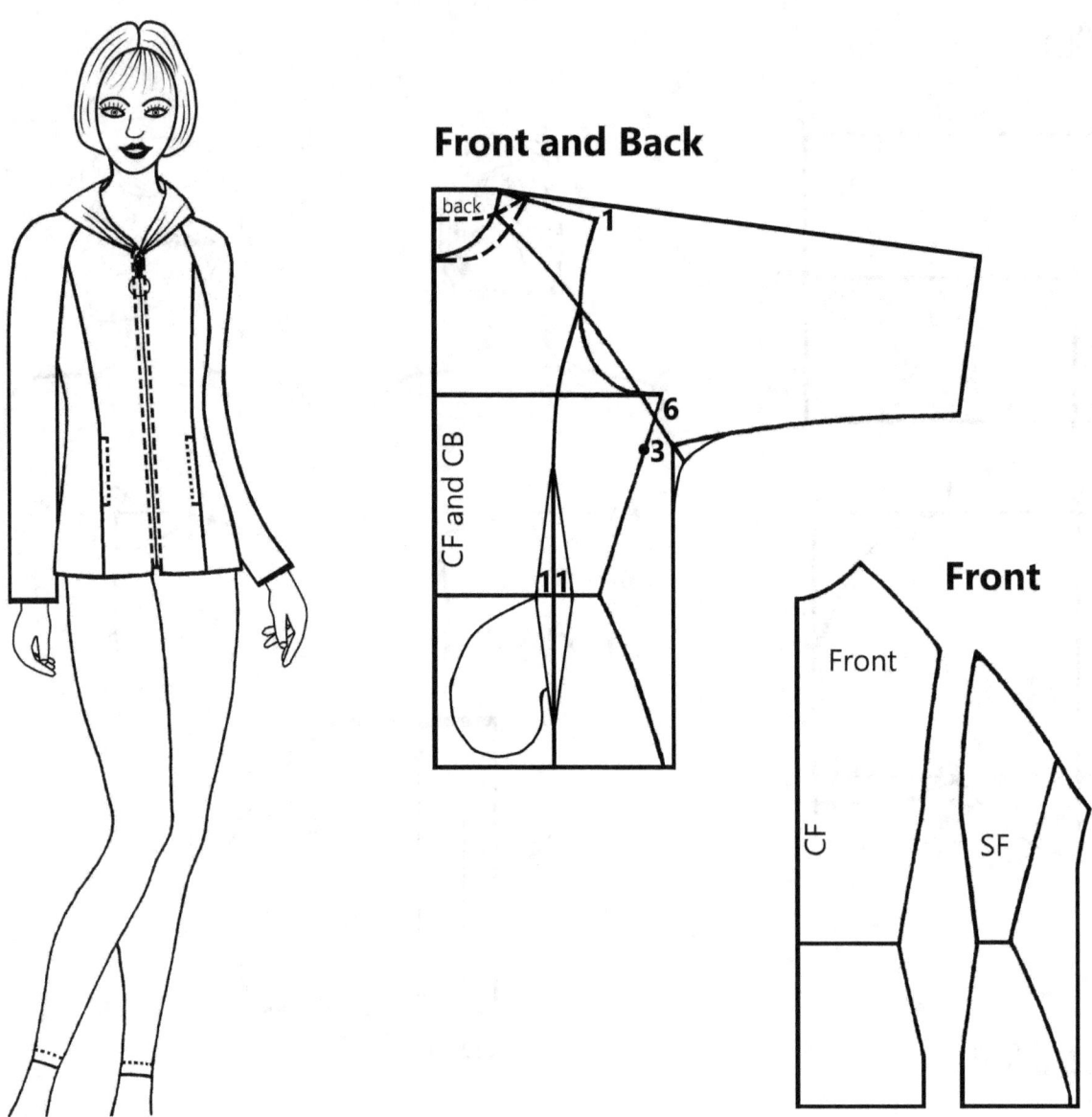

Front and Back

Front

TRACKSUIT TOP WITH HOOD

Trace the basic front kimono block. Adjust the bodice length as desired. Draw the sleeve to the desired length and the sleeve hemline to the desired width. Scoop the neckline by **2 cm (¾ in)** or as desired. Draw the back neck as illustrated. Measure **4 cm (1 ½ in)** down the neck and draw the raglan seam. Draw the panels as illustrated. Draw a pocket and trace it off. Trace the front off. Trace the back from the front without panels. Trace the front and back sleeve sections off and align them next to each other on paper. Secure the centre of the sleeve sections with tape. Draft the hood as illustrated on the previous page. Add grain lines, notches, hem, and seam allowances to all pattern pieces.

TRACKSUIT TOP WITH HOOD

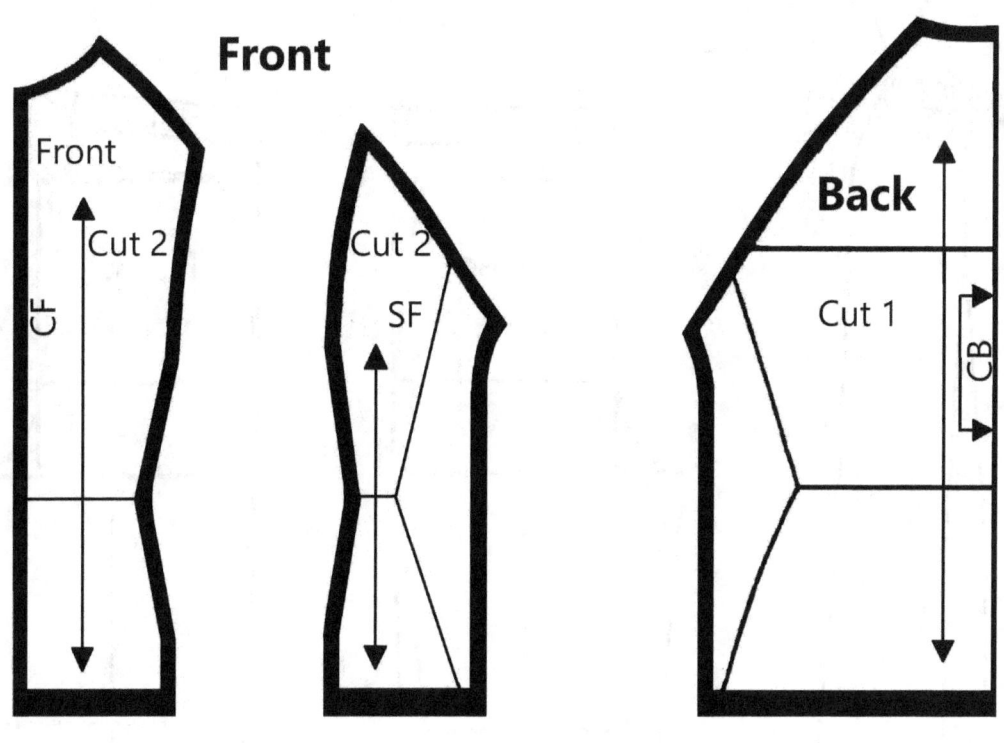
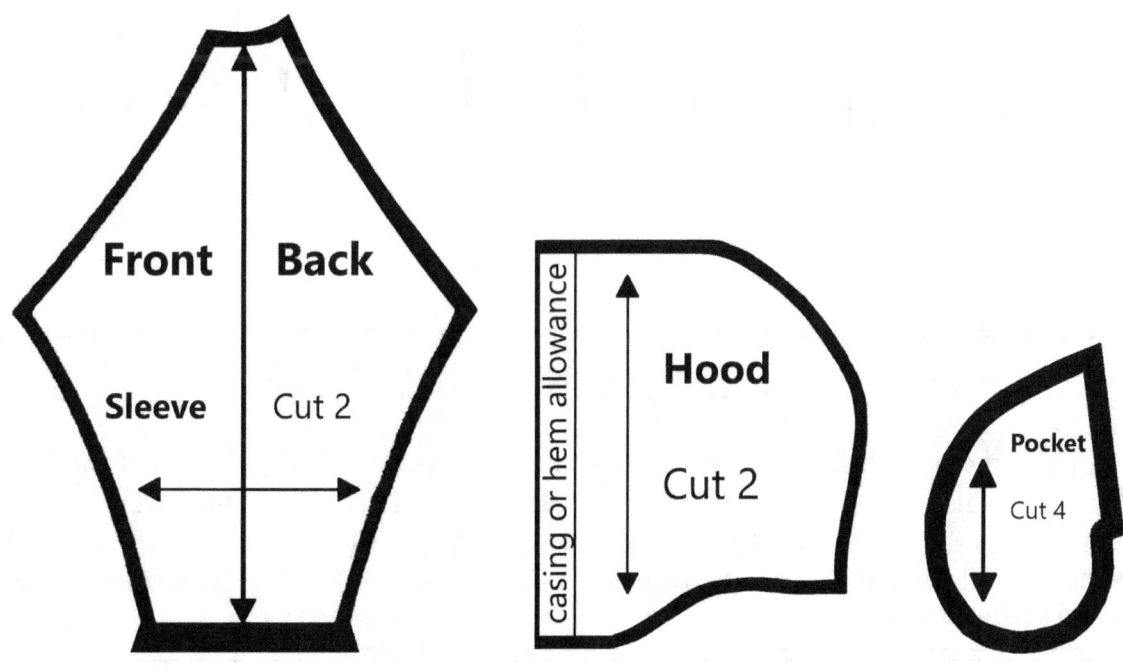

~ 233 ~

SPORTSWEAR

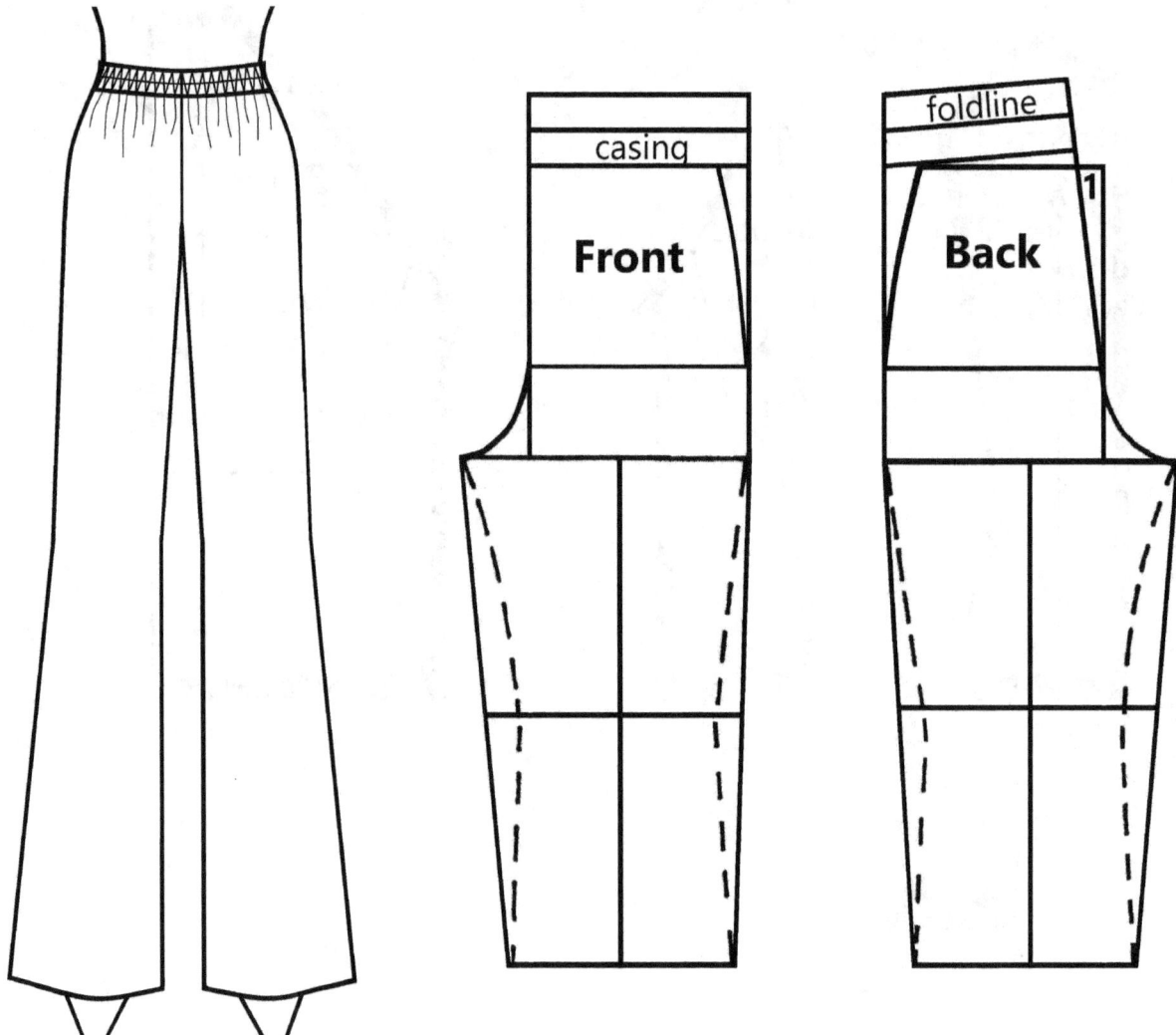

PANTS WITH ELASTICIZED WAISTBAND

Draft the basic trouser pattern without darts. Measure **1 cm** (**⅜ in**) in at the centre back. Raise the waistline to allow for a casing. The casing should be twice the width of the elastic plus **6 mm** (**¼ in**). Shape the legs to the required width. Complete the pattern as illustrated. Trace the front and back patterns off. Add grain lines, notches, hem, and seam allowances.

PANTS WITH ELASTICIZED WAISTBAND

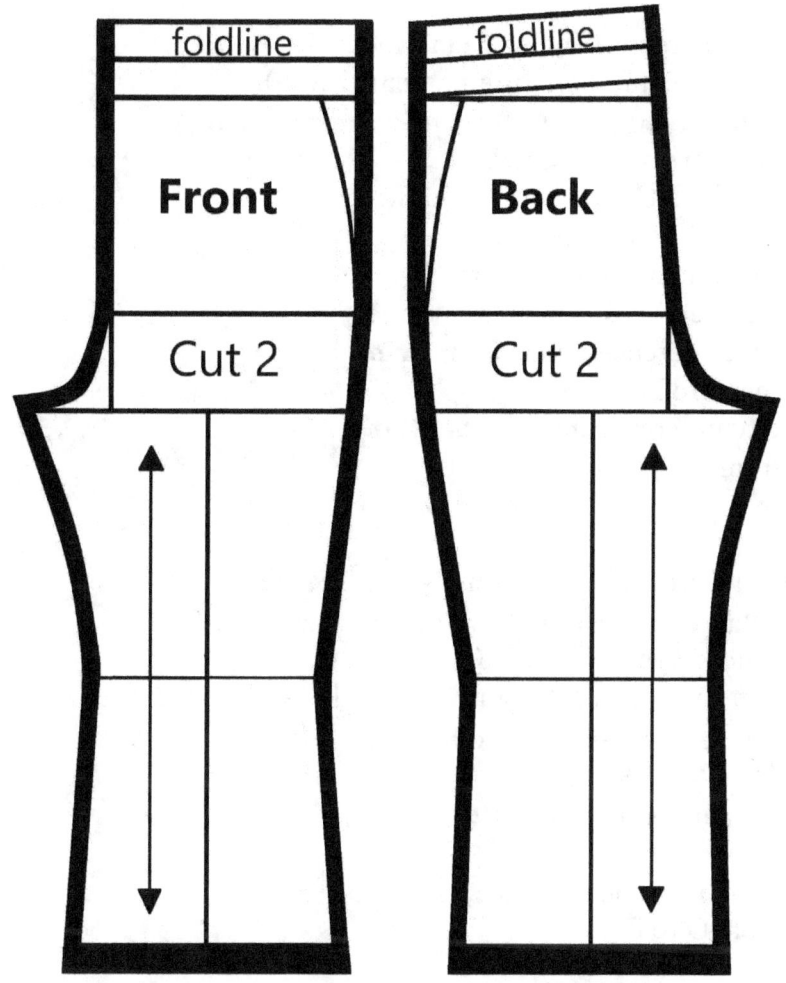

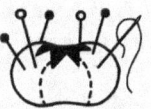

Method one of three for sewing elasticized waistbands:
Neaten raw edges of front and back side seams, inner leg seams, and crotches with overlocking. Stitch each front panel to each back panel at the inside leg seams, right sides together. Press the seams open. Stitch the front and back crotch seams, right sides together, matching the inside leg seams. Reinforce the crotch with a second row of stitches. Press the seam open. Stitch the side seams, right sides together. Press. Turn under **6 mm (¼ in)** on the casing's raw edge, and press or finish the raw edge with overlocking. Turn the casing to the wrong side to the required width and pin it in place. Stitch along the lower edge, leaving an opening to insert elastic. Insert the required length of elastic with a bodkin or safety pin. Overlap the elastic ends **1.5 cm (⅝ in)** and secure them with zigzag stitches. Stitch the opening in the casing closed. One or multiple rows of topstitching with even spacing can be sewn in the centre of the casing. Stretch the elastic while sewing. Neaten the hem's raw edges. Fold the hems up and press. Tack and stitch in place. Press.

SPORTSWEAR

LEGGINGS DRAFT

Front
A-B: Waist to ankle measurement minus **6 cm (2 ¼ in)**.
A-C: Quarter of the hip circumference minus **4 cm (1 ½ in)**.
C-D: Crotch depth. Rule a line from **C** down to **D** and across to **G**.
D-E: One third the measurement of **C** to **D**.
Measure **2 cm (¾ in)** in from **C** and rule a line down to **E**.
D-F: One fifth the measurement of **A** to **C**.
Draw a curve with the French curve from **E** to **F**.
G-H: Half the measurement of **B** to **G**.
H-I: Half the knee circumference minus **2 cm (¾ in)**.
Rule a curved line from **F** to **I**.
B-J: Half the ankle circumference minus **2 cm (¾ in)**.
Rule a straight line from **I** to **J**.

Back
A-K: Quarter of the hip circumference minus **4 cm (1 ½ in)**.
K-L: Crotch depth. Rule a line from **K** down to **L** and across to **G**.
L-M: One third the measurement of **K** to **L**.
Measure **2 cm (¾ in)** in and **3 cm (1 ¼ in)** up from **K**. Rule a line across to **A** and down to **M**.
L-N: One quarter the measurement of **A** to **K**.
Draw a curved line from **M** to **N**.
H-O: Half the knee circumference minus **2 cm (¾ in)**.
Rule a curved line from **N** to **O**.
B-P: Half the ankle circumference minus **2 cm (¾ in)**.
Rule a straight line from **O** to **P**.

SPORTSWEAR

LEGGINGS

 Draft the leggings block as described on the previous page. Trace the pattern off and add a casing twice the width of the elastic. Add a grain line, notches, hem, and **6 mm (¼ in)** seam allowances.

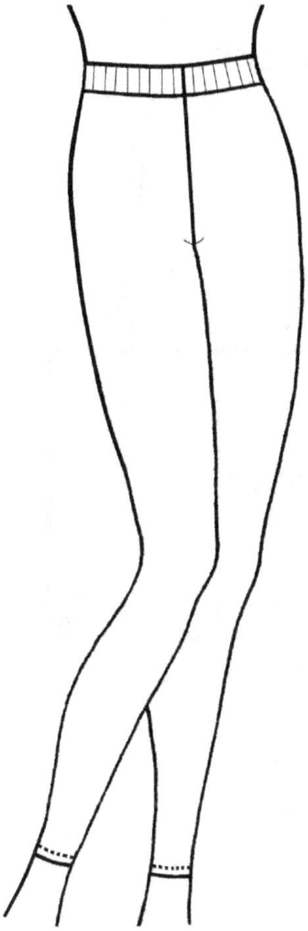

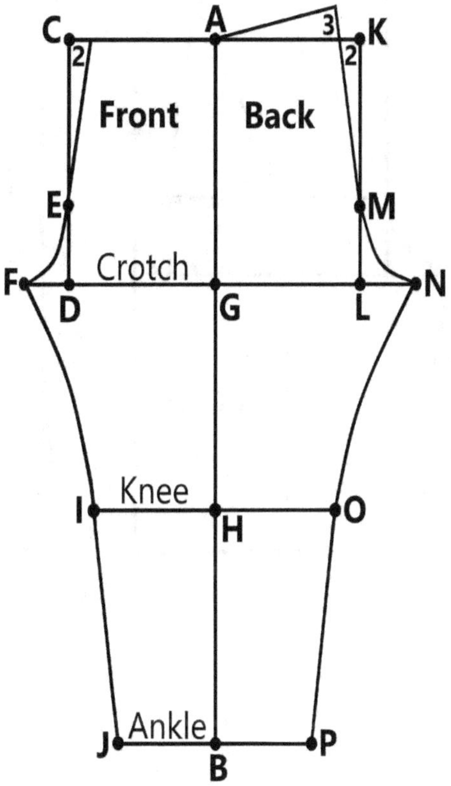

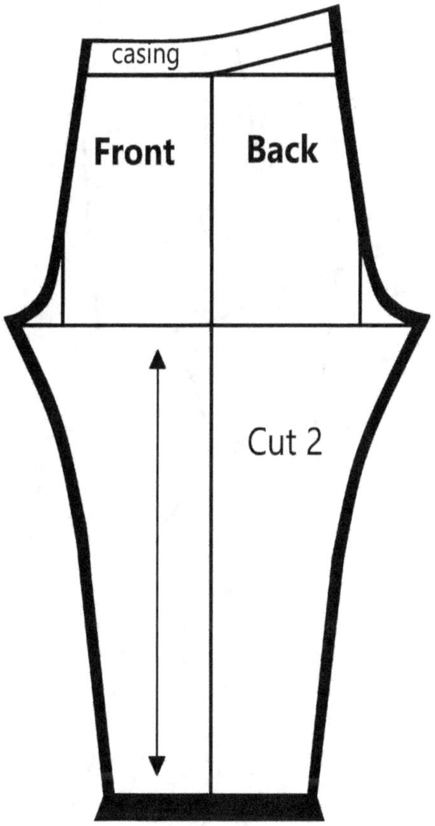

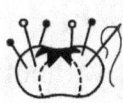 Use good-quality Spandex/Lycra fabric. Pin the inner leg seam of one leg, right sides together. Stitch the seam using four-thread overlocking and stitch length **2-2 ½**. Repeat the same for the other leg. Turn one leg right side out and slip it into the other leg, right sides together. Pin and stitch the crotch seam with the overlocker, using four-thread overlocking. Cut elastic to a desired length and overlap it to form a circle. Secure the ends with the sewing machine and a zigzag stitch. Quarter pin mark the elastic and the garment waistline. Pin the elastic to the wrong side of the garment, matching the pins up. Overlock or zigzag the waist edge, while stretching the elastic. Fold the elastic over to the wrong side, pin, and stitch in place. Neaten the hem edges with overlocking. Turn the hem edges up and press. Stitch the hem edges in place with the sewing machine using a twin stretch needle.

~ 237 ~

SPORTSWEAR

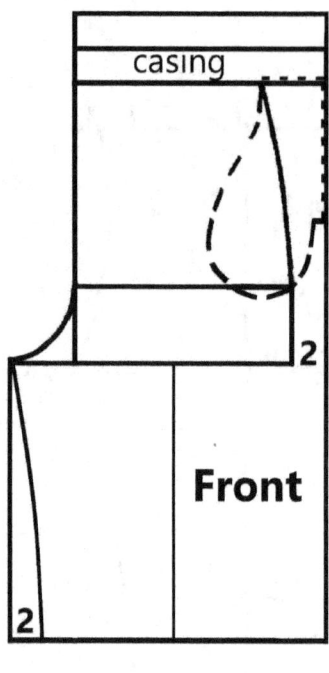

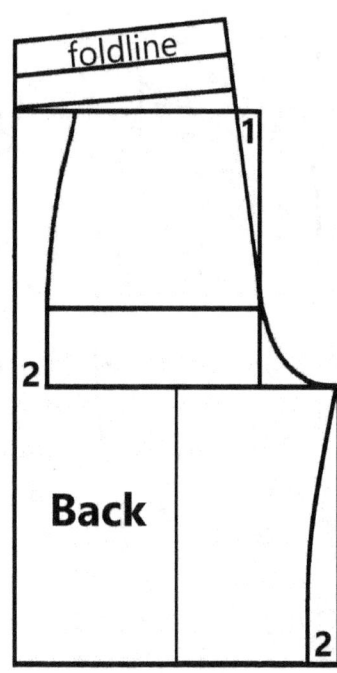

SHORTS WITH IN-SEAM POCKETS

Draft the basic trouser block without darts. Raise the front and back waistline as illustrated. Measure **1 cm (⅜ in)** in at the centre back. Draw the pocket as illustrated. Scoop the legs as illustrated or by the desired amount. Add a casing twice the width of the elastic plus **1 cm (⅜ in)**. Trace the front, back, and pocket pattern off. Add grain lines, notches, hem, and seam allowances.

SHORTS WITH IN-SEAM POCKETS

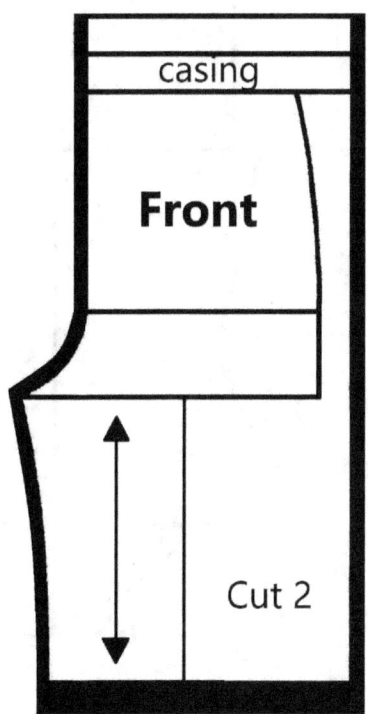
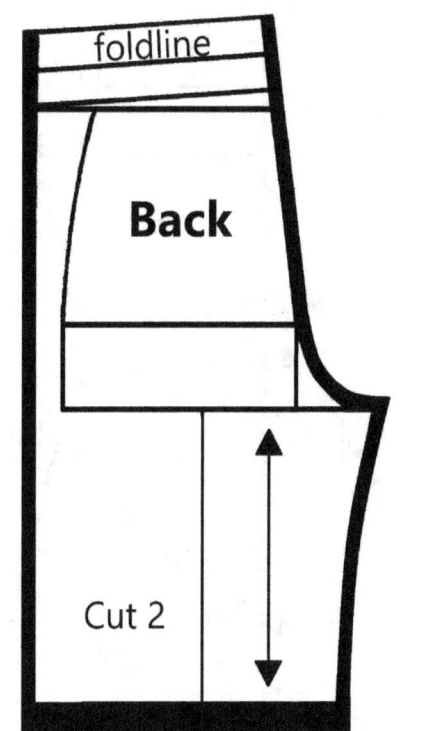
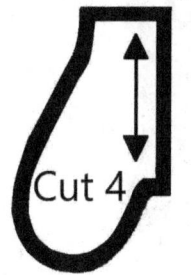

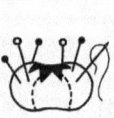 Neaten the inside leg seams and crotch seams of the front and back with overlocking or a zigzag stitch. Stitch the front to the back at the inside leg seams, right sides together. Pin and stitch the front and back crotch seams together. Reinforce the crotch with a second row of stitches. With right sides together, pin and stitch the pocket to the side edges of the front and back, using a **1 cm (⅜ in)** seam allowance. Neaten the side seams. Press the seam allowance toward the pockets. Pin the front and back at the sides, matching notches. Pin the pocket edges together. Stitch from the lower edge up to the marked pocket opening, and continue around the pocket to the upper edge. Clip back the seam allowance below the pockets. Press the side seams open. Turn pockets towards the front and press. Baste the upper edge of the pockets to the front. The pockets will be held in place by the casing. Overlock the raw edge of the waistline. Turn the casing to the wrong side to the required width and pin in place. Edgestitch close to the foldline. Join the ends of the required length of elastic to form a circle. Place the elastic inside the casing. Stitch next to the elastic, using a zipper foot. From the right side of the garment, stitch in the ditch through the waistband, at the centre front, centre back, and side seams. Turn under **6 mm (¼ in)** on the hem raw edge and press. Turn up the required amount for the hem and press. Pin and stitch the hem in place. Press.

SPORTSWEAR

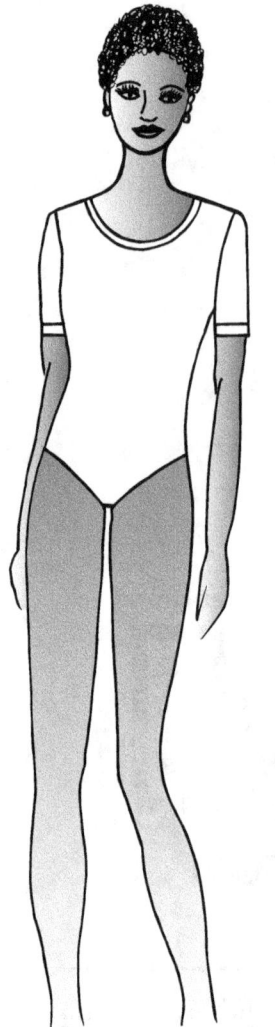
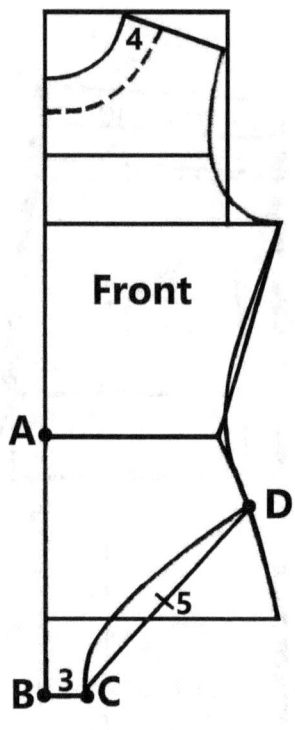
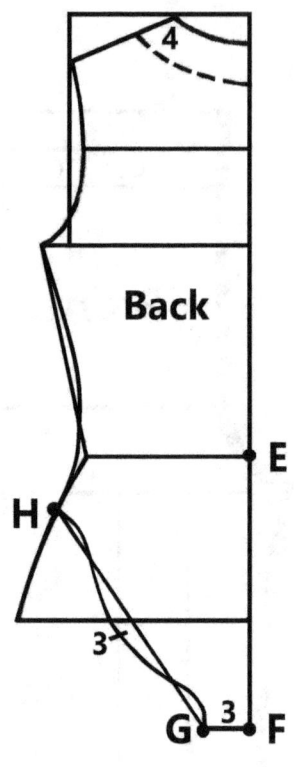

ALL-IN-ONE SPENCER

Draft the basic front and back bodice blocks. Scoop the necklines as desired. Complete the pattern as illustrated. Use the **knit sleeve** draft on page **222** to complete the pattern.

Front

A-B: Crotch depth plus **5 cm (2 in)**.
B-C: Rule a line measuring **3 - 3.5 cm (1 ¼ - 1 ⅜ in)** for the crotch.
C-D: Rule a line to a desired hip height and divide the line in half. Draw a curved line **4 - 5 cm (1 ½ - 2 in)** from the line for a high-cut legline.

Back

E-F: Crotch depth plus **8 cm (3 ⅛ in)**.
F-G: Rule a line measuring **3 - 3.5 cm (1 ¼ - 1 ⅜ in)** for the crotch.
G-H: Rule a line up to the same hip height as measured for the front. Draw a curved line **3 cm (1 ¼ in)** from this line. Trace all pattern pieces off. Add **6 mm (¼ in)** seam allowances at the shoulders and side seams, and **1 cm (⅜ in)** at the neckline and legline.

ALL-IN-ONE SPENCER

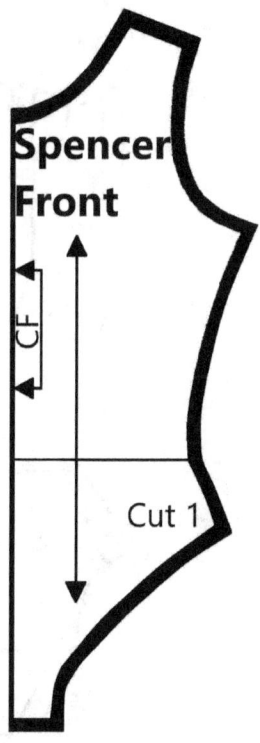
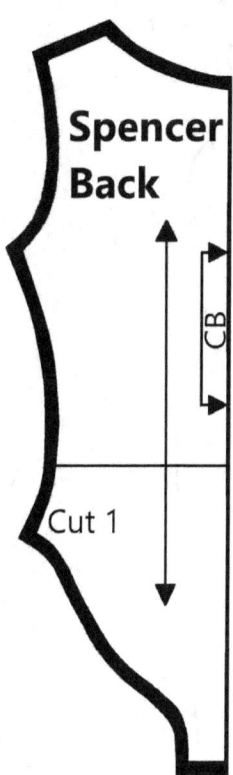

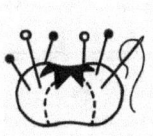
Use good-quality stretch fabric or stretch lace, matching sewing thread, **1 cm (⅜ in)** wide brief leg elastic, nylon, or satin ribbon, and poppers or snap fasteners. Reinforce the shoulder seams as described on page **221**. Lay the garment on a flat surface and measure the neckline. Cut the elastic to three-quarters of this measurement. Join the elastic to form a circle. Quarter pin mark the elastic and the neckline. Pin the elastic to the wrong side of the garment, matching up the pins. Stitch the elastic to the neckline using three-thread overlocking while holding the elastic and the garment at the front and back. Fold the elastic to the wrong side so that the elastic is encased. Stitch the neckline on the right side using a sewing machine and a twin stretch needle. With right sides together, pin the sleeve into the armhole, matching notches and the underarm seam. Stitch the sleeve in place using overlocking. Repeat for the other sleeve. With right sides together, pin and sew the sleeve seams and side seams using overlocking. Stitch the sleeve hems with the twin stretch needle. Lay the garment flat and measure the leg openings. Cut elastic to three-quarters of this measurement. Quarter pin mark the elastic and the leg opening. Pin the elastic to the wrong side of the leg opening, matching up the pins. Stitch the elastic to the leg opening using three-thread overlocking. Fold the elastic to the wrong side to encase the elastic. Stitch the leg opening on the right side of the garment with a twin stretch needle. Repeat for the other leg opening. Fold the raw edges of both crotch edges **1 cm (⅜ in)** to the wrong side and press. Pin ribbon on the wrong side of both crotch edges, folding the raw edges of the ribbon in. Stitch around the edges of the ribbon using a sewing machine and a small zigzag stitch. Insert poppers or snap fasteners.

SPORTSWEAR

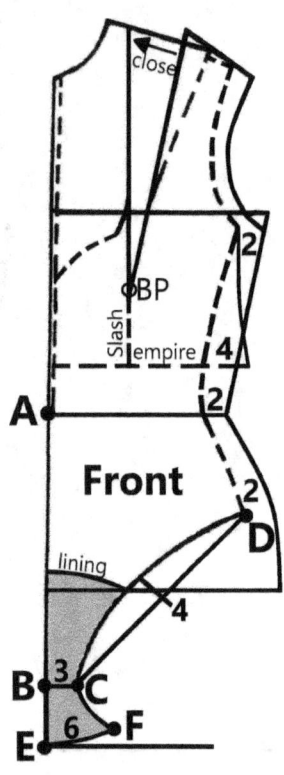
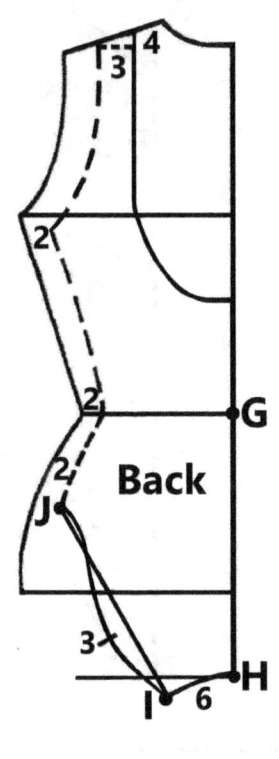

ONE-PIECE SWIMSUIT

Draft the front bodice block with the shoulder dart and the basic back bodice block. Add the style lines as illustrated. Add **4 cm (1 ½ in)** to the side of the empire for more gathers.

Front

A-B: Crotch depth plus **5 cm (2 in)**.

B-C: Rule a line measuring **3 cm (1 ¼ in)** across to **C**.

C-D: Rule a line up to a desired hip height. Divide the line in half and draw a curve **4 - 5 cm (1 ½ -2 in)** from this line for a high-cut legline.

B-E: Rule a line **4 cm (1 ½ in)** down.

E-F: Draw a **6 cm (2 ¼ in)** curved line for the crotch, ending **1 cm (⅜ in)** above the straight line.

Join **C** and **F**. Draw a curved line for the gusset lining (shaded area), as illustrated, and trace it off. Add **6 mm (¼ in)** seam allowance at the shoulders and side seams and **1 cm (⅜ in)** for the neckline and legline. Add a **1 cm (⅜ in)** seam allowance on the gusset lining side seams (legline).

Back

G-H: Crotch depth plus **4 cm (1 ½ in)**.

H-I: Draw a **6 cm (2 ¼ in)** curved line for the crotch, ending **1 cm (⅜ in)** below the straight line.

I-J: Rule a line up to the same hip height as the front and draw a curved line **3 cm (1 ¼ in)** from the line. Trace all pattern pieces off and add grain lines, notches, and seam allowances.

ONE-PIECE SWIMSUIT

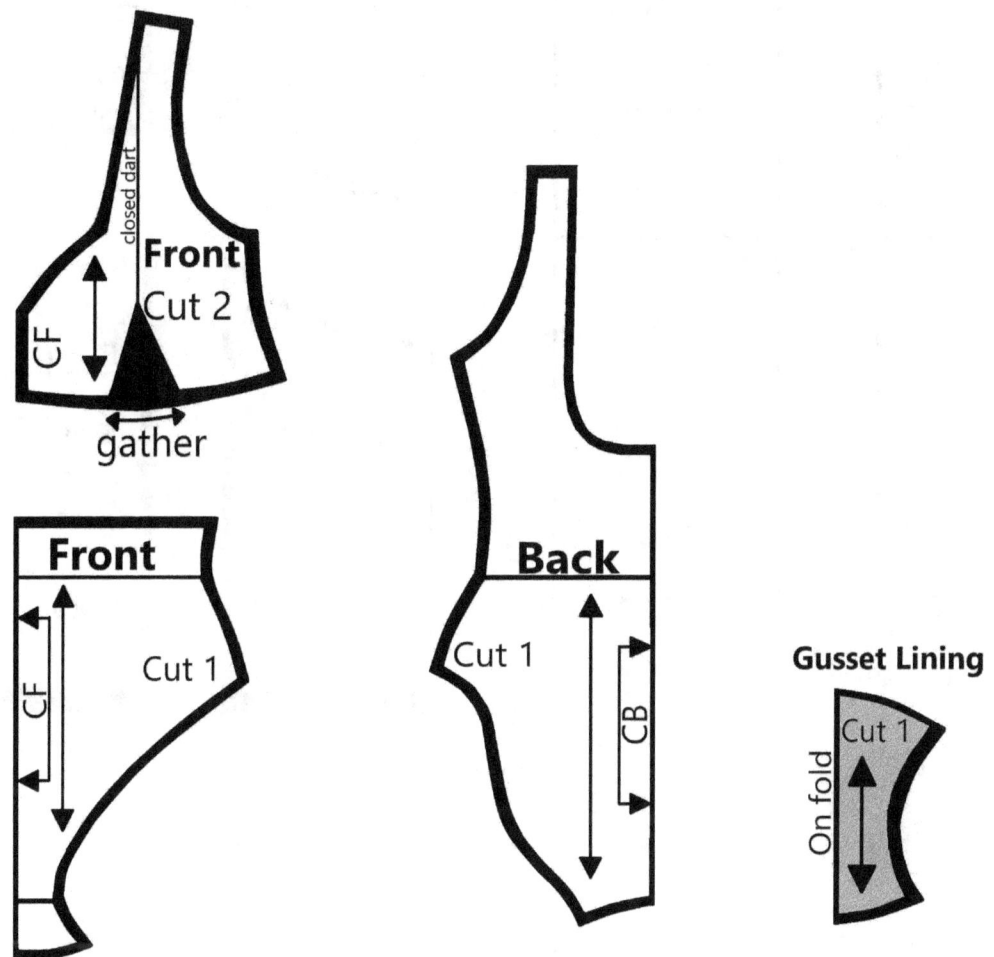

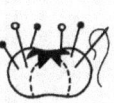
Use good-quality spandex, swimwear lining, brief leg elastic, and matching thread. Secure the pattern pieces to the fabric with magic tape, weights or pins. Cut out with a rotary cutter or sharp scissors. Pin the right side of the gusset lining to the wrong side of the back crotch. Pin the front and back crotches, right sides together and tack them in place. Sew together with the overlocker. Lay the swimsuit flat and tack the gusset lining around the leg openings. Stitch the two upper centre front panels together. Sew two rows of stitches **1 cm** (**⅜ in**) from the edge of the bodice and gather to fit the lower front panel. Stitch the bodice to the lower front panel. Reinforce the seam with a narrow strip of cotton tape. Pin and stitch the shoulders of the front and back together. Pin and stitch the side seams together using four-thread overlocking. Fit the costume and check the side seams and armholes. Adjust if necessary. Measure the arm, leg, and neckline openings. Cut a length of elastic to three-quarters of these openings, or **10 cm** (**4 in**) less than the circumference of each opening. Quarter pin mark each opening and the elastic. Finish off as described before, using three-thread overlocking and a twin stretch needle for topstitching.

MATERNITY WEAR

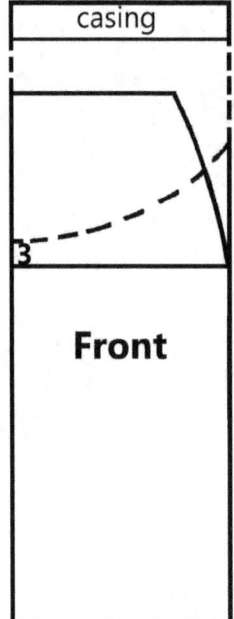
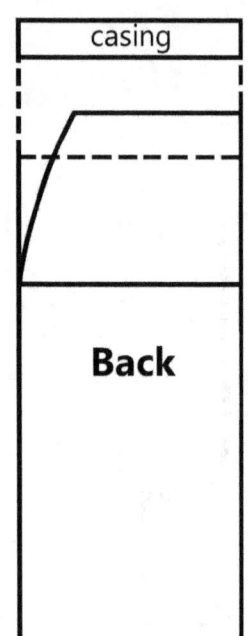
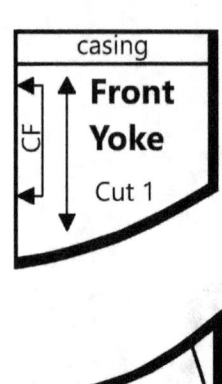
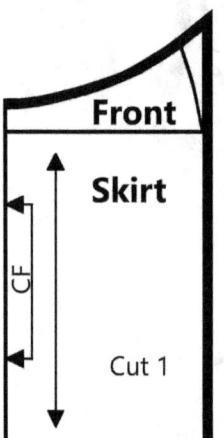
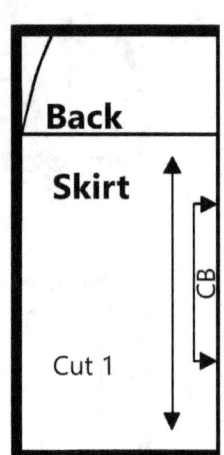

MATERNITY SKIRT

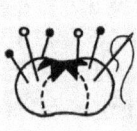 Draft the basic skirt block without darts. Draw a front and back yoke as illustrated. Ensure that the front and back side seams are the same length. Add a casing to the front and back pattern for elastic. Trace all pattern pieces off and add grain lines, notches, hem, and seam allowances.

The front and back yokes must be cut from stretch fabric or cut non-stretch fabric on the true bias. Stitch the yokes to the front and back panels. With right sides together, pin and stitch the side seams of the skirt. Press. Stitch the casing and waist elastic as described before. Finish the hem off and press the skirt.

MATERNITY WEAR

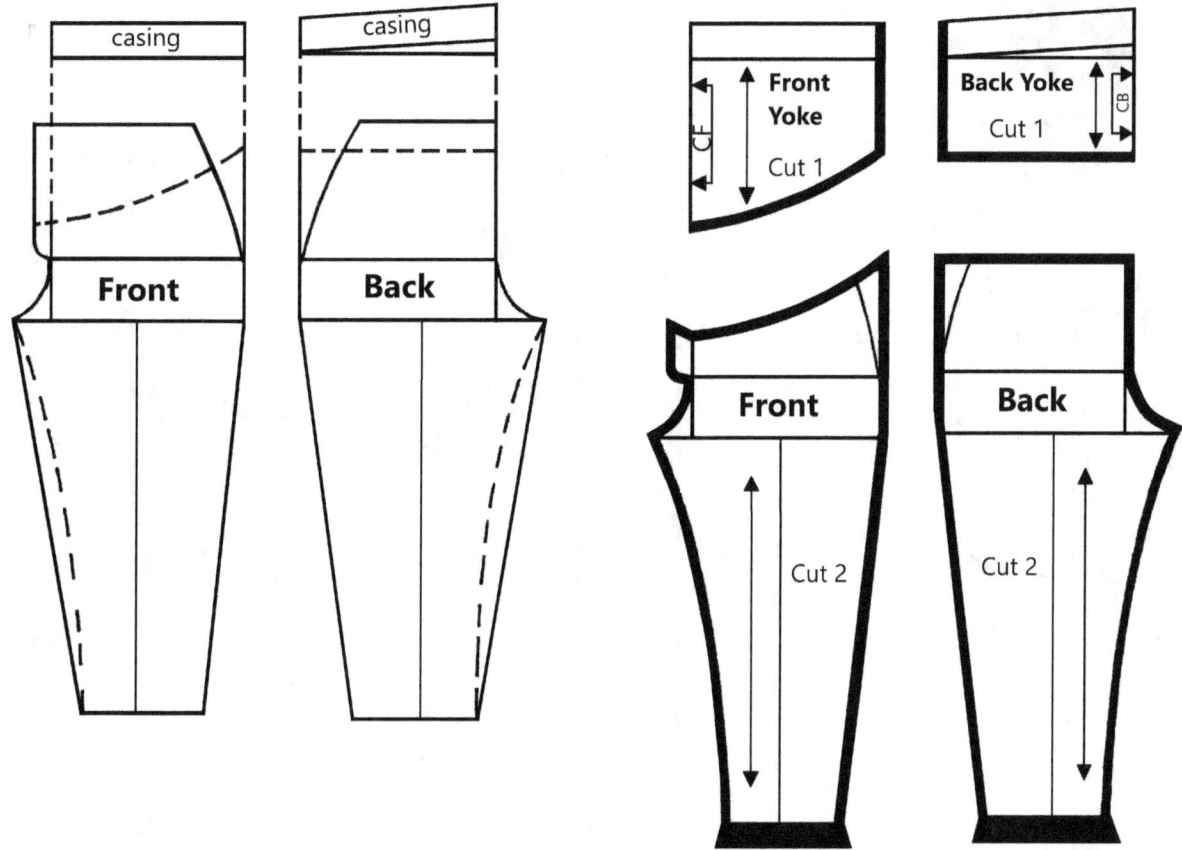

MATERNITY PANTS

Draft the basic front and back trouser pattern without the darts. Draw the yokes on the front and back pattern at a desired height. Check that the side seams of the front and back are the same length. Scoop the legs to a desired width. Add ease on the sides as desired. Trace the pattern pieces off. Add grain lines, notches, hem, and seam allowances.

Sew the front crotch seams and mock fly on the front panels, right sides together. Neaten the raw edges with overlocking. Press the mock fly to one side and stitch the fly seam to the front panel to form the mock fly. Pin and sew the back crotch seams, right sides together. Overlock the raw edges. Cut the yokes from stretch fabric. Pin and sew the front yoke to the front pants section. Repeat for the back pants section. Pin and sew the side seams of the front and back pants sections, right sides together. Pin and sew the front and back inner leg seams, right sides together. Complete the elasticized waist as described before. Sew the hem and press the garment.

MATERNITY WEAR

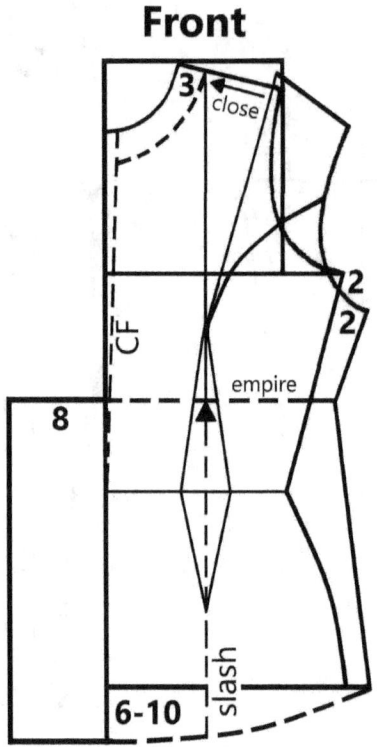
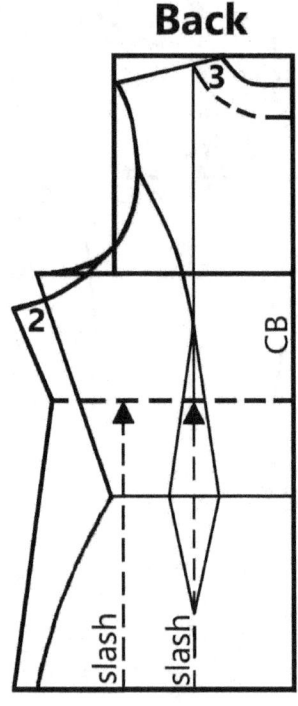

PLEATED EMPIRE WAIST TOP

Draft the front bodice with the shoulder dart and the basic back bodice. Scoop the neckline as desired. Drop the centre front hemline between **6** and **10 cm** (**2 ¼ - 4 in**) or as desired. Extend the centre front by **8 cm** (**3 ⅛ in**) for a pleat. Complete the back as illustrated. Trace the front and back sections off. Slash the front dart line up to the empire and spread it **8 cm** (**3 ⅛ in**) for a pleat. Draw a curved hemline. Slash the back up to, not through the empire and spread to a desired amount. Trace front and back neck facings off. Use the basic sleeve draft on page **58** to complete the pattern. Add grain lines, notches, hem, and seam allowances.

PLEATED EMPIRE WAIST TOP

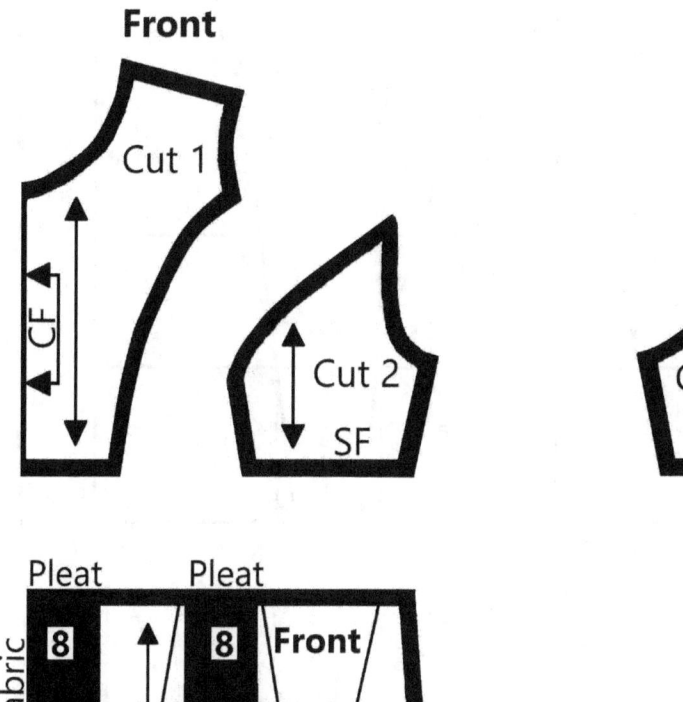
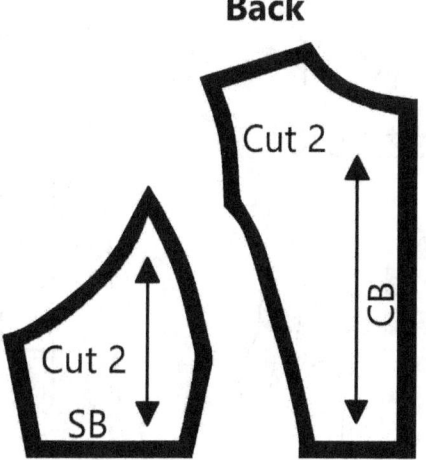
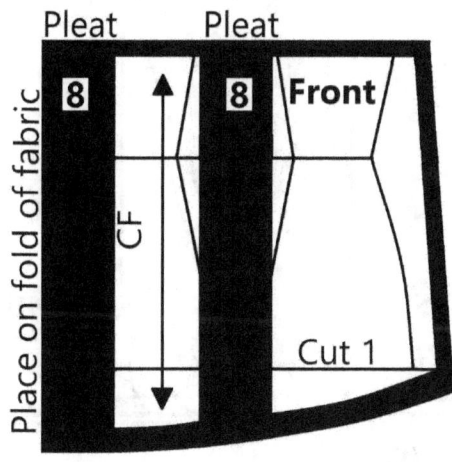
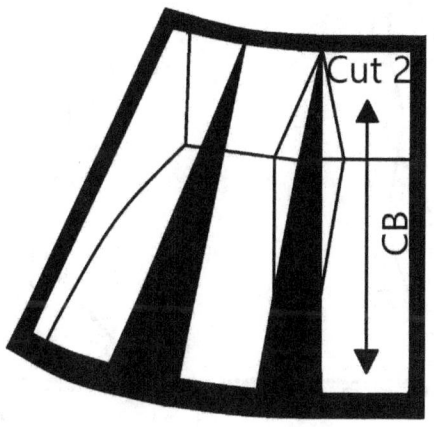

This top can be made from stretch or non-stretch fabric. With right sides together, pin and stitch the front and side front bodice panels together. Pleat the lower front section and attach it to the front bodice. Stitch the back and side back bodice panels together and attach them to the lower back section. Stitch the centre back seam up to the marked zipper opening. Insert a zipper in the centre back seam. Pin and stitch the side seams of the front and back, right sides together. Press. Complete the sleeves as described on page **73**. Sew the garment and sleeve hems. Press the garment.

MATERNITY WEAR

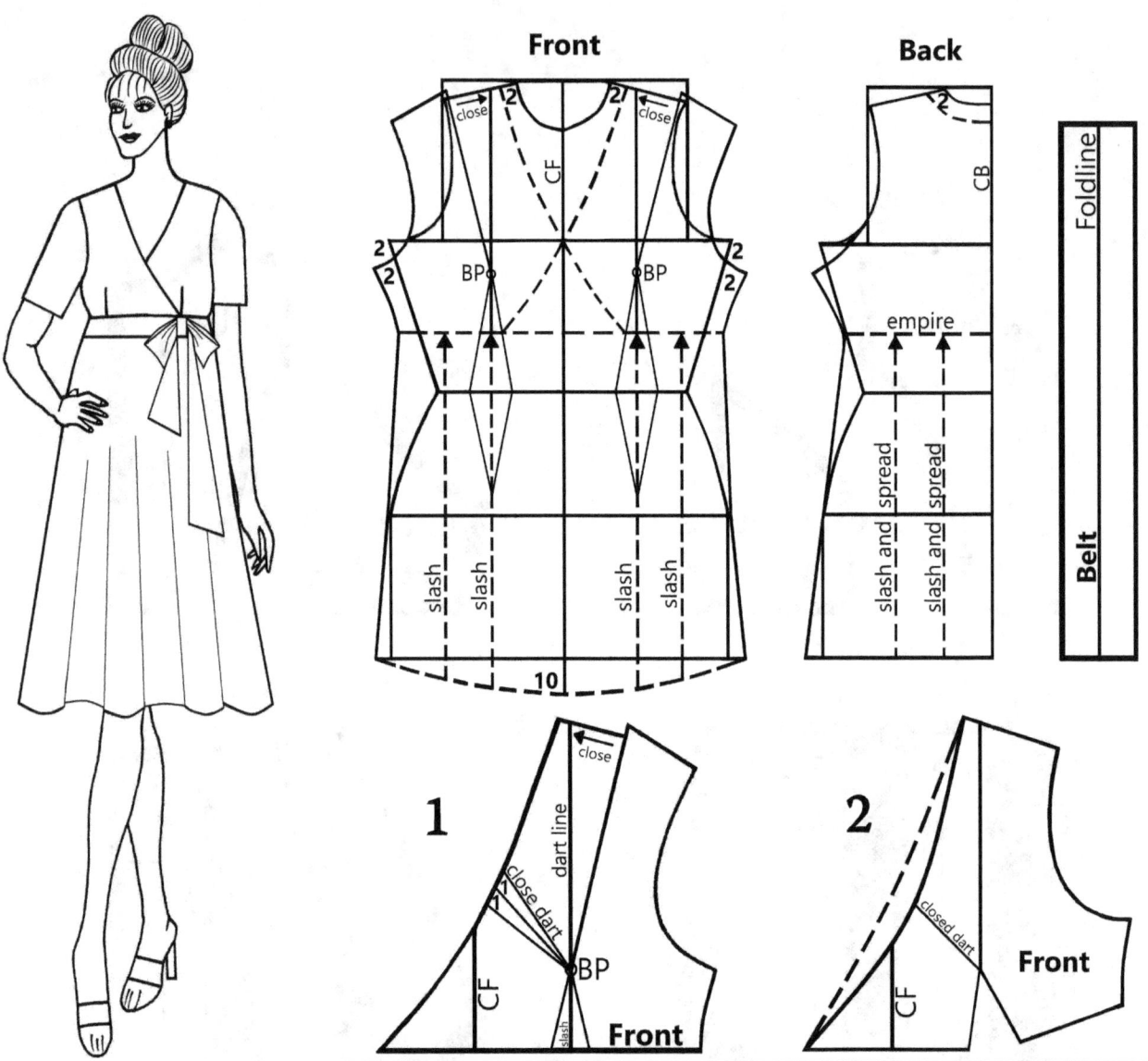

EMPIRE WAIST DRESS

Draft the basic front bodice block with the shoulder dart on the fold of a sheet of paper. Trace the lines through. Open the sheet and draw the style lines as illustrated. Drop the centre front by **10 cm** (**4 in**) or more. Draft the basic back bodice and draw the empire line at the same height as the front. Scoop the front and back necklines by **2 cm** (**¾ in**) or more.

1. Trace the front empire off. Slash the dart line up to the bust point. Draw a **2 cm** dart on the front neck as illustrated.
2. Close the shoulder dart and secure it with tape. Close the dart on the neck and redraw a curved or straight neckline as illustrated.

Trace the front and back skirt sections off. Slash the front skirt up to the empire and fold the dart close. Slash the side front line and spread it to a desired amount. Slash and spread the back skirt section. Trace the back empire off. Add grain lines, notches, hem, and seam allowances.

~ 248 ~

EMPIRE WAIST DRESS

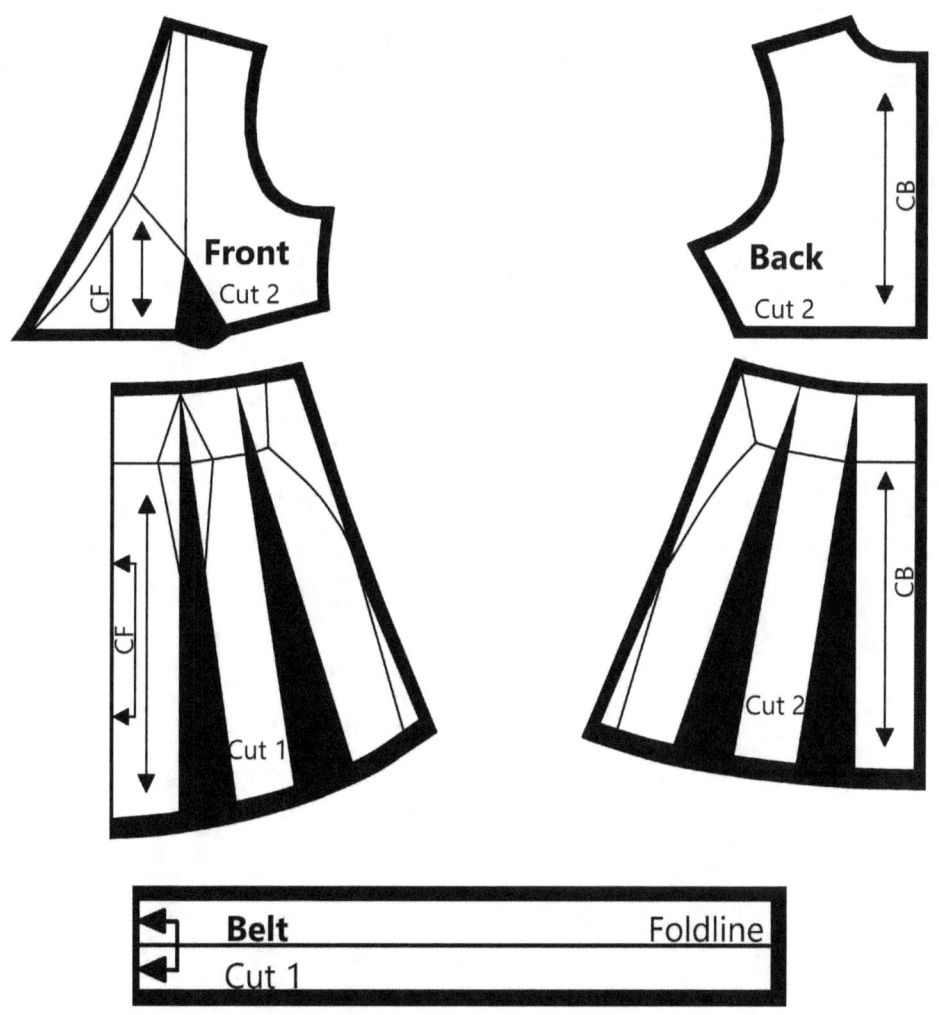

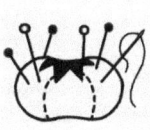

This dress can be made from stretch or non-stretch fabric. The centre back seam can be omitted if using a stretch fabric. The darts can be replaced with gathers. The neckline can be finished off with binding or facing. Trace front and back facings off and iron suitable interfacing on. Stitch the darts in the front bodice panels. Stitch the front and back shoulder seams, right sides together. Press the the seams. Stitch the facing shoulder seams together and press. Pin and stitch the facing to the garment neckline, right sides together. Trim, clip, and grade the seam allowance. Understitch the facing to the seam allowance. Tack the facing around the neckline on the inside of the garment and press. Overlap the front bodice panels at the centre front notches and baste them together. Pin and stitch the front bodice to the front skirt, right sides together. Repeat for the back bodice and back skirt sections. Stitch the centre back seam up to the marked zipper opening. Insert a zipper of your choice. Pin and stitch the front and back side seams, right sides together. Press. Complete the sleeves as described on page **73**. Sew the skirt and sleeve hems. Draw and sew a belt, if a belt is desired. Press the garment.

www.ingramcontent.com/pod-product-compliance
Lightning Source LLC
Chambersburg PA
CBHW051209290426
44109CB00021B/2394